BUTTERFLIES
THROUGH
BINOCULARS

FLORIDA

Field Guide Series
edited by Jeffrey Glassberg

Butterflies through Binoculars: The Boston-New York-Washington Region
by Jeffrey Glassberg

Butterflies through Binoculars: The East
by Jeffrey Glassberg

Butterflies through Binoculars: Florida
by Jeffrey Glassberg, Marc C. Minno, and John V. Calhoun

Dragonflies through Binoculars: North America
by Sidney W. Dunkle

Butterflies through Binoculars: The West
by Jeffrey Glassberg

BUTTERFLIES THROUGH BINOCULARS

FLORIDA

Jeffrey Glassberg
Marc C. Minno
John V. Calhoun

OXFORD
UNIVERSITY PRESS
2000

OXFORD
UNIVERSITY PRESS

Oxford New York
Athens Auckland Bangkok Bogotá Buenos Aires
Calcutta Cape Town Chennai Dar es Salaam Delhi
Florence Hong Kong Istanbul Karachi Kuala Lumpur
Madrid Melbourne Mexico City Mumbai Nairobi Paris
São Paulo Singapore Taipei Tokyo Toronto Warsaw
and associated companies in
Berlin Ibadan

Copyright © 2000 by Jeffrey Glassberg

Published by Oxford University Press, Inc.
198 Madison Avenue, New York, New York 10016

Oxford is a registered trademark of Oxford University Press, Inc.

Library of Congress Cataloging-in-Publication Data
Glassberg, Jeffrey.
Butterflies through binoculars : a field, finding, and gardening guide
to butterflies in Florida / by Jeffrey Glassberg,
Marc C. Minno, John V. Calhoun.
p. cm. (Field guide series)
Includes bibliographical references.
ISBN 978-0-19-511249-8
1. Butterflies—Florida. 2. Butterflies—Florida
Identification. 3. Butterfly gardening—Florida.
I. Minno, Marc C. II. Calhoun, John V. III. Title.
IV. Series : Butterflies [and others] through binoculars field guide series
QL551.F6 G58 2000 595.78'9'09759—dc21 99–35929

Contents

Acknowledgments

MANY PEOPLE HAVE CONTRIBUTED TO THE CREATION OF THIS FIELD GUIDE. Contributing butterfly reports and locality information that helped J.G. find butterflies for photography were Dave Bagget, John Calhoun, Rick Cech, Harry Darrow, Alana Edwards, Tom Emmel, Kathy Malone, Marc Minno, and Charles Sekerman. The able field help provided to J.C. and M.M. by Craig Huegel, Tom Neal, and Jeff Slotten is gratefully acknowledged.

Tom Emmel and Richard Curry (the Resource Coordinator of Biscayne National Park) generously arranged the logistics of a trip by J.G. to Elliot Key to see and photograph Schaus' Swallowtail. Amazingly, the full-body antimosquito suit that was provided wasn't even needed!

Patricia T. Harden of Walt Disney World Co. and Steve Gatewood and Jennifer Hess of The Nature Conservancy kindly facilitated a visit by J.G. to the Walt Disney Wilderness Preserve.

In preparing this work, there were many occasions when we examined museum specimens for information about identification features and also about geographical and temporal distributions. We thank Jim Miller, Fred Rindge, and Cal Snyder at the American Museum of Natural History, NY; Michael Thomas and John Heppner at the Florida State Collection of Arthropods, Gainesville, FL; and John Burns and Bob Robbins at the United States National Museum, Smithsonian Institution, Washington, DC for allowing us to examine specimens under their care.

Our sincere thanks to Alana Edwards and Teri Jebour for sharing a wealth of information about Florida butterfly gardening with us and our readers and to Roger Hammer, Mark Salvato, and Roberta Wooster for contributing important information to the locality section.

One of the most critical features of this book is the photographs.

ACKNOWLEDGMENTS

Although J.G. traveled extensively in Florida for years, searching for and photographing butterflies, still, in the end, there were some much needed photos for this book that he did not have. The following individuals generously provided their own photographs to fill the gaps (see photo credits appendix for specific list of photos): Ron Boender, Derb Carter, Jaret Daniels, Harry Darrow, Tom Emmel, Valerie Giles, Jim Nation, Philip Nordin, Peter W. Post, Charlie Rose, Jane Ruffin, and Joe Spano.

INTRODUCTION

THE SUNSHINE STATE AND SUN-SEEKING BUTTERFLIES—what a natural combination! Butterflies add color, drama, and movement to the natural areas where they live and to your garden. Their brilliant colors, graceful flight, ephemeral lives, and the magical transformations that convert caterpillars into butterflies, have caused humans to associate butterflies with such concepts as freedom and the human soul. Certainly, if you become involved with butterflies—searching for them in the wild or planning your garden to encourage their presence—your sense of personal freedom will grow and your soul will be nourished. Actually, prolonged field-time with butterflies will result in increased mental health, better physical fitness, and a more satisfying sex life—but these subjects are beyond the scope of this book.

The purpose of this book is to enable you to find and identify the adult butterflies that occur in Florida and this book treats all species known to have been found within the state. The world of butterflies is multifaceted, and as you learn to identify butterflies you will almost certainly become interested in many other aspects of their world. In this guide, however, many interesting topics related to butterfly study are either not included, or are not treated in depth, because inclusion of this material would create a bulkier, less portable book—a book that would work less well as a field guide. If you are interested in learning more about butterfly natural history, systematics, ecology, or gardening, please refer to the bibliography where many fine books covering these and related subjects are listed.

Binoculars

We strongly urge you to get a pair of close-focusing binoculars. Butterflies are generally small making them difficult to see well with the naked eye. Good, close-focusing binoculars will present a sharp image when the butterfly you are viewing is less than six feet away. The butterfly will fill your field of vision, giving you a new view of the world. Although you'll be able to identify many butterflies without binoculars, you won't see much of the incredible detail, and shimmering colors that make butterflying so rewarding. Without close-focusing binoculars, identifying skippers and hairstreaks may well be hopeless. If you use standard-issue binoculars, you will be backing up constantly, making the butterfly appear smaller and defeating the purpose for which you brought along the binoculars in the first place.

Other factors to consider in buying a pair of binoculars are power, size, weight, field of view, clarity, and brightness. Two numbers (for example 8 x 42) describe some basic features of binoculars. The first number indicates the power of magnification. Eight-power binoculars will make an object eight feet away appear as large as if it were one foot away. The second number is the diameter of the objective lens (in millimeters). In general, the larger this number the brighter the image will be.

As of this writing, binoculars that have the requisite close-focusing feature for butterflying are: Bausch & Lomb 8x42 and 10x42 Elites; Cabela 8x and 10x; Celestron 8x42 Regals; Minolta 8x22 and 10x25 Pocket binoculars; and Swift 7x42 Eaglets and 10x42 Viceroys. We are sure that others will soon appear. Ask your butterflying friends what binoculars they are using, or visit the North American Butterfly Association's web site at www.naba.org for the latest information. Test the binoculars you intend to buy for close-focusing, and to ensure that they feel comfortable to you. Which pair is best is a matter of personal preference.

How to Identify Butterflies

If you are just beginning to butterfly, the first step is to learn to recognize the six families of butterflies found in Florida—swallowtails, whites and yellows, gossamer-wings, metalmarks, brushfoots, and skippers. This shouldn't be too difficult because, in general, butterflies belonging to these different families have different wing shapes, sizes, colors, and behaviors. Certain subfamilies are also easy to rec-

ognize, for example, hairstreaks and blues among the gossamer-
wings, and spread-wing skippers and grass-skippers among the skippers. Refer to the short discussion of each butterfly family and
subfamily directly preceding the species accounts for that family or
subfamily. Once you know what family or subfamily the butterfly
belongs to, go to the appropriate plate(s) and see if you recognize the
butterfly you have found. Many species, such as the Zebra Swallowtail on plate 1, are so distinctive that you will probably immediately
recognize the illustration.

**With butterflies, you can make identification much simpler by asking
yourself: Where am I? What time of the year is it? What habitat is this?
Is this butterfly closely associating with a particular plant?** Many
species are found only in certain areas in Florida. Some fly only in the
early spring, others are most common late in the year. Most species are
found in certain habitats and not others, while different species often
use different caterpillar foodplants. Imagine that you are observing a
medium-sized brushfooted butterfly perched with its wings closed.
The color is mainly a gray-brown and there are some small black postmedian eye-spots on the hindwing (HW) and some white on the
forewing (FW). Looking at plates 21 and 22 you see that both Common Buckeye and Dingy Purplewing fit this description. If your butterfly is perched on low vegetation in an open field in northern
Florida, it is overwhelmingly likely to be a Common Buckeye. On the
other hand, if your butterfly is perched 12 feet up on a tree trunk or
leaf in a hardwood hammock in the Florida Keys, it almost certainly
isn't a Common Buckeye and may be a Dingy Purplewing.

If you are seriously motivated to learn butterfly identification,
probably the best approach is to look at the plates in this book whenever possible. This way you can burn the images of the different
species into your brain so that when you encounter a species in the
field that you have never seen before, it will look familiar to you. You
should also read the full species accounts, which often include more
identification information than is included on the pages facing the
plates.

Remember that **the appearance of a species of butterfly can vary
greatly from individual to individual** and that the appearance of the

same individual can vary with the quality and quantity of light. So, the individual you see in the field may not exactly match the individual illustrated on the plate. Often when a species undergoes a population explosion the range of variation increases even more. Additionally, the appearance of the same individual butterfly will change over time. When it first emerges from its chrysalis it will be very bright and in pristine condition. Often its wings will have a beautiful sheen. As the adult butterfly ages, scales will be lost and wings will become frayed and torn. Its color may fade. Distinguishing very worn Southern and Northern broken-dashes can be a real challenge! Sometimes identifying an individual butterfly is too great a challenge for anyone and it should be left as unidentified. This might be because the butterfly was too worn, not seen well enough, or was too easy to confuse with similar species. As you gain experience, you will begin to identify an ever greater percentage of the butterflies you encounter. We strongly recommend that you **use more than one field mark to identify a butterfly that is unusual for the location, habitat, or season in which you find it.** It is possible to find aberrant individuals that lack a certain spot, or have an extra line, or have a different color. For real rarities, it is best to rely on a combination of marks.

How to Find Butterflies

Location, location, location. Butterflies are found throughout Florida and, once you begin looking, you'll see butterflies everywhere. Some areas, however, are a tad more productive than others. The most productive habitats for butterflies, those that have the greatest diversity of species and the largest numbers of individuals, are open areas with natural vegetation. Butterflies are more common in open areas because, as with people, most butterflies like sunshine. They are more common in areas with native plants because, for the most part, these are the plants that caterpillars require as foodplants. So, for example, you will find very few species of butterflies on large manicured lawns—these are essentially biological deserts.

Look for areas with a great variety of vegetation—butterfly diversity is usually correlated with the complexity of the landscape. Some specialized and geographically limited habitats harbor special butterfly species. Boundaries between two different types of habitats will usually have more butterflies than either habitat by itself. Thus butterflying an open field adjacent to a woodland will be more productive than searching either in a woodland or in a field that is distant from a woodland.

How do you find butterfly habitats? One great way to start is by visiting the butterflying localities listed beginning on page 159. Almost all the species found in Florida can be found at these sites. A second method is to search for power line cuts or railroad rights-of-way and walk along these corridors. These narrow corridors often slice through a variety of habitats and may provide excellent habitats themselves. Another approach is to randomly drive along roads, looking for abandoned fields and other likely habitats. Lastly, for many species, the location at which the photograph of that butterfly was taken may be a good area to find the butterfly (this information is given on the pages facing the plates).

Timing is important. Although many of Florida's butterflies fly throughout the warmer months, some species are much more seasonal. Elfins fly only in the early spring while Schaus' Swallowtails are best found in May and June. Other species, while occurring throughout much of the year, have population peaks in the fall. Because behavioral patterns differ among species, you will find the most butterflies by searching at different times of the day. Some butterflies become active at dawn. However, luckily for people who prefer a leisurely breakfast, the peak of butterfly activity is probably from around 10:30 A.M. to about 3:00 P.M.

Friends are important too. Unless you teach third grade you don't have eyes in the back of your head. Butterflying with a small group of friends allows each of you to spot some butterflies that the others would have missed.

Butterfly Concentrators

Having found a likely looking habitat for butterflies, you now will want to search for the butterflies themselves. Sometimes butterflies are everywhere, by the thousands. But many times, the numbers of butterflies are much smaller. When this is the case, your search for butterflies can be helped by locating certain environmental features that concentrate butterflies.

Flowers. The great majority of adult butterflies feed by nectaring at flowers. Almost all flowers are used at some time by some butterflies, but some flowers are much more attractive to butterflies than others. Some of the best, widespread, wild nectar sources for spring, summer, and fall are listed on p. 7. Other plants may be important in your area. Locating stands of attractive flowers is the easiest way to find many butterfly species. If you are not familiar with these plants, you will probably want to consult a wildflower guide.

Hilltops. Many butterflies will congregate on the tops of hills. Although there aren't many hills in Florida, sometimes bumps will do. Actually, butterflies will sometimes concentrate around the tops of tall trees, but it is usually harder for you to join them there. See the behavior section, below, for more about hilltopping.

Mud puddles. A wide variety of species will congregate at damp sand or gravel.

Trails and dirt roads. Not only are butterflies easier to see along a trail but the trail itself serves to concentrate some of them. Believe it or not, many butterflies, such as buckeyes, prefer trails to undisturbed vegetation. If the trail is through a woodland, it needs to be wide enough to allow in sunshine to be a useful butterfly concentrator.

Caterpillar foodplants. Many species of butterflies have caterpillars that use only a few, or even just one, plant species as a foodplant. These special plants act to concentrate the adult butterflies as well, since females will come to these plants to lay their eggs. So, look for narrow-leaved croton to find Bartram's Hairstreak, and for yuccas to find Yucca Giant-Skippers. Each species account includes a section on caterpillar foodplants.

What is a Butterfly?

Butterflies are a group of evolutionarily related animals. They are grouped as part of the class Insecta, and together with the moths constitute the order Lepidoptera. This word derives from the Greek words for scale (*lepid*) and wing (*ptera*). True butterflies (superfamily Papilionoidea) and skippers (superfamily Hesperioidea) are usually con-

SPRING
Blueberries *(Vaccinium)*
Blackberries/dewberries *(Rubus)*
Plums *(Prunus)*
White sweet clover *(Melilotus alba)*

SUMMER
Spanish needles *(Bidens alba)*
Redroot *(Lachnanthes caroliniana)*
Lantana *(Lantana camara)*
Thistle *(Cirsium horridulum)*
Fogfruit *(Lippia nodiflora)*
Mexican clover *(Richardia)*

FALL
Spanish needles *(Bidens alba)*
Blazing stars *(Liatris)*
Deer-tongue *(Carphephorus)*
Lantana *(Lantana camara)*
Ironweed *(Vernonia gigantea)*
Summer farewell *(Dalea pinnata)*
Yellow buttons *(Balduina angustifolia)*
Pickerelweed *(Pontederia cordata)*

sidered together as butterflies, and separately from moths. It is generally easy to distinguish butterflies and moths.

Almost all of our butterflies are active exclusively during the day while the great majority of moths are active only at night. Some moths are active during the day, but these can usually be identified by their flight, which is characteristically stiff and very erratic. In part, this is because most moths have structures, called a frenulum and a retinaculum, that hook the forewing to the hindwing. Butterflies lack these structures and thus, in general, fly much more gracefully than most moths. When seen clearly, our butterflies are distinguished from moths by the shape of their antennas. Butterflies and skippers have a club (a swelling) at the end of their antennas while almost all moths do not (see p. 40).

Butterfly Biology

Life Cycle

Each butterfly goes through four distinct stages in its life: egg, caterpillar, pupa (chrysalis), and adult. The change from caterpillar to pupa to adult butterfly involves major changes in appearance. This process of great physical change, called "metamorphosis," has captured the imagination of peoples throughout the world. Many native peoples in the Americas, including the Papagos and the Aztecs, have myths and gods based upon butterfly transformations.

EGG

An adult female that has mated has the capacity to lay fertilized eggs. A considerable part of her day is spent searching for appropriate plants on which to lay her eggs. The butterfly usually recognizes the right plant by a combination of sight and smell. Butterflies have a very acute sense of smell. They have chemoreceptors (cells that respond to "tastes" and "smells") both on their antennas and the bottom ends of their legs. Most species lay their eggs on a plant that the newly hatched caterpillar will eat. Most species lay only one, or a few, eggs per plant. Others place a mass of eggs together. Some species lay their eggs mainly on flower buds; others place them on the undersides of leaves; still others lay their eggs at the base of a tree. How many eggs a particular female lays varies greatly from species to species. Over the course of their lives some butterflies will lay only a few dozen eggs. Most probably lay a few hundred, while some, such as Regal Fritillaries, lay a few thousand. The eggs themselves are quite interesting, with the eggs of each butterfly family having a different architecture.

CATERPILLAR

When the egg hatches, usually after less than a week, a tiny caterpillar emerges. This voracious eating machine spends almost all of its time eating and growing. As it rapidly increases in size, it outgrows its outer skin (called an exoskeleton). The old skin splits and is shed, revealing a new, larger, and baggier skin below. This process happens a number of times (usually three or four) over the course of about two or three weeks. The great majority of caterpillars do not successfully become butterflies. Most are either eaten by predators, especially wasps and birds, or they are parasitized, usually by one of many species of parasitic wasps or flies, or they succumb to fungal or viral diseases. The world of caterpillars is a fascinating one, with varied shapes and colors and full of interesting behavior—much of it used to avoid predators. However, identifying caterpillars is a vast subject—requiring its own book.

PUPA

When a caterpillar has grown to full size, it attaches itself to a support and becomes a pupa. Sometimes this happens on the caterpillar food-plant itself, but more often the caterpillar wanders away from the foodplant and attaches itself to a twig or a blade of grass. The moulted caterpillar, now encased in a hard outer shell (chrysalis), becomes a pupa—seemingly lifeless and inert. But inside this shell, an amazing transformation is taking place. The tissues and structures of the cater-pillar are being broken down and replaced with the tissues and struc-tures of the adult butterfly. If development is proceeding without impediment, within a week or two an adult butterfly will emerge. If not, the pupa may enter a resting state for a few months, or over-winter.

ADULT

Eventually, when the adult inside the chrysalis is fully formed, the chrysalis splits open, and the adult butterfly emerges. Often this happens very early in the morning. In the chrysalis, the wings are wrapped tightly around the butterfly's body. After the adult emerges, its wings unfurl as fluid pumps through the wing veins. This is a very vulnerable time in a butterfly's life, as it basks in the sunshine to warm itself and to harden and set its wings. Once the adult butterfly emerges from the chrysalis it grows no larger. So if you see a small butterfly, it is not a baby butterfly—it is a fully formed adult.

Lifespan

Most adult butterflies live for a relatively brief time. Some small blues may live only a few weeks, while large brush-footed butterflies, such as Mourning Cloaks and Monarchs, may live up to about eight months. Most adult butterflies can live about two to four weeks, if they are not eaten by predators, such as spiders, dragonflies, birds, and lizards.

Broods

The adults of some species of butterflies fly only at a particular time of the year. Adults of single-brooded species all emerge from their chrysalids at roughly the same time, i.e., over a period of a few weeks or, less commonly, a few months. For example, Henry's Elfins fly only in the early spring, then the adults mate and the females lay eggs. The caterpillars that soon hatch feed on flowers and young fruit for about three weeks and then pupate. The pupas enter a resting period (diapause) during the summer, fall, and winter and new adults emerge the following spring. So, Henry's Elfins are single-brooded.

Some species have two or more broods each year. Adult Juniper Hairstreaks, closely related to Henry's Elfins, also fly in the spring. But when the caterpillars grow up, many of the resulting pupas, rather than overwintering as the Henry's Elfins do, develop quickly into adult butterflies and this second brood then flies in the mid- to late-summer. The offspring of this second brood then overwinter as pupas and the resulting adults fly the next spring. Often, the adults of an early brood will have subtle differences in appearance from those of a later brood.

Further north many species have but one or two broods per year, but most species in Florida have three or more broods per year. Even those species that perhaps only have two broods in Florida may have asynchronous emergences of adults, leading to very long flight periods. Especially in southern Florida, many species can be found throughout much of the year.

Behavior

Because so little is known about butterfly behavior, this is an area where patient observation can increase our knowledge. Here are a few types of behaviors to look for when you are watching butterflies.

BASKING

Butterflies are cold-blooded—their body temperature largely depends on the ambient temperature. When it is cold outside, butterflies want to warm up and employ two different basking strategies to do so. Some butterflies sit in the sunshine in an exposed spot (or even better, on a warm rock) and open their wings. This allows the sun's rays to warm them. Other butterflies engage in lateral basking. These butterflies sit in the sunshine with their wings closed. They then tilt their bodies so that the plane of their wings is perpendicular to the sun's rays, the most efficient way to capture the warming energy of the sun.

HILLTOPPING

Many humans go to singles bars because prospective mates may be concentrated at these locations. Hilltops are the butterfly equivalent of singles bars. Especially in mountainous areas (such as the American West), males of many butterfly species may be most easily found by climbing to the top of the highest hill in the vicinity, especially if the top of the hill is open and if at least some of the slopes are quite steep. Here, the males patrol the area looking for females or they select a favored perch and wait. Unmated females also fly up here (otherwise the system wouldn't work), but already mated females spend more time elsewhere, looking for hostplants and nectar.

MUDPUDDLING

Many butterflies, especially males, congregate at damp sand or soil. Here they imbibe salts along with the water. The salts are passed along to the female at mating and contribute to the nourishment of the eggs. Seeing a large mud puddle party with many species of swallowtails and other butterflies is a thrilling experience.

COURTSHIP

We have little detailed knowledge about most butterflies' courtship patterns. Males of many species stake out territories. They then police these, either by flying back and forth, or by occasionally sallying forth from a favored perch, making sure that they're the only male around when a female saunters into the territory. Although the main objective would seem to be to drive away other males of the same species, some aggressive males try to drive off everything that moves, including birds and sometimes humans! Some butterflies have almost no courtship displays. The males simply fly up to a landed female, and if she is receptive, mate immediately.

Other butterflies behave differently. Most male hairstreaks set up territories, then fly up to greet a female flying through their territory. He flies with her until she lands, then lands next to her, usually facing her, and fans his wings. This disperses the "mating perfume" (a pheromone) that most male hairstreaks have in special patches of scales on the upper side of the their forewings. Many other butterflies are also territorial, while another group of males, taking the initiative, uses patrolling behavior to locate females—they just keep flying till they find them. Male Barred Yellows land alongside a female and flick open their forewing closest to the female. They place their forewing right in front of the female, touching her antennas, presumably to dazzle her with their great-looking and smelling (because of the mating perfume) bar! Most males of a given species will generally engage in either patrolling or territorial behavior, but not both. But males can sometimes switch between perching and patrolling and this may be related to population density.

Migration

Perhaps surprisingly, many butterfly species undertake migrations. We know very little about these movements. Here again is an area where careful observation by the increasing number of butterfliers will provide important new information.

While all butterflies move around, most don't migrate in the traditional sense. What they do is to disperse in a random direction from the site where they emerged from the chrysalis. Some adults immediately fly away from their emergence site, others stay around for most of their lives, then wander off as they get older, while some never leave. If none of the population ever left the original site, butterflies would never be able to colonize new, suitable sites. Since many butterfly species live in habitats that disappear over time (fields being replaced by forests, etc.), this dispersal is critical to the survival of butterfly species. So, a stray butterfly can appear almost anywhere.

Many butterflies that spend the summer in the eastern United States cannot survive northern winters. Each year, as the weather becomes warmer, butterflies from Florida fly north to repopulate these regions. Species that move northward each year include Cloudless Sulphur, Little Yellow, Gulf Fritillary, Red Admiral, Common Buckeye, Long-tailed Skipper,. Clouded Skipper, Fiery Skipper, Sachem, and Ocola Skipper. For most species these northward dispersals are gradual, but, in especially good years, one can see Cloudless Sulphurs or Clouded Skippers streaming northward along the Atlantic coast.

For many species the reverse migration, south in the fall, is more obvious, especially in north Florida. From late August through mid November, the same species that move northward in the spring migrate back into Florida. Like many people, some butterflies, such as Mourning Cloaks, may reside in Florida mainly as winter visitors.

Monarchs are the most well-known of migratory butterflies. But even here our knowledge is limited. We know that most of the Monarchs from central North America spend the winter in roosts in the mountains of central Mexico. But what about the Monarchs from the Atlantic seaboard? Although it seems that many of them also migrate to the same Mexican mountain overwintering sites, others may travel to, and through, Florida, perhaps flying on to undiscovered sites in the Caribbean and/or the Yucatan Peninsula. On the other hand, perhaps many northern Monarchs that enter the peninsula don't survive the winter and, for them, Florida is a dead end. Some Monarchs do overwinter in Florida, but these may be largely members of resident, nonmigratory, populations. At this point, we just don't know.

Butterfly Gardening

If you have a garden, even a small one, the chances are good that you can enjoy butterflies right at home. Many common garden flowers, such as marigolds and black-eyed susans, are attractive to butterflies. If you plant special plants such as pentas (*Pentas lanceolata*) and lantana (*Lantana camara*) you will attract many of the butterflies in your neighborhood to your garden while these plants are in bloom. Although somewhat more difficult to obtain and maintain than common garden flowers, we encourage you to try some of the native wildflowers that are excellent nectar sources for butterflies (see the list on page 15). One advantage of this approach is that the butterflies in your neighborhood may already be familiar with these plants, and thus have learned to come to them for nectar. Of course, the species of butterflies that you attract will depend on the species that are present in your vicinity. If you live close to natural areas, you will attract many more species than if you live in a suburban development. Even flower gardens in urban Miami or Jacksonville can attract a fair number of species.

An important point to keep in mind when planning a butterfly garden is that you must have caterpillars before you can have adult butterflies. The best butterfly gardens include many caterpillar foodplants (see Table 1) so the butterfly garden will "grow" butterflies, not just waylay some of the adults that happen to be in the neighborhood. If you are interested in a specific butterfly species, look up the account for that species and note its caterpillar foodplant and the gardening suggestions, if any. If you live within the range of the butterfly, and if there are natural populations close by, planting the indicated foodplant, either the native species or one especially suited to gardens, will give you a chance to enjoy this butterfly in your garden. Unlike many moth caterpillars, most butterfly caterpillars will not destroy the plants they are eating (well, sometimes they *do* become overexuberant). In addition, because they eat only very specific plants, you do not need to worry about them spreading to your roses or your azaleas. They will not eat these plants, or the vast majority of others that happen to be in your garden.

Blue porterweed *(Stachycarpheta jamaicensis and S. utricifolia)*
Butterfly bush *(Buddleia davidii)*
Butterfly sage *(Cordia globosa)*
Butterfly weed *(Ascelpias tuberosa)*
Climbing aster *(Aster caroliniensis)*
Coral honeysuckle *(Lonicera sempervirens)*
Firebush *(Hamelia patens)*
False heather *(Cuphea hyssopifolia)*
Golden dewdrop *(Duranta repens)*
Hibiscus *(Hibiscus denudatus)*
Lantana *(Lantana camara)*
Mexican sunflower *(Tithonia rotundifolia)*
Pentas *(Pentas lanceolata)*
Purple coneflower *(Echinacea purpurea)*
Spanish needles *(Bidens alba)*
Verbena *(Verbena)*

The more complex your garden becomes, the more attractive it is likely to be to butterflies. Try using many kinds of caterpillar foodplants and different nectar sources, but remember that planting masses of the same caterpillar foodplant or nectar source is usually much more successful than planting a single solitary plant. Because butterflies fly from early spring to late fall, your garden should contain a procession of flowers that bloom through the seasons. In addition, many butterfly species feed on small, inconspicuous plants that most gardeners would regard as weeds. If possible, allow a few areas of your garden, perhaps areas that are not easily seen, to become weedy. You'll be amazed by the beautiful butterflies that these areas will export to your more formal garden!

Besides plants, you should consider a few other features for your butterfly garden. As we saw in the behavior section, butterflies like to bask in the sun, and they like to sip moisture at damp sand or gravel.

Table 1 Some Caterpillar Foodplants (Suitable for the Florida Garden) of Widespread Butterflies

PLANT NAME	FOODPLANT FOR THESE CATERPILLAR SPECIES
Asters (*Aster*)	Pearl Crescent
Cassias (*Cassia*)	Little Yellow, Sleepy Orange, Cloudless Sulphur, Orange-barred Sulphur
Citrus (*Citrus*)	Giant Swallowtail
False Nettle (*Boehmeria cylindrica*)	Red Admiral
Fennel (*Foeniculum vulgare*)	Black Swallowtail
Fog fruit (*Lippia nodiflora*)	Phaon Crescent, Common Buckeye, White Peacock
Hackberries (*Celtis*)	American Snout, Hackberry Emperor, Tawny Emperor, Question Mark
Mallows/Hollyhocks	Gray Hairstreak, Common Checkered-Skipper, Tropical Checkered-Skipper
Milkweeds (*Asclepias*)	Monarch, Queen
Parsley (*Petroselinum*)	Black Swallowtail
Passion-vines (*Passiflora*)	Gulf Fritillary, Zebra (Heliconian), Julia (Heliconian), Variegated Fritillary
Pawpaw (*Asimina triloba*)	Zebra Swallowtail
Pearly-everlastings (*Gnaphalium*)	American Lady
Pipevines (*Aristolochia*)	Pipevine Swallowtail, Polydamas Swallowtail
Sassafras (*Sassafras albidum*)	Spicebush Swallowtail
Snapdragon (*Antirrhinum major*)	Common Buckeye

You can provide a basking area by placing some flat stones in a shel- tered, but sunny, location. If you don't have an area that is naturally damp, try burying a bucket or container filled with sand, adding water as necessary.

Butterfly Photography for Nonphotographers

Butterflies are often very approachable. This approachability makes butterflies easy to photograph. With a little patience, a little experience, and most important of all, the right equipment, anybody, even the photographically inept, like J.G., can take great photographs of butterflies *while still enjoying the butterflies themselves.*

In contrast, birds and flowers, for different reasons, are difficult to photograph, and, at least for birds, the photographer needs to focus single-mindedly on photography at the expense of seeing many birds. While a professional photographer may also take this approach with butterflies—spending the whole day hoping for one great picture—you needn't.

Why Take Photographs?

You can certainly enjoy butterflies without photographing them, and photography does take some time away from observation and can cost quite a bit. Why do it? Well, for one thing it's the easiest way to share your butterflying experiences with others. You can describe your experiences to others with words, but you need to be a talented speaker or author to do justice to the beauty of butterflies and the thrills of butterflying. But, with modern photographic equipment, you do not need to be a talented photographer to let people see the actual butterfly that you saw—or the field of flowers in which it flew—you just need to push the button.

Another reason to take photographs is that you can document the species that you see. You know, when you see some strange species and describe it to others, they may say "that can't occur around here, you must have misidentified it." When a European butterfly, the Small Tortoiseshell, appeared in New York City, photographers were able to document its occurrence so that there was no question of the validity of the report.

Photographs also allow you to hone your identification skills. By looking carefully at series of photographs that you have taken, you will be able to notice small identification points not mentioned elsewhere. In the rest of this section we try to provide information that will allow you to obtain clear, in-focus, well-lit photographs of a large percentage of the butterflies that you see and that can be used for identification and illustration purposes. If you are interested in obtaining a much smaller number of spectacular photographs that you can sell to national magazines, then your approach will be different.

Equipment

CAMERA BODY

Most people will find that a 35 mm single-lens reflex camera gives them the best results. J.G. strongly recommends using a model that has autofocusing and automatic shutter speed and aperature setting programs. Minolta autofocusing has always worked well for butterflies. Although the older Canon and Nikon autofocusing models did not work well for butterflies, the newer models are greatly improved. Two advantages of the autofocusing are that, it's probably more accurate than most people, and it frees up one of your hands to do other things. If you want to get close to the ground to approach a butterfly, you can put one of your hands down to help balance yourself, then lean forward and shoot the scene with the other hand. Or, if there's a butterfly over your head, you can lift the camera over your head and just point it, the camera will do the rest. With manual focus the requirement that your hand turns the barrel of the camera to focus it increases the chances of the butterfly detecting this movement and flying off.

LENS

Although it is possible to obtain passable photographs using a standard 50 mm lens, to take consistently good shots you should use a 100 mm macro lens. Make sure that you are getting a true macro lens, one that at closest focus results in a life-size image on the film. Many lenses listed as "macro" lenses, including all of those that are also zoom lenses do not have this feature. Without the 100 mm macro lens the butterflies

will generally look small in your pictures; with such a lens, the butterflies will fill the frame.

FLASH

Some photographers like to shoot all their pictures using natural light. They feel that the resulting photos look more natural. This puzzled J.G. for a long time, because while one can certainly obtain some great photographs using natural light, his experience is that, for the type of pictures most people take, the butterflies in the photographs taken using natural light often look highly unnatural! J.G. now believes that what they mean is that the background is not darkened relative to the butterfly, and so the background looks more natural. By and large, with flash the butterflies look more natural (that is, more like they appear to your eyes in the field) and so if you are interested in show-ing people how butterflies appear in the field, flash is extremely useful. In addition, the less available light one has, the longer one must expose the film (slower shutter speed) to obtain the same brightness. Since butterflies often move and your hands move also, using slow shutter speeds is not often an option—unless you've stuck a frozen butterfly on a flower (see below). Also, at closest focus, a 100 mm macro lens has a very shallow depth of field, so with available light one is not likely to get the entire butterfly in focus, let alone parts of the foreground and background. All of this argues for the use of a flash to provide extra light.

For the nonphotographer photographer there are really two choic-es for flash arrangements. The first is the standard flash mounted on the top of the camera. This can work fairly well. An advantage to these flashes over ring flashes is that they have much more power, creating good illumination of butterflies that are quite distant. One drawback, however, is that the angle of the flash may not be entirely suitable for illuminating butterflies at the closest focusing distance, leading to unwanted shadows. Also, using a flash mounted on the camera body, you will have only a fixed, point source of light and sometimes it is advantageous to illuminate the butterfly from an angle, or with light from more than one angle.

The second type of flash is a ring flash. Rather than sit on the top of the camera body, the ring flash fits around the end of the macro lens. An advantage of this system is that the flash is always aimed properly, yielding a very high percentage of eminently usable photos. Another advantage is that with four lights in the ring, you can vary the angle of light if you want to. A disadvantage of this system is that ring flashes are underpowered (they are intended for very close macro photography) making it difficult to properly illuminate targets at a distance, such as swallowtails. Another disadvantage, for some purposes, is that although the butterfly will be sharp and well-illuminated, this system tends to produce a higher percentage of photographs in which the background is black than does a camera-mounted flash. Black backgrounds result when the available light on the butterfly is much greater than the available light on the background. On many camera settings, the flash will overpower any natural light and because the light from the flash drops off as the square of the distance from the flash, only objects very close to the focal plane of the butterfly will be properly illuminated. (The same effect happens with all flashes, but because the ring flash is closer to the butterfly the effect is accentuated with a ring flash.) For the purposes of showing other people just how the butterfly looks, black backgrounds may be a plus, because one's attention is focused on the butterfly. However, in terms of a beautiful photograph, some people find a black background objectionable (except for Elvis pictures). Since most of the photographs in this book were taken using the ring flash system, you can judge for yourself if this system might be suitable for you.

FILM

In a few years time, the performance of digital cameras will equal or surpass that of traditional cameras. But, for now, film is still superior and the basic choice is between print and slide film. An advantage to prints is that you can easily view them yourself or with a small group of people. However, there are many advantages to slides—you can use them for talks to groups of people, they are easier to store, and their resolution is better. Since only slide film was used for the photographs shown here, we can't really make a recommendation about which print film is best. Sharper pictures are possible when you use film with lower ASA numbers. ASA 25 film will yield much sharper pictures, that can be greatly enlarged, than will ASA 200 film, but, the ASA 200 film can be used under much lower light conditions. If you are photographing without a flash, you will want to use ASA 200 film, or higher. With a flash, you can use ASA 25 or 64 film. J.G. uses Kodachrome 64 film, believing that, overall, its color veracity is the best. This film also has a reputation for long-term color stability.

ACCESSORIES

For most butterfly photographs it is a good idea to keep an ultraviolet filter over your lens. You'll want a strap for your camera. A good wide one will do less damage to your shoulder than a narrow one. You'll probably also want to take extra batteries and film with you on hikes. A small pouch that fits around your waist is useful for carrying extra rolls of film, extra sets of batteries for your flash, and an extra battery for the camera itself.

Taking the Photo

APPROACHING THE BUTTERFLY

When you see a butterfly you want to photograph, you naturally want to rush right up to it and grab its picture. Unfortunately, butterflies are pretty good motion detectors. So, you need to slow down. And be more graceful. The more slowly and gracefully you move the less likely you will frighten the butterfly. But, let's get real. If you move slowly enough the butterfly is guaranteed to have flown before you get in place for your photograph. So, you need to strike a balance. Just where that balance lies is best learned by experience. It will also vary from butterfly species to species, and from butterfly individual to individual. Some butterflies that are nectaring, or, that are mud puddling, will sit still forever. Others almost never stop. If you have a choice, find one that stops. If you are trying to photograph a Georgia Satyr and there are a number of individuals present, watch for an individual who is landing more frequently and for longer periods of time than others. It will probably continue to do so as you try to photograph it.

The same type of advice applies to those times when you especially want the upperside of the butterfly, or alternatively, the underside. Whatever you want, the butterflies will be doing the opposite. The few individuals who occasionally open their wings may well continue to do so. Focus on them.

If you have a choice, it is best to approach the butterfly from a low position, rather than from over its head. This way you'll be less likely to startle it. You'll also be less likely to startle it if you avoid having your shadow pass over the butterfly.

FRAMING THE BUTTERFLY

Proper framing is important for both aesthetically desirable results and easy identification of the butterflies in your photos. To clearly see your butterfly you should strive to have the butterfly's wings parallel to the plane of the film in your camera. Many times you will need to be on one knee, or on your belly, and/or with your body contorted into ludicrous positions to effectively accomplish proper framing. If the angle of the butterfly is off just a little, this will distort the perspective and make it more difficult to examine spot shapes and patterns that are important for identification. Of course, if you just want an interesting angle, that is a different story. Another decision you will make is what to include in the frame along with the butterfly. This is an aesthetic decision that depends upon your "eye"—what looks good to you. Like anything else in this world, some people are better than others in creating pleasing photographic compositions. However, unless you want to sell your photos to mass circulation magazines, this may not matter to you.

Another important point of this section is that late breaking research shows that Mourning Cloaks and Ruddy Daggerwings, playing a dark butterfly version of the old cat and mouse game, are often responsible for the missing fig newtons. Photos show them, fig-legged, skulking around fruit! Then again, maybe they were framed.

Photo Etiquette

Photo etiquette requires consideration for other people, for the butterfly, and for the environment. As more and more people take up

butterflying and butterfly photography, this will become more
important.

If you are with other people, you should consider their needs. A record shot from a distance, without a flash, is okay, but going right up to a butterfly to photograph it, or using a flash, carries the risk with it of frightening the butterfly away. When J.G. leads groups of people on butterflying trips he asks photographers to wait until everyone has had a careful look at the butterfly. (Of course, some people probably think that J.G. is not so good at policing himself!) If there is more than one photographer present, you might try a system of alternating who photographs first, although some butterflies are very cooperative and allow more than one person to photograph them at the same time. If a butterfly is sitting on the ground with its wings closed, but occasionally opening them, there can be a photographer on each side of the butterfly, each photographing its underside, while another photographer is behind the butterfly, waiting for its wings to open to photograph its upperside. Believe it or not, this has worked on a surprising number of occasions.

You should also consider the butterfly. Some photographers will do almost anything to obtain a photograph. They will capture a butterfly, place it in an ice chest to cool it, then pose the almost frozen butterfly on some colorful flower or background so they can photograph it to their heart's content. Putting aside the fact that there are times when butterflies are injured just by capturing them (and any injury to a butterfly is probably fatal), my opinion is that while photographers may believe that photographs obtained in this way are okay, if they don't inform readers that this is how the photographs were obtained then they are inadvertently deceiving the public. People looking at these photographs will believe that these artificial poses and situations can normally be found in nature. They cannot.

Last, but not least, you should consider the environment. When you walk up to butterflies for your photograph, do not trample flowers and other plants along the way. Any human actions cause environmental problems, especially when repeated by large numbers of people. Although it's impossible to avoid accidents, you can minimize the damage your activities cause by being aware of potential trampling problems and exercising care when you photograph.

Care of Your Photographs

RECORD KEEPING

More than just being pretty pictures, your photographs can be important records of what kinds of butterflies were in what locations at what times. We urge you to label your photographs. Not with some type of arcane code, but with the date the photograph was taken and the locality where it was taken written directly on the slide holder, or on the back of the print. A code is close to useless. Sure *you* know the code, you've even written it down in a notebook. But, as the years go by you'll forget the code or lose the notebook. And, we won't be the first to tell you, you will die. Invariably, eventually, your photographs will become separated from your code. Ask any museum curator, and they will tell you that butterfly specimens that do not have date and locality data, written on a label that is on the same pin as the specimen, have almost no value.

In order to write this information on your photographs, you will need to record it when you take the pictures. Relying on your memory is a bad idea and will eventually lead to mistakes that are misleading to others and embarrassing to yourself. Carry a small notebook with you. Number each roll of film you shoot, by year and sequence, e.g., 97-11 would be the 11th roll of film in 1997. Then in your field notebook, after the heading 97-11, the first hand-written entry might read "1. Great Southern White, Homestead, Miami-Dade Co., FL 3/25." When your slides from roll 11 come back developed, refer to your field notebook and write the information on the slide. If you have taken more than one photograph of what *you are sure* is the same individual butterfly (the butterfly has never left your sight), then indicate that in your notebook, and cross-label all the slides of the same individual by saying something like, see 1-5T, writing that same instruction on all five slides of the Great Southern White. This is especially important when you want to study the upperside and underside of the same butterfly, either for ID, or to see if certain upperside characteristics are associated with certain underside characteristics.

STORAGE AND PHOTOGRAPH RETRIEVAL

You should protect your photographs from excessive heat, high humidity, dust, and light. Prints can be stored in photo albums, or just in envelopes. Some people store their slides in carousels, others store them in the boxes in which the developed slides are returned, while others use special enamel slide cabinets. J.G. stores his slides in clear plastic pages with compartments for individual slides. Use only plastic pages that are labeled as archival for slides, others contain polyvinyl chloride, which can destroy your photos over time. These clear plastic pages, generally of polyethylene or of polyester polypropylene, then fit into three ring binders.

Some photographers store their photographs by trip, or by time period. J.G. stores his butterfly slides in taxonomic sequence. This makes it very easy to find slides of particular butterfly species to illustrate articles or talks.

VIEWING YOUR PHOTOGRAPHS

If you want to share your photos with groups of people, you need to project them onto a screen or a white wall using a slide projector. For viewing yourself, it is best to use a loupe, a type of magnifying glass especially made especially for viewing slides. Although you can just hold the slides up to a light and look through the loupe, many people probably prefer placing the slides on a light box. Loupes and light boxes are available from camera supply stores.

Conservation

Throughout the United States, when we talk about butterflies to people that we meet, their response is often "there certainly are fewer butterflies now than when I was a child." Unfortunately, this is especially true in Florida. Although only one Florida butterfly is included on the federal list of endangered species, this list is more a reflection of politics than of natural history. The sad reality is that Florida probably has more seriously threatened species of butterflies than any other state. Without concerted conservation efforts in the near term, we believe that many of our tropical hammock species will disappear. Most of these species are not found anywhere else in the United States. What a loss for future generations, not to be able to find Schaus' Swallowtails, Dina Yellows, Mimosa Yellows, Amethyst Hairstreaks, Bartram's Scrub-Hairstreaks, Martial Scrub-Hairstreaks, Miami Blues, Dingy Purplewings, Florida Purplewings, or Zestos Skippers in the United States.

As you study the range maps that accompany the photographic plates, you will notice that some species have part of their range colored bright red. This indicates that the species has disappeared from a large area it formerly inhabited. The red color really understates the loss of butterflies in our region because it does not include all those areas where species that were formerly common have become rare, or areas where there now exist only a few colonies where previously there were many. While in some cases the reasons for a species' loss are mysterious, the decline of most species has been due to human activities (see Table 2).

The main reason we are losing so many butterflies is that humans continue to expand their realm and destroy the habitats that butterflies need to survive. Wetlands are drained, woodlands are cut, fields are converted to parking lots or lawns. Of course, habitat loss affects almost all wildlife, but butterflies carry an added burden. Many of our butterflies flourish in habitats that are ephemeral, i.e., these habitats will disappear in a relatively short period of time due to natural succession. Many open areas, left to their own devices, will become woodlands. Woodlands do support some butterflies, but far fewer than open areas, especially when the woodland is "pure," without open disturbed areas either within it or adjacent to it. These open areas (often human-disturbed) are critical to butterfly populations because it is here that the greatest concentrations of flowers that serve as nectar sources are found. Perhaps surprisingly, it is often the availability of nectar sources for the adult butterflies, rather than foodplants for the caterpillars, that limits the size of a butterfly population.

In the past, naturally caused fires often created large open areas with ample nectar sources, and man-made fires can play an important role in creating or maintaining these areas today. Unfortunately, some of the conservation community and groups charged with the man-

Table 2 Florida butterflies that have declined over at least part of their range in the past 25 years.

SPECIES	REASONS FOR DECLINE
Schaus' Swallowtail	Habitat destruction; anti-mosquito spraying
Bartram's Scrub-Hairstreak	Habitat destruction
Miami Blue	Habitat destruction and perhaps other unknown factors
Zestos Skipper	Habitat destruction
Golden-banded Skipper	Unknown
Mottled Duskywing	Unknown
Arogos Skipper	Habitat destruction

agement of our natural areas have made a devil's embrace of fire—"fire is good at keeping areas open, let's burn like crazy." Yes, fire can be an effective tool in maintaining open habitats, but one needs to carefully control burns so that only *portions* of the habitat are burned every few years, always leaving refuges for species so that they can then recolonize the burned areas. Burning large areas without leaving refuges for the resident butterflies destroys the butterfly populations present (along with myriad other species of insects and plants). For example, one of the few places in Florida where Arogos Skippers could still be found until recently was in Ocala National Forest. Although the Forest Service was alerted to the presence of this rare species and of the danger of fire, in June of 1996, the Forest Service burned the northern section of the colony and then, in July, burned the southern portion. Arogos Skippers have not been seen there since.

The good news is that, with proper planning, human and butterfly habitations are compatible. Because most butterfly populations do not need very large expanses of habitat, preservation of most species is feasible by creating an interconnecting network of small protected habitat units along with a few larger units. Small habitat units, perhaps as small as the yards of a few concerned neighbors, are sufficient to support small populations of many species, especially if these small units are loosely connected to other small units. However, butterfly populations are commonly subject to very large fluctuations in numbers. In especially bad years for a particular species of butterfly, perhaps due to drought, or to a disease epidemic, the small units, with their small populations, will probably not survive. However, larger preserves support large and varied populations and habitats that will ensure that some individuals survive a calamity. Then, when the population rebounds, the larger preserves serve as butterfly reservoirs and overflow individuals will repopulate the small units.

A second factor reducing butterfly populations is pollution of the environment, especially pollution with pesticides. These pesticides are employed mostly for mass sprayings against pests such as med flies and mosquitoes, and for use by farmers and private homeowners. Mosquito control has had a devastating effect on a number of Florida's butterflies, especially those found in South Florida and the Keys.

Some people might ask: Why save butterfly species? Are they of any value? An extensive consideration of this question is outside the scope of this book but we would like to put forward a few short answers. (See *Why Preserve Natural Variety?* by B.G. Norton for a recent comprehensive discussion.) In many areas, butterflies play an important role in the pollination of flowers. In addition, each species may possess unique properties useful to humans that will be irretrievably lost should it become extinct. The recent discovery of a potent anticancer drug, taxol, in a species of yew that had been considered a "trash species" highlights this possibility. Because ecological systems are interrelated in complicated ways, the removal of a single species can have a much greater adverse effect than might have been anticipated. In many cases, the extinction of but a single species will result in the removal of a number of other species that are, in some way, dependent on the first species. Often, the fact that a species of butterfly is close to extinction can be seen as a symptom that an entire unique habitat is about to be destroyed. The collapse of many of the earth's ecosystems may result in a world hostile, at best, to humans.

In addition to these practical arguments for the preservation of but-

terflies, there are clearly aesthetic and moral reasons to insist that butterflies survive. Only recently have human beings seen peoples from
other tribes as similar to themselves and thus "real human beings"
worthy of protection. As people become ever more conscious of their
environment, they may come to see that all biological entities have
intrinsic value and are worthy of protection. Many years ago, the
Greeks equated butterflies with the souls of people, using the Greek
word *psyche* for both. One does not have to believe in Greek mytholo-
gy to know that in a world without butterflies, the souls of all people
would be greatly diminished.

The Florida Landscape

Travel guides characterize Florida as a warm vacation paradise, where
the sun eternally sets over a postcard landscape of palm trees, flowers,
and beaches. Sadly, this simplistic portrayal ignores the true beauty and
variety of Florida. It also disregards the diversity of plants and animals
that inhabit the state. Florida encompasses a wealth of natural won-
ders, which, if only noticed, would enrich the lives of residents and visitors alike. The noted Florida ecologist, Marjorie Harris Carr, wisely
advised that "the salvation of the Florida scene will come about only if
the public savors its beauty, understands its limitations, and speaks up
for its preservation."

Nearly 800 miles in length from the western edge of the Panhandle
to Key West, Florida is both temperate and tropical. From November to
May is a dry season, with limited precipitation and mild temperatures.
A wet season with higher temperatures and heavy afternoon rains
occurs from June through October. The humid subtropical climate
bathes a mostly flat, sandy countryside that is largely covered with
forests of pine. Deep stream valleys slice through portions of the Panhandle and gently rolling terrain is the standard across much of the
central peninsula. Lush deciduous forests, reminiscent of northern
woodlands, are strewn across the northwestern counties. Broad tidal
marshes, sand dunes, and impenetrable mangrove swamps occupy
the undeveloped portions of the state's one thousand-mile coastline.
Hundreds of barrier islands hug the coast and offshore coral reefs provide food and shelter for an endless array of marine life.

Water is a recurring theme in Florida. Beach lovers are comforted to know that no location in Florida is more than 60 miles from seawater. Inland, 34 major rivers and streams traverse the state, draining summer rains into both the Gulf of Mexico and the Atlantic Ocean. Among these is the fabled Suwannee River, which twists its way through dense forests of northern Florida. The Apalachicola River of the Panhandle is the largest, possessing a drainage basin that includes three states. Alligators silently patrol still waters and wading birds fish along the shorelines of over 7000 freshwater lakes. The largest is Lake Okeechobee, a shallow body of water over 700 square miles in size. Sharing this wetland pallet is a myriad of swamps, marshes, and freshwater springs. An unmistakable denizen of many swamps is cypress (*Taxodium* sp.). These stately trees, festooned with gently swaying Spanish moss (*Tillandsia usneoides*), are perennial symbols of the deep South. In southern Florida, the most prominent wetland feature is the Everglades, a vast ecosystem encompassing nearly 4000 square miles. Much of urban southern Florida obtains its water supply from this fragile "river of grass."

At the southern tip of Florida are the Keys, a rocky chain of islands projecting southwestward into the Gulf of Mexico. Key West, the Marquesas Keys, and the Dry Tortugas flirt with Cuba as the southernmost locations in the United States. The Keys are regarded as extensions of the West Indies where numerous tropical species maintain a precarious existence at the northern edge of their ranges.

Native plants in Florida number over 4000 and inspired Juan Ponce de León in 1513 to describe the newly discovered land before him as "Pescua Florida," the place of flowers. This botanical heritage contributes to a rich assemblage of habitats that support a multitude of butterfly species. A brief overview of these communities can be used as a guide to the habitats discussed in this book.

The most prevalent upland natural habitats in Florida are **pine flatwoods**. Flatwoods consist of slash and longleaf pine (*Pinus elliotii* and *P. palustris*) forests and support a rich undergrowth of grasses and saw palmettos (*Serenoa repens*). These dry habitats are abundant throughout much of the southeastern states, including Florida. Flatwoods support many butterflies, including Palmetto Skippers, Pipevine Swallowtails,

Southern Dogfaces, Barred Yellows, Little Metalmarks, Queens,
duskywings, and cloudywings. **Dry prairies** are distributed sparingly in
northern and central Florida, especially to the north and west of Lake
Okeechobeee. These open, grassy expanses are similar to flatwoods,
but lack a pine overstory. Many butterflies found in flatwoods also
inhabit dry prairies. **Pine rockland** occurs where pine forests grow on
limestone outcroppings of the extreme southeastern mainland and
the Keys. The National Key Deer Refuge on Big Pine Key is largely
composed of pine rockland. Butterflies mostly limited to this habitat
are Florida Duskywing, Bartram's Scrub-Hairstreak, and Florida
Leafwing. **Sandhills** are dry habitats where scrub oaks, particularly
turkey oak (*Quercus laevis*), form an understory in more open
pinelands. Sandhills are scattered across the northern half of Florida,
but possess qualities attractive to development and many have been
destroyed. Butterflies are diverse in sandhill environments and
include such uncommon species as Frosted Elfin, Goatweed Leafwing,
Dotted Skipper, Meske's Skipper, Arogos Skipper, Dusted Skipper, and
Cofaqui Giant-Skipper.

Hammocks are widely distributed in Florida. The term *hammock* is
loosely used to describe various types of hardwood forests. **Moist** or
temperate hardwood hammocks are composed of broad-leaved deciduous trees and occur primarily in the northern half of Florida. These rich
forests support many butterflies typically found further north, such as
Coral Hairstreak, King's Hairstreak, Summer Azure, Silvery Checkerspot, Red-spotted Purple, Golden-banded Skipper, Little Glassywing, Zabulon Skipper, and Northern Broken-Dash. San Felasco
Hammock State Preserve, Gold Head Branch State Park, and Torreya
State Park contain exemplary hardwood communities. **Tropical hammocks** are broad-leaved evergreen forests of primarily tropical trees.
Confined to the extreme southern mainland and the Keys, several
mainland tropical hammocks were severely damaged in 1992 by Hurricane Andrew. A few remaining fragments are being protected, such
as in the North Key Largo Hammocks State Botanical Site. Some tropical butterflies found in and around these habitats are Schaus' Swallowtail, Florida White, Mimosa Yellow, Dina Yellow, Amethyst
Hairstreak, Martial Scrub-Hairstreak, Dingy Purplewing, Florida Pur-

plewing, Ruddy Daggerwing, Zestos Skipper, and Hammock Skipper. **Coastal hammocks** are found along the coasts of northern and central Florida. These hammocks differ in that they mostly contain oaks, cabbage palm (*Sabal palmetto*), and southern red cedar (*Juniperus silicicola*). Excellent examples of coastal hammocks can be observed at Canaveral National Seashore and in the vicinity of Yankeetown, Levy County. The most notable butterfly of coastal hammocks is the Florida subspecies of Juniper Hairstreak ('Sweadner's' Juniper Hairstreak).

Scrubs are limited to northern and central Florida, especially along the low sandy ridges of the central peninsula. Thickets of shrubs and small trees dominate these dry habitats where sand pines (*Pinus clausa*) are sometimes abundant. Scrubs are rapidly being reduced by development, but extensive tracts can still be found within Ocala National Forest. Sleepy Duskywings and Eastern Pine Elfins can be found in scrub habitats.

Swamps are conspicuous communities in Florida. Many types of these forested wetlands occur in the state. **Mangrove swamps** extend along the coasts of southern and central Florida and are dominated by red mangrove (*Rhizophora mangle*), black mangrove (*Avicennia germanans*), and white mangrove (*Laguncularia racemosa*). Few butterflies occur in mangrove swamps, but Mangrove Skippers and Mangrove Buckeyes may commonly be found. **Hardwood swamps** are dominated by hardwood deciduous trees and are limited to northern and central Florida. Florida Caverns State Park and Suwannee River State Park maintain diverse tracts of bottomland hardwood swamps. Butterflies such as Dukes' Skipper, Seminole Crescent, and Appalachian Brown are found primarily in hardwood swamps. Hardwood swamps of northern Florida frequently contain dense stands of cane (*Arundinarea gigantea*) that are known as **canebreaks**. Butterflies associated with cane are Southern Pearly-Eye, Yehl Skipper, and Lace-winged Roadside-Skipper. **Cypress swamps**, dominated by bald and pond cypresses (*Taxodium distichum* and *T. ascendens*), are widespread and common in Florida, but do not support many butterflies. **Bay swamps (bayheads)**, dominated by sweet bay (*Magnolia virginiana*) and swamp bay (*Persea palustris*), are widespread in the northern half of Florida. Palamedes Swallowtails can usually be seen in the vicinity of bay swamps or other swamps containing an abundance of swamp bay. Hessel's Hair-streaks occur only in swamp habitats containing Atlantic white cedar (*Chamaecyparis thyoides*), such as in the Blackwater River State Forest and the Apalachicola National Forest.

Freshwater **marshes** are treeless wetlands dominated by herbaceous (nonwoody) vegetation. They are often established around the margins of lakes. Vast expanses of saw grass (*Cladium jamaicense*) marsh dominate the Everglades ecosystem. A number of butterflies, particularly skippers, inhabit marsh habitats. Notable examples include Least Skipper, Broad-winged Skipper, Palatka Skipper, Dion Skipper, Berry's Skipper, and Delaware Skipper. **Wet prairies** can also be considered a type of marsh where water levels limit the amount of invasive woody vegetation. Superior wet prairies can be found in Paynes Prairie State Preserve near Gainesville. Georgia Satyrs and many of the butterflies typical of marshes can be found in wet prairies. Various grasses and rushes usually dominate **salt marshes**. Salt marshes are closely associated with the coast where they are regularly inundated by salt water. Higher portions of salt marshes (salt flats) often support an abundance of saltwort (*Batis maritima*) and glasswort (*Salicornia* spp.). Salt marsh vegetation is widespread along stretches of coastal Florida where wave action is limited, such as within St. Marks and Merritt Island National Wildlife Refuges. Butterflies associated with salt marshes are Great Southern Whites, Eastern Pygmy-Blues, Salt Marsh Skippers, and Obscure Skippers. Natural lowland **savannas** are moist grassy habitats where trees are sparse. Savannas are found sparingly in northern Florida, including portions of the Apalachicola National Forest. Common Wood-Nymphs, Crossline Skippers, Palmetto Skippers, Dion Skippers, and Berry's Skippers can be found in savannas.

Without a doubt, the most common Florida habitats are not natural. Pastures, drainage ditches, cultivated field edges, citrus groves, avocado groves, brushy wood lots, roadsides, residential yards, and urban parks offer food plants and nectar sources for a variety of butterflies. Species frequently found in these **disturbed situations** include Giant Swallowtail, Checkered White, Cloudless Sulphur, Orange-barred Sulphur, Little Yellow, Sleepy Orange, Dainty Sulphur, Ceraunus Blue, Gulf Fritillary, Phaon Crescent, Pearl Crescent, Common Buck-

INTRODUCTION

eye, White Peacock, Long-tailed Skipper, Dorantes Longtail, Common Checkered-Skipper, Tropical Checkered-Skipper, Fiery Skipper, and Whirlabout.

A Fluid Fauna

The butterfly fauna of Florida is continually changing. This is most apparent in the southern half of the state where tropical influences are more pronounced. Many tropical butterflies appear to have colonized Florida within the last century, most of them within the past 40 years. Like many Americans, the following species are recent immigrants: Orange-barred Sulphur, Dina Yellow, Silver-banded Hairstreak, Gray Ministreak, Fulvous Hairstreak, Tropical Buckeye, Malachite, Soldier, Dorantes Longtail, and Monk Skipper. Androgeus Swallowtails became established in southeastern Florida in the mid-1970s, but disappeared after several seasons. Very recently, Nickerbean Blues have taken up residence in the lower Keys, perhaps only temporarily. Tropical species such as Orbed Sulphur, Boisduval's Yellow, Caribbean Peacock, Many-banded Daggerwing, Antillean Daggerwing, and Violet-banded Skipper, have been found in Florida on only one or two occasions.

Migratory movements, especially from Cuba—only 90 miles away—play a major role in the appearance of unusual butterfly species in Florida. In 1973, large numbers of the Yellow Angled-Sulphur came ashore in the lower Keys, but completely vanished after a few days. It has been suggested that extensive cutting of coastal forests in northern Cuba caused the dispersal of many tropical species into the lower Keys during the early 1970s.

Some butterflies probably enter Florida as stowaways on ships or planes carrying produce and other plant materials. Thousands of insects are discovered and destroyed each year during agricultural inspections at Florida ports of entry, but many more presumably go unnoticed. The Ruddy Hairstreak and Cramer's Eighty-eight that were found in Florida, both South American, may have arrived in this fashion. This probably also explains the unexpected sighting of a spectacular blue Morpho in southern Florida several decades ago—certainly a memorable event!

Tropical breezes probably also contribute to the movement of

species into Florida. The tropical climate influencing Florida gen-
erates powerful storms during the wet season. Some of these dis-
turbances attain hurricane strength, producing high winds and
traveling great distances during their development. These storm
systems can extend over 400 miles in diameter and produce winds
in excess of 200 mph. They can be enormously destructive, radi-
cally altering the landscape in their wake. Despite this intense
destructive power, tropical storms probably transport butterflies to
Florida from neighboring West Indian islands or, conceivably, from
the Central American mainland. These delicate creatures may be
swept into rising air currents and carried many miles with no apparent ill effects.

The devastation wreaked by tropical storms is not entirely detri-
mental. Some butterfly species are negatively affected, while others
take advantage of newly created habitat. Though valuable tropical
hammock habitat was lost to Hurricane Andrew in 1992, Dina Yellows
benefited from the resulting spread of their food plant, Mexican alvaradoa (*Alvaradoa amorphoides*), in ravaged hammocks.

Butterfly jailbreak is another potential means of entry into Florida.
The mild Florida climate is perfect for the creation of butterfly
"houses"—essentially zoos for butterflies. Several such exhibits have
opened in recent years and are extremely popular. Although most
attractions employ strict measures to prohibit escape, a butterfly from
South America or Africa may someday be seen sipping nectar in a
yard in Fort Lauderdale or a park in Winter Haven.

The large number of tropical species that have recently become
established in south Florida may be related to the growing, and now
prolific, use of exotic tropical plants for landscaping. However, since
Florida is outside the normal range of many visiting butterflies, even if
a mated female survives an arduous journey to Florida, manages to
locate suitable foodplants and produces offspring, the colony may not
survive more than a few seasons. Harsh weather conditions, competi-
tion with other species, or other factors may ultimately lead to the
population's demise. In the years to come, we will doubtlessly see
other butterfly species enter Florida. Some will attempt to stay, others
will merely be tourists. Fortunate are those who encounter these way-
faring visitors during their fleeting existence in Florida.

About the Plates

Photographs

The 376 photographs (356 by Jeffrey Glassberg) on the 43 color plates represent a first. The *Through Binoculars* books are the first field guides to any group of organisms that use photographs in a true field guide format. Unlike other books that use photographs, the species in the photographs in this book are presented in the **correct size relationships** to the other species on the plate—the photographs having been carefully enlarged or reduced to provide this relationship. On the top right of the facing page to each plate, you learn the magnification or reduction from life size of that plate.

When males and females differ greatly in their appearance, both sexes are shown. In general, if the illustration is unlabeled as to sex, it can be assumed that both sexes are quite similar (although experienced butterfliers can probably discern the sex of most individuals by subtle differences).

Photographs were chosen and arranged so that similar species are shown in similar poses, making comparisons for identification easier. Almost all of the photographs were taken using the same camera equipment and film, so in general there is a visual consistency to the photographs, making them easy to compare to each other. Additional factors influencing the choice of photograph to illustrate each species were quality of the photograph, and condition and typicality of the butterfly illustrated. Of course, in some cases there was little choice. For example, the photographs of Dusky Roadside-Skipper and Cofaqui Giant-Skipper show the only individuals of these species J.G. had ever seen. When possible, we have used photographs of butterflies photographed in Florida. Photos taken outside of Florida show individuals that are substantially identical to those of the same species that occur in Florida.

Unless otherwise indicated, all photographs by J.G. were taken in the wild, of unrestrained, unmanipulated butterflies. Two photographs, of very rare species for which no photographs of wild butterflies were available, are of museum specimens.

The black and white lines that appear on some of the photographs have been placed over the photographs to draw your eye to field

Recognizing which wing of a grass-skipper one is viewing may require some practice. Remember that grass-skippers hold their HWs flat but their FWs are held at an angle. So, depending upon one's angle of view, one may see the right FW on the right side and the left HW on the left side. For example, photograph 12, on plate 37, is of a Clouded Skipper. On the right side of the skipper one sees a wing with white spots. This is the right FW. On the left side one sees a wing that is unmarked. This is the left HW. The left FW is not readily visible, it is angled edge on toward the viewer. The right HW is partially visible as a crescent "northeast" of the right FW. Most of the photos of the upper surfaces of grass-skippers follow this pattern.

Facing Page Notes

The notes on the pages facing the plates are intended to serve as a quick reference to the most important identification features'. In addition, the notes on these pages tell you where and when each of the photographs was taken, when known. Dates are shown as month/day/year. This information can be useful in locating the species. Also, when an important flower is well-illustrated in a photo, we tell you the name of the flower as an aid to recognizing these resources.

Maps

The range maps tell you where a species is normally found. If an area is colored on a particular map, this means that we believe there are **resident populations** of the species in this area, or, if the species is an immigrant, that an **active field observer is likely to see the species in this area at least once every two to three years.**

It is important to remember that butterflies have wings and will wander outside their normal range, occasionally for a great distance. Just because your location is not included in the normal range of a species doesn't mean it is impossible to see that species where you live, just that it becomes increasingly unlikely the farther from the normal range you go.

ABBREVIATIONS

A	abundant, you are likely to encounter more than 20 individuals per field trip to the right locality at the right time
C	Central Florida subregion—Citrus, Sumter, Lake, and Volusia counties south to include Sarasota, De Soto, Highlands, Okeechobee, and St. Lucie counties
C	common, you are likely to encounter between 4 and 20 individuals per field trip to the right locality at the right time
Co.	county
C.R.	county road
FW	forewing
H	historically occurred but no longer present
HW	hindwing
K	Florida Keys subregion—includes Sands Key southward
L	local, not generally distributed, even within the range shown, absent from many areas with seemingly suitable habitat
N	Northern Florida subregion—Levy, Marion, Putnam, and Flagler counties north to Georgia and west to Jefferson County
NF	national forest
NP	national park
NWR	national wildlife refuge
R	rare, rarely seen even at the right place at the right time
S	Southern Florida subregion—Charlotte, Glades, and Martin counties south through mainland Florida
S	stray, not part of the region's normal fauna and not seen most years
SF	state forest
SP	state park
SR	state road
U	uncommon, you are likely to see 0–3 individuals per field trip to the right place at the right time
W	Florida panhandle subregion—Jefferson County westward
WMA	wildlife management area
X	not normally found in this subregion
♂	male
♀	female

STATE ABBREVIATIONS

AR	Arkansas		**NH**	New Hampshire
AZ	Arizona		**NJ**	New Jersey
CA	California		**NY**	New York
CO	Colorado		**PA**	Pennsylvania
CT	Connecticut		**TN**	Tennessee
FL	Florida		**TX**	Texas
GA	Georgia		**VA**	Virginia
IA	Iowa		**VT**	Vermont
LA	Louisiana		**WV**	West Virginia
NC	North Carolina			

In addition to showing the ranges of butterflies, to our knowledge, these maps are among the first to provide information about butterfly broods (see the discussion of broods on page 10). The different colors on the map indicate the number of broods a species normally has in each portion of its range. Yellow indicates one brood, green indicates two broods, and blue indicates three or more broods. In general, you will need to search for a single-brooded species at a particular time of the year, while three-brooded species will be present during most of the warm season.

A fourth color, red, is used in the range maps to indicate that portion of a species' former range, from which it has been extirpated, i.e., it no longer is found there. Red is used only if the best available information suggests that there are no longer any resident populations within that portion of its historic range.

A purple dot indicates that the species' range in this area is much smaller than the actual area covered by the purple dot.

BUTTERFLY WING AREAS AND BODY PARTS

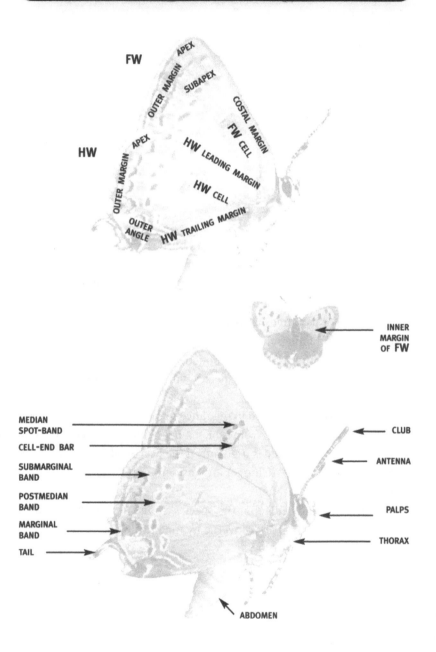

FW

APEX

OUTER MARGIN

SUBAPEX

COSTAL MARGIN

FW CELL

HW

APEX

OUTER MARGIN

HW LEADING MARGIN

HW CELL

OUTER ANGLE

HW TRAILING MARGIN

INNER MARGIN OF FW

MEDIAN SPOT-BAND

CELL-END BAR

SUBMARGINAL BAND

POSTMEDIAN BAND

MARGINAL BAND

TAIL

CLUB

ANTENNA

PALPS

THORAX

ABDOMEN

LIST OF PLATES

PLATES INTRODUCTION

Photos

Photographs on the following 44 plates show butterflies in the correct size comparison to others on the same plate. The absolute size is indicated at the top of the plate.

Unless otherwise indicated, either on the facing page or in the photo credits appendix, photographs are by Jeffrey Glassberg and were taken in the wild, of unrestrained, unmanipulated butterflies. Date and locality information are given when known. Dates are shown as month/day/year.

Maps

If an area is colored on a particular map, this means that we believe there are **resident populations** of the species in the area, or, if the species is an immigrant, that **an active field observer is likely to see the species in this area at least once every two to three years**.

We have divided Florida into 5 areas to provide more detail about flight times and abundance. At the top left of the Florida map is the Panhandle Region. At the top right is the Northern Region. Below it is the Central Region. Below it is the Southern Region. Range in the Key's Region is indicated by color, or lack thereof, on a disproportionally enlarged "Key West."

See the introductory text for more information about the maps.

RANGE MAP COLORS

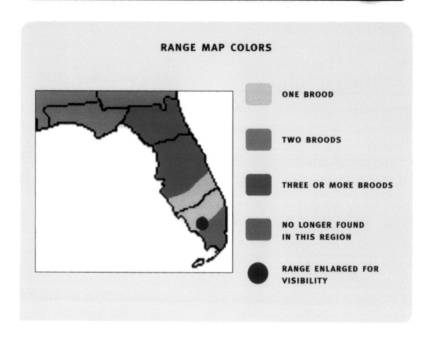

RANGE MAP COLORS

ONE BROOD

TWO BROODS

THREE OR MORE BROODS

NO LONGER FOUND
IN THIS REGION

RANGE ENLARGED FOR
VISIBILITY

NORTHERN CLOUDYWING

SILVER-SPOTTED SKIPPER

TROPICAL CHECKERED-SKIPPER

SACHEM

WHIRLABOUT

SWARTHY SKIPPER

GRAY HAIRSTREAK

CERAUNUS BLUE

AMERICAN SNOUT

LITTLE METALMARK

E

PIPEVINE SWALLOWTAIL

EASTERN TIGER SWALLOWTAIL

CLOUDLESS SULPHUR

CHECKERED WHITE

LITTLE YELLOW

F

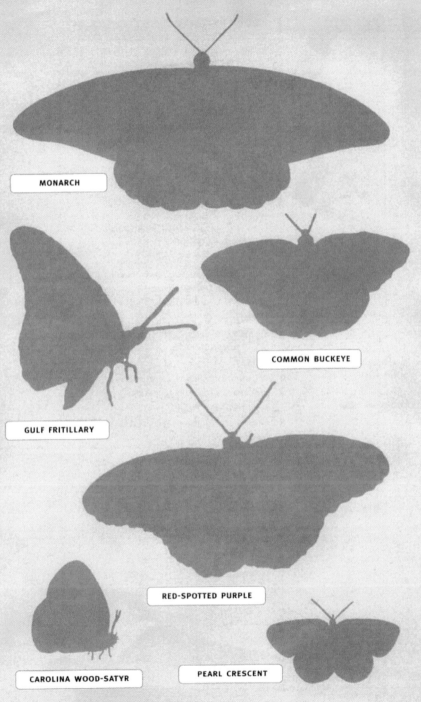

MONARCH

COMMON BUCKEYE

GULF FRITILLARY

RED-SPOTTED PURPLE

CAROLINA WOOD-SATYR

PEARL CRESCENT

G

1 Pipevine Swallowtail *Battus philenor*. **p. 45**
Below. 8/23/91 Newman's Lake, Alachua Co. FL
Single orange spot-band on iridescent blue **HW**.

2 Above. 1987 Gainesville, Alachua Co. FL
Iridescent blue **HW**.
Very dark **FW**.
No **FW** markings.

3 Polydamas Swallowtail *Battus polydamas*. **p. 46**
Below. 3/30/97 Ft. Lauderdale, Broward Co. FL
No tails.
Dull red **HW** marginal spots and red spots on the body.

4 Above. Ft. Lauderdale, Broward Co. FL
No tails.
Wide dirty-yellow postmedian band.
Constantly in motion.

5 Zebra Swallowtail *Eurytides marcellus*. **p. 46**
Spring form below. 3/17/94 Ocala NF, Marion Co. FL
Black and white and red stripes.
Long tails.

6 Spring form above. 3/17/94 Ocala NF, Marion Co. FL
Black and white stripes.
Long tails.

7 Summer form below. 6/6/87 Ocala NF, Marion Co. FL
Black and white and red stripes.
Very long tails.

8 Summer form above. 8/24/91 Ocala NF, Marion Co. FL
Black and white stripes.
Very long tails.

1 Pipevine Swallowtail

2 Pipevine Swallowtail

3 Polydamas Swallowtail

4 Polydamas Swallowtail

5 Zebra Swallowtail

6 Zebra Swallowtail

7 Zebra Swallowtail

8 Zebra Swallowtail

1 **Black Swallowtail** *Papilio polyxenes.* **p.47**
Below. 5/17/94 Gainesville, Alachua Co. FL
HW median and submarginal orange spot-bands.
HW median orange spot-band complete.
HW yellow/orange cell-spot.
FW median yellow spot-band reaches costa.

2 ♀ above. 5/19/94, Gainesville, Alachua Co. FL
Blue on **HW**.
Yellow **FW** subapical spot.
Often flies with low nondirectional flight.
Open areas and gardens.

3 ♂ above. 8/25/91 Newnan's Lake, Alachua Co. FL
Bright yellow spot-bands, **FW** and **HW**.

4 **Spicebush Swallowtail** *Papilio troilus.* **p. 51**
♀ above. 5/11/97 Gainesville, Alachua Co. FL
Blue on **HW**.
Lacks yellow **FW** subapical spot.
Marginal spots greenish and large.

5 Below. 5/11/97 Gainesville, Alachua Co. FL
HW median and submarginal orange spot-bands.
HW median spot-band missing 1 orange spot.
Lacks **HW** yellow/orange cell spot.
FW median yellow spot-band doesn't reach costa.

6 ♂ above. 3/20/94 Gulf Hammock, Levy Co. FL
Greenish-blue cast on the **HW**.
Usually flies with rapid, directional flight.
Woodlands and adjacent fields.

7 **Eastern Tiger Swallowtail** *Papilio glaucus.* **p. 50**
Black ♀ below. 9/23/94 Chassahowitzka, Citrus Co. FL
No postmedian orange spot-band.
Usually retains shadow of tiger pattern.

8 Above. 9/23/94 Chassahowitzka, Citrus Co. FL
Yellow with black stripes.

PLATE 2

1 Black Swallowtail

2 Black Swallowtail ♀

3 Black Swallowtail ♂

4 Spicebush Swallowtail ♀

5 Spicebush Swallowtail

6 Spicebush Swallowtail ♂

7 Eastern Tiger Swallowtail ♀

8 Eastern Tiger Swallowtail

1 Giant Swallowtail *Papilio cresphontes.* **p. 48**
Below. 2/3/96 Tavernier, Monroe Co. FL
Cream-colored wings and body.
HW with blue median spot-band.

2 Above. 8/25/91 Newnan's Lake, Alachua Co. FL
Brown-black.
Yellow spot-bands form x's near **FW** apexes.
Yellow spot within tail.

3 Schaus' Swallowtail *Papilio aristodemus.* **p. 49**
Below. 5/24/94 Elliott Key, Miami-Dade Co. FL
(marked individual for population study).
Large rusty patch in the **HW** median band.
Males with bright yellow antennal clubs.
Lacks yellow spot in tail.

4 ♂ above. 5/25/94 North Key Largo, Monroe Co. FL
Yellow bands duller than Giant or Palamedes.
Yellow bands do not form an x near **FW** apex.
Males with bright yellow antennal clubs.
Lacks yellow spot in tail.
Found in tropical hardwood hammocks.

5 Bahamian Swallowtail *Papilio andraemon.* **p. 49**
Below. 6/5/85 Elliott Key, Miami-Dade Co. FL
(individual to be marked for population study).
Rusty "brick" juts into the **HW** postmedian band.
Males with bright yellow antennal clubs.

6 Above. 5/9/85 Elliott Key, Miami-Dade Co. FL
Yellow bar in the **FW** cell.
FW with submarginal yellow band of very faint dashes.
Found in tropical hardwood hammocks.

7 Palamedes Swallowtail *Papilio palamedes.* **p. 51**
Below. 3/29/99 Big Cypress National Preserve, Collier Co. FL
Brown-black wing bases.
Yellow stripe along the base of the wings.

8 Above. 3/26/97 Fakahatchee Strand, Collier Co. FL
Wide yellow **HW** postmedian band.

PLATE 3

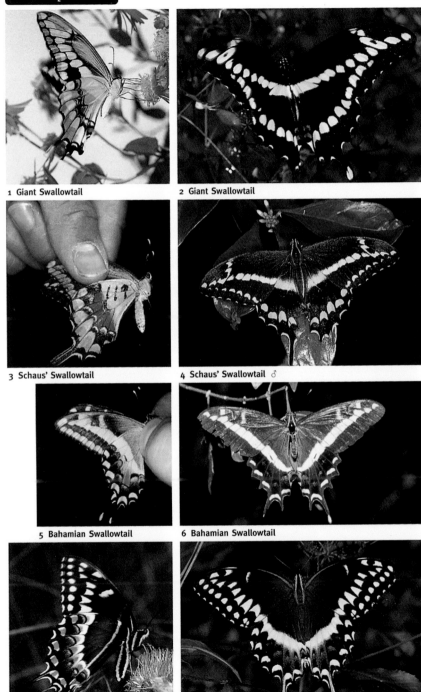

1 Giant Swallowtail

2 Giant Swallowtail

3 Schaus' Swallowtail

4 Schaus' Swallowtail ♂

5 Bahamian Swallowtail

6 Bahamian Swallowtail

7 Palamedes Swallowtail

8 Palamedes Swallowtail

1 **Great Southern White** *Ascia monuste*. **p. 54**
♀ below. 5/21/94 W. Summerland Key, Monroe Co. FL
Varies from white to smoky-gray-brown as shown.
Antennal clubs are turquoise.

3 ♂ below. 5/22/94 W. Summerland Key, Monroe Co. FL
Antennal clubs are turquoise.
No orange at base of **HW** leading margin.
HW sometimes with prominent markings.

5 ♀ above. 3/25/97 Homestead, Miami-Dade Co. FL
Varies from white to smoky-gray-brown as shown.
FW with cell-end bar.
Black **FW** border tends to follow veins inward.
Antennal clubs are turquoise.

7 ♂ above. 5/21/94 W. Summerland Key, Monroe Co. FL
Black **FW** border tends to follow veins inward.
Antennal clubs are turquoise.

2 **Florida White** *Appias drusilla*. **p. 52**
♀ below. 3/28/97 Matheson Hammock, Miami-Dade Co. FL
Antennal clubs are pale, not turquoise.
FW usually with orange at base.
Mainly in tropical hardwood hammocks.

4 ♂ below. 3/28/97 Matheson Hammock, Miami-Dade Co. FL.
Antennal clubs are pale, not turquoise.
Orange at base of **HW** leading margin.
Usually more opalescent than Great Southern White.
Mainly in tropical hardwood hammocks.

6 ♀ above. Same individual as 2.
Antennal clubs are pale, not turquoise.
Black **FW** border doesn't follow veins inward.
No **FW** cell-end bar.
Mainly in tropical hardwood hammocks.

8 ♂ above. 3/25/90 Matheson Hammock, Miami-Dade Co. FL
Black **FW** border, if present, doesn't follow veins inward.
Antennal clubs are pale, not turquoise.
Mainly in tropical hardwood hammocks.

1 Great Southern White ♀

2 Florida White ♀

3 Great Southern White ♂

2 Florida White ♂

5 Great Southern White ♀

2 Florida White ♀

7 Great Southern White ♂

8 Florida White ♂

1 Checkered White *Pontia protodice.* **p. 53**
♀ below. 3/29/97 Homestead, Miami-Dade Co. FL
Veins lined with greenish brown.
Black patch on mid **FW** costa.
Most common in disturbed and agricultural areas.
Flight is erratic and close to the ground.

2 ♀ above. 5/25/94 Homestead, Miami-Dade Co. FL
Many black spots on white background.

3 ♂ below. 3/29/97 Homestead, Miami-Dade Co. FL
Black patch on mid **FW** costa.

4 ♂ above. 3/25/97 Homestead, Miami-Dade Co. FL
Black spots on white background, not as extensive as on
female.

5 Cabbage White *Pieris rapae.* **p. 54**
Below. 5/18/94 Rock Bluff, Liberty Co. FL
Black spot on **FW**.
Flight is graceful.

6 ♀ above. 10/4/92 Chappaqua, Westchester Co. NY
Solid gray **FW** apex.
Two black spots on **FW**.

8 ♂ above. 6/14/91 Cross River, Westchester Co. NY
Solid gray **FW** apex.
One black spot on **FW**.

7 Orange Sulphur *Colias eurytheme.* **p. 55**
♀ white form below. 6/20/91 Cross River, Westchester Co. NY
Silvered spot in center of **HW**.
Black borders of **FW** above can be seen in flight and through
the wing.

PLATE 5

1 Checkered White ♀

2 Checkered White ♀

3 Checkered White ♂

4 Checkered White ♂

5 Cabbage White

6 Cabbage White ♀

7 Orange Sulphur ♀

8 Cabbage White ♂

1 Southern Dogface *Colias cesonia.* **p. 56**
Below. 10/1/95 Ocala NF, Marion Co. FL
Large.
Bold black outline of a dog's head can be seen through **FW**.
Pointed **FW**.
Fall form with **HW** suffused with pink.

2 Above (caught in spider web). 10/26/95 La Gloria, Starr Co. TX
Bold dog's face pattern on **FW**.
Bright yellow.
Upperside normally visible only in flight.

3 Orange Sulphur *Colias eurytheme.* **p. 55**
♂ below. 7/29/94 Blowing Rock, Watauga Co. NC
Shows at least some orange on the **FW**.
Males have a solid **FW** black border.

4 ♂ above (road killed). 9/19/93 Anza-Borrego SP, CA
Ranges from extensive bright orange to just a blush of
orange on the **FW** disc.
Upperside normally visible only in flight.

5 ♀ below. 6/5/96 Jones Knob, Macon Co. NC
Females have the **FW** black border w/ paler spots.

6 Shy Yellow *Eurema messalina.* **p. 151**
Below. 2/6/94 New Providence, Bahamas
West Indian—possible stray to Florida.
Black subapical mark on **FW**.
White **FW** disc. See text.

7 Dainty Sulphur *Nathalis iole.* **p. 63**
Dry season (winter) form.
Below. 2/3/96 Homestead, Miami-Dade Co. FL
Tiny.
Variable below.
Greenish **HW**.
Black spots in **FW** submargin.
Flies low to ground.

8 Wet season (summer) form below.
10/2/95 Daytona Beach, Volusia Co. FL

9 Above (in flight). 5/1/98 Garden Canyon, Cochise Co. AZ
FW with a dark bar.
Does not normally open wings while landed.
See Barred Yellow, plate 7.

PLATE 6

1 Southern Dogface

2 Southern Dogface

3 Orange Sulphur ♂

4 Orange Sulphur ♂

5 Orange Sulphur ♀

6 Shy Yellow

7 Dainty Sulphur

8 Dainty Sulphur

9 Dainty Sulphur

1 Little Yellow *Eurema lisa.* **p. 60**
♂ below. 7/26/93 Chappaqua, Westchester Co. NY
Bright yellow above. Black antennas.
FW black border wide at apex (visible through wing).
Rapid, straight, and low flight in open situations.

2 ♀ below. 9/29/95 Gainesville, Alachua Co. FL
HW with two basal black spots. Pink spot at **HW** apex.

3 Mimosa Yellow *Eurema nise.* **p. 61**
♂ below. 10/8/95 Bauer Park, Miami-Dade Co. FL
Lacks **HW** basal black spots of Little Yellow.
FW black border at apex narrower than Little Yellow.
Flies within edge of woodland.

4 ♀ below. 2/3/96 Bauer Park, Miami-Dade Co. FL
Lacks **HW** basal black spots of Little Yellow.
FW black border at apex narrower than Little Yellow.
Flies within edge of woodland.

5 Dina Yellow *Eurema dina.* **p. 62**
♂ below. 5/23/94 Bauer Park, Miami-Dade Co. FL
Bright orange above. Very narrow **FW** black border.
FW without dark spot in cell.
HW with a dark spot in the cell.

6 ♀ below. 5/20/94 Homestead, Miami-Dade Co. FL
Yellow above. **FW** without a dark spot in cell.
HW with a dark spot in the cell.

7 Sleepy Orange *Eurema nicippe.* **p. 62**
Wet season (summer) form below. 5/6/97 Trilby, Pasco Co. FL
Bright orange above. **FW** with cell-end bar.
Diagonal brown markings on **HW.**

8 Dry season (winter) form below.
10/27/96 Peñitas, Hidalgo Co. TX
Bright orange above. **FW** with cell-end bar.
Diagonal brown markings on **HW.**

9 Barred Yellow *Eurema daira.* **p. 60**
Wet season (summer) form below.
8/23/91 Gainesville, Alachua Co. FL
Small. Base of **FW** costal margin not yellow.

10 Dry season (winter) form below.
3/19/94 Gainesville, Alachua Co. FL
Suffused with rusty-brown.
Small.
Base of **FW** costal margin not yellow.

11 Above. (not to scale) 1/19/97 Catemaco, Veracruz, Mexico
Black bar on male **FW** (on left, courting).
White or yellow above.
♂ above with black bar along **FW** lower margin.

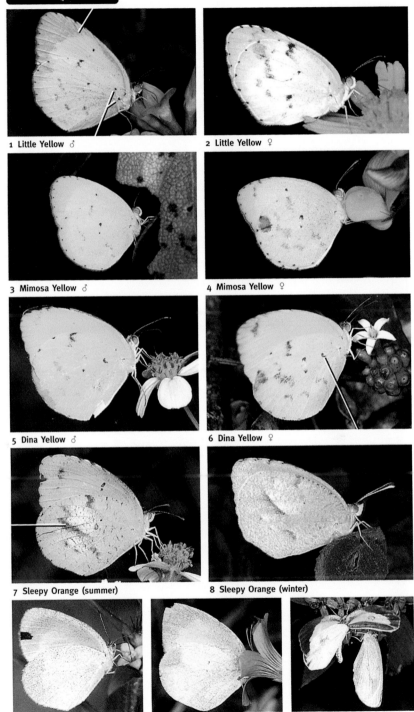

PLATE 7

1 Little Yellow ♂

2 Little Yellow ♀

3 Mimosa Yellow ♂

4 Mimosa Yellow ♀

5 Dina Yellow ♂

6 Dina Yellow ♀

7 Sleepy Orange (summer)

8 Sleepy Orange (winter)

9 Barred Yellow (summer)

10 Barred Yellow (winter)

11 Barred Yellow

1 Cloudless Sulphur *Phoebis sennae.* **p. 56**
♂ below. 9/29/95 Gainesville, Alachua Co. FL
Larger than *Colias* sulphurs and yellows.
Bright yellow above (see plate 9).
Green-yellow below with cell-end spots on **FW** and **HW**.

2 ♀ below. 9/23/94 Chassahowitzka, Citrus Co. FL
Larger than *Colias* sulphurs and yellows.
Cell-end spots on **FW** and **HW**.
Line from **FW** apex broken.
Yellow above.

3 Orange-barred Sulphur *Phoebis philea.* **p. 57**
♂ below. 3/22/94 Kendall, Miami-Dade Co. FL
Rich yellow to orange.
Can be almost unmarked orange-yellow or as well-marked
  as shown.
Line from **FW** apex broken.
Above, with large orange patches (see plate 9).
Mainly an immigrant, Sept.–Oct., northward.

4 ♀ below. 3/31/97 Kendall, Miami-Dade Co. FL
Similar to Cloudless Sulphur but more extensive pink.
Above, with large pink-orange patches on **HW**.
Mainly an immigrant, Sept.–Oct., northward.

5 Large Orange Sulphur *Phoebis agarithe.* **p. 58**
♂ below. 3/22/94 Kendall, Miami-Dade Co. FL
Orange.
Line from **FW** apex straight.
Bright orange above (see plate 9).

6 ♀ below. 5/24/94 Elliott Key, Miami-Dade Co. FL
Line from **FW** apex straight.
Above, orange or whitish.

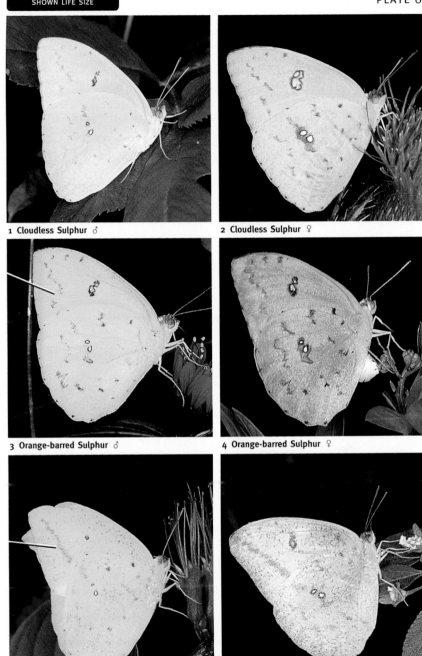

1 Cloudless Sulphur ♂

2 Cloudless Sulphur ♀

3 Orange-barred Sulphur ♂

4 Orange-barred Sulphur ♀

5 Large Orange Sulphur ♂

6 Large Orange Sulphur ♀

1 Cloudless Sulphur *Phoebis sennae.* **p. 56**
♂ above (road-killed).
10/27/96 La Joya, Starr Co. TX
Larger than *Colias* sulphurs and yellows.
Bright yellow.
Upperside normally visible only in flight.

2 Large Orange Sulphur *Phoebis agarithe.* **p. 58**
♂ above (road-killed).
10/23/95 Roma, Starr Co. TX
Larger than *Colias* sulphurs and yellows.
Bright orange.
Upperside normally visible only in flight.

3 Statira Sulphur *Phoebis statira.* **p. 58**
Below. 10/19/93 Santa Ana NWR, Hidalgo Co. TX
Some yellow at base of **FW** costa and along **FW** disc.
Usually with a pink patch at **FW** apex.
Outer 1/3 of the wings are "puckered."
Most frequent on the coast.

4 Lyside Sulphur *Kricogonia lyside.* **p. 59**
Below. 10/28/96 Peñitas, Hidalgo Co. TX
Usually with green tinge and whitened vein as shown but
    can be very pale without whitened vein.
Above, varies from yellow to white.
Stray or very rare resident.

5 Yellow Angled-Sulphur *Anteos maerula.* **p. 150**
Below. 10/26/93 Mission, Hidalgo Co. TX
Rare stray to the Keys and south Florida.
Very large.
Veined leaf effect.
Bright yellow above.

6 Orange-barred Sulphur *Phoebis philea.* **p. 57**
♂ above (in flight)(not to scale).
3/26/90 South Miami, Miami-Dade Co. FL
Yellow with bright orange patches.

7 Boisduval's Yellow *Eurema boisduvaliana.* **p. 151**
Below. 2/9/95 Mismaloya, Jalisco, Mexico
Very rare stray to south Florida and the Keys.
HW with small pointed "tail."
Bright orange-yellow above. See text.

1 Cloudless Sulphur ♂

2 Large Orange Sulphur ♂

3 Statira Sulphur

4 Lyside Sulphur

5 Yellow Angled-Sulphur

6 Orange-barred Sulphur ♂

7 Boisduval's Yellow

1 Harvester *Feniseca tarquinius.* **p. 63**
Below. 6/12/93 Wentworths Location, NH
HW with delicate white tracings.
Local and rare in moist woodlands with alders.
Mainly March–May, Aug.–Oct.

2 Above. 5/24/95 Morristown, Morris Co. NJ
Orange.
Inky-black spots in **FW** cell and near apex.
Local and rare in moist woodlands with alders.
Mainly March–May, Aug.–Oct.

3 Little Metalmark *Calephelis virginiensis.* **p. 83**
Below. 3/26/97 Fakahatchee Strand, Collier Co. FL
Found in open pine flats, wet prairies.
Metallic silver markings on orange ground.

4 Above. Same individual as in 3.
Small.
Rich orange-brown.
Metallic markings.

5 American Snout *Libytheana carinenta.* **p. 84**
Below. 8/25/91 Gainesville, Alachua Co. FL
Extremely long palps.
Grond color variable.

6 Below. 8/22/88 Vernon, Sussex Co. NJ
Extremely long palps.
Ground color variable.

7 Above. 10/21/93 La Joya, Starr Co. TX
Extremely long palps.
Orange basally, wide blackish brown borders.
White subapical spots.

PLATE 10

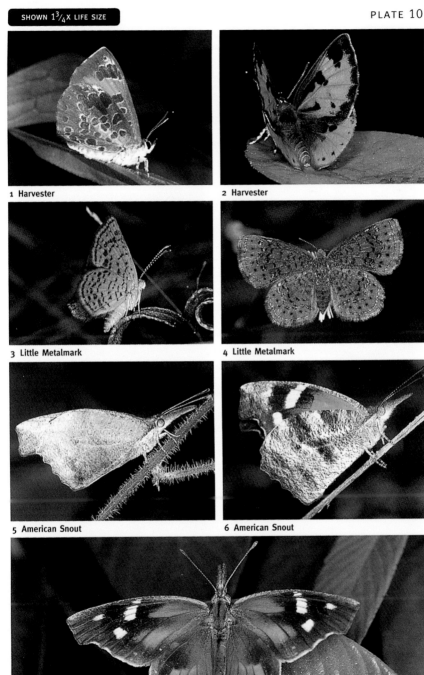

1 Harvester

2 Harvester

3 Little Metalmark

4 Little Metalmark

5 American Snout

6 American Snout

7 American Snout

1 Great Purple Hairstreak *Atlides halesus.* **p. 65**
♂ above (caught by crab spider—legs at top left).
9/24/94 Gainesville, Alachua Co. FL
Brilliant iridescent blue (not purple) normally visible only
  in flight.
♀ above has more restricted, noniridescent blue.

2 Below. 9/24/94 Gainesville, Alachua Co. FL
Large.
Bright red spots at wing bases.
White spots on body.
Iridescent turquoise on **FW** disc.

3 Atala *Eumaeus atala.* **p. 64**
Below. 3/25/90 South Miami, Miami-Dade Co. FL
Brilliant orange abdomen.
HW with iridescent blue spot-bands.
Usually close to cycads.

4 Caterpillar (not to scale).
10/3/95 Fairchild Gardens, Miami-Dade Co. FL
Bright red and yellow on cycads.

5 Pupas (not to scale)
2/4/96 Del Rey Beach, Palm Beach Co. FL

6 White M Hairstreak *Parrhasius m-album.* **p. 73**
Below. 9/26/94 Gainesville, Alachua Co. FL
Brilliant iridescent blue above normally visible only in flight
  (seen here through tear in **HW**).

7 Below. 9/26/94 Gainesville, Alachua Co. FL
White spot at center of leading edge of **HW**.
HW red spot set inward from margin.
Lacks cell-end bar.

PLATE 11

1 Great Purple Hairstreak ♂

2 Great Purple Hairstreak

3 Atala

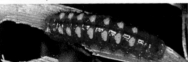

4 Atala caterpillar

5 Atala pupas

6 White M Hairstreak

7 White M Hairstreak

1 **'Sweadner's' Juniper Hairstreak** *Callophrys gryneus sweadneri.* **p. 71**
Below. 3/20/94 Yankeetown, Levy Co. FL
Smooth, olive-green ground color.
Prominent white postmedian band.
Found amidst stands of red cedars.

2 **Hessel's Hairstreak** *Callophrys hesseli.* **p. 72**
Below. 5/1/90 Chatsworth, Ocean Co. NJ
Emerald green ground color.
Top white spot on **FW** postmedian band displaced outwardly.
Found in white cedar swamps.
Very local, with widely separated colonies within the range shown.

3 **Silver-banded Hairstreak** *Chlorostrymon simaethis.* **p. 66**
Below. 5/21/94 Tavernier, Monroe Co. FL
Bright acid green ground color.
HW postmedian line white and straight.

5 ♂ above. 10/27/98 Santa Ana NWR, Hidalgo Co. TX
Iridescent purple.

6 ♀ above. 10/24/98 Santa Ana NWR, Hidalgo Co. TX

4 **Amethyst Hairstreak** *Chlorostrymon maesites.* **p. 65**
Below. Collected 6/25/35 Brickell Hammock, Miami, Miami-Dade Co. FL
[this specimen was the model for Fig. 10, Plate 15 in Klots (1951)]
No white postmedian line on **FW**.
HW with maroon marginal patch.
Extremely rare.

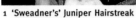

1 'Sweadner's' Juniper Hairstreak

2 Hessel's Hairstreak

3 Silver-banded Hairstreak

4 Amethyst Hairstreak

5 Silver-banded Hairstreak ♂

6 Silver-banded Hairstreak ♀

1 Coral Hairstreak *Satyrium titus.* **p. 67**
Below. 5/18/94 Rock Bluff, Liberty Co. FL
Coral red marginal spots on **HW**.
No tail.
No blue marginal eye-spot.

2 Banded Hairstreak *Satyrium calanus.* **p. 67**
Below. 6/28/95 Lakehurst, Ocean Co. NJ
Common and variable.
Postmedian band with white dashes outwardly, occasionally
with white on both sides of band.

3 King's Hairstreak *Satyrium kingi.* **p. 68**
Below. 6/6/96 Southern Pines, Moore Co. NC
Strong orange "bar" over **HW** blue spot.
Cell-end bars not aligned with bars above them.
Postmedian band composed of rectangles.
Local and rare.

4 Striped Hairstreak *Satyrium liparops.* **p. 69**
Below. 7/2/96 Five Ridge Preserve, Plymouth Co. IA
Striped appearance.
Orange cap on **HW** blue spot.
Cell-end bars aligned with bars above them.

5 Southern Hairstreak *Satyrium favonius.* **p. 69**
'Southern' Southern Hairstreak *S.f. favonius*
5/6/97 Pasco Co. FL
Extensive red-orange on **HW** submargin.
White spot at center of leading edge of **HW** (sometimes
faint).
Long tails.

6 'Northern' Southern Hairstreak *S. f. ontario*
Below. 6/22/89 Cross River, Westchester Co. NY
Lacks cell-end bar. Brown ground color.
Usually no **HW** white spot at center of leading edge of **HW**,
but sometimes present.

1 Coral Hairstreak

2 Banded Hairstreak

3 King's Hairstreak

4 Striped Hairstreak

5 'Southern' Southern Hairstreak

6 'Northern Southern' Hairstreak

1 Eastern Pine Elfin *Callophrys niphon.* **p. 71**
5/23/96 Voluntown, New London Co. CT
Stunningly banded.
Orange-brown patches on ♀ above, visible in flight.
Found in pine woodlands.
Mainly found in March.

2 Henry's Elfin *Callophrys henrici.* **p. 70**
Below. 4/24/94 Larenim Park, Mineral Co. WV
Frosted **HW** margin.
Bold white marks at ends of **HW** postmedian band.
Short, tail-like protuberance on **HW**.
Prefers moist to wet woodlands.

3 Frosted Elfin *Callophrys irus.* **p. 70**
Below. 4/25/94 Bratton's Run, Rockbridge Co. VA
Larger than Henry's Elfin. Frosted **HW**.
Short, tail-like protuberance on **HW**.
Black spot near tailed area.
Found in dry habitats with lupine.

4 Red-banded Hairstreak *Calycopis cecrops.* **p. 76**
Below. 3/15/94 Walt Disney Wilderness Preserve, Osceola Co. FL
Small and dark.
Prominent red postmedian band on both wings.
Some blue above in flight.

5 Fulvous Hairstreak *Electrostrymon angelia.* **p. 76**
Below. 5/21/94 Key Largo, Monroe Co. FL
HW postmedian line disrupted, with an isolated white spot
    at leading edge of **HW**.
FW postmedian line with no white.
Copper-colored above, sometimes visible in flight.

6 Gray Ministreak *Ministrymon azia.* **p. 77**
Below. 3/15/88 Margarita Island, Venezuela
Tiny.
Pale gray ground color.
Irregular red postmedian band.
Red marginal line.
Red on crown of head.

1 Eastern Pine Elfin

2 Henry's Elfin

3 Frosted Elfin

4 Red-banded Hairstreak

5 Fulvous Hairstreak

6 Gray Ministreak

1 Gray Hairstreak *Strymon melinus.* **p. 73**
Below. 9/23/94 Levy Co. FL
Common and widespread.
HW large orange marginal spot usually flat inwardly with
black line on inward side.
Postmedian line with white outside, black adjacent, and
often with some red on inward side.

2 ♀ above. 8/23/91 Gainesville, Alachua Co. FL
Red-orange on crown of head.

3 Martial Scrub-Hairstreak *Strymon martialis.* **p. 74**
Below. 3/24/94 Big Pine Key, Monroe Co. FL
Bold white postmedian line on both **HW** and **FW.**
HW without white basal spots.

7 Above. 3/24/94 Big Pine Key, Monroe Co. FL
Both male and female with blue above.

4 Bartram's Scrub-Hairstreak *Strymon acis.* **p. 75**
Below. 3/27/99 Big pine Key, Monroe Co. FL
Two white basal spots on **HW.**
Pine rocklands with narrow-leaved croton.
Local and threatened.

8 Above. Same individual as in 4.
White, or off-white, spot over orange outer angle spot.

5 Mallow Scrub-Hairstreak *Strymon columella.* **p. 75**
Below. 3/25/94 Key West, Monroe Co. FL
Postmedian band of black and white crescents.
Strong black spot near base of **HW.**
Spot by tail often triple-colored—black, red, orange.

6 Disguised Scrub-Hairstreak *Strymon limenia.* **p. 152**
Below. 2/26/96 Vega Alta, Puerto Rico
Very rare stray to Florida Keys.
Browner than Mallow Scrub-Hairstreak.
Extra black spot along **HW** trailing margin.
Red outer angle lobes above.
See text.

1 Gray Hairstreak

2 Gray Hairstreak ♀

3 Martial Scrub-Hairstreak

4 Bartram's Scrub-Hairstreak

5 Mallow Scrub-Hairstreak

6 Disguised Scrub-Hairstreak

7 Martial Scrub-Hairstreak

8 Bartram's Scrub-Hairstreak

1 **Eastern Pygmy-Blue** *Brephidium isophthalma.* **p. 78**
Below. 3/24/94 Big Pine Key, Monroe Co. FL
Salt marsh tidal flats.
Tiny.
Four bold marginal eye-spots on **HW**.

2 **Cassius Blue** *Leptotes cassius.* **p. 78**
Below. 3/22/90 Royal Palm, Everglades NP, Mimai-Dade Co. FL
"Zebra" striped.
10 ♀ and ♂ above. 3/27/97 Homestead, Miami-Dade Co. FL
♀ with very pale bluish-white ground color.
♂ with pale violet ground color.

3 **Spring Azure** *Celastrina ladon.* **p. 82**
Below. 6/29/94 Springdale, Sussex Co. NJ
Grayish-white ground color.
No prominent eye-spots or orange.
No tail.

4 **Ceraunus Blue** *Hemiargus ceraunus.* **p. 80**
Below. 9/28/95 Ocala NF, Marion Co. FL
HW with 1 strong marginal eye-spot.
HW with 2 strong black spots on the basal 1/2 of the leading
margin.
9 ♀ above. 3/22/90 Flamingo, Everglades NP, Monroe Co. FL
FW with wide black borders and blue basally.
11 ♂ above. 2/3/96 Homestead, Miami-Dade Co. FL

5 **Miami Blue** *Hemiargus thomasi.* **p. 79**
Below. 5/19/72 Islamorada, Monroe Co. FL
Broad white postmedian band on both **HW** and **FW**.
Two black eye-spots near **HW** outer angle.
HW with 4 basal spots and crescent-shaped orange spot.
7 ♂ above. 5/19/72 Islamorada, Monroe Co. FL
No orange spot at **HW** outer angle.
♀ above. Not Illustrated.
Crescent-shaped orange spot near **HW** outer angle.

6 **Nickerbean Blue** *Hemiargus ammon.* **p. 79**
Below. 3/25/99 Big Pine Key, Monroe Co. FL
Broad white postmedian band on both **HW** and **FW**.
Two black eye-spots near **HW** outer angle.
HW with 3 basal spots and bullet-shaped orange spot.
♂ above. Orange-pink spot at **HW** outer angle.
8 ♀ above. 3/18/98 Big Pine Key, Monroe Co. FL
Bullet-shaped orange spot near **HW** outer angle.

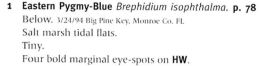

PLATE 16

1 Eastern Pygmy-Blue

2 Cassius Blue

3 Spring Azure

4 Ceraunus Blue

5 Miami Blue

6 Nickerbean Blue ♂

7 Miami Blue ♂

8 Nickerbean Blue ♀

9 Ceraunus Blue ♀

10 Cassius Blue ♀ and ♂

11 Ceraunus Blue ♂

1 Gulf Fritillary *Agraulis vanillae.* **p. 84**
Below. 8/23/91 Lake Delancey, Ocala NF, Marion Co. FL
HW heavily silvered.
FW long and narrow.

2 ♂ above. 3/21/90 Homestead, Miami-Dade Co. FL
Red-orange.
Bright black-ringed white spots in **FW** cell.
♀ is similar but browner above.

3 Julia (Heliconian) *Dryas iulia.* **p. 85**
Below. 10/8/95, Bauer Park, Miami-Dade Co. FL
Long wings.
Brown with white and red at **HW** base.

4 ♂ above. 10/8/95 Bauer Park, Miami-Dade Co. FL
Bright brownish-orange.
Long narrow wings.

5 ♀ above. 3/28/99 Tavernier, Monroe Co. FL
Brownish-orange.
Long narrow wings.
Black band across **FW**.

6 Zebra (Heliconian) *Heliconius charitonius.* **p. 85**
Below. 10/4/95 Royal Palm, Everglades NP, Miami-Dade Co. FL
Black with yellow stripes.
Long narrow wings.

7 Above. 3/21/91 Homestead, Miami-Dade Co. FL
Black with yellow stripes.
Long narrow wings.

8 Variegated Fritillary *Euptoieta claudia.* **p. 86**
Below. 6/29/91 Pelham Bay Park, Bronx, NY
Mottled **HW** with pale median and marginal patches.

9 Above. 1998. Gainesville, Alachua Co. FL
Dull orange-brown.
Chunky shape.
Black spots around submargin of **FW** and **HW**.

PLATE 17

SHOWN ³/₄X LIFE SIZE

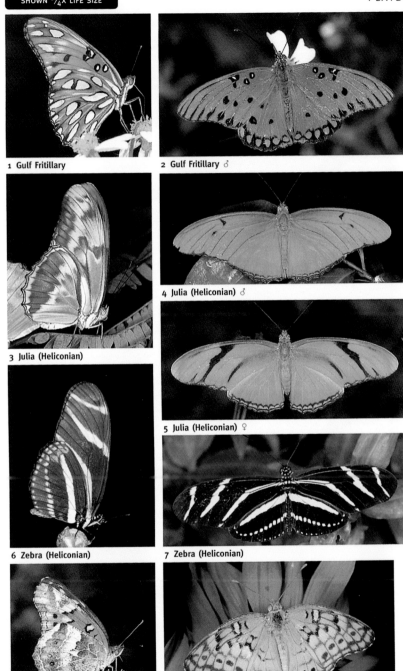

1 Gulf Fritillary

2 Gulf Fritillary ♂

3 Julia (Heliconian)

4 Julia (Heliconian) ♂

5 Julia (Heliconian) ♀

6 Zebra (Heliconian)

7 Zebra (Heliconian)

8 Variegated Fritillary

9 Variegated Fritillary

1 **Phaon Crescent** *Phyciodes phaon.* **p. 88**
Below. 9/23/94 Cedar Key, Levy Co. FL
HW tan with darker markings.
FW disc bright orange.
FW with cream-colored median band.
HW marginal crescent inwardly bounded by black line.

2 Above. 5/10/97 St. Augustine, St. Johns Co. FL
FW with cream-colored median band.

3 **Pearl Crescent** *Phyciodes tharos.* **p. 89**
Below. 3/26/97 Big Cypress Preserve, Collier Co. FL
HW reticulated.
HW with pale marginal crescent.
Extremely variable.

4 Above. 9/25/94 east of Deland, Volusia Co. FL
Orange with black reticulations.
Extremely variable.

5 **Cuban Crescent** *Phyciodes frisia.* **p. 87**
Below. 5/21/94 W. Summerland Key, Monroe Co. FL
FW outer margin with a concave section.
Usually quite a bit brighter than this worn individual.

6 Above. Same individual as 3.
FW with three large orange-brown spots.
FW outer margin with a concave section.
HW submarginal line more angled.

7 **'Seminole' Texan Crescent** *Phyciodes texana seminole* **p. 87**
Below. 5/7/97 Gulf Hammock, Levy Co. FL
HW mottled dark with white median band.

8 Above. 5/7/97 Gulf Hammock, Levy Co. FL
Black with red-orange basally.
HW with white median band.

1 Phaon Crescent

2 Phaon Crescent

3 Pearl Crescent

4 Pearl Crescent

5 Cuban Crescent

6 Cuban Crescent

7 'Seminole' Texan Crescent

8 'Seminole' Texan Crescent

1 Question Mark *Polygonia interrogationis.* **p. 90**
Below. 10/24/98 Hidalgo Co. TX
HW with silvered "question-mark."

2 Above. 7/9/95 Mt. Kisco, Westchester Co. NY
FW black horizontal subapical mark.
Violaceous **HW** margin.
"Orange" form lacks black on **HW**.

3 Eastern Comma *Polygonia comma.* **p. 90**
Below. 8/22/92 Great Dismal Swamp NWR, Suffolk, VA
HW with silvered "comma."

4 Above. 7/12/95 Lunenburg, Essex Co. VT
Smaller than Question Mark.
Lacks **FW** black horizontal subapical mark.
"Orange" form lacks black on **HW**.

5 Red Admiral *Vanessa atalanta.* **p. 92**
Below. 3/29/97 Homestead, Miami-Dade Co. FL
HW dark and mottled.
Red, white and blue along **FW** costal margin.

6 Above. 3/20/90 S. Miami, Miami-Dade Co. FL
FW with bright red-orange median band.
HW with bright red-orange marginal band.
Appears small and dark during its rapid flight.

7 Mourning Cloak *Nymphalis antiopa.* **p. 91**
Below (not to scale, 3/4× life size). 7/11/95 Gorham, NH
Very dark striated brown.
Cream-yellow borders.

8 Above (not to scale, 3/4× life size).
7/25/91 Moose River Plains, Hamilton Co. NY
Deep brown.
Cream-yellow borders.

1 Question Mark

2 Question Mark

3 Eastern Comma

4 Eastern Comma

5 Red Admiral

6 Red Admiral

7 Mourning Cloak

8 Mourning Cloak

1 American Lady *Vanessa virginiensis.* **p. 91**
Below. 9/26/94 Gainesville, Alachua Co. FL
HW with "cobwebbing."
Remember, "American Ladies have big eyes."
HW with two large eye-spots.

2 Above. 5/18/94 Live Oak, Suwannee Co. FL
FW black median markings usually not connected.
FW often with small white spot in orange ground. (often more prominent than on this individual.)

3 Painted Lady *Vanessa cardui.* **p. 92**
Below. 9/13/91 Snug Harbor, Staten Island, Richmond Co. NY
HW with "cobwebbing."
HW with four smallish eye-spots.

4 Above. 6/12/95 Roaring River SP, Barry Co. MO
FW with bold black median band forming semicircle.
FW often flushed with pink.
No white spot in orange ground.

5 Hackberry Emperor *Asterocampa celtis.* **p. 100**
Below. 5/18/94 Torreya SP, Liberty Co. FL
Creamy gray-brown.
Prominent eye-spots on **HW** and **FW**.
FW cell with two black spots.

6 Above. 7/2/96 Plymouth Co. IA
Dark brown.
FW with white spots.
FW with a black eye-spot.

7 Tawny Emperor *Asterocampa clyton.* **p. 100**
Below. 6/17/94 Corkscrew Swamp Sanctuary, Collier Co. FL
Pale golden-brown.
No eye-spots on **FW**.
FW cell with black line across it.

8 Above. 5/17/94 Newnan's Lake, Alachua Co. FL
Warm orange-brown.
FW without white spots.
FW without black eye-spot.

1 American Lady

2 American Lady

3 Painted Lady

4 Painted Lady

5 Hackberry Emperor

6 Hackberry Emperor

7 Tawny Emperor

8 Tawny Emperor

1 Common Buckeye *Junonia coenia.* **p. 93**
Below. 9/29/95 Gainesville, Alachua Co. FL
HW pale with darker lines.
FW usually with white on inside of large eye-spot.

2 Above. 3/26/97 Big Cypress Preserve, Collier Co. FL
Prominent eye-spots on both wings.
Two orange bars in the **FW** cell.
FW usually with white or tan on inside of large eye-spot.
FW band just past cell usually off-white.
Contrasting orange patch by eye-spot at **FW** tornus.
Two **HW** eye-spots unequal in size.
HW orange submarginal band is wide.

3 Mangrove Buckeye *Junonia evarete.* **p. 93**
Below. 3/23/94 Mrazek Pond, Everglades NP, Miami-Dade Co. FL
Most of **HW** fairly unicolorous dull brown.

4 Above. 3/25/94 Little Hamaca Park, Key West, Monroe Co. FL
Large **FW** eye-spot completely surrounded by orange.
FW band just past cell is orange.
Two **HW** eye-spots fairly similar in size.
HW orange submarginal band is wide.

5 Tropical Buckeye *Junonia genoveva.* **p. 94**
Below. 12/4/94 New Providence, Bahamas
HW with prominent pale median stripe.

6 Above. 12/4/94 Same individual as 5.
Brown or pale brown to the inside of large **FW** eye-spot.
FW band just past cell is wide and flushed with pink.
HW orange submarginal band is narrow.

7 White Peacock *Anartia jatrophae.* **p. 95**
Below. 5/23/94 Miami, Miami-Dade Co. FL
Pearly white with darker markings.
Pale orange margins.

8 Above. 10/2/95 Tree Tops Park, Broward Co. FL
Pearly gray-white with darker markings.
Orange margins.

1 Common Buckeye

2 Common Buckeye

3 Mangrove Buckeye

4 Mangrove Buckeye

5 Tropical Buckeye

6 Tropical Buckeye

7 White Peacock

8 White Peacock

1 Red-spotted Purple *Limenitis arthemis astyanax.* **p. 96**
Below. 3/17/94 Ocala NF, Marion Co. FL
Red-orange spots at wing bases and in a submarginal band.

2 Above. 1997. Gainesville, Alachua Co. FL
Iridescent blue **HW**.
No tails.

3 Viceroy *Limenitis archippus.* **p. 96**
Below. 5/17/94 Gainesville, Alachua Co. FL
(nectaring at buttonbush, *Cephalanthus occidentalis*)
HW with black postmedian band.

4 Above. 5/17/94 Gainesville, Alachua Co. FL
Deep orange-brown.
Smaller than Monarch.
HW with black postmedian band.
Can be lighter orange northward.

5 Malachite *Siproeta stelenes.* **p. 95**
Below. 10/2/95 Tree Tops Park, Broward Co. FL
Large.
Green.

6 Above. 10/6/95 Sugarloaf Key, Monroe Co. FL
Large.
Green.

7 Florida Purplewing *Eunica tatila.* **p. 98**
Below. 11/11/89 Bentsen SP, Hidalgo Co. TX
Dark brown with a squared off **FW** apex.
FW with two subapical white spots with a black spot
between them.
Local and rare.
Flies in the interior of tropical hardwood hammocks.

8 Dingy Purplewing *Eunica monima.* **p. 97**
Below. 1/22/88 Castellow Hammock, Miami-Dade Co. FL
Warm mauve gray-brown.
FW apex rounded.
HW with circular line enclosing two spots, bottom spot
black, top spot gray-white.
Local and rare.
Flies in the interior of tropical hardwood hammocks.

PLATE 22

1 Red-spotted Purple

2 Red-spotted Purple

3 Viceroy

4 Viceroy

5 Malachite

6 Malachite

7 Florida Purplewing

8 Dingy Purplewing

1 **Goatweed Leafwing** *Anaea andria.* **p. 99**
Below. 1997 Gainesville, Alachua Co. FL
FW apex usually hooked.
Dead leaf pattern.
HW without submarginal line.

2 Above. 1995 Gainesville, Alachua Co. FL
Orange-brown (males brighter).
HW with short tail.

3 **Florida Leafwing** *Anaea floridalis.* **p. 99**
Below. 3/26/99 Big Pine Key, Monroe Co. FL
Mottled gray.
FW with hooked apex.
HW with short tail.
HW with submarginal line (sometimes faint).
Usually lands on tree limbs or trunks.

4 Above (caught by green lynx spider). 10/4/95 Long Pine Key, Everglades NP, Miami-Dade Co. FL
Bright red-orange.

5 **Ruddy Daggerwing** *Marpesia petreus.* **p. 98**
Below. 3/21/90 South Miami, Miami-Dade Co. FL
Mauve-gray-brown wings.
White body and wing bases.
FW sharply angled by apex.
HW with long tail.

6 Above. 3/25/90 Matheson Hammock, Miami-Dade Co. FL
Bright orange with black stripes across **FW** and **HW**.
FW sharply angled by apex.
HW with long tail.

7 **Many-banded Daggerwing** *Marpesia chiron.* **p. 154**
Above (Not to scale). 2/12/95 Mismaloya, Jalisco, Mexico
Stray, one report from Florida Keys.
Brown with black stripes across **FW** and **HW**.
HW with long tail.
Smaller than Ruddy Daggerwing.

8 **Antillean Daggerwing** *Marpesia eleuchea.* **p. 154**
Above (Not to scale). 2/12/87 Montego Bay, Jamaica
Stray, one report from Florida Keys.
FW median band has sharp angle.
Smaller than Ruddy Daggerwing.

1 Goatweed Leafwing

2 Goatweed Leafwing

3 Florida Leafwing

4 Florida Leafwing

5 Ruddy Daggerwing

6 Ruddy Daggerwing

7 Many-banded Daggerwing

8 Antillean Daggerwing

1 Southern Pearly-eye *Enodia portlandia.* **p. 101**
Below. 9/29/95 Newnan's Lake, Alachua Co. FL
Large and gray-brown.
Usually with much white.
Prefers rich bottomland woods with cane.

2 Common Wood-Nymph *Cercyonis pegala.* **p. 105**
Below. 6/20/95 Abita Springs, St. Tammany Parish, LA
Large and dark brown.
FW with large yellow-orange postmedian patch.
Prefers open grassy fields or open pine flats.

3 Appalachian Brown *Satyrodes appalachia.* **p. 102**
Below. 6/23/96 WPR, Westchester Co. NY
Pale brown.
Each **HW** eye-spot surrounded by pale circle.

4 Above. 6/23/96 WPR, Westchester Co. NY
Prefers wet wooded areas.

5 Little/Viola's Wood-Satyr *Megisto cymela/viola.* **p. 104**
Below. 3/16/94 Newnan's Lake, Alachua Co. FL
Prominent silver markings between eye-spots.
Mainly March–May.

9 Above. 3/16/94 Newnan's Lake, Alachua Co. FL
Large eye-spots. Mainly March–May.

6 Carolina Satyr *Hermeuptychia sosybius.* **p. 103**
Below. 3/15/94 Walt Disney Wilderness Preserve, Osceola Co. FL
No lower **FW** eye-spot. **HW** with cell-end bar.
Abundant and widespread.
February–November.

10 Above. 3/15/94 Walt Disney Wilderness Preserve, Osceola Co. FL
No eye-spots.

7 Georgia Satyr *Neonympha areolata.* **p. 103**
Below. 10/4/95 Long Pine Key, Everglades NP, Miami-Dade Co. FL
Orange-brown ring surrounds **HW** eye-spots.
HW eye-spots quite elongated.
FW spots faint or absent.
Savannas in open pine woods; wet prairies.

8 Gemmed Satyr *Cyllopsis gemma.* **p. 102**
Below. 3/19/94 Newnan's Lake, Alachua Co. FL
"Gemmed" with a silvery-gray **HW** marginal patch.
No **FW** eye-spots.

1 Southern Pearly-eye

2 Common Wood-Nymph

3 Appalachian Brown

4 Appalachian Brown

5 Viola's Wood-Satyr

6 Carolina Satyr

7 Georgia Satyr

8 Gemmed Satyr

9 Viola's Wood-Satyr

10 Carolina Satyr

1 Monarch *Danaus plexippus.* **p. 105**
Below. 9/24/94 Gainesville, Alachua Co. FL
Large. Dull orange.
Black border with double marginal row of white spots.
White spots on body.

2 ♂ above. 7/30/94 Roan Mtn., Carter Co. TN
Bright orange.
HW without black postmedian band.
HW with black sex patch that ♀ lacks.
Glides with wings held in a "V."
Flies with deep powerful wingbeats.

4 ♀ above. 10/13/96 Morristown, Morris Co. NJ
Same as ♂ but lacks **HW** black sex patch.

3 Viceroy *Limenitis archippus.* **p. 96**
Below. 7/30/90 Kisco Swamp, Westchester Co. NY
Not related to monarchs, shown for comparison.
Smaller than Monarch.
HW with black postmedian band.
Glides on flat wings.
Flies with shallow wingbeats.
Darker in most of Florida (see plate 22).

5 Queen *Danaus gilippus.* **p. 107**
Below. 9/23/94 Levy Co. FL
Darker and browner than Monarch.
FW postmedian area with white spots.
FW without black subapical band.

6 ♂ above. 9/23/94 Levy Co. FL
Rich mahogany brown.
FW postmedian area with white spots.
FW without black subapical band.
FW veins not blackened.

7 Soldier *Danaus erisimus.* **p. 107**
Below. 3/29/99 Fakahatchee Strand, Collier Co. FL
HW with a postmedian pale patch.
FW postmedian area without white spots (area covered by
HW in photo).
FW veins blackened.

8 ♀ above. 3/25/97 Chekika Unit, Everglades NP, Miami-Dade Co. FL
FW postmedian area without white spots, usually with two
faint yellowish spots.
FW veins blackened.

PLATE 25

1 Monarch

2 Monarch ♂

3 Viceroy

4 Monarch ♀

5 Queen

6 Queen ♂

7 Soldier

8 Soldier ♀

1 Mangrove Skipper *Phocides pigmalion.* **p. 109**
Below. 3/23/90 Key Largo, Monroe Co. FL
Much iridescent cobalt blue.
Iridescent turquoise bands on **HW**.

2 Above. 5/22/93 Stock Island, Monroe Co. FL
Very large.
Much iridescent cobalt blue.
Iridescent turquoise on **HW**.

3 Hammock Skipper *Polygonus leo.* **p. 110**
Below. 3/25/94 Stock Island, Monroe Co. FL
Often lands upside down under a leaf.
Blue-tinged gray-brown ground color.
Black spot near base of the **HW**.

4 Above. 3/21/90 South Miami, Miami-Dade Co. FL
Blackish-brown with blue iridescent sheen.
Three large white spots on the **FW**.
Three small subapical white spots on the **FW**.

5 Hoary Edge *Achalarus lyciades.* **p. 112**
Below. 8/1/94 Fort Bragg, Cumberland Co. NC
Rare in Florida.
A large dark skipper.
Large white patch on **HW** margin.
Generally stays low to the ground.

6 Zestos Skipper *Epargyreus zestos.* **p. 109**
Below. 5/22/94 Stock Island, Monroe Co. FL
Looks like a Silver-spotted without the silver spot.
Will often fly up into trees of hardwood hammock.
Local, rare and declining on the Florida Keys.

7 Silver-spotted Skipper *Epargyreus clarus.* **p. 110**
Below. 8/24/91 Ocala NF, Marion Co. FL (nectaring at lantana)
Large.
Large silvered spot in the middle of the **HW**.

8 Above. 8/23/91 Gainesville, Alachua Co. FL
FW is angular.
Brown-gold **FW** spot-band.

PLATE 26

1 Mangrove Skipper

2 Mangrove Skipper

3 Hammock Skipper

4 Hammock Skipper

5 Hoary Edge

6 Zestos Skipper

7 Silver-spotted Skipper

8 Silver-spotted Skipper

1 **Long-tailed Skipper** *Urbanus proteus.* **p. 111**
Below. 3/25/90 Miami-Dade Co. FL
Long tail on **HW**.
FW postmedian dark band continuous.

2 Above. 5/22/94 Stock Island, Monroe Co. FL
Long and broad tails.
Blue-green iridescence on body and wing bases.

3 **Dorantes Longtail** *Urbanus dorantes.* **p. 111**
Below. 3/20/90 South Miami, Miami-Dade Co. FL
Long tail on **HW**.
FW postmedian dark band interrupted by ground color
pushing out toward wing margin.

4 Above. 9/24/94 Gainesville, Alachua Co. FL
Long tails.
No blue-green iridescence.

5 **Golden-banded Skipper** *Autochton cellus.* **p. 112**
Below. 8/15/89 Box Canyon, Pima Co. AZ
Luminous yellow band on **FW**.
No white patch on **HW**.
Rare and local.

6 Above. 9/3/97 Monterrey, Nuevo Leon, Mexico
Luminous yellow band on **FW**.
Found in wooded ravines.
Rare and local.

PLATE 27

1 Long-tailed Skipper

2 Long-tailed Skipper

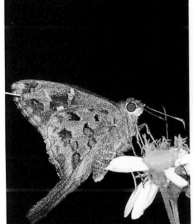

3 Dorantes Longtail

4 Dorantes Longtail

5 Golden-banded Skipper

6 Golden-banded Skipper

1 Northern Cloudywing *Thorybes pylades.* **p. 114**
Below. 3/17/94 Lake Delancey, Ocala NF, Marion Co. FL
"Face" brown or dark gray.

2 Above. 3/17/94 Lake Delancey, Ocala NF, Marion Co. FL
Uniform brown ground color.
White spots usually restricted.

3 Confused Cloudywing *Thorybes confusis.* **p. 114**
Below. 8/23/91 Gainesville, Alachua Co. FL
"Face" white or pale gray.
Outer 1/3 of **FW** often pale.
See text.

4 Above. 8/23/91 Gainesville, Alachua Co. FL
White spots vary from very restricted to extensive.
Middle spot of lower group of three spots usually a pale thin
line (if present at all).
Individuals with extensive markings resemble Southern
Cloudywings but lack the white patch at the bend in
antennal club.
See text.

5 Southern Cloudywing *Thorybes bathyllus.* **p. 113**
Below. 5/18/94 Torreya SP, Liberty Co. FL
"Face" white or pale gray.

6 Above. 3/17/94 Riverside Island, Ocala NF, Marion Co. FL
Uniform brown ground color.
White spots usually large.
FW with second from the costa, white median spot often
shaped like an hourglass.
White patch at bend in antennal club.

1 Northern Cloudywing

2 Northern Cloudywing

3 Confused Cloudywing

4 Confused Cloudywing

5 Southern Cloudywing

6 Southern Cloudywing

1 **Juvenal's Duskywing** *Erynnis juvenalis.* **p. 117**
♂ above. 3/18/94 Yankeetown, Levy Co. FL
White spots large on **FW**.
Pale spot near end of **FW** cell (sometimes faint).
Usually with much gray on the **FW**.

2 ♀ above. 4/15/95 Busch, Carroll Co. AR
White spots large on **FW**.
Pale spot near end of **FW** cell.

3 Below. 3/17/94 Riverside Island, Ocala NF, Marion Co. FL
Two pale subapical spots on **HW** (almost always).

4 **Horace's Duskywing** *Erynnis horatius.* **p. 117**
Below. 5/18/94 Gretna, Gadsden Co. FL
No pale subapical spots on **HW**.

5 ♂ above. 8/22/91 Gainesville, Alachua Co. FL
Pale spot near end of **FW** cell (sometimes faint).
Fairly uniform brown without gray.
White line over eye. Four **FW** subapical spots in a row.
See Zarucco Duskywing, plate 30.

6 ♀ above. 3/25/90 Matheson Hammock, Miami-Dade Co. FL
White spots large on **FW**.
Pale spot near end of **FW** cell.
Very strong pattern.
Large, dark submarginal spots on paler **HW** ground.

7 ♂ above. Worn individual.
3/15/94 Walt Disney Wilderness Preserve, Osceola Co. FL
Pale spot near end of **FW** cell (sometimes faint).
Fairly uniform brown without gray.
White line over eye. Four **FW** subapical spots in a row.
See Zarucco Duskywing, plate 30.

8 **Florida Duskywing** *Ephyriades brunneus.* **p. 116**
♂ above. 3/22/90 Long Pine Key, Everglades NP, FL
Semicircle of white spots near the **FW** apex.
Brown ground color fairly uniform.
Prefers pine rocklands.

9 Below. 3/24/94 National Key Deer Refuge, Monroe Co. FL

10 ♀ above. 3/22/90 Long Pine Key, Everglades NP, FL
Semicircle of white spots near the **FW** apex.
Violaceous sheen when fresh.
Prefers pine rocklands.

PLATE 29

1 Juvenal's Duskywing ♂

2 Juvenal's Duskywing ♀

3 Juvenal's Duskywing

4 Horace's Duskywing

5 Horace's Duskywing ♂

6 Horace's Duskywing ♀

7 Horace's Duskywing ♂

8 Florida Duskywing ♂

9 Florida Duskywing

10 Florida Duskywing ♀

1 Sleepy Duskywing *Erynnis brizo.* **p. 116**
♂ above. 3/17/94 Riverside Island, Ocala NF, Marion Co. FL
No white spots on **FW**.
Broad chain-like postmedian band on **FW**.
Open flatwoods and scrubs.

2 ♀ above. 3/17/94 Riverside Island, Ocala NF, Marion Co. FL
No white spots on **FW**.
Broad chain-like postmedian band on **FW**.
Pale brownish patch at **FW** "wrist."
March–April.

3 Wild Indigo Duskywing *Erynnis baptisiae.* **p. 119**
♂ above. 5/29/92 Oakridge, Sussex Co. NJ
Rare. Subapical white spots on **FW**.
Usually without (or faint) pale spot in **FW** cell.

4 ♀ above. 7/11/96 Troy Meadows, Morris Co. NJ
Subapical white spots on **FW**.
Usually without (or faint) pale spot in **FW** cell.
HW with small pale spots on dark brown.
HW usually with pale, straight, and thin cell-end bar.
See Horace's and Zarucco duskywings females.

5 Below. 5/22/91 Chappaqua, Westchester Co. NY
Small pale spots on dark brown **HW**.

6 Mottled Duskywing *Erynnis martialis.* **p. 118**
Above. 4/15/95 Busch, Caroll Co. AR
More mottled than other duskywings.
Narrow and sharp **HW** postmedian dark band.
Violet sheen when fresh. May be gone from Florida.

7 Zarucco Duskywing *Erynnis zarucco.* **p. 118**
Below. 8/1/94 Fort Bragg, Cumberland Co. NC

8 ♀ above. 8/23/91 Gainesville, Alachua Co. FL
HW with no cell-end bar (or an ill-defined one).
Very similar to Wild Indigo Duskywing female.

9 ♂ above. 3/25/94 Little Hamaca Park, Key West. FL
West Indian race, see 10 for ID info.

10 ♂ above. 5/11/97 Gainesville, Alachua Co. FL
FW relatively narrow and angled.
Pale brown "wrist" patch at end of **FW** cell.
FW cell and costal fold usually evenly black.
FW subapical white spots with fourth (bottom) spot (if pre-
sent) usually smaller and displaced outwardly.
Usually with no (or faint) white eyeline.
Often with neck gray.
See male Horace's Duskywing, plate 29.

PLATE 30

1 Sleepy Duskywing ♂

2 Sleepy Duskywing ♀

3 Wild Indigo Duskywing ♂

4 Wild Indigo Duskywing ♀

5 Wild Indigo Duskywing

6 Mottled Duskywing

7 Zarucco Duskywing

8 Zarucco Duskywing ♀

9 Zarucco Duskywing ♂

10 Zarucco Duskywing ♂

1 Common Checkered-Skipper *Pyrgus communis.* **p. 120**
Below. 9/24/94 Gainesville, Alachua Co. FL
"Clean" white and tan bands.
No brown spot in the middle of the **HW** leading margin.

2 ♂ above. 5/19/94 Gainesville, Alachua Co. FL
White and black with blue-gray body hairs.
FW marginal row of small white spots missing apical spot.
FW with white spot just beyond cell-end white bar absent or
very small.
HW marginal white spots usually minute.

4 ♀ above. Same individual as 1.
White and black. See number 2 for more ID information.

3 Tropical Checkered-Skipper *Pyrgus oileus.* **p. 121**
Below. 3/20/90 South Miami, Miami-Dade Co. FL
White and tan pattern "smudged."
Brown spot in the middle of the **HW** leading margin.

6 ♂ above. 5/17/94 Newnan's Lake, Alachua Co. FL
FW marginal row of small white spots complete with apical
spot.
FW with white spot just beyond cell-end white bar present
and large.
HW marginal white spots usually not so small.

9 ♀ above. 5/20/94 Bauer Park, Homestead, Miami-Dade Co. FL
White and black.
See number 6 for more ID information.

5 Common Sootywing *Pholisora catullus.* **p. 121**
Above. 7/29/92 Somers, Westchester Co. NY
Small and brown/black with many tiny white spots.
White spots on the head.
Most likely in disturbed situations.
Rare and local in Florida.

7 Hayhurst's Scallopwing *Staphylus hayhurstii.* **p. 115**
♂ above. 8/23/91 U. of Florida, Gainesville, FL
Dark brown/black with a few small white spots.
Gold or silver flecking. **HW** with scalloped margin.

8 ♀ above. 9/29/95 Newnan's Lake, Alachua Co. FL
Brown with darker concentric bands.
FW with a few small white spots.
Gold or silver flecking. **HW** with scalloped margin.

1 Common Checkered-Skipper

2 Common Checkered-Skipper ♂

3 Tropical Checkered-Skipper

4 Common Checkered-Skipper ♀

5 Common Sootywing

6 Tropical Checkered-Skipper ♂

7 Hayhurst's Scallopwing ♂

8 Hayhurst's Scallopwing ♀

9 Tropical Checkered-Skipper ♀

1 Swarthy Skipper *Nastra lherminier.* **p. 122**
Below. 10/2/95 Daytona Beach, Volusia Co. FL
Yellow-brown.
Veins paler.

2 Above. 8/2/94 Fort Bragg, Cumberland Co. NC
Unmarked dark brown.

3 Neamathla Skipper *Nastra neamathla.* **p. 122**
Below. 9/23/94 Chassahowitzka, Citrus Co. FL
Usually duller brown than Swarthy Skipper.
Veins not paler.

4 Above. 8/23/91 Gainesville, Alachua Co. FL
Usually with two pale spots in the median **FW**.

5 Three-spotted Skipper *Cymaenes tripunctus.* **p. 123**
Below. 10/3/95 Matheson Hammock, Miami-Dade Co. FL
Long antennas—about 1/2 the **FW** length.
Yellowish-brown to brown ground.
HW usually with distinct postmedian spots.
See Eufala Skipper and Obscure Skipper, plate 41.

6 Above. 5/20/94 Bauer Park, Homestead, Miami-Dade Co. FL
Base of the **FW** costa often tawny orange.
Three white subapical spots are separate and curve out.

7 Eufala Skipper *Lerodea eufala.* **p. 143**
Below. 9/22/94 Pasco, Pasco Co. FL
Antennas less than 1/2 the **FW** length.
Pale gray-brown ground color.
HW with indistinct postmedian spots.
Immigrant northward.
See Three-spotted Skipper, this plate.

8 Above. 9/26/94 Gainesville, Alachua Co. FL
White subapical spots almost touch and are straight.

9 Southern Skipperling *Copaeodes minimus.* **p. 125**
Below. 5/17/94 Gainesville, Alachua Co. FL
Tiny.
Narrow white ray on **HW**.

11 Above. 5/10/97 St. Augustine, St. Johns Co. FL
Wings long and narrow.

10 Least Skipper *Ancyloxypha numitor.* **p. 124**
Below. 6/22/96 WPR, Westchester Co. NY.
Very small. Weak flight.
Rounded wings.

12 Above. 6/11/91 Goose Pond SP, Orange Co. NY
Small. Weak flight with black above.
Rounded wings.

1 Swarthy Skipper

2 Swarthy Skipper

3 Neamathla Skipper

4 Neamathla Skipper

5 Three-spotted Skipper

6 Three-spotted Skipper

7 Eufala Skipper

8 Eufala Skipper

9 Southern Skipperling

10 Least Skipper

11 Southern Skipperling

12 Least Skipper

1 Fiery Skipper *Hylephila phyleus*. **p. 125**
♂ below. 9/26/94 Gainesville, Alachua Co. FL
Small dark spots on a bright orange ground.
Widespread and common.

4 ♀ below. 8/24/91 Ocala NF, Marion Co. FL
Small dark spots on a dull orange ground.

7 ♂ above. 5/19/94 Gainesville, Alachua Co. FL
Jagged black borders on **FW** and **HW**.

10 ♀ above. 8/25/91 Gainesville, Alachua Co. FL
Jagged black border on **FW**.
"Arrow" pointing outward on **HW**.

2 Whirlabout *Polites vibex*. **p. 129**
♂ below. 8/25/91 Royal Park Plaza, Gainesville, Alachua Co. FL
Large smudged dark spots at corners of a square.

5 ♀ below. 8/23/91 Gainesville, Alachua Co. FL
Dull greenish-gray-yellow.
Large smudged dark spots at corners of a square.

8 ♂ above. 8/23/91 Gainesville, Alachua Co. FL
Jagged black border on **FW**.
Relatively smooth black border on **HW**.

11 ♀ above. 3/26/97 Fakahatchee Strand, Collier Co. FL
Brown with small pale spots on **FW**.
No spot in the **FW** cell.

3 Sachem *Atalopedes campestris*. **p. 132**
♂ below. 5/17/94 Gainesville, Alachua Co. FL
Squarish brown patch at center of **HW** trailing margin.

6 ♀ below.7/29/94 Blowing Rock, Watauga Co. NC
Yellow-brown.
Large, pale postmedian chevron on **HW**.
Very variable.

9 ♂ above. 9/26/94 Gainesville, Alachua Co. FL
Large, black, rectangular stigma on **FW**.

12 ♀ above. 5/19/94 Gainesville, Alachua Co. FL
Black patch at the center of **FW**.
Two large white hyaline spots on **FW**.

PLATE 33

1 Fiery Skipper ♂

2 Whirlabout ♂

3 Sachem ♂

4 Fiery Skipper ♀

5 Whirlabout ♀

6 Sachem ♀

7 Fiery Skipper ♂

8 Whirlabout ♂

9 Sachem ♂

10 Fiery Skipper ♀

11 Whirlabout ♀

12 Sachem ♀

1 **Dotted Skipper** *Hesperia attalus.* **p. 126**
Below. 9/27/94 Riverside Island, Ocala NF, Marion Co. FL
HW usually with distinct bright white dots.
FW with two subapical pale spots.

2 ♂ above. 7/25/90 Lakehurst, Ocean Co. NJ
Uncommon and local in sandy, grassy, open flatwoods.
HW with postmedian spot-band.

3 ♀ above. Riverside Island, Ocala NF, Marion Co. FL
HW with postmedian spot-band.

15 Below. 9/27/94 Ocala NF, Marion Co. FL
Variant with more pronounced spots.

4 **Crossline Skipper** *Polites origenes.* **p. 129**
Below. 6/28/92 Hauppauge, Suffolk Co. NY
Usually warm yellow-brown with postmedian spot-band.
Low contrast between **HW** color and **FW** costal margin.

5 ♂ above. 7/9/95 Mt. Kisco, Westchester Co. NY
FW stigma not as intense as in Tawny-edged.
Stigma narrows toward the base of the **FW**.
Additional pale yellow spot distally adjacent to stigma.

6 ♀ above. Sandhills Gamelands, Scotland Co. NC
HW with broad dark border and hint of orange on disc.

7 **Tawny-edged Skipper** *Polites themistocles.* **p. 128**
Below. 9/25/94 Daytona Beach, Volusia Co. FL
Usually drab olive-brown with no (or faint) pale band.
Strong contrast between color of **HW** and bright **FW** costal
   margin.

8 ♂ above. 9/26/94 Gainesville, Alachua Co. FL
Intense, thick, black stigma on **FW**.
Rectangular orange spot at end of stigma.

9 ♀ above. 9/26/94 Gainesville, Alachua Co. FL
HW with narrow dark border and very little orange.

13 Below. 5/31/91 Chappaqua, Westchester Co. NY
Variant with more pronounced postmedian band.

10 **Baracoa Skipper** *Polites baracoa.* **p. 127**
Below. 10/4/95 Long Pine Key, Everglades NP, FL
Usually with chunky, pale postmedian band.

11 ♂ above. 3/28/99 Homestead, Miami-Dade Co. FL
Dark ray inward from **FW** margin passes end of stigma.

12 ♀ above. 3/21/90 Homestead, Miami-Dade Co. FL
See text.

14 Below. 5/20/94 Bauer Park, Homestead, Miami-Dade Co. FL
Variant without pale postmedian band.

1 Dotted Skipper

2 Dotted Skipper ♂

3 Dotted Skipper ♀

4 Crossline Skipper

5 Crossline Skipper ♂

6 Crossline Skipper ♀

7 Tawny-edged Skipper

8 Tawny-edged Skipper ♂

9 Tawny-edged Skipper ♀

10 Baracoa Skipper

11 Baracoa Skipper ♂

12 Baracoa Skipper ♀

13 Tawny-edged Skipper

14 Baracoa Skipper

15 Dotted Skipper

1 Southern Broken-Dash *Wallengrenia otho.* **p. 130**
Below. 5/9/97 Gainesville, Alachua Co. FL
Reddish-brown ground color.
HW postmedian band often in shape of a 3.
Broad gray **FW** fringe.

2 ♂ above. 3/20/90 South Miami, Miami-Dade Co. FL
Rectangular orange spot at end of stigma.

3 ♀ above. 9/25/94 Daytona Beach, Volusia Co. FL
Rectangular orange spot on **HW**.

4 Northern Broken-Dash *Wallengrenia egeremet.* **p. 130**
Below. 9/29/95 Gainesville, Alachua Co. FL
Yellow-brown ground color.
Wide postmedian **HW** band often in shape of a 3.

5 ♂ above. 5/19/94 Gainesville, Alachua Co. FL
Rectangular pale orange spot at end of stigma.

6 ♀ above. 9/25/94 Daytona Beach, Volusia Co. FL
Rectangular pale spot at end of stigma.

7 Little Glassywing *Pompeius verna.* **p. 131**
Below. 5/7/97 Gulf Hammock, Levy Co. FL
Dark brown ground color.
White patch just below antennal club.
HW usually has postmedian line with discrete spots.

8 ♂ above. 8/1/94 Fort Bragg, Cumberland Co. NC
White patch just below antennal club.
Large rectangular white spot in middle of **FW**.

9 ♀ above. 5/7/97 Gulf Hammock, Levy Co. FL
White patch just below antennal club.
Large square white spot in middle of **FW**.
White spot in **FW** cell.

10 Dun Skipper *Euphyes vestris.* **p. 139**
Below. 9/25/94 Daytona Beach, Volusia Co. FL
Faint, if any, **HW** postmedian band.
Head of males often golden.

11 ♂ above. 3/18/89 Disney World, Orlando, FL.
Completely dark with black stigma (pale patch on this individual is abraded scales, not part of pattern).
Also see Clouded Skipper, plate 37.

12 ♀ above. 8/23/91 Newnan's Lake, Alachua Co. FL
FW with two small white central spots.
Also see Clouded Skipper, plate 37 and Twin-spot Skipper, plate 37.

PLATE 35

1 Southern Broken-Dash

2 Southern Broken-Dash ♂

3 Southern Broken-Dash ♀

4 Northern Broken-Dash

5 Northern Broken-Dash ♂

6 Northern Broken-Dash ♀

7 Little Glassywing

8 Little Glassywing ♂

9 Little Glassywing ♀

10 Dun Skipper

11 Dun Skipper ♂

12 Dun Skipper ♀

1 **Delaware Skipper** *Anatrytone logan.* **p. 133**
Below. 10/4/95 Long Pine Key, Everglades NP, FL.
Clear, bright, unmarked yellow-orange.
HW fringe orange to tan.

2 ♂ above. 3/30/99 Big Cypress National Preserve, Collier Co. FL
Black **FW** cell-end bar.
Black veining on **FW**.

3 ♀ above. 10/4/95 Long Pine Key, Everglades NP, FL
Black **FW** cell-end bar.
Black at base of **FW**.

4 **Arogos Skipper** *Atrytone arogos.* **p. 132**
Below. 10/1/95 Riverside Island, Ocala NP, Marion Co. FL
Orange-yellow.
HW with whitish veins. **HW** fringe white.
Local and rare.

5 ♂ above. 7/8/97 Fort Collins, CO
No black **FW** cell-end bar.
No black veining on **FW**.

6 ♀ above. 7/24/96 Fort Dix, Ocean Co. NJ
Broad black borders on **FW** and **HW**.
Long, thin black mark in middle of basal half of **FW**.

7 **Byssus Skipper** *Problema byssus.* **p. 133**
Below. 8/25/91 Newnan's Lake, Alachua Co. FL
Bright orange-brown.
Pale area in middle of **HW**.
HW often with paler veins.
FW with subapical pale spots.

8 ♂ above. 5/7/97 Gulf Hammock, Levy Co. FL
Orange band sweeps across entire **FW**.

9 ♀ above. 9/24/94 Gainesville, Alachua Co. FL

10 **Meske's Skipper** *Hesperia meskei.* **p. 127**
Below. 9/29/95 Gainesville, Alachua Co. FL
Yellow-orange to rusty-orange.
HW with pale postmedian band faint to distinct.
FW with two subapical pale spots.
Scarce.

11 ♂ above. 10/5/96 Sandhills Gamelands, NC

12 ♀ above. Same individual as 10.
FW costal margin white.
FW with unbroken postmedian spot-band.

1 Delaware Skipper

2 Delaware Skipper ♂

3 Delaware Skipper ♀

4 Arogos Skipper

5 Arogos Skipper ♂

6 Arogos Skipper ♀

7 Byssus Skipper

8 Byssus Skipper ♂

9 Byssus Skipper ♀

10 Meske's Skipper

11 Meske's Skipper ♂

12 Meske's Skipper ♀

1 Dusted Skipper *Atrytonopsis hianna.* **p. 140**
Below. Aug. 1996. Duval Co. FL
"Masked" appearance.
HW with basal and postmedian white spots.

2 Below. 4/24/94 Goshen, Rockbridge Co. VA
More northern populations often lack the extensive white
HW spots (this form very rare in Florida).

3 Above. 6/7/91 WPR, Westchester Co. NY
White eye-line.

4 Twin-spot Skipper *Oligoria maculata.* **p. 143**
Below. 3/26/97 Big Cypress Preserve, Collier Co. FL
Chestnut-brown ground color.
Usually with three bold white spots on **HW**, with two
together (the twins). (Spots are occasionally faint.)

5 Above. 5/17/94 Gainesville, Alachua Co. FL

6 Zabulon Skipper *Poanes zabulon.* **p. 134**
♂ above. 5/20/97 Morris Co. NJ
Black cell-end bar on **FW**.
FW black border very uneven.

7 ♀ below. 8/17/96 Heard Museum, McKinney, TX
Silvery white margin at **HW** apex.

8 ♂ below. 8/1/94 Fort Bragg, Cumberland Co. NC
Yellow with brown patch at **HW** base enclosing yellow.

9 ♀ above. 8/16/96 Heard Museum, McKinney, TX
White **HW** margin at apex visible.

10 Clouded Skipper *Lerema accius.* **p. 124**
Below. 8/30/95 3/16/94 Gainesville, Alachua Co. FL
FW with gray patch.
Vertical dark patch in center of wing.
Lacks two white submarginal spots that Hobomok has.

11 ♂ above. 3/16/94 Newnan's Lake, Alachua Co. FL
FW subapical spots curve outward.
Also see Dun Skipper above, plate 35.

12 ♀ above. 8/25/91 Gainesville, Alachua Co. FL
FW subapical spots curve outward.
FW with oval cell spot.
Also see Dun Skipper above, plate 35.

1 'Florida' Dusted Skipper

2 Dusted Skipper

3 Dusted Skipper

4 Twin-spot Skipper

5 Twin-spot Skipper

6 Zabulon Skipper ♂

7 Zabulon Skipper ♀

8 Zabulon Skipper ♂

9 Zabulon Skipper ♀

10 Clouded Skipper

11 Clouded Skipper ♂

12 Clouded Skipper ♀

1   Broad-winged Skipper *Poanes viator.* **p. 136**
Below. 10/1/96 Hutchinson Island, Savannah, GA
Dull, **HW** with paler ray flanked by pale spots.
Subapical spot(s) on **FW**.
Often lands with its head up and body vertical.

2   ♂ above. 10/1/96 Hutchinson Island, Savannah, GA

3   ♀ above. 8/9/90 Mt. Kisco, Westchester Co. NY
Large.
Yellow ray at **HW** outer angle.

4   Yehl Skipper *Poanes yehl.* **p. 135**
Below. 8/22/92 Great Dismal Swamp NWR, Suffolk, VA
Rusty-orange fading to dull yellow.
Three or four pale postmedian spots on **HW**.

5   ♂ above. 8/22/92 Great Dismal Swamp NWR, Suffolk, VA
Black border along **HW** leading edge narrows near apex.

6   ♀ above. 8/24/92 Great Dismal Swamp NWR, Suffolk, VA
Lacks yellow ray at **HW** outer angle of previous species.

7   Aaron's Skipper *Poanes aaroni.* **p. 134**
Below. 8/26/90 Higbeetown, Atlantic Co. NJ
Dull.
HW with a narrow, pale ray that usually extends the length
of the wing.
Pale ray often flanked by two pale dots.
No subapical spot on **FW**.

8   ♂ above. 5/10/97 Osceola NF, Baker Co. FL

9   ♀ above. 5/10/97 Osceola NF, Baker Co. FL

10 Palatka Skipper *Euphyes pilatka.* **p. 137**
Below. 3/26/97 Fakahatchee Stand , Collier Co. FL
Very large.
Rusty-brown.
Prefers brackish sawgrass marshes and adjacent areas.

11 ♂ above. 3/24/90 Big Cypress Preserve, Collier Co. FL
FW usually has thin black line parallel to costal margin.

12 ♀ above. 3/26/97 Big Cypress Preserve, Collier Co. FL

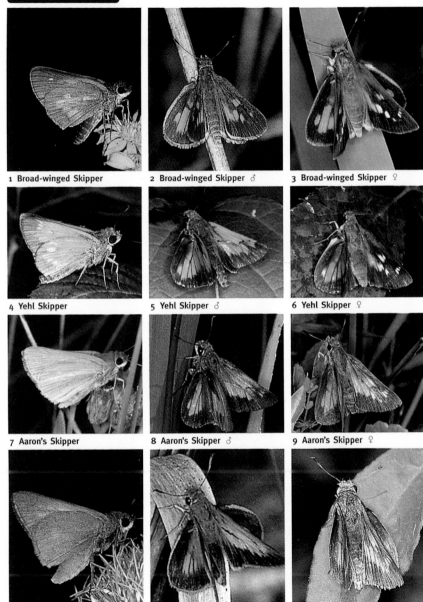

1 Broad-winged Skipper

2 Broad-winged Skipper ♂

3 Broad-winged Skipper ♀

4 Yehl Skipper

5 Yehl Skipper ♂

6 Yehl Skipper ♀

7 Aaron's Skipper

8 Aaron's Skipper ♂

9 Aaron's Skipper ♀

10 Palatka Skipper

11 Palatka Skipper ♂

12 Palatka Skipper ♀

1 Dion Skipper *Euphyes dion.* **p. 137**
Below. 9/26/94 Gainesville, Alachua Co. FL
Bright orange to dull reddish-orange.
HW with one or two pale rays, top ray usually not extending
the entire length of wing.
Prefers open wetlands.

2 ♂ above. 7/11/96 Troy Meadows, Morris Co. NJ

3 ♀ above. 9/29/95 Gainesville, Alachua Co. FL

4 Dukes' Skipper *Euphyes dukesi.* **p. 138**
Below. 9/22/94 Trout Creek, Hillsborough Co. FL
Rich orange-brown to sooty-brown.
HW with one or two pale rays.
FW disc black.
Prefers shady, fresh-water swamps.

5 ♂ above. 9/22/94 Trout Creek, Hillsborough Co. FL
Very dark with black stigma.

6 ♀ above. 8/31/95 Chesapeake, VA
Dark brown without markings.

7 Palmetto Skipper *Euphyes arpa.* **p. 136**
Below. 9/26/94 Gainesville, Alachua Co. FL
Large and orange.
Golden head and mantle.

8 ♂ above. 8/25/91 Gainesville, Alachua Co. FL
Golden head and mantle.
Long, narrow, black stigma.

9 ♀ above. Same individual as 7.

10 Berry's Skipper *Euphyes berryi.* **p. 138**
Below. 9/25/94 Daytona Beach, Volusia Co. FL
Dull brownish-orange.
Whitened **HW** veins.
FW without subapical pale spots.
Local and rare. See text.

11 ♂ above. 9/25/94 Same individual as 10.
Thin stigma on **FW**.
Black ray inward from margin about 1/3 **FW** length.

12 ♀ above. (Collected 9/16/42 Orlando, FL by Dean F. Berry—for whom this
species is named.)
FW cell spot.
Some tawny on the **HW**.

1 Dion Skipper

2 Dion Skipper ♂

3 Dion Skipper ♀

4 Dukes' Skipper

5 Dukes' Skipper ♂

6 Dukes' Skipper ♀

7 Palmetto Skipper

8 Palmetto Skipper ♂

9 Palmetto Skipper ♀

10 Berry's Skipper

11 Berry's Skipper ♂

12 Berry's Skipper ♀

1 Lace-winged Roadside-Skipper *Amblyscirtes aesculapius.*
p. 141
Below. 5/7/97 Gulf Hammock, Levy Co. FL
Cobwebby white veins.
In or near cane-brakes.

2 Above. 8/25/91 Newnan's Lake, Alachua Co. FL

3 Dusky Roadside-Skipper *Amblyscirtes alternata.* **p. 142**
Below. 3/20/94 Riverside Island, Ocala NF, Marion Co. FL
Dark with some bluish scales.
Almost no white or pale markings.
Blunt antennal clubs.

4 Above. Same individual as 3.
Only a few faint **FW** subapical spots.

5 Common Roadside-Skipper *Amblyscirtes vialis.* **p. 142**
Below. 5/21/91 Nottingham Barrens Co. Park, Nottingham, PA
Small and black.
Outer portions of wings are "frosted."
Fringes are strongly checkered.
FW subapical white spots usually much wider at margin.

6 Above. 8/2/94 Fort Bragg, Cumberland Co. NC
Flies April–May and Aug.–Sept.

7 Pepper and Salt Skipper *Amblyscirtes hegon.* **p. 141**
Below. 6/12/93 Wentworths Location, NH
Yellowish tinged gray-brown ground color.
Prominent cream-colored postmedian band on **HW**.
Rare and local.
April–May.

8 Above. 6/5/96 Jones Knob, Highlands, Macon Co. NC
FW with strong spot-band.
Rare and local.
April–May.

1 Lace-winged Roadside-Skipper

2 Lace-winged Roadside-Skipper

3 Dusky Roadside-Skipper

4 Dusky Roadside-Skipper

5 Common Roadside-Skipper

6 Common Roadside-Skipper

7 Pepper and Salt Skipper

8 Pepper and Salt Skipper

1 Ocola Skipper *Panoquina ocola*. **p. 146**
Below. 8/24/91 Lake Delancey, Ocala NF, Marion Co. FL
Long, narrow wings.
Dark line running along side of abdomen.
Distal 1/4 of **HW** darker.
Occasionally with white postmedian spots on **HW**.

2 Above. 5/19/94 Gainesville, Alachua Co. FL
FW median pale spot is bullet-shaped.

3 Below. 8/24/91 Lake Delancey, Ocala NF, Marion Co. FL
Purplish sheen when fresh.

4 Salt Marsh Skipper *Panoquina panoquin*. **p. 145**
♂ above. 9/29/96 Black River, Savannah, GA
Long narrow wings.
Dark line running along side of abdomen.
Found in salt marshes and adjacent areas.

5 Below. 9/23/94 Cedar Key, Levy Co. FL
Cream-colored streak on **HW**.
Long narrow wings.
Dark line running along side of abdomen.
Yellow-brown ground color.
Paler yellow veining.
Found in salt marshes and adjacent areas.

6 ♀ above. 9/30/96 Black River, Savannah, GA
Long narrow wings.

7 Obscure Skipper *Panoquina panoquinoides*. **p. 145**
Below. 3/24/94 Big Pine Key, Monroe Co. FL
Dull brown.
Dark line running along side of abdomen.
Paler veins.
Usually with three small white spots on **HW** postmedian.
No cream-colored streak on **HW**.
Found in salt marshes and adjacent areas.
Also see Three-spotted Skipper, plate 32.

8 Above. 2/26/99 Big Pine Key, Monroe Co. FL
Obscure.

1 Ocola Skipper

2 Ocola Skipper

3 Ocola Skipper

4 Salt Marsh Skipper ♂

5 Salt Marsh Skipper

6 Salt Marsh Skipper ♀

7 Obscure Skipper

8 Obscure Skipper

1 Cofaqui Giant-Skipper *Megathymus cofaqui.* **p. 147**
Below. 3/18/89 Disney World, Orlando, FL
See Yucca Giant-Skipper (this plate).
Gray ground color.
White spot near **HW** leading margin not so large.
Variable number of small white postmedian spots.
Often flies at dawn and dusk.

2 Yucca Giant-Skipper *Megathymus yuccae.* **p. 147**
Below. 3/19/94 Royal Park Plaza, Gainesville, Alachua Co. FL
Huge.
Very dark brown with some marginal frosting.
Large white spot near the leading margin of the **HW**.
Tan-yellow **HW** fringe.

3 Monk Skipper *Asbolis capucinus.* **p. 140**
Below. 5/22/94 Key West, Monroe Co. FL
Dark red-orange-brown.

4 Above. 5/22/93 Stock Island, Monroe Co. FL
Rich chestnut color.

5 Brazilian Skipper *Calpodes ethlius.* **p. 144**
Below. 10/25/98 Mission, Hidalgo Co. TX
HW with three or four translucent spots in an angled line.

6 Above. 9/22/94 Trout Creek, Hillsborough Co. FL

1 Cofaqui Giant-Skipper

2 Yucca Giant-Skipper

3 Monk Skipper

4 Monk Skipper

5 Brazilian Skipper

6 Brazilian Skipper

1 **Mimic** *Hypolimnas misippus.* **p. 153**
♀ below. November, 1986 Royal Palm, Everglades NP, FL
Rare stray to south Florida.
FW with bold white subapical stripe.
Appearance above is similar.

2 ♂ above. 9/9/76 Subic Bay, Grande Island, Philippines
Rare stray to south Florida.
Extremely large white spots on black ground.
Appearance below is vaguely similar to female below, with
bold white median patches on **FW** and **HW**.

3 **Mercurial Skipper** *Proteides mercurius.* **p. 155**
Below. 2/10/94 Hill Bank, Orangewalk District, Belize
Very large for a skipper.
Bright orange head.

4 **Orion** *Historis odius.* **p. 154**
Below. March 1996, Hill Bank, Orangewalk District, Belize
Huge size.
Wing shape and pattern resemble dead leaf.
Possible stray to south Florida.

5 **Funereal Duskywing** *Erynnis funeralis.* **p. 155**
Above. 11/10/89 Santa Ana NWR, Hidalgo Co. TX
Stray to Florida panhandle region.
Bold white fringe on **HW**.
Otherwise, extremely similar to Zarucco Duskywing.

6 **Violet-banded Skipper** *Nyctelius nyctelius.* **p. 156**
Below. 10/29/93 Mission, Hidalgo Co. TX
Alternating pale and dark bands.
Pale bands with violaceous sheen when fresh.
Black spot near the middle of **HW** leading margin.
Abdomen with black and white rings.
One record from Florida Keys.

7 **Pale Cracker** *Hamadryas amphichloe.* **p. 153**
Above. Feb. 1999. Guanica Dry Forest Preserve, Puerto Rico
Large.
Gray with pale **FW** subapical patches.
Usually lands head-down on tree trunks.
Strays to south Florida.

1 Mimic ♀

2 Mimic ♂

3 Mercurial Skipper

4 Orion

5 Funereal Duskywing

6 Violet-banded Skipper

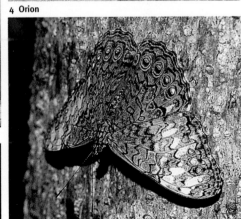

7 Pale Cracker

1 **Fogfruit** *Lippia nodifolia*
9/2/9/95 Gainesville, Alachua Co. FL

2 **Spanish needles** *Bidens alba*
Nov. 1995, Clay Co. Fl.

3 **Lantana** *Lantana camara*
June 1996, Gainesville, Alachua Co. FL

4 **Southern dewberry** *Rubus trivialis*
March 1995, Clay Co. FL

5 **Redroot** *Lachnanthes caroliniana*
Above. July 1986, Highlands Co. FL

6 **Hog Plum** *Prunus umbellata*
March 1991, Ordway Preserve, Putnam Co. FL

7 **Pickerelweed** *Pontederia cordata*
July 1991, Volusia Co. FL

8 **Thistle** *Cirsium horridulum*
April 1995, Clay Co. FL

9 **Highbush blueberry** *Vaccinium corymbosum*
Feb. 1998, Caravelle WMA, Putnam Co. FL

10 **Narrow-leaved croton** *Croton linearis*
March 1999, Big Pine Key, Monroe Co. FL

PLATE 44

1 Fogfruit

2 Spanish needles

3 Lantana

4 Southern dewberry

5 Redroot

6 Hog Plum

7 Pickerelweed

8 Thistle

9 Highbush blueberry

10 Narrow-leaved croton

ABOUT THE SPECIES ACCOUNTS

Name

English and scientific names follow the North American Butterfly Association's (NABA) *Checklist and English Names of North American Butterflies*. Before the NABA checklist was published in 1995, each author of a book about butterflies used whatever set of names struck his or her fancy. The result has been a confusing plethora of names that has bewildered the uninitiated and made it more difficult for the public to become involved with butterflies. We are now on the road toward standardization, although this process will take years to be completed. If a widespread, currently in-print field guide has used an English name different from the one used here, that name is also included in the index.

Although the scientific names used in this work follow the NABA list, in those cases where we disagree with the species status given in that list, we say so.

Size

The size of a butterfly can be difficult to determine in the field. Is the length of the forewing (FW) 9/16 inch or is it 11/16 inch? Because of this difficulty, we have opted for expressing the size of each species relative to other standard species. Most of these standard species are common and widespread, and thus you should rapidly become familiar with them. The sizes of the standard species themselves are given in Table 3 and in the species accounts for these species. **Perhaps the easiest way to visualize the size of the standard species is to look at the silhouettes in the beginning of the plates section. All of the size standard species are shown there at life size.** Because different groups of butterflies and skippers typically are seen with their wings in differ-

Table 3 Length of 1 Forewing

SIZE STANDARD SPECIES	COSTAL MARGIN (IN INCHES)
Pipevine Swallowtail	1 $^{12}/_{16}$
Eastern Tiger Swallowtail	2 $^3/_{16}$
Little Yellow	$^{11}/_{16}$
Checkered White	$^{15}/_{16}$
Cloudless Sulphur	1 $^5/_{16}$
Ceraunus Blue	$^7/_{16}$
Gray Hairstreak	$^{10}/_{16}$
Gulf Fritillary	1 $^9/_{16}$
Pearl Crescent	$^{11}/_{16}$
Common Buckeye	1
Red-spotted Purple	1 $^9/_{16}$
Carolina Satyr	$^{11}/_{16}$
Monarch	2
Tropical Checkered-Skipper	$^9/_{16}$
Northern Cloudywing	$^{12}/_{16}$
Silver-spotted Skipper	1 $^2/_{16}$
Swarthy Skipper	$^8/_{16}$
Whirlabout	$^9/_{16}$
Sachem, female	$^{11}/_{16}$

ent positions, we have chosen to use the length of the front margin of one FW, which should be visible in all cases, as the measure of size. The size given is the average size in inches. Symbols used in this section are: "=," meaning that the size of the species being discussed is equal to the size standard species, "<" meaning that the size of the species being discussed is less than the "size standard" species, "<<" meaning much less than, ">" meaning greater than, ">>" meaning much greater than, "≤" meaning less than or equal to, and "≥" meaning greater than or equal to.

In addition to using these size standards you can determine the actual size of a species by looking at the photographic plates. Each plate has the species on that plate in the correct size relationship to each other, and at the top left corner of the plate itself you are told whether the actual size of the butterflies is smaller or larger than shown. For example, the blues on plate 16 are shown at 2 × life size, i.e., the length of the FW costal margin of each butterfly in the photographs is about 2 times larger than the actual size of the HW costal margin.

When considering size, remember that the size of different individuals of the same species can vary dramatically. Occasionally a runt individual will be drastically smaller than is normal for the species. And, although in many species both sexes are a similar size, as a general rule, females are larger than males.

Similar Species

Here, we try to alert you to the possibility of confusion with another species. Generally, if one of a pair of similar species is common while the other is rare, we only mention the similar species in the account of the rare species to direct your attention to a more common look-alike.

Range

We describe, in very general terms, each species range **outside Florida**. Ranges within Florida are described only if the species is extremely local. Ranges are shown on the maps on the facing pages to the plates.

Abundance

The flight period and abundance for each species are given for five subregions of Florida—the panhandle (West), northern Florida (North), central Florida (Central), southern Florida (South), and the Florida Keys (Keys). The extent of these subregions is defined on page 38 under abbreviations and shown on the map in the beginning of the plates section.

We try to give information that will allow you to know when to search for a particular species and how likely you might be to find it. **We cannot emphasize enough that this section is intended as a rough guide.** Butterfly abundance can, and usually does, vary dramatically from year to year and from locality to locality. One of the pleasures of butterflying is that each year is certain to bring its quota of surprises. Flight dates can also vary tremendously depending upon the weather pattern of the year. When we list a species as flying "All year," this does not necessarily mean that you will see this species whenever you visit the region where it is found. It means that there is a reasonable chance of seeing the species in that region whenever you visit. Finding the species at a particular time in a particular year may depend upon the vagaries of that year's brood sequence and abundance level.

Major Foodplant

Listed as an aid to finding the adult butterflies are the major plant(s), or group of plants that are eaten by the caterpillars. For many uncommon butterflies the easiest way to locate colonies is to search for sites where the foodplant is common.

Garden Suggestions

Here we list specific garden-worthy plants that have been used successfully by Florida gardeners to attract certain species into their gardens. Remember that a mass planting is often more successful than a single plant. Since these plants will be used as caterpillar foodplants, don't remove the caterpillars that are eating them or you won't have any adult butterflies!

Comments

Here we include assorted information and/or thoughts that didn't fit easily into one of the above-listed categories.

SPECIES ACCOUNTS

Swallowtails
(family Papilionidae)

Swallowtails are our largest butterflies. Their long tails and often slow flight make them among our most graceful.

Pipevine Swallowtail *Battus philenor* Plate 1

SIZE	1 13/16 inch.
SIMILAR SPECIES	Spicebush Swallowtail, Black Swallowtail, Red-spotted Purple.
IDENTIFICATION	A very dark swallowtail above with strongly iridescent blue HW. Below, note the large **single** orange spot-band on **iridescent blue**. Spicebush and Black Swallowtails have blue that is not iridescent and **two** orange spot-bands. Red-spotted Purple lacks tails.
HABITAT	Wide-ranging, this swallowtail can be encountered almost anywhere, but is found primarily in open situations near sparse woodlands, including gardens.
RANGE	Also, north to Connecticut and Kansas, west to California, south to southern Mexico.
ABUNDANCE	3 or more broods. **W:** C, early Feb.–early Nov., most common March–April, late July–early Oct. **N:** C, early Feb.–early Nov., most common March–April, late July–early Oct. **C:** C, early Feb.–early Nov., most common March–April, late July–early Oct. **S:** S. **K:** X.
MAJOR FOODPLANT	Pipevines (*Aristolochia*) including ornamental vines and the native host *A. serpentaria*.
GARDEN TIPS	Dutchman's pipe (*Aristolochia macrophylla*).
COMMENTS	This species has a rapid flight near the ground, but readily visits flowers such as thistles, blackberries, wild plums, and paintbrush (*Carphephorus corymbosus*).

Polydamas Swallowtail *Battus polydamas* Plate 1

SIZE ≥ Pipevine Swallowtail.

SIMILAR SPECIES Black Swallowtail.

IDENTIFICATION A rapidly flying Polydamas Swallowtail is easy enough to identify when one gets a good look at it—something that is not so easy to do! They are generally fast fliers, more powerful than Black Swallowtails, and when nectaring they continue to rapidly beat their wings. This species lacks tails (but, of course, Black Swallowtails sometimes lose theirs) and has a wide dirty **yellow postmedian band above**. Male Black Swallowtails have narrower, bright yellow median bands and yellow marginal spots above. Below, Polydamas Swallowtails are dark with **dull red marginal spots** on the HW and **red spots on the body**.

HABITAT Gardens and vacant lots, edges of woodlands, beaches of the Keys. Reliably found only in the vicinity of gardens with Duchman's Pipe.

RANGE Also, the West Indies and south Texas, south through tropical Americas.

ABUNDANCE LU, March–Nov. RS, north to Gainesville. 3 or more broods. **W:** X. **N:** LR, early March–late Nov. **C:** LR, all year, most common March–June, Aug.–Nov. **S:** LU, all year, most common March–June, Aug.–Nov. **K:** LR, records from mid April–late June, but probably all year.

LOCALITIES Kanapaha Botanical Garden, Gainesville, Alachua Co.; Cypress Gardens, Winter Haven, Polk Co.; Bok Tower Gardens, Lake Wales, Polk Co.; Tradewinds Park in Fort Lauderdale (especially outside of Butterfly World); Fairchild Tropical Garden, Miami-Dade Co.; Biscayne NP.

MAJOR FOODPLANT Pipevines (*Aristolochia*).

GARDEN TIPS Dutchman's pipe (*Aristolochia elegans* or *A. macrophylla*). You probably need several well-established plants. Polydamas Swallowtail caterpillars are heavy feeders and can totally decimate a plant.

COMMENTS Even though they lack tails, the Polydamas Swallowtails are closely related to the Pipevine Swallowtails. Planting *Aristolochia* often results in the sudden appearance of the caterpillars of this species where no adults had previously been seen. Adults readily come to pentas, lantana, and other flowers.

Zebra Swallowtail *Eurytides marcellus* Plate 1

SIZE ≤ Pipevine Swallowtail.

IDENTIFICATION The aptly named Zebra Swallowtail can be confused with none of

Florida's other butterflies. The black-striped white triangular wings with graceful tails are distinctive. Also note the bright red median HW stripe below.

HABITAT　Open brushy fields and woodlands, that support the foodplant, including scrubs, sandhills, flatwoods, and pastures.

RANGE　Also, north to Maryland, Ohio, and west to east Texas and Missouri.

ABUNDANCE　3 or more broods. **W:** C, Feb.–late Oct., most common early March–late April, late July–late Sept. **N:** C, late Jan.–late Oct., most common early March–late April, late July–late Sept. **C:** C, late Jan.–early Nov., especially March–April, Aug.–Sept. **S:** LU, late Jan.–early Nov., most common Feb.–March, late July–early Sept. **K:** S.

MAJOR FOODPLANT　Paw-paws (*Asimina triloba, A. parviflora* and *A.reticulata*).

GARDEN TIPS　Paw-paws.

COMMENTS　Summer individuals are larger with broader black bands and longer tails than spring individuals. Flight is usually lower to the ground than Florida's other swallowtails and is very direct with rapid wingbeats.

Black Swallowtail *Papilio polyxenes* **Plate 2**

SIZE　= Pipevine Swallowtail.

SIMILAR SPECIES　Spicebush Swallowtail, Pipevine Swallowtail, Eastern Tiger Swallowtail (black females).

IDENTIFICATION　Throughout much of Florida, there are five species of "black" swallowtails: Black Swallowtail, Spicebush Swallowtail, Pipevine Swallowtail, Polydamas Swallowtail, and the black form of the female Eastern Tiger Swallowtail. Below, Black and Spicebush Swallowtails have two rows of orange spots; the Pipevine and black female Eastern Tiger Swallowtails, only one; Polydamas Swallowtail, none. Below, the **yellow. HW cell spot** or the FW subapical yellow spot distinguish this species from all others. Also note that the **FW postmedian and marginal yellow spots go all the way to the costal margin** while in Spicebush Swallowtail, they stop short. Also below, **the HW median orange spot-band is complete** (Spicebush Swallowtails lack one of the orange spots). Above, males, with their bright yellow spot-bands across both wings are obvious. Some females can appear surprisingly similar to some female Spicebush Swallowtails but can be separated from this and other species by the presence of a yellow FW subapical spot. Black Swallowtails usually have a less powerful flight than Spicebush Swallowtails.

SWALLOWTAILS

HABITAT	Open wet or disturbed areas. Marshes, wet prairies, and roadside ditches, as well as old fields, vacant lots, and gardens.
RANGE	Also, north to southern Canada, west to southern California and south in the mountains to Peru.
ABUNDANCE	3 or more broods. **W:** U, late Feb.–late Oct., most common mid March–mid May, Aug.–Sept. **N:** U, late Feb.–late Oct., most common mid March–mid May, Aug.–Sept. **C:** U, all year, especially April–May, Sept.–Oct. **S:** U, all year, especially April–May, Sept.–Oct. **K:** S.
MAJOR FOODPLANT	Many carrot family (umbellifera) plants, including parsley, fennel, carrot (wild or not) and water dropwort (*Oxypolis filiformis*).
GARDEN TIPS	Fennel and parsley.
COMMENTS	Males sometimes patrol and perch in small territories around patches of the foodplant. Adults readily visit flowers and tend to stay closer to the ground than other black-colored swallowtails.

Giant Swallowtail *Papilio cresphontes* **Plate 3**

SIZE	≥ Eastern Tiger Swallowtail.
SIMILAR SPECIES	Palamedes Swallowtail.
IDENTIFICATION	At a distance, note the contrast between the dark wings above and the pale wings below. Above, the wings are dark brown (almost black) with prominent yellow bands. Note the x's these bands form near the apexes of the FWs and the yellow spot in the HW tails. Below, note the striking cream-colored body and cream-colored wings with HW blue median spot-band.
HABITAT	Open woodlands and fields, citrus groves, and gardens near woodlands.
RANGE	Also, north to Virginia and Iowa, west to southern Arizona, south to West Indies and northern South America.
ABUNDANCE	3 or more broods. **W:** C, late Feb.–mid Nov., most common March–May, Aug.–Sept. **N:** C, early Feb.–mid Nov., most common March–May, Aug.–Sept. **C:** C, all year, especially March–April, June–July, Sept.–Oct. **S:** C, all year, especially March–April, June–July, Sept.–Oct. **K:** C, all year, especially March, June, Aug.–Sept.
MAJOR FOODPLANT	Rutaceae: Cultivated citrus, Wafer Ash (*Ptelea trifoliata*), wild lime (*Zanthoxylum fagara*), and Hercules-club (*Zanthoxylum clavaherculis*).
GARDEN TIPS	Grapefruit (*Citrus maxima*), lemon (*Citrus limon*), and wild lime.
COMMENTS	One of the largest butterflies in the eastern United States, the caterpillars, called "orange dogs" are sometimes a pest of citrus

crops. Closely associated with the caterpillar foodplants and may not be present in areas of potential habitat.

Schaus' Swallowtail *Papilio aristodemus* **Plate 3**

SIZE ≤ Eastern Tiger Swallowtail.

SIMILAR SPECIES Giant Swallowtail, Palamedes Swallowtail, Bahamian Swallowtail.

IDENTIFICATION Above, yellow bands are narrower and duller than on Giant Swallowtails or Palamedes Swallowtails, and unlike Giant Swallowtail, bands do not form an X near the FW subapex. **Note the bright yellow antennal clubs (of males) and lack of yellow spots in tails.** Below, there is an extensive, **rusty-colored patch in the HW median.** Flight is usually lower than Giant Swallowtail (within 3–4 feet of ground). Ground color above is paler brown and bands are paler, duller yellow, so there is less contrast than in Giant Swallowtail. Overall shape is much squarer than elongated Giant Swallowtail.

HABITAT Tropical hammocks.

RANGE Upper Florida Keys, especially the larger islands of Biscayne National Park and the northern end of Key Largo. Recently reintroduced to a few parks in the south Miami area. Also, the West Indies, including the Bahamas and Cuba.

ABUNDANCE 1 Brood. **W:** X. **N:** X. **C:** X. **S:** LR, late March–late June, most common mid May–mid June. **K:** LR, late March–late June, most common mid May–mid June.

LOCALITIES Elliott Key, Biscayne NP, Miami-Dade Co.; North Key Largo Hammocks State Botanical Site, Monroe Co.

MAJOR FOODPLANT Torchwood (*Amyris elemifera*) and wild lime (*Zanthoxylum fagara*).

COMMENTS This species, federally listed as an endangered species, is the subject of recovery and reintroduction efforts on the Keys and the southern mainland, where it came close to extinction, mainly due to habitat loss and mosquito control programs. Males have a rapid, darting flight along trails and hammock edges. Females are more often found fluttering in the hammocks as they search for host plants.

Bahamian Swallowtail *Papilio andraemon* **Plate 3**

SIZE ≤ Black Swallowtail.

SIMILAR SPECIES Giant Swallowtail, Schaus' Swallowtail, Palamedes Swallowtail.

IDENTIFICATION Remember, Bahamians have bars and bricks (not the Bahamian people who are, in my experience, warm and hospitable, but rather the swallowtails). Above, the **yellow bar** in the FW cell separates this species from either Giant or Schaus' Swallowtail but be careful, the larger Palamedes Swallowtail also has a yellow bar in the cell. Male antennal clubs have yellow. Below, note the **"brick"**—a squared off rusty-colored patch jutting into the postmedian band.

HABITAT Tropical hammocks.

RANGE Upper Florida Keys (Biscayne NP and the northern tip of Key Largo). Also, the West Indies.

ABUNDANCE 2–3 broods. **W**: X. **N**: X. **C**: X. **S**: S. **K**: LR, mid May–late Nov., most common late Aug.–mid Sept.

LOCALITIES Biscayne NP, Miami-Dade Co.; North Key Largo Hammocks State Botanical Site, Monroe Co.

MAJOR FOODPLANT Torchwood (*Amyris elemifera*) and other Rutaceae.

COMMENTS One of the most (the most?) geographically restricted resident U.S. butterflies, this rare species, when found, is usually in the same areas as Schaus' Swallowtail. The Bahamian Swallowtail was once considered a federally threatened species, but was later taken off the list when a few surveys failed to find any individuals. However, it was still extant in Florida in the mid 1990s. Males have a rapid flight.

Eastern Tiger Swallowtail *Papilio glaucus* **Plate 2**

SIZE 2 3/16 inch.

SIMILAR SPECIES Spicebush Swallowtail (black form females).

IDENTIFICATION This boldly colored swallowtail is one of Florida's most spectacular and familiar butterflies. Bright yellow wings with black stripes make this usually very large swallowtail immediately identifiable. Females are dimorphic (have two forms) with some that are yellow, and some that are black. Below, these are easy to differentiate from other black" swallowtails because they lack the HW median orange spot-band of Black and Spicebush Swallowtails and the iridescent blue of Pipevine Swallowtails. They also usually retain a shadow of the "tiger" pattern.

HABITAT Deciduous woodlands and swamps, especially woodland edges and wooded watercourses and including residential areas.

RANGE Also, north to New Hampshire and Nebraska and south through Mexico.

ABUNDANCE 2 asynchronous broods or 3 broods. **W**: C, Feb.–late Oct., most common March–April, Aug.–Sept. **N**: C, mid Jan.–early Nov., most common March–April, Aug.–Sept. **C**: C, Jan.–Nov., especially March–July, Sept.–Nov. **S**: C, Jan.–Nov., especially March–July, Sept.–Nov. **K**: X.

SWALLOWTAILS

MAJOR FOODPLANT Sweet bay (*Magnolia virginiana*), wild black cherry (*Prunus serotina*), and tulip tree (*Liriodendron tulipifera*).

GARDEN TIPS Sweet bay, and swamp bay (*Persea palustris*).

COMMENTS Females sometimes exceed the Giant Swallowtail in size. Light and dark females are about equally abundant in Florida.

Spicebush Swallowtail *Papilio troilus* **Plate 2**

SIZE ≥ Pipevine Swallowtail.

SIMILAR SPECIES Black Swallowtail, Pipevine Swallowtail, black-form female Eastern Tiger Swallowtail.

IDENTIFICATION Below, note **two orange spot-bands (marginal and postmedian) on the HW**, the absence of a yellow spot in the HW cell, and one **missing orange spot in the HW median spot-band**. Pipevine and black form female Tiger Swallowtails have only one orange spot-band while Black Swallowtails have a yellow spot in the cell and a complete orange median spot-band. Above, males are easily recognized by the beautiful cloud of bluish-green on the HW (although there is much individual variation in the amount of blue or green).

HABITAT Open woodlands and their borders, bay swamps, flatwoods, scrubs, and residential areas.

RANGE Also, north to New York and Missouri, west to eastern Texas.

ABUNDANCE Probably 2 or 3 broods. **W**: C, mid Feb.–late Oct., most common March–April, late July–late Sept. **N**: C, early Feb.–late Oct., most common March–April, late July–late Sept. **C**: C, Feb.–Nov., especially Feb.–March, Sept.–Nov. **S**: LR, Feb.–Nov. **K**: X.

MAJOR FOODPLANT Laurel family, especially sassafras (*Sassafras albidum*), bays (*Persea*) and camphor tree (*Cinnamonmum camphora*).

GARDEN TIPS Red bay (*Persea borbonia*).

COMMENTS Look on the caterpillar foodplants for the late instar caterpillars. Penultimate instar caterpillars are adorable, while last instar individuals are flamboyant mini-dragons. Adult males sometimes gather at mud puddles.

Palamedes Swallowtail *Papilio palamedes* **Plate 3**

SIZE = Eastern Tiger Swallowtail.

SIMILAR SPECIES Giant Swallowtail.

IDENTIFICATION A large, very dark brown and yellow swallowtail of southern swamps. Below, note the **yellow stripe along the base of the wings**. Above, note the **wide yellow HW postmedian band**.

In flight the yellow "flash" on the HWs distinguishes Palamedes from Giant Swallowtail. The dark brown/black fades to brown.

HABITAT Woodlands, swamps, scrubs, and adjacent open areas.

RANGE Also, north to southern Maryland and west along the Gulf to eastern Texas. Also, northeastern Mexico.

ABUNDANCE Probably 3 broods. **W**: C–A, mid Feb.–late Oct., most common March–April, June–July, Aug.–Sept. **N**: C–A, mid Jan.–late Oct., most common March–April, June–July, Aug.–Sept. **C**: C–A, all year, especially March–May, June–Aug., Sept.–Oct. **S**: C–A, all year, especially March–May, June–Aug., Sept.–Oct. **K**: S.

MAJOR FOODPLANT Bays (*Persea*).

GARDEN TIPS Red bay (*Persea borbonia*).

COMMENTS Palamedes Swallowtails are so common that some people forget how gorgeous they are. Despite their color and pattern differences, Palamedes and Spicebush swallowtails are closely related. Both have similar courtship flights, with a female flying a foot or two above the ground and a male flying slowly about 1 or 2 feet above her. Sometimes the two species will court each other!

Pierids, or Whites and Yellows (family Pieridae)

Pierids are white and yellow butterflies that range in size from small to large. The white and yellow colors are due to the presence of pteridines, pigments that are characteristic of pierids and that are rarely found in other families of butterflies. Their fairly rapid and low flight, usually with only short stops for nectar, draws one's eye to them as they nervously course about open fields. Usually, they will not sit still to allow you a leisurely study of their appearance. In general, whites will open their wings while landed, but yellows and sulphurs will not. You will only be able to see the yellow or orange color, often useful for identification, while the butterfly is flying, or on those very rare occasions when you come across a courting pair. So ubiquitous are they that many people believe that the word "butterfly" derives from a common European yellow.

Florida White *Appias drusilla* **Plate 4**

SIZE ≥ Cabbage White.

SIMILAR SPECIES Great Southern White.

IDENTIFICATION Very difficult to distinguish from the much more common Great

Southern Whites on the wing. At rest, unlike Great Southern Whites, the **antennal clubs are white**, not turquoise. Above, the black margin on the FW doesn't extend inward along the veins as it does in Great Southern White. Below, Florida Whites have **orange at the base of HW leading margin** that Great Southern Whites lack.

HABITAT Tropical hammocks.

RANGE The Keys and coastal areas of the southern mainland. Occasionally strays northward along the coast to the Sarasota and Titusville areas. Also, south through West Indies and tropical Americas.

ABUNDANCE LU–LC. All year in southern Florida, irregularly straying north to Gainesville. 3 or more broods. **W**: X. **N**: S. **C**: S. **S**: LU–C, all year, most common May–July. **K**: LU–C, all year, especially May–June, Aug.

LOCALITIES Hugh Taylor Birch State Recreation Area, Broward Co.; Fakahatchee Strand State Botanical Site, Collier Co.; Matheson Hammock Park, Miami-Dade Co.; Biscayne NP, Miami-Dade Co.; North Key Largo Hammocks State Botanical Site, Monroe Co.; John Pennekamp SP, Monroe Co.

MAJOR FOODPLANT Capers (*Capparis* and *Drypetes*).

GARDEN TIPS Jamaican capertree (*Capparis cynophallophora*) and flexible capertree (*Capparis flexuosa*)(may require a wooded site, not just an isolated plant).

COMMENTS Florida Whites often fly in the shade and dappled light along narrow trails through hardwood hammocks.

Checkered White *Pontia protodice* **Plate 5**

SIZE 15/16 inch.

SIMILAR SPECIES Cabbage White.

IDENTIFICATION When well seen, the extensive black or dark brown wing markings are distinctive. Females have more extensive markings than males. In flight, this species is similar to Cabbage White but the white ground color appears chalky with a slight bluish tinge. Its flight tends to use deeper wingbeats and to be more direct than the swerving flight of Cabbage Whites.

HABITAT Disturbed open areas, especially edges of cultivated fields, roadsides, abandoned railroad tracks along the coast, and other sandy areas.

RANGE Also, north to New York, west to California, and south to northern Mexico.

ABUNDANCE 3 or more broods. **W**: LR, late Feb.–early Nov. **N**: LC–A, early

Feb.–early Nov., most common Feb.–May. **C:** LC–A, late Feb.–early Nov. **S:** LU, Feb.–Dec. **K:** S, March, May. Populations of this species are ephemeral.

MAJOR FOODPLANT Crucifers, especially peppergrass (*Lepidium*).

GARDEN TIPS Peppergrass (*Lepidium*).

COMMENTS Flight is quick, erratic and low to the ground.

Cabbage White *Pieris rapae* Plate 5

SIZE = Checkered White.

SIMILAR SPECIES Clouded/Orange Sulphur (white females).

IDENTIFICATION This European introduction is an often high-flying white with a fairly strong but erratic (swerving) flight. Seen well, Cabbage Whites have either 1 (males) **or 2** (females) **black spots and a dark subapex on the FW above** but early spring individuals sometimes have these markings greatly diminished. Below, there is usually a strong yellowish cast to the HW.

HABITAT Any type of open or lightly wooded terrain, especially gardens, roadsides, and agricultural lands. Also present in urban areas.

RANGE Also, throughout most of North America and Eurasia.

ABUNDANCE 3 or more broods. **W:** LU–LC, early Feb.–late Nov., most common April–May. **N:** LU–LC, early Feb.–late Nov., most common April–May. **C:** LU, March–Nov. **S:** LR–LU, March–Dec. **K:** S, Jan.

MAJOR FOODPLANT Crucifers.

GARDEN TIPS Cabbage and broccoli.

COMMENTS Although probably the most ubiquitous butterfly in North America, Cabbage Whites are not common in Florida. Although many people disparage this species, because it is so common throughout most of its range and because it is not native, close observation reveals it to be one of the most graceful inhabitants of the air.

Great Southern White *Ascia monuste* Plate 4

SIZE ≤ Cloudless Sulphur.

SIMILAR SPECIES Cabbage White, Florida White.

IDENTIFICATION The **turquoise antennal clubs** are distinctive. Females can be white, dark smoky brown, or anything in between.

HABITAT Open situations, especially along the coast, including dunes, salt marshes, fields, and gardens.

RANGE Also, north along the coast to South Carolina and west along the coast to Texas then south through tropical Americas.

ABUNDANCE 3 or more broods. Rarer inland than along the coast. **W:** X. **N:** U, March–Oct. **C:** C–A, March–Nov. **S:** A, all year, most common

March–April, June–July, Sept., and Dec. **K**: A, all year, especially Jan., April–May, Aug.–Oct., and Dec.

MAJOR FOODPLANT   Saltwort (*Batis maritima*) and peppergrass (*Lepidium*).

GARDEN TIPS   Arugula (but then no salad for you!), nasturtium, and sea rockets (*Cakile lanceolata*).

COMMENTS   This species frequently undergoes tremendous population explosions—sometimes sending emigrants out through the continent. Dark females are more common in coastal populations, especially in summer and autumn, and are not limited to seasons of migratory activity during population outbreaks.

Falcate Orangetip *Anthocharis midea* Not Illustrated, see *Butterflies through Binoculars: The East.*

SIZE   < Checkered White.

SIMILAR SPECIES   Checkered White.

IDENTIFICATION   This is a small, early spring white. Males, with their bright orange wingtips contrasting with otherwise white wings, gladden the heart and are unmistakable. Females have blunt (falcate) FWs and are heavily marbled below. Flight is fairly weak and very close to the ground, rarely rising more than a couple of feet high.

HABITAT   Open deciduous woodlands with small crucifers; slope forests of ravines and swamps near rivers.

RANGE   Panhandle. Thus far it has been found only along the Ochlockonee River in Liberty and Wakulla counties. Also, discontinuously north to New York and west to Kansas and south Texas.

ABUNDANCE   1 Brood. **W**: LR, probably late Feb.–late March. The few Florida sightings have been in mid March. Found singly or in small numbers. **N**: X. **C**: X. **S**: X. **K**: X.

LOCALITIES   Porter Lake Recreation Area, Liberty Co.; southwest of Sanborn, Wakulla Co. (both localities are in the Apalachicola NF).

MAJOR FOODPLANT   Probably spring cress (*Cardamine bulbosa*) but possibly other crucifers.

COMMENTS   Only a few individuals of this delicate butterfly have been seen in Florida.

Orange Sulphur *Colias eurytheme* **Plates 5 & 6**

SIZE   = Checkered White.

SIMILAR SPECIES   Clouded Sulphur.

IDENTIFICATION   A strong-flying medium-sized sulphur of open fields. Above with at least some orange (this can usually be seen in flight).

Clouded Sulphurs lack any orange either below or above. (See comments.)

HABITAT Open fields, roadsides, agricultural areas, etc.

RANGE Also, most of North America and south to central Mexico.

ABUNDANCE 3 or more broods. **W**: LU, mid-Feb.–early Nov., most common in March–June. **N**: LU, all year, most common in March–June. **C**: LU, May–Oct., especially Aug. **S**: LU, May–Oct., especially Aug. **K**: S, July, Oct. Populations are ephemeral.

MAJOR FOODPLANT Clover (*Trifolium*), white sweet clover (*Melilotus alba*) and other Fabaceae.

COMMENTS Forms with a mostly yellow ground color are found mainly in the spring, and are sometimes mistaken for Clouded Sulphurs which have not been recorded in the state for many decades.

Southern Dogface *Colias cesonia* **Plate 6**

SIZE > Checkered White.

SIMILAR SPECIES Clouded Sulphur.

IDENTIFICATION A bright yellow sulphur, slightly larger than Clouded Sulphur, with a bold black outline of a dog's head above. Below, note pointed FWs and the outline of dog's head pattern through the FW. The fall form has the HW below suffused with pink.

HABITAT Dry roadsides and fields, usually near, or in, open woodlands.

RANGE Also, north to South Carolina and South Dakota, west to southern California, south through the Americas.

ABUNDANCE 3 or more broods. **W**: LU–C, March–early Nov., most common March–April, Sept.–Oct. **N**: LU–C, March–early Nov., most common March–April, Sept.–Oct. **C**: LU–C, March–early Nov., most common March–April, Sept.–Oct. **S**: LR, all year, especially Jan.–June, Aug.–Nov. **K**: X.

MAJOR FOODPLANT Leadplant (*Amorpha*) and summer farewell (*Dalea pinnata*).

COMMENTS Flight is fast and erratic. The fall generation is marked with pink on the underside of the hindwings and overwinters in a reproductive resting phase.

Cloudless Sulphur *Phoebis sennae* **Plates 8 & 9**

SIZE 1 5/16 inch.

SIMILAR SPECIES Orange-barred Sulphur.

IDENTIFICATION Size alone will usually suffice to distinguish giant-sulphurs from yellows or other sulphurs. This is by far the most common and widespread giant-sulphur, especially northward. It has a high, directional, sailing flight with characteristic deep, powerful wingbeats. This species can usually be separated on the wing from its congeners by its yellow upperwings. Males are pale yellow; females vary from orange-yellow to off-white. Green-yellow below, males have few markings while females' more extensive markings include a broken FW postmedian line. Large Orange Sulphurs are bright orange above. Orange-barred Sulphurs are usually larger and have deep orange markings above, but these can sometimes be difficult to see in flight.

HABITAT A wide variety of open situations.

RANGE Also, north to New York and Missouri, south through tropical Americas.

ABUNDANCE 3 or more broods. **W**: A, early Feb.–late Nov., most common Feb.–April, Aug.–Oct. **N**: A, all year, most common Feb.–April, Aug.–Oct. **C**: A, all year, especially March–April, Sept.–Oct. **S**: A, all year, especially March–April, Sept.–Oct. **K**: C–A, all year, most common March, Sept.–Oct.

MAJOR FOODPLANT Cassias.

GARDEN TIPS Chapman's wild sensitive plant (*Cassia chapmanii*), privet wild sensitive plant (*Cassia ligustrina*), and partridge pea (*Cassia fasciculata*).

COMMENTS A highly mobile species, Cloudless Sulphurs move north in small numbers in the springtime, then move back southward by the millions in September and October. Numbers fluctuate markedly from year to year. They prefer to nectar at red flowers.

Orange-barred Sulphur *Phoebis philea* Plates 8 & 9

SIZE ≥ Cloudless Sulphur.

SIMILAR SPECIES Cloudless Sulphur, Large Orange Sulphur.

IDENTIFICATION Above, males are **yellow with orange patches** on both the FWs and HWs. Females range from yellow to white above, lack the FW orange patches, usually have rich reddish HW borders above and often have rich reddish suffusions below. Below, FW postmedian line is broken as in Cloudless Sulphur. Cloudless Sulphurs are all yellow, Large Orange Sulphurs are all orange and have a straight FW postmedian line below.

HABITAT Gardens, open woodlands and pinelands in subtropical areas.

RANGE Also, south Texas south through tropical Americas.

ABUNDANCE 3 or more broods. **W**: S. **N**: LU, March–Dec., most common Sept.–Oct. **C**: LU, all year, most common Sept.–Oct. **S**: LU, all year, especially March–May, June–July, Sept.–Oct., Dec. **K**: LU, all year. Most common May, July, and Oct.

MAJOR FOODPLANT Shrubby sennas (*Cassia*) such as *Cassia alata*, *C. bicapsularis*, and *C. fistula*.

GARDEN TIPS Chapman's wild sensitive plant (*Cassia chapmanii*), privet wild sensitive plant (*Cassia ligustrina*).

COMMENTS The image of this species is commonly used in advertisements, probably because its cheerful bright yellow and orange pattern fits many people's idea of a butterfly. Wide-ranging, this species colonized south Florida (presumably from Mexico) in the 1930s. It moves northward as the season progresses. Flight is often high, rapid, and erratic.

Large Orange Sulphur *Phoebis agarithe* Plates 8 & 9

SIZE = Cloudless Sulphur.

SIMILAR SPECIES Orange-barred Sulphur.

IDENTIFICATION A very large sulphur that is **bright orange above**. Below, note the **diagonal, straight line on the FW**. Orange-barred Sulphurs are yellow with orange patches above and have a broken postmedian line on the FW below.

HABITAT General in open tropical and subtropical situations, including gardens and woodland edges.

RANGE Also, south Texas and south through tropical Americas.

ABUNDANCE 3 or more broods. **W**: X. **N**: S. **C**: U, May–Dec., especially July–Nov. **S**: C–A, all year, especially March, June–July, Oct., Dec. **K**: A, all year, most common March–May, Aug.–Oct.

MAJOR FOODPLANT Wild tamarind (*Lysiloma latisiliquum*) and blackbead (*Pithecellobium keyense*).

GARDEN TIPS Wild tamarind (*Lysiloma latisiliquum*) and blackbead (*Pithecellobium keyense*).

COMMENTS Like Orange-barred Sulphurs, this species migrates northward as the season progresses. Adults fly rapidly about the forest canopy and even over the ocean between islands of the keys.

Statira Sulphur *Phoebis statira* Plate 9

SIZE = Cloudless Sulphur.

SIMILAR SPECIES Cloudless Sulphur, Lyside Sulphur.

IDENTIFICATION Above, similar to Cloudless Sulphur. Below, females are either marked as shown on plate 12 or are immaculate ivory white, but with **some yellow at the base of the FW costal margin and along the FW disc**. Males are similar but are tinged yellow-green. In Florida, most, if not all, females resemble the individual shown on plate 12. The FW cell-end markings below are dark pink, usually pretty much "filled in," and have a smaller projection toward the costal margin. There are no markings on the basal 1/2 of the HW. Other giant-sulphurs have FW cell-end markings that are larger, of nearly equal size, and that are not so filled in. Usually has a pinkish patch at the apex of the FW. Note the **puckered appearance of the outer 1/3 of the wings.** Lyside Sulphur is smaller, greener, usually with a characteristic whitened HW vein.

HABITAT   Open areas near salt marshes or mangroves—near stands of *Dalbergia*; occasionally inland residential areas.

RANGE   Also, south Texas and the West Indies, south through tropical Americas.

ABUNDANCE   3 or more broods. **W**: X. **N**: X. **C**: LR–LU, all year, most common March, June–July, Oct. **S**: LR–LU, all year, most common March, June–July, Oct. **K**: LR or S.

LOCALITIES   Bonita Beach, Lee Co.; Blowing Rocks Preserve, Martin Co.; Juno Beach Scrub Preserve, Palm Beach Co.; Hugh Taylor Birch State Recreation Area, Broward Co.

MAJOR FOODPLANT   Coinvine (*Dalbergia ecastophyllum*).

COMMENTS   This species is very easy to overlook amid the much more common Cloudless Sulphurs, especially since the two species are extremely difficult to differentiate on the wing. It is fond of red flowers.

Lyside Sulphur *Kricogonia lyside* **Plate 9**

SIZE   = Checkered White.

SIMILAR SPECIES   Statira Sulphur, White Angled-Sulphur.

IDENTIFICATION   Extremely variable. Above, varies from yellow to white with yellow patches, to white. Below, often distinctively green with a prominently whitened vein running through the HW and a yellow flush to the FW disc, but can be pale yellowish to almost white without the whitened vein.

HABITAT   Margins of tropical hammocks, salt marshes, and mangroves.

RANGE   West Indies, including the Bahamas and Cuba, and southern Texas south to Venezuela.

ABUNDANCE   **W**: X. **N**: X. **C**: X. **S**: LR(S?), July–Oct. **K**: LR(S?), July, Sept. Rarely encountered most years, but occasionally locally common.

LOCALITIES   North Key Largo Hammocks State Botanical Site, Monroe Co.

MAJOR FOODPLANT   Not known to breed in Florida, but uses lignum vitae (*Guaiacum sanctum*) elsewhere in the Caribbean.

COMMENTS   Most often observed on the northern Keys, Lyside Sulphurs easily may be mistaken for the more common species of whites.

Barred Yellow *Eurema daira* **Plate 7**

SIZE ≤ Little Yellow.

SIMILAR SPECIES Little Yellow, Dainty Sulphur.

IDENTIFICATION A very small, weak-flying yellow. Above, yellow, or white, or with FW yellow and HW white. Males have a black bar along the FW lower margin that can sometimes be seen either in flight or through the wings when landed. Below, HW with weak pattern, winter individuals suffused with rusty-brown. The HW apex is usually vaguely darker with an inwardly directed line. Base of FW at costal margin is white or tan with darker flecking, Little Yellow is pure yellow here. Dainty Sulphur is smaller with darker markings below.

HABITAT Disturbed open situations—roadsides, vacant fields, gardens, etc.— and sparse woodlands.

RANGE Also, north to South Carolina west to Louisiana. Also south Texas south through tropical Americas.

ABUNDANCE 3 or more broods. **W**: U, March–Oct., especially Aug.–Sept. **N**: A, all year, most common June–Nov. with peaks in Aug.–Sept. **C**: A, all year, especially Feb.–March, Oct.–Dec. **S**: A, all year, especially Jan., Nov.–Dec. **K**: A, all year, most common Jan., Sept.–Dec.

MAJOR FOODPLANT Pencil flowers (*Stylosanthes*) and joint vetches (*Aeshonymene*).

COMMENTS ·Migrates southward from north to south Florida in the fall. Southward, some males possess white HWs and females can be white, rather than yellow. This is probably due to immigrants from the West Indies (where these are the typical color forms) breeding with resident populations in southern Florida. During courtship, a male lands next a female and places one of his FWs in front of the female (keeping his other wings closed), presumably to wow her with his great black bar and its associated perfume.

Little Yellow *Eurema lisa* **Plate 7**

SIZE 1 1/16 inch.

SIMILAR SPECIES Other rare yellows.

IDENTIFICATION A small yellow, very bright yellow above, with a rapid, low, and straight flight path, is likely to be this species. If seen landed, note the scattered smudged dark markings on the HW below and the **black** (not dull pink) antennas. The extent of markings below is quite variable. Most individuals have a pink spot at the HW apex, although this spot is often diminished or absent in males.

HABITAT	Most common in disturbed open areas, especially dry, sandy, grassy fields. Also found in sparse woodlands.
RANGE	Also, north to New York and Iowa and south to Costa Rica and the West Indies.
ABUNDANCE	3 or more broods. **W**: LC, all year, most common May–Nov. with peaks in Aug.–Oct. **N**: LC, all year, most common May–Nov. especially Aug.–Oct. **C**: LC, all year, especially Sept.–Oct. **S**: LC, all year, especially Sept.–Oct. **K**: C, all year. Most common Oct.–Dec.
MAJOR FOODPLANT	Partridge peas (*Cassia fasciculata* and *C. nictitans*).
GARDEN TIPS	Partridge pea (*Cassia fasciculata*) and Chapman's wild sensitive plant (*Cassia chapmanii*).
COMMENTS	By far Florida's most widespread and common yellow (*Eurema*). White females are generally uncommon, but may be locally frequent in some years.

Mimosa Yellow *Eurema nise* **Plate 7**

SIZE	≤ Little Yellow.
SIMILAR SPECIES	Little Yellow.
IDENTIFICATION	Mimosa Yellows fly at the edges of woodlands. Unlike similar Little Yellows, they rarely venture into the open adjacent areas, and if they do they usually do not remain for long. Beside behavior, note two marks to distinguish this rare species from Little Yellow. First, look carefully at the black border at the FW apex (this can usually be seen from below, looking through the wing). Mimosa Yellow has a much narrower border than does Little Yellow. Second, Mimosa Yellow lacks a black spot near the base of the HW below that Little Yellow has.
HABITAT	In U.S., edges of tropical hammocks.
RANGE	Also, West Indies and southern Texas south through tropical Americas.
ABUNDANCE	3 or more broods. **W**: X. **N**: X. **C**: X. **S**: LR, April–Dec., most common Sept.–Dec. **K**: LR, April, June–July, Sept.
LOCALITIES	Biscayne NP, Miami-Dade Co.; Castellow Hammock Preserve, Miami-Dade Co.; Camp Owaissa Bauer, Miami-Dade Co.
MAJOR FOODPLANT	Wild tamarind (*Lysiloma latisilaquum*).
COMMENTS	When disturbed, Mimosa Yellows retreat into the shaded forest margins, while Little Yellows remain in the sunlight. Populations of this butterfly, occurring only from the Homestead area east and southeast to the upper Keys, are **rare and ephemeral**, appearing sporadically at a location and then disappearing.

WHITES & YELLOWS

Dina Yellow *Eurema dina* Plate 7

SIZE	≥ Little Yellow.
SIMILAR SPECIES	Little Yellow.
IDENTIFICATION	Yet another denizen of tropical hammocks (and especially their brushy edges), Dina Yellow is larger and more orange-flushed than Little Yellow. Males are bright orange-yellow with a very narrow black FW border. Females are yellow with an orange flush. Below, note the **pinkish-brown apexes of both FW and HW**. Little Yellow lacks a pinkish patch on the FW apex.
HABITAT	Tropical hammocks, citrus groves, and avocado orchards.
RANGE	Also, West Indies, Mexico to Panama.
ABUNDANCE	3 or more broods. **W**: X. **N**: X. **C**: X. **S**: LR, all year, especially Sept.–Dec. **K**: S.
LOCALITIES	Camp Owaissa Bauer, Miami-Dade Co.; Castellow Hammock Preserve, Miami-Dade Co.
MAJOR FOODPLANT	Mexican alvaradoa tree (*Alvaradoa amorphoides*).
COMMENTS	First found in south Florida in 1962, this species arrived from the Bahamas. Now **extremely local** in the Homestead area with a few reports from Key Largo. Flight is relatively slow. Adults stay in the vicinity of the host plant, but readily nectar at nearby patches of Spanish needles, lantana, and other weedy flowers. When disturbed they fly into the forest.

Sleepy Orange *Eurema nicippe* Plate 7

SIZE	= Checkered White.
SIMILAR SPECIES	Orange Sulphur.
IDENTIFICATION	This butterfly is bright orange above with black borders. It flies closer to the ground than Orange Sulphur, with weaker wing-beats and is a darker orange above. Seen well, note the black antennas (Orange Sulphur—dull pink) and the characteristic **diagonal brown markings** on the HW below. This species has two color forms and the HW ground color below can be either yellow or a dull reddish color.
HABITAT	Roadsides, open fields, and open pine woodlands.
RANGE	Also, north to New Jersey and Kansas, west to southern California, south to West Indies and Mexico south to Costa Rica.
ABUNDANCE	3 or more broods. **W**: C–A, all year. Most common late Aug.–late Oct. **N**: C–A, all year. Most common late Aug.–late Oct. **C**: C, all year, especially Aug.–Dec. **S**: C, all year, especially Aug.–Dec. **K**: C, all year.
MAJOR FOODPLANT	Shrubby *Cassia*.
GARDEN TIPS	Sicklepod (*Cassia obtusifolia*) and Christmas senna (*Cassia bicapsularis*).

COMMENTS   The name "sleepy" does not refer to this species' flight—which is quite perky. Rather, the cell-end spots on the FW above look like closed eyes. See also, Sleepy Duskywing.

Dainty Sulphur *Nathalis iole* **Plate 6**

SIZE   ≤ Little Yellow.

SIMILAR SPECIES   Barred Yellow, Little Yellow.

IDENTIFICATION   A tiny sulphur, more greenish yellow above than Little Yellow. Flight, even lower to the ground than Barred Yellow. Below, note the dark greenish HW and the **black spots on the FW submarginal area**.

HABITAT   Fields, roadsides, and other disturbed habitats.

RANGE   Also, north to Nebraska, west to southern California and south to West Indies and Guatemala.

ABUNDANCE   3 or more broods. **W**: R. **N**: U, all year, most common in April and Dec. **C**: A, early March–Dec., especially March–April, Sept.–early Nov. **S**: A, all year, especially April–June. **K**: A, all year, most common April, June, Aug.–Oct.

MAJOR FOODPLANT   Spanish needles *(Bidens alba)*.

COMMENTS   Quite variable in detail, this butterfly is still distinctive. The few sightings from the Panhandle may be of strays from more western states, rather than of individuals from the more sedentary peninsular populations.

Lycaenids or Gossamer-wings (family Lycaenidae)

This is a very large worldwide family of butterflies consisting, in Florida, of harvester, hairstreaks, and blues. Most species are quite small, although a few tropical hairstreaks are larger than an American Lady. Many gossamer-wings are myrmecophilous (ant-loving). The caterpillars secrete a "honey-dew" from special glands that attracts certain species of ants. These ants then "tend" the caterpillars helping to protect them from predator species. The caterpillars of many gossamer-wings (including some in Florida) feed on flower parts.

Harvester *Feniseca tarquinius* **Plate 10**

SIZE   = Gray Hairstreak.

IDENTIFICATION   A medium-sized lycaenid, bright orange above with bold black markings. Below, note the orange disc of the FW and dull reddish-brown HW with **delicate white markings**.

HABITAT	Woodlands, especially near watercourses or wet areas with alders.
RANGE	Also, north to New Brunswick and west to Manitoba and east Texas.
ABUNDANCE	At least 3 broods. **W**: LR, March–May, Aug.–Oct. **N**: LR, March–May, Aug.–Oct. **C**: LR, March–May, Aug.–Oct. **S**: X. **K**: X.
LOCALITIES	Torreya SP, Liberty Co.
CATERPILLAR FOOD	Woolly aphids, usually on alders (*Alnus serrulata*) or greenbriers (*Smilax*).
COMMENTS	Harvesters are Florida's only butterflies with carnivorous caterpillars. The caterpillars feed on other insects (woolly aphids) rather than on plants. Adults don't come to flowers but can sometimes be found sunning themselves on tree leaves in woodland glades or mudpuddling at damp soil.

Hairstreaks
(subfamily Theclinae)

The name of these small but intricately patterned butterflies is thought to be derived either from the many lines or streaks that tend to appear on the HW below or from the usual presence of fine, hair-like tails. Twenty-two species occur in Florida while about 1000 species of hairstreaks inhabit Central and South America. Many species have an eye-spot near the outer angle of the HW below that tends to attract the attention of predators to the wrong end of the butterfly. The subterfuge is usually enhanced by tails that resemble antennas. When the hairstreak lands with its head facing downward and its tails move in the air as it "saws" its HWs back and forth, the effect is complete. Many tropical species have this eye-spot pattern greatly developed and it is not unusual to find individuals who have sacrificed the missing portions of their HWs to birds. Almost all of Florida's species keep their wings closed while landed.

Atala *Eumaeus atala* Plate 11

SIZE	>> Gray Hairstreak.
SIMILAR SPECIES	Great Purple Hairstreak.
IDENTIFICATION	This sensational animal is difficult to misidentify, except in flight when it looks remarkably mothlike. The bright orange abdomen and red on the base of the HW can remind one of a Great Purple Hairstreak but the triple spot-band of iridescent aquamarine spots on the HW below is unique.

HABITAT	Anyplace its foodplants want to be, including urban and suburban plantings. Occasionally even found in natural habitats!
RANGE	Also, West Indies.
ABUNDANCE	3 or more broods. **W**: X. **N**: X. **C**: LR, all year. **S**: LU, all year, most common March–April, Oct.–Dec. **K**: S, March, June.
LOCALITIES	Hugh Taylor Birch State Recreation Area, Broward Co.; Fairchild Tropical Garden, Miami-Dade Co.
MAJOR FOODPLANT	Coontie (*Zamia pumila*) and a number of introduced ornamental cycads.
GARDEN TIPS	Coontie.
COMMENTS	Not too long ago, this species was thought to be gone from the U.S., a victim of the rapid development of South Florida. But since 1970, landscape gardeners and butterfly gardeners have planted increasing numbers of coontie and other cycads and the population of this butterfly, one of the more sensationally colored, is now booming.

Great Purple Hairstreak *Atlides halesus* **Plate 11**

SIZE	>> Gray Hairstreak.
SIMILAR SPECIES	Atala.
IDENTIFICATION	A very large, dramatically marked hairstreak. When it flies, one can see the flash from the shining iridescent blue (not purple) scales covering the entire wings above. Females have more restricted, noniridescent, blue above. Below, the FW has an iridescent turquoise patch, while both the FW and the HW have large red spots near their bases. Note the striking orange abdomen.
HABITAT	Edges of moist woodlands.
RANGE	Also, north to Delaware, west to California and south to Guatemala.
ABUNDANCE	At least 3 broods. **W**: U–C, Feb.–early Nov., most common mid April–May, Sept.–Oct. **N**: U–C, all year, most common mid April–May, Sept.–Oct. **C**: U–C, all year, most common mid April–May, Sept.–Oct. **S**: X. **K**: X.
MAJOR FOODPLANT	Mistletoe (*Phoradendron serotinum*).
COMMENTS	Adults spend most of their time in the canopy of trees infected with mistletoe (especially oaks), but also come readily to flowers. The flight is very rapid and erratic.

Amethyst Hairstreak *Chlorostrymon maesites* **Plate 12**

SIZE	<< Gray Hairstreak.
SIMILAR SPECIES	Silver-banded Hairstreak.

IDENTIFICATION This tiny green hairstreak has a maroon marginal patch on the HW below, not extending to the HW leading edge and **lacks a FW white postmedian line**. Silver-banded Hairstreak has a HW maroon marginal border extending to the HW leading edge and has a white postmedian line on the FW below.

HABITAT Tropical hammocks.

RANGE Also, the Bahamas and the Antilles.

ABUNDANCE LR or no longer found in Florida. Probably all year, but mainly late May–mid June. 3 or more broods. **W**: X. **N**: X. **C**: X. **S**: X. Previously rare here but not seen on the mainland for many years. **K**: R, all year, especially May–June and Oct.–early Dec. Mostly seen singly or in very small numbers.

LOCALITIES North Key Largo Hammocks State Botanical Site, Monroe Co.; Stock Island Botanical Site, Monroe Co.

MAJOR FOODPLANT Uncertain; one report from Jamaica on balloon-vine (*Cardiospermum*), other reports suggest that it may use a wide variety of caterpillar foodplants, including leguminous trees, especially woman's tongue (*Albizia lebbeck*).

COMMENTS We know of no reports of this species in the past five years. Perhaps a combination of rarity and a behavioral pattern that keeps this species high in the trees has caused it to be overlooked. But, with the continuing destruction of hammock environments in the Florida Keys, it is possible that this species has been extirpated. This species is (was) a true tropical gem of southern Florida. It sometimes occurs (occurred) with the more common Silverbanded Hairstreak.

Silver-banded Hairstreak *Chlorostrymon simaethis* Plate 12

SIZE < Gray Hairstreak.

SIMILAR SPECIES Amethyst Hairstreak.

IDENTIFICATION Bright acid green below with a prominent **white, straight, postmedian line**. Above, males are iridescent purple, females blue-gray (both sexes sometimes opening their wings while landed).

HABITAT Areas with balloon-vine, including tropical hammock edges, and disturbed areas.

RANGE Also, southern Texas and southern California, West Indies, south through tropical Americas.

ABUNDANCE LR–LU. 3 or more broods. **W**: X. **N**: X. **C**: X. **S**: LU, all year, most common Oct.–early Dec. **K**: LU, all year, especially May–June.

LOCALITIES North Key Largo Hammocks State Botanical Site, Monroe Co.; Tavernier, Monroe Co.

MAJOR FOODPLANT	Balloon-vines (*Cardiospermum*); the caterpillars are easily found by looking through the semitransparent, inflated seedpods (the balloons) of the host for accumulations of frass, although some may be Miami Blues or Gray Hairstreaks, which also feed on balloon-vines.
GARDEN TIPS	Balloon-vines (*Cardiospermum*).
COMMENTS	First found in south Florida in 1973 but now apparently declining. Plantings of its caterpillar foodplant by south Florida butterfly gardeners should increase the population of this tiny, but brilliant, butterfly.

Satyrium **Hairstreaks**

The five Satyrium hairstreaks in Florida are similar. All are basically brown to brownish-gray to gray. Although they have rapid and very erratic flight paths, they are easier to follow than one would think since they often alight not far from where they began! Like many groups of hairstreaks, male *Satyrium* hairstreaks have scent pads on the FWs above. These pads contain specialized scales through which a pheromone (a specialized type of scent) is released. Females sense the male's perfume during courtship rituals and, presumably, how good he smells influences her decision to mate or reject her suitor.

Coral Hairstreak *Satyrium titus* **Plate 13**

SIZE	= Gray Hairstreak.
IDENTIFICATION	A brown, **tailless** hairstreak. It has a prominent marginal row of red-orange spots but no blue marginal eye-spot.
HABITAT	Edges of moist woodlands.
RANGE	Also, north to Quebec and west to British Columbia.
ABUNDANCE	1 brood. **W:** LR, mid May–mid June. **N:** X. **C:** X. **S:** X. **K:** X.
LOCALITIES	Torreya SP, Liberty Co.
MAJOR FOODPLANT	Chickasaw plum (*Prunus angustifolius*) and probably wild cherry (*Prunus serotinum*).
COMMENTS	Orange milkweed (*Asclepias tuberosa*) is a magnet for this butterfly, much more so than for any other hairstreak. The short flight period and localized occurrence make this species difficult to find.

Banded Hairstreak *Satyrium calanus* **Plate 13**

SIZE	= Gray Hairstreak.
IDENTIFICATION	A widespread and variable hairstreak, Banded Hairstreak has well-marked postmedian bands on both FWs and HWs. The

band is outwardly strongly edged with white while inwardly the white edging varies from absent to strong. This butterfly is larger and has longer tails southward in Florida. In addition, many Florida individuals have more extensive orange than does the individual illustrated.

HABITAT Prefers open fields or glades, with nectar sources, adjacent to oak/hickory woodlands.

RANGE Also, north to New Brunswick and west to Manitoba and Colorado.

ABUNDANCE 1 brood. **W:** LU, late April–early June. **N:** LU, mid April–early May, especially mid–late April. **C:** LU, mid April–mid May. **S:** R, late April. **K:** X.

LOCALITIES Torreya SP, Liberty Co.; McKethan Lake, SR 476 at Istachatta Trail, Withlacoochee SF.

MAJOR FOODPLANT Oaks (*Quercus*) and hickories (*Carya*).

COMMENTS Most often seen at the flowers of sparkleberry (*Vaccinium arboreum*) and white sweet clover.

King's Hairstreak *Satyrium kingi* Plate 13

SIZE = Gray Hairstreak.

SIMILAR SPECIES Banded Hairstreak, Striped Hairstreak.

IDENTIFICATION Looks like a Banded Hairstreak with a **strong orange bar over blue "thecla" spot.** Striped Hairstreak also has orange over its blue "thecla" spot, but this orange is usually (but not always) in the form of an inwardly directed chevron, not a flat bar. Unlike Striped, FW white cell-end bars are set off from the postmedian band and two white dashes closest to HW leading margin are not aligned with white cell-end bars below. The flight of King's Hairstreak is more direct, easier to follow, than the whirling flight of Banded Hairstreak.

HABITAT Moist woodlands where the caterpillar foodplant is present.

RANGE Also, north to Maryland and west to east Texas.

ABUNDANCE 1 brood. **W:** LU, mid May–Aug., most common in early June. **N:** X. **C:** X. **S:** X. **K:** X.

LOCALITIES Torreya SP, Liberty Co.; Blackwater River SP, Santa Rosa Co.

MAJOR FOODPLANT Common sweetleaf (*Symplocos tinctoria*).

GARDEN TIPS Common sweetleaf (*Symplocos tinctoria*) (also called horsesugar).

COMMENTS The range of this species essentially follows the range of its caterpillar foodplant, but within that range it is inexplicably local and rare. Males perch at about 3–4 feet, often on the hostplant, during the middle of the day.

Striped Hairstreak *Satyrium liparops* **Plate 13**

SIZE = Gray Hairstreak.

SIMILAR SPECIES Banded Hairstreak.

IDENTIFICATION On first impression appears to have many more white lines and be "stripier" but actual differences are rather subtle. The white lines are set farther apart and **aligned** so as to form stripes. Also note the **orange cap** on the blue outer angle eye-spot.

HABITAT Thickets, woodland openings and brushy edges.

RANGE Also, north to southern Canada and west to Colorado.

ABUNDANCE 1 brood. **W:** LU, late April–early June. **N:** LU, early April–late May, especially mid–late April. **C:** LU, early April–late May, especially mid–late April. **S:** X. **K:** X.

LOCALITIES Torreya SP, Liberty Co.; McKethan Lake, S. R. 476 at Istachatta Trail, Withlacoochee SF.

MAJOR FOODPLANT Sparkleberry (*Vaccinium arboreum*) and hawthorns (*Crataegus*).

COMMENTS Males often perch on the leaves of trees and shrubs along the margins of deciduous forest. Both sexes visit the flowers of sparkleberry and white sweet clover for nectar. The flight is rapid and erratic. This species is particularly active late in the afternoon.

Southern Hairstreak *Satyrium favonius* **Plate 13**

SIZE ≤ Gray Hairstreak.

SIMILAR SPECIES White M Hairstreak, Gray Hairstreak.

IDENTIFICATION This species has a clean appearance (as do White M and Gray hairstreaks) due to the lack of cell-end bars. On the Florida peninsula most individuals have an extensive HW red-orange patch, running from the blue eye-spot to the leading edge of the HW and are distinctive ('Southern' Southern Hairstreaks). Northward and westward, this patch is much less extensive, more orange, and broken into individual spots ('Northern' Southern Hairstreaks). Then note that the large red-orange spot outwardly edged with black reaches, or almost reaches, the HW margin. White M Hairstreak has this spot displaced inwardly. Distinguished from Gray Hairstreak by brownish (rather than gray) ground color.

HABITAT Woodlands, scrubs, sandhills, hammocks, and nearby roadsides and vacant lots with an abundance of flowers.

RANGE Also, north to Massachusetts and west to New Mexico.

ABUNDANCE 1 brood. **W:** U–C, early April–early June, most common early–mid April. **N:** U–C, early April–early June, most common early–mid April. **C:** U–C, early April–early June, most common early–mid April. **S:** LR–U, late March–late April. **K:** X.

MAJOR FOODPLANT	Various oaks (*Quercus*).
COMMENTS	One of the most common hairstreaks in Florida. Until recently, the Florida and more northern populations were considered separate species, Southern and Northern Hairstreaks, respectively. But there is a blend zone where every combination of characters can be found. In Florida, this blend zone extends west and north from about Tallahassee.

Frosted Elfin *Callophrys irus* Plate 14

SIZE	≤ Gray Hairstreak.
SIMILAR SPECIES	Henry's Elfin.
IDENTIFICATION	A ground-hugging hairstreak with "frosted" HW margin and short tail-like protuberances. Note the **black spot on the HW near the "tailed" area**. FW white postmedian line is not smooth. Henry's Elfin has richer, reddish-brown color and has a smooth continuous white FW postmedian line below. Also note pale area between FW postmedian and marginal lines of Frosted Elfin. Henry's Elfin lacks this.
HABITAT	Sandy or rocky acidic areas cleared by fire or, much more often, by man; such as power-line cuts, railroad right-of-ways, and roadsides with good stands of its foodplant.
RANGE	Also, north to Massachusetts and west to Michigan and east Texas.
ABUNDANCE	1 brood. **W:** not yet recorded from this region, but should be present. **N:** LR, late Feb.–early April. **C:** X. **S:** X. **K:** X.
LOCALITIES	Jennings SF; St. Marys River SF.
MAJOR FOODPLANT	Sundial lupine (*Lupinus perennis*).
COMMENTS	Extremely local.

Henry's Elfin *Callophrys henrici* Plate 14

SIZE	< Gray Hairstreak.
SIMILAR SPECIES	Frosted Elfin.
IDENTIFICATION	A bright brown elfin of woodlands. Note the frosted HW margin and the bold white marks at either end of the HW postmedian line. Tail-like protuberances are usually visible. Frosted Elfin has a black spot on the HW near the "tailed" area, has duller, paler ground color and little contrast between ground color on either side of postmedian line.
HABITAT	A wide variety of moist woodlands with brushy understories, including wet pinelands, bayheads and swamps.
RANGE	Also, north to Quebec and Manitoba and west to New Mexico.
ABUNDANCE	1 brood. **W:** LU, late Feb.–late April., most common in mid

March. **N:** LU, late Feb.–late April, most common in mid March.
C: LU, early March–mid April. **S:** X. **K:** X.

LOCALITIES Torreya SP, Liberty Co.; Porter Lake Campground and White-
head Lake Recreation Area in the Apalachicola NF; Mike Roess
Gold Head State Branch SP, Clay Co.; Highlands Hammock SP,
Highlands Co.; Juniper Springs, Ocala NF; Welaka SF.

MAJOR FOODPLANT Dahoon holly (*Ilex cassine*) and American holly (*Ilex opaca*), but
some populations in the Panhandle may use redbud (*Cercis canadensis*).

COMMENTS Willows, often visited for nectar, are a good indicator of when to
look for this butterfly since the blooming period closely matches
the flight season of Henry's Elfin.

Eastern Pine Elfin *Callophrys niphon* Plate 14

SIZE = Gray Hairstreak.
IDENTIFICATION Stunningly banded with rich reddish-brown and black.
HABITAT Sand Pine scrubs and mixed hardwood and pine forests.
RANGE Also, north to Canada and west to Alberta and east Texas.
ABUNDANCE 1 brood. **W:** LR–LU, late Feb.–early April, most common
early–mid March. **N:** LR–LU, late Feb.–early April, most common
early–mid March. **C:** LR–LU, late Feb.–early April, most com-
mon early–mid March. **S:** X. **K:** X.
LOCALITIES Two miles east of Lake Delancy Campground, Ocala NF.
MAJOR FOODPLANT Sand pine (*Pinus clausa*) and probably other pines.
COMMENTS Adults spend much of their time in the crowns of pines. Occasionally they can be found perching on the needles of young
sand pines. They can also be found at the margins of mud puddles along dirt roads and at the flowers of wild cherries (*Prunus*).

Juniper Hairstreak *Callophrys gryneus* Plate 12

SIZE ≤ Gray Hairstreak.
SIMILAR SPECIES Hessel's Hairstreak.
IDENTIFICATION In Florida, its bright olive-green color separates this crowd pleas-
er from all Florida's other hairstreaks except its close relative,
Hessel's Hairstreak in the north. Range does not overlap with
Florida's other green-colored hairstreaks.
HABITAT Almost any areas with red cedar and nectar sources for both the
spring and fall broods.
RANGE Also, north to Canada and west to California (as 'Siva' Juniper
Hairstreak).
ABUNDANCE 2 broods. **W:** LU, March–late Sept. **N:** LU, early March–mid
Oct., most common March–May, Sept.–Oct. **C:** LU, early

March–mid Oct., most common March–May, Sept.–Oct. **S:** X.
K: X. Although formerly considered to be very rare, 'Sweadner's' Juniper Hairstreak is actually widespread, although fairly
local and uncommon, in much of northern and central Florida.

LOCALITIES Torreya SP, Liberty Co.; Suwannee River SP; Anastasia State
Recreation Area, S. Johns Co.; Cedar Key, Levy Co.; Yankeetown, Levy Co.; Salt Springs, Ocala NF.

MAJOR FOODPLANT Southern red cedar (*Juniperus silicicola*).

GARDEN TIPS Southern red cedar (*Juniperus silicicola*).

COMMENTS This butterfly tends to remain very close (usually on) its host.
Most easily found by thumping on the red cedars and watching
the Juniper Hairstreak whirl up. Florida's population is 'Sweadner's' Juniper Hairstreak (*C.g.sweadneri*), a Florida endemic that
is more of a flower visitor than other Juniper Hairstreaks.

Hessel's Hairstreak *Callophrys hesseli* **Plate 12**

SIZE < Gray Hairstreak.

SIMILAR SPECIES Juniper Hairstreak.

IDENTIFICATION Normally, only found in Atlantic white cedar swamps (although
individuals must disperse to new areas). Brighter, **more emerald green** than Juniper Hairstreak from which it can usually be
separated by habitat preference alone. Juniper Hairstreaks
inhabit dry, often hilly fields with good stands of their host, red
cedar. Hessel's Hairstreak are found in white cedar swamps. Note
the **top white spot on the FW postmedian band displaced
outwardly** and the **brown patches distal to the postmedian line**, especially on the HW. Juniper Hairstreak has the top
white spot of the FW postmedian band aligned with the spot
below it and lacks the brown patches distal to the postmedian line.

HABITAT Edges of swamps and bottomland forests containing the caterpillar foodplant.

RANGE Also, north along the Atlantic coast (in disjunct populations) to
southern New England.

ABUNDANCE 3 broods? **W:** LR, mid March–early May, mid June–late July,
Sept.–Oct. **N:** X. **C:** X. **S:** X. **K:** X.

LOCALITIES New River east of Sumatra, Apalachicola NF; Alligator Creek,
Blackwater River SF, Santa Rosa Co.

MAJOR FOODPLANT Atlantic white cedar (*Chamaecyparis thyoides*).

COMMENTS This small butterfly perches near the tops of white cedar trees,
often 20 or more feet above the ground. Hot, humid conditions
coupled with masses of blood-thirsty tabanid flies make this one
of the more challenging butterflies to observe in Florida. Adults

occasionally descend from the treetops to visit damp soil but have not been observed visiting flowers in Florida.

White M Hairstreak *Parrhasius m-album* Plate 11

SIZE ≥ Gray Hairstreak.

SIMILAR SPECIES Southern Hairstreak (northern forms).

IDENTIFICATION With its flashing iridescent blue upper wings, White M Hairstreak is a worthy representative of a largely tropical group. Unfortunately for us, its beautiful blue is usually only visible during its rapid and erratic flight. Below, the white spot near the base of the HW will separate this species from all of Florida's other hairstreaks except Southern. Note the inwardly displaced orange and black spot on the HW. 'Northern' Southern Hairstreaks have this spot at the usual position at the HW margin. 'Southern' Southern Hairstreaks have an extensive red-orange patch near the HW margin.

HABITAT Open brushy areas with abundance of flowers adjacent to, or within, pine/oak woodlands.

RANGE Also, north to Massachusetts and west to eastern Kansas and Texas.

ABUNDANCE 3 broods. **W:** U–C, early March–mid Dec., most common April–May and Sept.–Oct. **N:** U–C, early March–mid Dec., most common April–May and Sept.–Oct. **C:** U–C, early March–early Nov., especially April–May, Sept.–Oct. **S:** U–C, late Feb.–late Dec. **K:** X.

MAJOR FOODPLANT Oaks (*Quercus*).

COMMENTS Adults frequent the tops of large oak trees, where they can often be seen perching and chasing each other late in the afternoon. They also come readily to flowers.

Scrub-Hairstreaks
(genus *Strymon*)

There are about 60 species of scrub-hairstreaks, all restricted to the New World. Unlike most of Florida's other hairstreaks, scrub-hairstreaks sometimes perch with their wings open and thus allow a view of their topsides.

Gray Hairstreak *Strymon melinus* Plate 15

SIZE 10/16 inch.

SIMILAR SPECIES Southern Hairstreak (northern forms).

IDENTIFICATION A widespread hairstreak with a true gray ground color below (rarely gray-brown). Note the prominent HW postmedian line, white outwardly and black inwardly (often with reddish-orange inwards of the black).

HABITAT Most common in disturbed open habitats but can be encountered in almost any habitat.

RANGE Also, most of North America and south through Central America to northern South America.

ABUNDANCE 3 or more broods. **W:** C, early March–early Nov., most common April–Oct. with a peak in June–July. **N:** C, early March–early Nov., most common April–Oct. with a peak in June–July. **C:** C, early Feb.–late Nov. **S:** C, all year, especially July–Oct. **K:** C, all year, especially Jan., March–April, June, and Aug.–Oct.

MAJOR FOODPLANT Beggarweeds (*Desmodium*), milk-peas (*Galactia*), and many others.

GARDEN TIPS Marsh mallow (*Kosteletzkya virginica*) and broomweed (*Sida acuta*).

COMMENTS This is the only widely distributed scrub-hairstreak in North America. Because the shade of gray, and intensity and coloration of the HW postmedian line, are quite variable, many butterfliers attempt to convert sightings of Gray Hairstreaks into sightings of more exotic species.

Martial Scrub-Hairstreak *Strymon martialis* **Plate 15**

SIZE = Gray Hairstreak.

SIMILAR SPECIES Gray Hairstreak, Bartram's Hairstreak.

IDENTIFICATION Both sexes with some blue above. Below, note the **bold white postmedian line** on both HW and FW. Gray Hairstreak's white postmedian line is more divided into dashes, not so bold, not so straight, and not as angled inwards. Bartram's Hairstreak has two white basal spots on the HW that this species lacks.

HABITAT Open and brushy sites with the foodplant, especially shrubby shorelines and the margins of tropical hammocks.

RANGE Also, Bahamas, Cuba, Cayman Islands, and Jamaica.

ABUNDANCE 3 or more broods. **W:** X. **N:** X. **C:** X. **S:** LU–LC, all year, most common May, Aug.–Oct. **K:** LU, all year, most common May, Aug.–Oct.

LOCALITIES Cactus Hammock, Big Pine Key; Long Key State Recreation Site; North Key Largo Hammocks State Botanical Site; (all of these are in Monroe Co.).

MAJOR FOODPLANT Bay cedar (*Suriana maritima*) and Florida trema (*Trema micrantha*).

GARDEN TIPS   Bay cedar (*Suriana maritima*).

COMMENTS   Best bet is to find good stands of the foodplant. The extensive stands of bay cedar at cactus hammock have recently been destroyed by Hurricane Georges. Hopefully, they will recover.

Bartram's Scrub-Hairstreak *Strymon acis* Plate 15

SIZE   ≤ Gray Hairstreak.

SIMILAR SPECIES   Gray Hairstreak, Martial Scrub-Hairstreak.

IDENTIFICATION   Below, note the **bold white postmedian line** on both HW and FW and the **two white basal spots on the HW**. Gray Hairstreak's white postmedian line is more divided into dashes, not so bold, not so straight, and not as angled inwards. Martial Scrub-Hairstreak lacks the two white HW basal spots.

HABITAT   Pine rockland with the hostplant.

RANGE   Also, West Indies.

ABUNDANCE   LU. All year. 3 or more broods. **W**: X. **N**: X. **C**: X. **S**: LR–LU, all year, especially March–May, July–Aug., Dec. **K**: LR–LU, all year, especially March–May, July–Aug., Dec.

LOCALITIES   Long Pine Key, Everglades NP; National Key Deer Refuge, Big Pine Key, Monroe Co.

MAJOR FOODPLANT   Narrow-leaved croton (*Croton linearis*).

GARDEN TIPS   Narrow-leaved croton (*Croton linearis*).

COMMENTS   Usually seen on croton, nectaring, courting, or egg-laying. Hurricane Andrew appears to have destroyed some mainland populations of this butterfly.

Mallow Scrub-Hairstreak *Strymon columella* Plate 15

SIZE   < Gray Hairstreak.

SIMILAR SPECIES   Gray Hairstreak, Ceraunus Blue.

IDENTIFICATION   This is a small, relatively inconspicuous hairstreak. HW below has a prominent black postmedian line and **two basal black spots** (sometimes the more distal spot is faint). Florida's population often has a tricolored tail-spot. Gray Hairstreak lacks the basal spots. Ceraunus Blue lacks tails, has extra dark spots on the basal half of the HW, and flies more slowly and less erratically.

HABITAT   Disturbed, weedy fields and roadsides.

RANGE   Also, south to the West Indies and through Central America to Bolivia.

ABUNDANCE   3 or more broods. **W**: X. **N**: X. **C**: X. **S**: U–C, all year, most common Jan., May, Aug.–Sept., Dec. **K**: U–C, all year, most common Jan., May, Aug.–Sept., Dec.

MAJOR FOODPLANT Various mallows (Malvaceae). Also, bay cedar (*Suriana mariti-ma*)(at least on Big Pine Key).

COMMENTS Males of this confusingly variable butterfly can sometimes be found perching with open wings 10–25 feet up at the tops of shrubs and small trees in the late afternoon.

Fulvous Hairstreak *Electrostrymon angelia* Plate 14

SIZE < Gray Hairstreak.

SIMILAR SPECIES Southern Hairstreak, White M Hairstreak.

IDENTIFICATION Note the disrupted HW postmedian line with an isolated prominent white spot along the HW leading edge. In flight the copper-colored upperside can sometimes be seen. Southern and White M hairstreaks have more continuous HW postmedian lines and have white postmedian lines on the FW that this species lacks.

HABITAT Gardens, disturbed shrubby areas, margins of tropical hammocks.

RANGE Also, West Indies.

ABUNDANCE 3 or more broods. **W:** X. **N:** X. **C:** R, Oct.–Nov. **S:** U–C, all year, most common March–April, June, Sept.–Oct. **K:** U, all year, especially April–June, Aug.–Oct.

MAJOR FOODPLANT Brazilian pepper (*Schinus terebinthifolius*).

COMMENTS Fulvous Hairstreaks formed a beachhead in southern Florida in the early 1970s, feeding on the introduced Brazilian pepper. They seem to be still spreading northward, although some more northerly populations may be only temporary, dying back after the winter. Brazilian pepper is considered to be an invasive pest—perhaps someone can develop a noninvasive variety.

Red-banded Hairstreak *Calycopis cecrops* Plate 14

SIZE < Gray Hairstreak.

IDENTIFICATION A small dark hairstreak with an **obvious red postmedian band** on both the HW and FW below. Above, shows some bright blue in flight.

HABITAT A wide variety of woodland openings and edges; also, brushy, overgrown, sandy fields.

RANGE Also, north to southern Connecticut and west to eastern Kansas and Texas.

ABUNDANCE 3 or more broods. **W:** C–A, all year, most common mid Feb.–March, May–July, Sept.–Oct. **N:** C–A, all year, most common mid Feb.– March, May–July, Sept.–Oct. **C:** C–A, all year, especially March–April, Sept.–Oct. **S:** C–A, all year, most common March–July. **K:** U, all year, especially March–May, Oct.–Dec.

MAJOR FOODPLANT   A wide variety of detritus (rotting leaves), especially near mango (*Manifera indica*), Brazilian pepper (*Schinus terebinthifolius*) and other trees.

GARDEN TIPS   Wax myrtle (*Myrica cerifera*).

COMMENTS   This is the most common hairstreak in Florida. It is the only species of the approximately 70 species of groundstreaks—a genus of tropical hairstreaks, most of which look very similar—that ranges widely into the United States.

Gray Ministreak *Ministrymon azia* Plate 14

SIZE   << Gray Hairstreak.

SIMILAR SPECIES   Red-banded Hairstreak.

IDENTIFICATION   A tiny, pale-gray hairstreak with irregular red postmedian bands. Note red marginal lines on FW and leading half of HW, and **red on head**. Red-banded Hairstreak is browner with much straighter HW postmedian band and lacks red marginal line and red on head.

HABITAT   Open scrub and disturbed areas.

RANGE   Also, West Indies and southern Texas south to Argentina.

ABUNDANCE   3 or more broods. **W**: X. **N**: X. **C**: LR, Oct.–Nov. **S**: LR–LU, all year, most common Sept.–Dec. **K**: LR–LU, all year, most common Sept.–Dec.

LOCALITIES   North Key Largo Hammocks State Botanical Site, Monroe Co.

MAJOR FOODPLANT   Lead tree (*Leucaena leucocephala*).

COMMENTS   Found in South Florida for the first time in 1973. It is very close-ly associated with its caterpillar foodplant—find it and you may see the butterfly. On several occasions, this species has been found along the west coast of Florida as far north as Pasco County, probably representing temporary populations that do not survive cold winters.

Blues
(subfamily Polyommatinae)

Most blues can be recognized as blues on the wing. They are generally blue above (surprise!) and their flight is usually less rapid and erratic than hairstreaks. Although blues are largely found in temperate and northern regions, most of Florida's blues have affinities with tropical groups.

Eastern Pygmy-Blue *Brephidium isophthalma*
Plate 16

SIZE	< Ceraunus Blue.
IDENTIFICATION	A tiny blue of salt marsh tidal flats, where it may be locally abundant but inconspicuous, flying very close to the ground. Note the **four prominent black marginal HW eye-spots**.
HABITAT	Coastal flats and salt marshes.
RANGE	Also, north along the coast to South Carolina and west to East Texas. Also, North Bimini Island (Bahamas).
ABUNDANCE	3 or more broods. **W**: R. **N**: LU, early March–early Oct. **C**: LU, early March–early Oct. **S**: LU, all year, especially March, June–July. **K**: LU, all year, especially Jan., March–April, Aug.–Oct., Dec.
MAJOR FOODPLANT	Glassworts (*Salicornia*) and probably saltwort (*Batis maritima*).
COMMENTS	Unlike their western cousins, Eastern Pygmy-Blues rarely open their wings while landed. Abundance fluctuates markedly from season to season, and from year to year. The caterpillars of this species are tended by ants, which may be a factor in causing its distribution to be localized.

Cassius Blue *Leptotes cassius* Plate 16

SIZE	≥ Ceraunus Blue.
IDENTIFICATION	Its zebra-striping distinguishes Cassius Blue from all Florida's other blues.
HABITAT	Generally distributed in open habitats, including pine woods and the edges of tropical hammocks.
RANGE	Also, West Indies and south Texas to Argentina.
ABUNDANCE	C, south Florida, all year. R, immigrant to northern Florida. 3 or more broods. **W**: X. **N**: R, Aug.–Oct. **C**: U, early March–early Nov. **S**: C, all year, especially June–July, Oct.–Dec. **K**: C–A, all year, most common March–June, Aug.–Sept.
MAJOR FOODPLANT	A wide variety, especially legumes.

GARDEN TIPS   Leadworts (*Plumbago scandens, auriculata alba, auriculata* "Cape Royal").

COMMENTS   Although often found low to the ground, it is not uncommon to find Cassius Blues nectaring high in flowering trees. Flight of males is generally more rapid and erratic than the fluttering flight of females. Most frequent near the coast.

Miami Blue *Hemiargus thomasi* Plate 16

SIZE   ≥ Ceraunus Blue.

SIMILAR SPECIES   Nickerbean Blue, Ceraunus Blue, Cassius Blue.

IDENTIFICATION   Below, note the **bright orange spot near the HW outer angle**, the white postmedian band, **especially on the FW** and the **two eyespots near the HW outer angle**. Ceraunus Blues have a very dull orange spot near the HW outer angle, in Florida, they normally have only a single eyespot near the outer angle (some individuals have a 2nd partial eye-spot—but this is above, not below the usual eye-spot), and have a more uniform ground color. Cassius Blues lack bold black spots at HW leading margin. Above, females have an orange spot near the HW outer angle that related blues lack. See Nickerbean Blue for discussion.

HABITAT   Beach scrub and hammock edges.

RANGE   Also, West Indies.

ABUNDANCE   All year. 3 or more broods. **W**: X. **N**: X. **C**: X. **S**: R or H, all year. **K**: R or H, all year, especially March–May, Sept.–Oct.

LOCALITIES   Biscayne NP, Miami-Dade Co.; North Key Largo State Botanical Site; Long Key State Recreation Area; National Key Deer Refuge, Big Pine Key; (all of these are in Monroe Co.).

MAJOR FOODPLANT   Balloon-vines (*Cardiospermum*).

GARDEN TIPS   Balloon-vines (*Cardiospermum*).

COMMENTS   This butterfly used to be common around Miami and was reported from much of south Florida (with temporary populations in central Florida). More recently it has been restricted to the Florida Keys, but finding it even there has become problematic. Although it may still occur in south Florida, we know of no verified reports since Hurricane Andrew in 1992. In addition, Nickerbean Blues now occur at some sites where Miami Blues previously were found.

Nickerbean Blue *Hemiargus ammon* Plate 16

SIZE   = Ceraunus Blue.

SIMILAR SPECIES   Miami Blue, Ceraunus Blue, Cassius Blue.

IDENTIFICATION The bright orange spot near the HW outer angle tells you this isn't a Ceraunus or Cassius Blue. Very similar to the native Miami Blue but somewhat smaller than that species. Note the following marks. Below, there **are only 3 dark spots near the base of the HW**. Miami Blue has 4 spots near the base of the HW (although the additional spot is sometimes faint). Near the HW outer angle, the **orange spot is bullet-shaped**, pushing into the white band. Miami Blue has a crescent-shaped orange spot that doesn't displace the adjacent white band. **The space distil to the HW cell-end bar is white**. Miami Blue has this space gray. Above, males have a pink-orange spot (occasionally faint or lacking) at the HW outer angle that male Miami Blues lack. Females have this spot bullet-shaped and orange, while in Miami Blue females this spot is crescent-shaped.

HABITAT This species' caterpillar foodplants occur in coastal hammocks and pine rockland.

RANGE Also, West Indies.

ABUNDANCE All year. 3 or more broods. **W**: X. **N**: X. **C**: X. **S**: X. **K**: U–C, probably all year.

LOCALITIES National Key Deer Refuge, Big Pine Key, Monroe Co.

MAJOR FOODPLANT Nickerbeans (*Caesalpinia*).

COMMENTS Native to the Bahamas and Cuba, a population of this species was discovered on Big Pine Key in December, 1997 by Mark Salvato (who understandably believed that they were Miami Blues) and independently by Jeff Slotten in March 1998, who correctly identified them. There is no way to know as of this writing whether Nickerbean Blues will firmly take hold in southern Florida or will die out, as Androgeus Swallowtails did in the 1970s and 1980s. Our guess is that, having arrived from the West Indies, they will find south Florida to their liking, and flourish.

Ceraunus Blue *Hemiargus ceraunus* **Plate 16**

SIZE 7/16 inch.

SIMILAR SPECIES Miami Blue, Mallow Scrub-Hairstreak.

IDENTIFICATION Ceraunus and Miami blues have two prominent black spots on the HW leading margin below. Other blues may have black spots here, but they are not so prominent relative to the other HW spots. Mallow Scrub-Hairstreak has tails, has fewer spots on the basal half of the HW, and flies faster and more erratically.

HABITAT	Generally distributed in open areas, especially in those that are disturbed.
RANGE	Also, west to southern California and south to Costa Rica and the West Indies.
ABUNDANCE	3 or more broods. **W:** U–C, early March–mid Oct., most common July–Oct. **N:** U–C, early March–mid Oct., most common July–Oct. **C:** C, all year, but most numerous Aug.–Oct. **S:** C–A, all year, especially May–July, Sept.–Oct., Dec. **K:** U–C, all year, most common Aug.–Sept., Dec.
MAJOR FOODPLANT	Flowers and young leaves of a wide variety of legumes.
GARDEN TIPS	Cow pea (*Vigna lutea*), butterfly pea (*Centrosema virginianum*), and milk-pea (*Galactia regularis*).
COMMENTS	This is the most common blue in Florida. Although Ceraunus Blues weakly flutter very close to the ground, like many blues, they usually try your patience waiting for them to actually alight.

Eastern Tailed-Blue *Everes comyntas*
Not Illustrated, see *Butterflies through Binoculars: The East.*

SIZE	≥ Ceraunus Blue.
SIMILAR SPECIES	Spring Azure.
IDENTIFICATION	The "tails" are diagnostic but occasionally are worn. Both above and below note the orange spot (often two or three) by the HW tails. Can usually be distinguished from Spring Azure by its ground-hugging flight and the darker blue of its males and some females and the graying color in other females.
HABITAT	Open areas in general.
RANGE	Also, north to Canada, west to the Dakotas and southeastern Arizona south to Costa Rica; and California (an introduction?).
ABUNDANCE	R. 3 or more broods. **W:** LR, probably early March–Nov., especially late Aug.–mid Oct. **N:** LR, probably early March–Nov. **C:** S. **S:** X. **K:** X.
LOCALITIES	Blackwater River SP, Santa Rosa Co.; Florida Caverns SP, Jackson Co.; University of North Florida nature trails, Duval Co.; Jennings SF, Clay Co.
MAJOR FOODPLANT	Pea family.
COMMENTS	Widespread and abundant to the north, Eastern Tailed-Blues are rare in Florida and usually found in small numbers. Males fly faster and higher above the ground than do male Ceraunus Blues.

Spring Azure *Celastrina ladon* Plate 16

Two subspecies of spring azures occur in Florida and, as these probably merit species status, we treat them separately.

'Edwards' Spring Azure *Celastrina ladon violacea.*

SIZE	> Ceraunus Blue.
SIMILAR SPECIES	Summer Azure, Eastern Tailed-Blue.
IDENTIFICATION	Clear azure blue above (females with black borders). Unlike Eastern Tailed-Blue, there are no tails and no orange. Flight is usually higher and stronger than Eastern Tailed Blue. Below, ground color is pale with various dark markings. Separation from Summer Azure is difficult. Male 'Edwards' Spring Azures have a flatter, less brilliant blue above. Flight times differ somewhat.
HABITAT	Temperate hardwood forests.
RANGE	Also, north to Massachusetts and west to Missouri.
ABUNDANCE	1 brood. **W:** LR, late Feb.–April. **N:** LR, late Feb.–April. **C:** X. **S:** X. **K:** X.
LOCALITIES	Eglin Air Force Base; Olustee SF, Baker County; Ralph E. Simmons SF, Nassau Co.; Torreya SP, Liberty Co.; O'Leno SP, Alachua and Columbia counties.
MAJOR FOODPLANT	Unknown in Florida.
COMMENTS	Only very recently have we realized that this butterfly occurs in northern Florida. Flight time is earlier than for Summer Azure but there is a period of overlap. It's appearance and behavior are similar to Summer Azure.

'Summer' Spring Azure *Celastrina ladon neglecta.*

SIZE	> Ceraunus Blue.
SIMILAR SPECIES	Eastern Tailed-Blue.
IDENTIFICATION	Clear azure blue above (females with black borders). Unlike Eastern Tailed-Blue, there are no tails and no orange. Flight is usually higher and stronger than Eastern Tailed Blue. Below, ground color is pale with various dark markings.
HABITAT	Temperate hardwood forests.
RANGE	Also, north to Canada and west to the Dakotas and Texas.
ABUNDANCE	Probably 3 broods. **W:** LR–U, late March–April, May–mid June, late July–Oct. **N:** LR, late March–April, May–mid June, late July–Oct. **C:** R. **S:** X. **K:** X.
LOCALITIES	Florida Caverns SP, Jackson Co.; Torreya SP, Liberty Co.; Apalachicola NF; Mike Roess Gold Head State Branch SP, Clay Co.

MAJOR FOODPLANT   A wide variety of plants from many different families.

COMMENTS   Although previously considered to be a 2nd brood of the Spring Azure, these summer-flying azures are almost certainly a distinct species—*Celastrina neglecta*. We have listed them as subspecies *neglecta* to be conservative and to be consistent with the NABA list. Ants often tend the caterpillars.

Metalmarks
(family Riodinidae)

Metalmarks derive their name, naturally enough, from the metallic marks that are often present on their wings. The variety of wing size, shape, and pattern of this very large tropical group is truly amazing. Some resemble hairstreaks, some resemble skippers, some resemble crescents, and some resemble heliconians! Compared to many of the brilliantly colored and patterned tropical species, Florida's representative of this family is rather a plain Jane, but still handsome nonetheless.

Little Metalmark *Calephelis virginiensis* Plate 10

SIZE   = Ceraunus Blue.

IDENTIFICATION   A small, but bright inhabitant of open pine woods. Above, bright, rich, red-orange-brown with silver metallic markings.

HABITAT   Grassy clearings in pine flatwoods, wet prairies and pastures.

RANGE   Also, north to North Carolina and west to East Texas.

ABUNDANCE   3 or more broods. **W**: LU–LC, early March–early Nov., most common April–May, Sept.–Oct. **N**: LU–LC, early March–early Nov., most common April–May, Sept.–Oct. **C**: LU–LC, late Feb.–mid Nov. **S**: LC, all year, especially March, May–June, Oct., Dec. **K**: extirpated.

LOCALITIES   Apalachicola NF, Liberty Co.; Ocala NF, Marion Co.

MAJOR FOODPLANT   Yellow thistle (*Cirsium horridulum*).

GARDEN TIPS   Yellow thistle (*Cirsium horridulum*).

COMMENTS   Flight is low to the ground. The wings are generally held flat while landed on leaves or when nectaring at flowers such as Godfrey's fleabane (*Pluchea rosea*) and mistflower (*Eupatorium coelestinum*).

Brushfoots
(family Nymphalidae)

Called brushfoots because of the greatly reduced male forelegs, this family includes many of Florida's best known and most conspicuous butterflies. They constitute a very diverse collection of species and some consider a number of the groups included here (such as the satyrs and the monarchs) as separate families.

American Snout *Libytheana carinenta* **Plate 10**

SIZE
> Pearl Crescent.

IDENTIFICATION
The extremely long snout (palps) is obvious on this mainly orange and brown butterfly. Below, it is very variable, ranging from quite pale with few markings to dark and mottled. While its flight can be rapid, it often seems erratic and mothlike.

HABITAT
Thickets and open woodlands with hackberries.

RANGE
Also, north to Massachusetts and west to southern California and south to Argentina and the West Indies.

ABUNDANCE
3 or more broods. **W**: U–C, Feb.–Oct., most common April–May. **N**: U–C, Feb.–Oct., most common April–May. **C**: U–C, Feb.–Oct., most common April–May. **S**: R, all year, especially Sept.–Oct. **K**: S, Jan., July, Oct., Nov.

MAJOR FOODPLANT
Hackberries (*Celtis*).

COMMENTS
The extremely long snout is hard to miss, but an understanding about its function has been elusive.

Gulf Fritillary *Agraulis vanillae* **Plate 17**

SIZE
1 9/16 inch.

SIMILAR SPECIES
Julia.

IDENTIFICATION
A long-winged, low-flying nymphalid. Deep reddish-orange above and heavily silvered below. Above, note the black-ringed white spots in the FW cell. Julias lack the silvering below and the white spots above.

HABITAT
Open fields, roadsides and gardens.

RANGE
Also, north to North Carolina, west to California and south to Argentina and the West Indies.

ABUNDANCE
3 or more broods. **W**: A, all year, especially April–Dec., most common Aug.–Oct. **N**: A, all year, especially April–Dec., most common Aug.–Oct. **C**: A, all year, especially March–July,

MAJOR FOODPLANT Passion-vines (*Passiflora*).

GARDEN TIPS Corky-stemmed passion-vine (*P. suberosa*), maypop (*P. incarnata*), and cerulean passion-vine (*P. caerulea* nonnative).

COMMENTS Truly a spangled dazzler, this is one of Florida's most extravagant butterflies. Luckily for us, it is common and widespread. During the fall, large numbers migrate into Florida from regions farther north.

Julia (Heliconian) *Dryas iulia* **Plate 17**

SIZE = Gulf Fritillary.

SIMILAR SPECIES Gulf Fritillary.

IDENTIFICATION Flying on narrow wings with shallow wingbeats, this orange heliconian is resident only in subtropical and tropical areas. Males are bright orange-brown, females duller orange-brown with a black band across the FW. Gulf Fritillaries are red-orange rather than orange-brown and have bright silvered spots below.

HABITAT A generalist, found in open and disturbed situations near tropical and subtropical woodlands.

RANGE Also, West Indies and south Texas south to Brazil.

ABUNDANCE 3 or more broods. **W:** X. **N:** X. **C:** S. Occasional individuals stray northward along the west coast to Sanibel Island and Sarasota. **S:** LC, all year, most common March–April, June–July, Oct.–Dec. **K:** C, all year, especially Jan., April–June, Aug.–Oct. Uncommon in the lower Keys.

MAJOR FOODPLANT Passion-vines (*Passiflora*).

GARDEN TIPS Corky-stemmed passion-vine (*P. suberosa*) and maypop (*P. incarnata*).

COMMENTS Flight is much faster and directional than that of the closely related Zebra (Heliconian). Widespread and very common in the tropics.

Zebra (Heliconian) *Heliconius charitonius* **Plate 17**

SIZE = Gulf Fritillary.

IDENTIFICATION It is difficult to misidentify the black and yellow striped Zebra (Heliconian) although I'm sure some have succeeded. Flying slowly and gracefully, usually in the dappled light of semi-shade, this species is characteristic of disturbed habitats throughout the tropics and subtropics.

HABITAT Woodland and hammock edges.

RANGE Also, West Indies and south Texas south to Ecuador.

ABUNDANCE	3 or more broods. **W:** R–U, Aug.–Oct. **N:** U–C, all year, most common Aug.–Oct. **C:** A, all year, especially March–April, June–July, and Oct.–Dec. **S:** A, all year, especially March–April, June–July, and Oct.–Dec. **K:** U–C, all year, most common April–June, Aug.–Sept., Dec.
MAJOR FOODPLANT	Passion-vines (*Passiflora*).
GARDEN TIPS	Corky-stemmed passion-vine (*P. suberosa*) and maypop (*P. incarnata*).
COMMENTS	This species, the State Butterfly of Florida, moves northward as the season progresses but does not survive cold winters. Groups of Zebra (Heliconians) often roost together at night, sometimes using the same site for weeks or months. Females gather balls of pollen (a source of amino acids) on the tip of the tongue and then digest the pollen externally.

Variegated Fritillary *Euptoieta claudia* Plate 17

SIZE	> Common Buckeye.
IDENTIFICATION	A **dull, orange-brown** fritillary whose behavior and overall appearance is more similar to an American Lady than to the greater fritillaries. Florida's other fritillaries are brighter orange above. Below, it is unlike any of Florida's other butterflies, with a pale, very wide, postmedian band on the HW.
HABITAT	Open fields with flowers, roadsides.
RANGE	Also north to Massachusetts and Manitoba, west to southern California and south to Argentina and the West Indies.
ABUNDANCE	3 or more broods. **W:** C, April–Oct., most common Aug.–Oct. **N:** U, March–early Nov. **C:** U, March–early Nov. **S:** R–U, all year. **K:** R–U, all year.
MAJOR FOODPLANT	Violets (*Viola*) and passion-vines (*Passiflora*).
COMMENTS	Flight is rapid and low to the ground. Variegated Fritillaries are very wary and difficult to approach closely, but readily visit flowers, such as Spanish needles.

Silvery Checkerspot *Chlosyne nycteis* Not Illustrated, see *Butterflies through Binoculars: The East.*

SIZE	> Pearl Crescent.
SIMILAR SPECIES	Pearl Crescent.
IDENTIFICATION	A small, orange and black nymphalid of woodland glades. Larger than Pearl Crescent with **wider FW black borders above**. Usually with at least some of the HW postmedian spots with paler pupils. Below, note the very broad **white median band** on the HW.
HABITAT	Sunny clearings in bottomland hardwood forests.

RANGE	Also, north to southern Canada and west to Colorado and Arizona.
ABUNDANCE	2 broods. **W**: LR, May–June, probably Aug.–Sept. **N**: X. **C**: X. **S**: X. **K**: X.
LOCALITIES	Florida Caverns SP, Jackson Co.; Three Rivers State Recreation Area, Jackson Co.
MAJOR FOODPLANT	Unknown in Florida but uses sunflowers (*Helianthus*) and other Compositae elsewhere.
COMMENTS	Usually flies within 1 foot of the ground or shrubs and basks in sunlit clearings. Often difficult to see the underside well.

'Seminole' Texan Crescent *Phyciodes texana* Plate 18

SIZE	≥ Pearl Crescent.
IDENTIFICATION	Black with white median spot-band and some red-brown basally. Darker than Florida's other crescents.
HABITAT	Margins, sunny clearings, and partly shaded areas of swamps, bottomlands, and moist forests.
RANGE	Also, north to South Carolina, west to the American southwest and south to Guatemala.
ABUNDANCE	3 or more broods. **W**: LU, late March–early Oct., most common March, Aug.–Sept. **N**: LU, late March–early Oct., most common March, Aug.–Sept. **C**: LR, early May–late Nov., especially Aug.–Nov. **S**: X. **K**: X.
LOCALITIES	Gum Root Swamp Conservation Area (Gum Root Park), Alachua Co.; Torreya SP, Liberty Co.; Florida Caverns SP, Jackson Co., Suwannee River SP.
MAJOR FOODPLANT	Water-willow (*Justicia*), dicliptera and probably other small Acanthaceae.
COMMENTS	A more leisurely flyer than Florida's other crescents. Some consider the Florida subspecies, 'Seminole' Texan Crescent, to be a distinct species from the Texan Crescents flying further west.

Cuban Crescent *Phyciodes frisia* Plate 18

SIZE	= Pearl Crescent.
SIMILAR SPECIES	Pearl Crescent, Phaon Crescent.
IDENTIFICATION	This crescent has the FW above with 3 large orange-brown spots against a black ground color. Below, note the pale zigzag submarginal bands.
HABITAT	Edges of subtropical hammocks and other open and sparsely wooded situations.
RANGE	Also, West Indies. ('Tulcis' Cuban Crescent, almost certainly a distinct species, is found in southern Texas south through South America.)

BRUSHFOOTS

ABUNDANCE	3 or more broods. **W**: X. **N**: X. **C**: RS, late Feb.–mid Oct. Known to breed during at least one season (1994). **S**: LU, all year. **K**: LU, all year, most common March–May, Aug.–Dec.
LOCALITIES	Biscayne NP; Collier-Seminole SP, Collier Co.; North Key Largo Hammocks State Botanical Site, Monroe Co.
MAJOR FOODPLANT	Crimson dicliptera (*Dicliptera assurgens*), shrimpflower (*Beloperone*), and perhaps other small Acanthaceae.
GARDEN TIPS	Red shrimpflower (*Beloperone*).
COMMENTS	Like so many other Florida butterflies, Cuban Crescents are usually found on Spanish needles. During courtship, males fly dizzingly in tight circles around the landed female.

Phaon Crescent *Phyciodes phaon* Plate 18

SIZE	≤ Pearl Crescent.
SIMILAR SPECIES	Pearl Crescent.
IDENTIFICATION	Above, note the **cream-colored FW median band**, contrasting with the orange postmedian band. Below, the cream-colored FW median band is visible. The HW is generally cream colored (with black markings), strongly contrasting with the brown-orange FW base. Pearl Crescents below don't have a cream-colored FW median band and their HW ground color is a warmer orange–tan, that contrasts less strongly with the orange color at the base of the FW.
HABITAT	Moist open situations with its low, mat-forming hostplants. Often along roadsides, trails, or lake beds.
RANGE	Also, north to North Carolina and Kansas, west to southern California, Cuba, and Mexico south to Guatemala.
ABUNDANCE	3 or more broods. **W**: U–C, mid March–early Nov. **N**: C–A, early March–mid Nov., especially March–April, Sept.–Oct. **C**: C–A, mid Feb.–early Dec., especially March–April, Sept.–Nov. **S**: C–A, all year, most common May–June, Aug.–Oct., Dec. **K**: C, all year, especially Jan., March–May, Aug.–Oct., Dec.
MAJOR FOODPLANT	Fogfruit (*Lippia*; sometimes placed in the genus *Phyla*).
GARDEN TIPS	Fogfruit (*Lippia nodiflora*; sometimes called frogfruit).
COMMENTS	It is easy to overlook these small crescents, even when they swarm on roadsides and lawns, because they fly very close to the ground. The fall generation of adults generally wait until springtime to mate. During observed courtship behavior, the male landed behind the female, walked up along-side of her (on right side) and open and shut his wings a few times. Then he moved back behind her and mating ensued.

Pearl Crescent *Phyciodes tharos* **Plate 18**

SIZE	11/16 inch.
SIMILAR SPECIES	Phaon Crescent.
IDENTIFICATION	Small, bright orange (when fresh) with a flight that is low to the ground and often involves gliding. Exact pattern can be quite variable. Males and females and different broods also differ to some degree. Note the orange above with extensive reticulate black markings. Phaon Crescents have a cream-colored FW median band that is visible from above or below.
HABITAT	Widespread in open situations, sandhills, flatwoods, fields, wet prairies, power-line cuts, etc.
RANGE	Also, north to southern Canada, west to Montana, and south through Mexico.
ABUNDANCE	3 or more broods. **W**: C, early March–early Nov., most common March–April, Sept.–Oct. **N**: C, early March–early Nov., most common March–April, Sept.–Oct. **C**: C, mid Feb.–early Dec., especially March–April, Sept.–Nov. **S**: C, all year, especially May–June, Aug.–Oct., Dec. **K**: U, all year, especially Jan., March, May–June, Aug.–Oct., Dec.
MAJOR FOODPLANT	Asters (*Aster*).
GARDEN TIPS	Climbing aster (*Aster caroliniensis*), aster (*Aster dumosus*), Walter's aster (*Aster walteri*), and other aster cultivars.
COMMENTS	This is one of the most common and widespread butterflies in North America.

Anglewings
(genus *Polygonia*)
and Tortoiseshells
(genus *Nymphalis*).

These two groups are best considered together, since they share many traits and are extremely closely related. Unlike most of Florida's butterflies, adult anglewings and tortoiseshells do not usually nectar at flowers. Instead, they often can be seen taking sap from trees, congregating at rotting fruit, or even deriving sustenance from animal scat or carrion.

Although these butterflies are essentially northern (also found throughout Eurasia), Question Marks, Eastern Commas, and Mourning Cloaks can be found in northern Florida.

Question Mark *Polygonia interrogationis* Plate 19

SIZE
> Common Buckeye.

SIMILAR SPECIES
Eastern Comma.

IDENTIFICATION
A medium-sized orangish butterfly of the woods and nearby open area. Flight is rapid but usually not very directional, often returning to the same area. Note the violaceous margin of the HW and, below, the silvered "question-mark." Above, the black or "summer" form has much black on the HWs while the orange or "fall" form is mainly orangish-brown. These forms correspond largely, but not completely, with the summer and fall broods. There are also two forms below, either fairly unicolored or heavily mottled.

HABITAT
Woodlands, swamps and adjacent open areas.

RANGE
Also, north to southern Canada, west to Colorado and southeastern Arizona, and south through the Mexican highlands.

ABUNDANCE
2 broods. 2nd brood overwintering as adults and flying again next spring. **W**: U–C, Feb.–May, Aug.–Dec., most common March–April. **N**: U–C, Feb.–May, Aug.–Dec., most common March–April. **C**: U–C, Feb.–May, Aug.–Dec., most common March–April. **S**: S. **K**: X.

MAJOR FOODPLANT
Elms (*Ulmus*) and hackberries (*Celtis*).

COMMENTS
The fall generation hibernates in wood piles and other protected places during Dec. and Jan.

Eastern Comma *Polygonia comma* Plate 19

SIZE
= Common Buckeye.

SIMILAR SPECIES
Question Mark.

IDENTIFICATION
Note the size, generally smaller than a Question Mark. Above, very similar to Question Mark but **lacks the horizontal black, subapical spot** of that species. Below, note silvered "comma." Like Question Mark there is an orange above "fall" form and a "summer" form with black on the HW. Eastern Commas can usually be told from Question Marks, even on the wing, by their generally smaller size and less robust flight with faster wingbeats.

HABITAT
More closely restricted to woodlands than Question Mark.

RANGE
Also, north to Quebec, and west to Manitoba and east Texas.

ABUNDANCE
2 broods. 2nd brood overwintering as adults and flying again next spring. **W**: R, Feb.–Dec., most common March–April. **N**: S or R. **C**: X. **S**: X. **K**: X.

LOCALITIES
Torreya SP, Liberty Co.; Kanapaha Botanical Garden, Alachua Co.

| MAJOR FOODPLANT | Elms (*Ulmus*). |
| COMMENTS | Eastern Commas are seldom encountered in Florida. They easily may be mistaken for the more abundant Question Mark. |

Mourning Cloak *Nymphalis antiopa* Plate 19

SIZE	≥ Red-spotted Purple.
IDENTIFICATION	Unmistakable. A large, dark nymphalid. Dark brown above with yellow borders and blue submarginal spots. Below, dark striated brown with pale yellow borders. Often glides in flight.
HABITAT	Hardwood forests.
RANGE	Also, all of North America, west through Eurasia, and south through Mexico.
ABUNDANCE	Probably 1 brood. **W**: R, primarily Feb.–April. **N**: R, primarily Feb.–April. **C**: R, primarily Feb.–April. **S**: X. **K**: X.
LOCALITIES	Torreya SP, Liberty Co.; Kanapaha Botanical Garden, Alachua Co.; University of North Florida nature trails, Duval Co.; Whitehead Lake Recreation Area, Apalachicola NF.
MAJOR FOODPLANT	Willows (*Salix*) and many other trees and shrubs.
COMMENTS	Although Mourning Cloaks may occasionally breed in northern Florida, most individuals found in Florida are probably winter visitors that have migrated into Florida from farther north.

American Lady *Vanessa virginiensis* Plate 20

SIZE	≥ Common Buckeye.
SIMILAR SPECIES	Painted Lady.
IDENTIFICATION	A medium-sized dull-orange butterfly with white spots on the black upper FW apex. Below, note the distinctive cobweb pattern on the HW and the pink patch on the FW. To distinguish from similar Painted Lady remember, "American Ladies have big eyes and a sharp cut." The big eyes refer to the 2 large eye-spots on the HW below. Painted Ladies have four smallish eye-spots on the HW below. The "sharp cut" refers to the shape of the FW. American Ladies have the FW sharply cut with the apex protruding, while Painted Ladies have a more regular outline. Most individuals have a white spot on the FW above that Painted Ladies lack.
HABITAT	Open spaces, including fields, roadsides, and coastal dunes.
RANGE	Also, north to southern Canada, west to California, and south through Mexico.
ABUNDANCE	3 or more broods. **W**: U–C, all year, most common Feb.–May. **N**: U–C, all year, most common Feb.–May with a peak in April. **C**: U–C, March–Aug., especially April. **S**: U–C, March–Aug., most common in April. **K**: RS, May, June, Oct.

MAJOR FOODPLANT	Pearly everlastings (*Anaphalis*) and other Compositae.
GARDEN TIPS	Pearly everlastings (*Anaphalis*).
COMMENTS	American Ladies hibernate during the coldest part of the winter.

Painted Lady *Vanessa cardui* **Plate 20**

SIZE	≥ Common Buckeye.
SIMILAR SPECIES	American Lady.
IDENTIFICATION	This widespread immigrant is generally larger than American Lady with a pinkish suffusion (American Lady is more orange). The median black FW band is much bolder (in fact, the entire gestalt of the butterfly is more dramatic). Above, American Lady usually has a white spot on the FW orange ground (sometimes small) that Painted Lady lacks. Below, note four roughly equal eye-spots on the HW. American Lady has two large eye-spots.
HABITAT	Can be encountered in any type of open habitat.
RANGE	Also, the rest of North America, south to northern South America, Eurasia, Africa, and India.
ABUNDANCE	An immigrant that may not breed in Florida. **W**: R–U, May–Dec., especially Sept.–Dec. with a peak in Oct. **N**: R–U, May–Dec., especially Sept.–Dec. with a peak in Oct. **C**: R–U, April–Nov., especially Oct.–Dec. **S**: R–U, April–Nov., especially Oct.–Dec. **K**: R–U, April, Sept.–Dec. This migratory butterfly fluctuates in numbers in Florida, and appears to be absent during some years.
MAJOR FOODPLANT	Thistles and many other species.
GARDEN TIPS	Yellow thistle.
COMMENTS	The most cosmopolitan butterfly in the world. Each year, Painted Ladies stream out of northern Mexico during March and April in impressive migratory swarms to repopulate the eastern United States. This repopulation, both as to numbers of butterflies and to the extent of the territory they reach, varies widely from year to year. Due to the path of the migration, butterflies often reach the northeastern United States and the northern plains before they reach Florida (Aug.).

Red Admiral *Vanessa atalanta* **Plate 19**

SIZE	≥ Common Buckeye.
IDENTIFICATION	A rapidly flying (often), medium-sized dark nymphalid. Naturally enough, Red Admirals are patriotic—sporting red, white, and blue along the FW costa below. Above, the reddish-orange bands on both FWs and HWs make confusion of this species with any other very difficult.

HABITAT	Open situations with flowers, including fields, beaches, suburbia, especially moist fields near woodlands.
RANGE	Also, the rest of North America and south through Central America, Eurasia, and Africa.
ABUNDANCE	Probably 2 broods in the north, perhaps 3 broods southward. **W**: C, Jan.–Aug., Nov.–Dec., most common March–April, Nov. **N**: C, Jan.–Aug., Nov.–Dec., most common March–April, Nov. **C**: C, all year, especially March–May. **S**: C, all year, especially March–May. **K**: RS, Jan.–March, May, Oct.
MAJOR FOODPLANT	False nettle (*Boehmeria cylindrica*), pellitory (*Parietaria*), and nettles (*Urtica*).
GARDEN TIPS	False nettle (*Boehmeria cylindrica*).
COMMENTS	Red Admirals hibernate in protected sites during the winter. They can often be seen basking along sandy roadsides or on the sides of sunlit buildings.

Common Buckeye *Junonia coenia* Plate 21

SIZE	1 inch.
SIMILAR SPECIES	In south Florida see Mangrove and Tropical buckeyes.
IDENTIFICATION	A brown nymphalid with **prominent eye-spots** along the margins of both wings and **two orange bars** in the FW cell.
HABITAT	Open fields, beaches, and many disturbed situations. Especially fond of sandy areas and paths where they can rest on the ground.
RANGE	Also, north to Massachusetts and South Dakota, west to California, and south through the West Indies and Mexico.
ABUNDANCE	3 or more broods. **W**: C–A, late Feb.–late Nov., most common March–May, Sept.–Nov. **N**: C–A, late Feb.–late Nov., most common March–May, Sept.–Nov. **C**: C–A, mid Feb.–mid Dec., especially June–July, Sept.–Nov. **S**: C–A, mid Feb.–mid Dec., especially June–July, Sept.–Nov. **K**: U–C, all year, most common Sept.–Oct.
MAJOR FOODPLANT	Gerardias (*Gerardia*), seymeria (*Seymeria*), toadflax (*Linaria*), and plantain (*Plantago*).
GARDEN TIPS	Fogfruit (*Lippia nodiflora*), snapdragon (*Antirrhinum major*).
COMMENTS	This is one of Florida's most familiar butterflies, as it is easily identified and is found around lawns and gardens—close to human habitations.

Mangrove Buckeye *Junonia evarete* Plate 21

SIZE	≥ Common Buckeye.
SIMILAR SPECIES	Common Buckeye, Tropical Buckeye.

IDENTIFICATION A large buckeye with much orange. Above, the FW subapical patch is pale to strong orange. Common Buckeyes' subapical patch is white. Note that the **large FW eye-spot is surrounded by orange.** Common Buckeyes usually have some white on the inner edge of the FW eye-spot and have a contrasting bright orange patch adjacent to the FW eye-spot by the FW tornus. Tropical Buckeyes lack orange on the inner edge of the FW eyespot. The two HW eye-spots tend to be more similar in size in Mangrove Buckeyes than in Common Buckeyes.

HABITAT Edges of black mangrove swamps and adjacent areas.

RANGE Also, the Antilles and the Caribbean coast of north Mexico and south Texas.

ABUNDANCE 3 or more broods. **W**: X. **N**: RS, July–Oct. **C**: LU, Feb.–Nov., especially April–May, Aug.–Oct. **S**: LU, all year, most common June–Oct. **K**: LU, all year, especially Jan., April–May, Aug.–Oct., Dec.

LOCALITIES Tampa Bay Sanctuaries, Hillsborough Co.; Merritt Island NWR, Brevard and Volusia Cos.; Terra Ceia Aquatic Preserve, Manatee Co.; Biscayne NP; Flamingo, Everglades NP; North Key Largo Hammocks State Botanical Site, Monroe Co.; National Key Deer Refuge, Big Pine Key, Monroe Co.

MAJOR FOODPLANT Black mangrove (*Avicennia germinans*).

COMMENTS Until very recently, the buckeye species situation was quite confused, and there are still some uncertainties.

Tropical Buckeye *Junonia genoveva* Plate 21

SIZE = Common Buckeye.

SIMILAR SPECIES Common Buckeye, Mangrove Buckeye.

IDENTIFICATION Above, **FW pale median band is wide and flushed with pink. Inner edge of the large FW eye-spot is usually brown, or pale brown** (very occasionally with some orange). **HW orange submarginal band is narrow.** Below, note the prominent pale median stripe. Common Buckeye usually has white along inner edge of FW eye-spot, has very unequal HW eye-spots, and has a broad orange HW submarginal band. Mangrove Buckeye has orange FW median band and FW eye-spot completely surrounded by orange.

HABITAT Open and/or disturbed areas in the tropics and subtropics.

RANGE Also, south throughout the American tropics.

ABUNDANCE Present in variable numbers in south Florida, mainly on Key Largo. 3 or more broods. **W**: X. **N**: X. **C**: X. **S**: LR, all year, most frequent Nov.–Dec. **K**: LR, all year, most frequent Jan., Oct., Dec.

LOCALITIES	Key Largo, Monroe Co.
MAJOR FOODPLANT	Blue porterweed (*Stachytarpheta jamaicensis*) and probably other Verbenaceae.
COMMENTS	Discovered in Florida relatively recently, this species' abundance waxes and wanes. It may be resident or it may periodically become established in southern Florida, only to eventually die out. Older museum specimens of Tropical Buckeyes from Florida were misidentified as Mangrove Buckeyes.

White Peacock *Anartia jatrophae* **Plate 21**

SIZE	= Common Buckeye.
IDENTIFICATION	An easy call—silvery white all over with an orange border.
HABITAT	A wide variety of moist open and/or disturbed areas.
RANGE	Also, throughout tropical Americas.
ABUNDANCE	3 or more broods. **W**: R immigrant, May–Dec., most common Sept.–Oct. **N**: R immigrant, May–Dec., most common Sept.–Oct. **C**: C, early March–early Dec., especially Aug.–Oct. **S**: C–A, all year, especially March, June–Dec. with a peak in Aug.–Oct. **K**: LU–LC, all year, most common Aug.–Oct.
MAJOR FOODPLANT	Smooth water-hyssop (*Bacopa monnieri*) and various verbenas (Verbenaceae).
GARDEN TIPS	Smooth water-hyssop (*Bacopa monnieri*), green shrimp-plant (*Blechum brownei*).
COMMENTS	This very attractive, essentially tropical, butterfly flies low to the ground with very shallow wingbeats.

Malachite *Siproeta stelenes* **Plate 22**

SIZE	≥ Red-spotted Purple.
IDENTIFICATION	How many other big, bright green butterflies have you seen flying around?.
HABITAT	Tropical hammocks and overgrown avocado and citrus groves.
RANGE	Also, south throughout tropical Americas.
ABUNDANCE	3 or more broods. **W**: X. **N**: X. **C**: RS, primarily Sept.–Dec. **S**: LU, all year, most common March–May, July–Oct., Dec. **K**: RS, Jan.–July, Oct.–Dec. Numbers seem to be increasing.
LOCALITIES	Tree Tops Park, Broward Co.; Fern Forest Nature Center, Broward Co.; Camp Owaissa Bauer, Miami-Dade Co.; Castellow Hammock Preserve, Miami-Dade Co.
MAJOR FOODPLANT	Green shrimp-plant (*Blechum brownei*).
GARDEN TIPS	Green shrimp-plant (*Blechum brownei*).
COMMENTS	Not many people can remain stoic having sighted one of these flying emeralds. Established in southern Florida within the recent

past, Malachites are becoming more common and expanding their range, although Hurricane Andrew set them back.

Red-spotted Purple *Limenitis arthemis astyanax* Plate 22

SIZE	1 9/16 inch.
SIMILAR SPECIES	Pipevine Swallowtail.
IDENTIFICATION	This magnificent butterfly is common in northern Florida, less so southward. Above, black with extensive iridescent blue. It has no tails. Below there are **red-orange spots** both in a submarginal band and **at the base of the wings**. Pipevine Swallowtail has tails and lacks the spots at the wing base.
HABITAT	Rich moist woodlands are preferred but Red-spotted Purples are widely distributed and are sometimes found in suburban areas.
RANGE	Also, north to Massachusetts and South Dakota, west to Texas and southeast Arizona, and south into northern Mexico.
ABUNDANCE	2 broods. **W**: U–C, March–Oct., most common March–May, Aug.–Oct. **N**: U–C, March–Oct., especially March–May, Aug.–Oct. **C**: U–C, March–Oct., most common March–May, Aug.–Oct. **S**: RS, Aug.–Sept. **K**: X.
MAJOR FOODPLANT	Cherry (*Prunus*) and others.
COMMENTS	Often attracted to mud puddles, fermenting fruit, and animal feces. On rare occasions, this species is known to breed with the closely related Viceroy butterfly, producing odd color variations.

Viceroy *Limenitis archippus* Plates 22 & 25

SIZE	≤ Red-spotted Purple.
SIMILAR SPECIES	Monarch, Queen.
IDENTIFICATION	Fairly large and **uniformly orange**. In northern Florida ground color can be similar to Monarch's, while in much of Florida the ground color is a darker brown-orange—mimicking Queens. Distinguished from Monarchs and Queens by the black postmedian band on the HW. Viceroys can be readily separated from Monarchs and Queens in flight by their smaller size (although size overlaps with Queens) and less powerful wingbeats. They often glide on flat wings while Monarchs and Queens "sail" with their wings in a "V."
HABITAT	Open areas adjacent to watercourses or wet areas with willows.
RANGE	Also, north through much of Canada, west to Washington State, and south into northern Mexico.

ABUNDANCE	Probably 2 broods, perhaps 3 in the south. **W**: C, March–Nov., most common March–May, July–Oct. **N**: C, March–Nov., especially March–May, July–Oct. **C**: C, Feb.–Dec., most common March–May, July–Oct. **S**: C, all year, especially May–Oct. **K**: RS, May, Aug.
MAJOR FOODPLANT	Willows (*Salix*).
GARDEN TIPS	Coastal plain willow (*Salix caroliniana*), grows best in a moist/wet area.
COMMENTS	Well known as a mimic of the Monarch. For a long time it was thought that birds avoided eating palatable Viceroys because they confused them with distasteful Monarchs. Recent evidence suggest that, at least here in Florida, Viceroys are also distasteful to birds. Presumably, a greater number of similar-looking, unpalatable individuals in an area results in a faster learning curve for birds, sparing butterflies.

Dingy Purplewing *Eunica monima* Plate 22

SIZE	< Common Buckeye.
SIMILAR SPECIES	Florida Purplewing.
IDENTIFICATION	Above, a dull, iridescent purple. Unfortunately, it doesn't normally open its wings while landed—usually on leaves on trees. Below, a warm gray-brown tinged with mauve. Note the HW postmedian circular areas, the upper circular area containing 2 spots—the top one gray-white. Florida Purplewing is larger, has a falcate FW apex, has a FW black subapical spot that this species lacks, and usually lacks the gray-white HW spot.
HABITAT	Tropical hammocks.
RANGE	South Miami-Homestead area and the Keys. Also, the Greater Antilles and southern Texas south to northern South America.
ABUNDANCE	3 or more broods. **W**: X. **N**: X. **C**: X. **S**: LR, all year, most common Oct.–Dec. **K**: LR, March, May, July, Aug., Oct.–Dec.
LOCALITIES	Camp Owaissa Bauer and Castellow Hammock Preserve, both in Miami-Dade Co.
MAJOR FOODPLANT	Gumbo-limbo (*Bursera simaruba*).
GARDEN TIPS	Gumbo-limbo (*Bursera simaruba*).
COMMENTS	Dingy Purplewings fly mostly in the forest canopy, only rarely descending near the ground. In the 1970s through the 1980s this species was regularly found in extreme southern Florida but searches the past few years have failed to find any, possibly due to loss of habitat in the wake of Hurricane Andrew. Given to strong migratory movements in the tropics.

Florida Purplewing *Eunica tatila* **Plate 22**

SIZE = Common Buckeye.
SIMILAR SPECIES Dingy Purplewing.
IDENTIFICATION Iridescent purple above. Below, dark brown, with a falcate FW apex. Usually one can see a black FW subapical spot between 2 white spots. See Dingy Purplewing.
HABITAT Tropical hammocks.
RANGE South Miami-Homestead area and the Keys. Also, West Indies and southern Texas south to Argentina.
ABUNDANCE 3 or more broods. **W**: X. **N**: X. **C**: X. **S**: LR, all year. **K**: LR, all year, most common Jan., March–June, Aug.–Sept.
LOCALITIES Elliott Key, Biscayne NP; North Key Largo Hammocks State Botanical Site, Monroe Co.; John Pennekamp SP, Monroe Co.
MAJOR FOODPLANT Crabwood (*Ateramus lucida*).
COMMENTS It is difficult to see this species' bright iridescent purple upperside, because it usually flies within the shade of tropical hammocks, lands on tree trunks, and usually keeps its wings closed while landed.

Ruddy Daggerwing *Marpesia petreus* **Plate 23**

SIZE = Red-spotted Purple.
SIMILAR SPECIES Julia.
IDENTIFICATION A good-sized orange nymphalid of the tropics and subtropics. In flight it could be mistaken for a bright orange Julia (but of course it isn't potable). Seen well, the straight black lines across the wings and especially the characteristically-shaped wings and tails are unmistakable. Usually lands with its head facing down, except when on the ground.
HABITAT Tropical hammock edges and openings.
RANGE Also, some Caribbean islands and south Texas south through the American tropics.
ABUNDANCE 3 or more broods. **W**: X. **N**: X. **C**: RS, along coast north to Tampa and New Smyrna Beach, April–mid Dec. **S**: U–C, all year, most common March–July, Oct.–Nov. **K**: U, all year, especially May–July, Sept.–Oct.
LOCALITIES Fern Forest Nature Center, Broward Co.; Matheson Hammock, Miami-Dade Co.; Camp Owaissa Bauer, Miami-Dade Co.; Castellow Hammock Preserve, Miami-Dade Co.; Fakahatchee Strand State Preserve, Collier Co.; Biscayne NP, Miami-Dade Co.; North Key Largo State Botanical Site, Monroe Co.
MAJOR FOODPLANT Figs (*Ficus*).
GARDEN TIPS Short-leaf fig (*Ficus citrifolia*).

COMMENTS Territorial males will often come down from on high to investigate bright orange objects. Try throwing an orange into the air or wave an orange cloth.

Florida Leafwing *Anaea floridalis* Plate 23

SIZE ≤ Red-spotted Purple.
SIMILAR SPECIES Goatweed Leafwing.
IDENTIFICATION Bright red-orange above, mottled grayish below, these boldly marked leafwings rush about the pine scrub barrens then suddenly alight on a tree limb with their wings closed. Goatweed Leafwings are similar, browner below and more orange above, but the two species are not normally found together. Also, Florida Leafwings have slightly uneven wing margins.
HABITAT Pine rockland.
RANGE Extreme southern mainland Florida and Big Pine Key.
ABUNDANCE 3 or more broods. **W**: X. **N**: X. **C**: X. **S**: LR, all year, most common Aug.–Oct. **K**: LR–LU, all year, especially Jan., March–May, Sept.–Oct.
LOCALITIES Long Pine Key, Everglades NP; National Key Deer Refuge, Big Pine Key, Monroe Co.
MAJOR FOODPLANT Narrow-leaved croton (*Croton linearis*).
COMMENTS Leafwings do not normally visit flowers, but are attracted by rotting fruit and carrion. Hurricane Andrew may have eliminated Florida Leafwing from several areas on the mainland, and the species appears to be declining. Some consider the Florida Leafwing a subspecies of the Tropical Leafwing (*A. troglodyta*).

Goatweed Leafwing *Anaea andria* Plate 23

SIZE ≤ Red-spotted Purple.
IDENTIFICATION Larger than anglewings. Red-orange to orange-brown above (males brighter), with a short HW tail. Behavior, flight, and wing-shape are different from other orange butterflies in its range.
HABITAT Open woodlands such as sandhills and the edges of hammocks near rivers.
RANGE Also, north to Illinois and west to Nebraska and Texas.
ABUNDANCE 2 broods. **W**: LR–LU, Feb.–Nov., especially March and Oct. **N**: LR–LU, June–Sept. (summer form), Oct.–April (winter form), most common in March and Oct. **C**: R. **S**: RS. **K**: RS, Aug.
LOCALITIES Ralph E. Simmons SF, Nassau Co.; Suwannee River SP; Kanapaha Botanical Garden, Alachua Co.; San Felasco Hammock, Alachua Co.

MAJOR FOODPLANT | Silverleaf croton (*Croton argyranthemus*) and other crotons.
GARDEN TIPS | Silverleaf croton.
COMMENTS | The leaf-like underside makes the butterfly nearly invisible while at rest. Often flies as if swooping up and down on ocean waves. Overwintering individuals have more pointed FWs than summer individuals.

Hackberry Emperor *Asterocampa celtis* **Plate 20**

SIZE | = Common Buckeye. Females usually larger than males.
SIMILAR SPECIES | Tawny Emperor.
IDENTIFICATION | A nervous, rapidly flying nymphalid that often appears quite pale in flight as the sun flashes off the creamy gray-brown undersurface. Above, warm brown. Note the **white subapical FW spots** above and the **black FW marginal eye-spot** both above and below. Tawny Emperor is a warm orange-brown above and lacks the white subapical spots and the black FW eye-spot.
HABITAT | Woodland edges, residential areas. Closely tied to hackberry trees.
RANGE | Also, north to Massachusetts and west to Colorado and Arizona.
ABUNDANCE | 2 to 3 broods. **W**: LC–A, late March–early Nov., most common April–May, July–Sept. **N**: LC–A, late March–early Nov., most common April–May, July–Sept. Can be extremely abundant in a limited area around the foodplant. **C**: LU–C, March–late Nov. **S**: RS. **K**: X.
MAJOR FOODPLANT | Hackberries (*Celtis*).
GARDEN TIPS | Hackberries (*Celtis*).
COMMENTS | An infrequent flower visitor, Hackberry Emperors can, not surprisingly, most often be found flying around a hackberry tree. When not on hackberry trees they often alight on people in search of the salts in our perspiration. Fermenting fruit is almost as attractive as people. Hackberry Emperors are also fond of landing on bright objects and simply holding a piece of white paper in the sun can attract males from their normal perches. The larger females are less active and therefore seen less than males.

Tawny Emperor *Asterocampa clyton* **Plate 20**

SIZE | ≥ Common Buckeye. Females usually much larger than males.
SIMILAR SPECIES | Hackberry Emperor, Painted Lady.
IDENTIFICATION | Above, warm orange-brown with HW borders that can be either mainly orange or mainly black. Note the prominent series of eye-spots on the HW on both surfaces. Hackberry Emperor has

white spots above, is paler and grayer below, and has black eye-spots on the FW. Painted Lady is much paler below.

HABITAT Woodland edges, forested residential areas. Closely tied to hackberry trees but seems to disperse more than Hackberry Emperor.

RANGE Also, north to Massachusetts and west to Minnesota and Arizona.

ABUNDANCE 2 to 3 broods. **W**: LC, late March–early Oct., most common April–May, Aug.–Sept. **N**: LC, late March–early Oct., most common April–May, Aug.–Sept. **C**: LU, March–early Nov. **S**: LR, Feb.–mid Nov. **K**: X.

LOCALITIES Chekika unit of Everglades NP, Miami-Dade Co.

MAJOR FOODPLANT Hackberries (*Celtis*).

GARDEN TIPS Hackberries (*Celtis*).

COMMENTS One frequently sees both Tawny Emperors and Hackberry Emperors in the same vicinity—if you are a really proficient butterflier you find them both alighted on you at the same time! Geographically variable, some populations, including those in Florida ('Flora' Tawny Emperor), have previously been considered separate species.

Satyrs or Browns
(subfamily Satyrinae)

The satyrs are a group of brown, medium-sized butterflies with a characteristic bouncy flight. They tend to remain low and weave among the grasses or sedges that are their caterpillar foodplants.

Southern Pearly-eye *Enodia portlandia* **Plate 24**

SIZE ≥ Common Buckeye.

SIMILAR SPECIES Appalachian Brown.

IDENTIFICATION A large, dark, woodland satyr. Below, note the prominent HW submarginal eye-spots that are **surrounded as a group, by one continuous white line**. Appalachian Brown is much paler brown and has HW submarginal eye-spots that are individually surrounded by white circles.

HABITAT Rich bottomlands, moist hammocks, and flatwoods with canebrakes.

RANGE Also, north to southeastern Virginia, west to Missouri, and east Texas.

ABUNDANCE 3 or more broods. **W**: LU, late Feb.–mid June, mid Aug.–early Nov., especially April, Aug.–Sept. **C**: LU, late Feb.–mid June, mid Aug.–early Nov., most common April, Aug.–Sept. **S**: X. **K**: X. This species can be very common near patches of the host plant.

LOCALITIES Torreya SP, Liberty Co.; Ralph E. Simmons SP, Nassau Co.; Kelly Park, Orange Co.; Florida Caverns SP, Jackson Co.; Kanapaha Botanical Garden, Alachua Co.

MAJOR FOODPLANT Switch cane (*Arundinaria gigantea*).

GARDEN TIPS Switch cane (*Arundinaria gigantea*).

COMMENTS Southern Pearly-eyes can be very common near patches of their hostplant but have an erratic flight that is difficult to follow in the dappled sunlight of its forest home. Adults land on the leaves of the host and tree trunks and readily come to fermenting fruit and sap flows.

Appalachian Brown *Satyrodes appalachia* Plate 24

SIZE ≥ Common Buckeye.

SIMILAR SPECIES Southern Pearly-eye.

IDENTIFICATION Appalachian Browns are easily distinguished from Little Wood-Satyrs by their larger size and large HW eye-spots below. They can be distinguished from Southern Pearly-eyes by their paler more subdued coloration and below, by the presence of a white outer ring around each HW eye-spot.

HABITAT Wet, wooded situations such as swamps and shaded drainage ditches.

RANGE Also, South Carolina and northern Mississippi north to Massachusetts and Minnesota.

ABUNDANCE Probably 3 broods. **W**: LR, late March–late Oct., most common May–June, Sept.–Oct. **N**: LR, late March–late Oct., most common May–June, Sept.–Oct. **C**: LR, late March–early Nov. **S**: X. **K**: X.

LOCALITIES University of North Florida nature trails, Duval Co.; Caravelle WMA, Putnam Co.; Crystal Springs, Pasco Co.; Juniper Springs, Ocala NF; Ralph E. Simmons SP, Nassau Co.

MAJOR FOODPLANT Sedges (*Carex*) and beakrush (*Rhynchospora inundata*).

COMMENTS A rare and exciting find anywhere in Florida, the abundance of this species varies greatly from year to year.

Gemmed Satyr *Cyllopsis gemma* Plate 24

SIZE = Carolina Satyr.

SIMILAR SPECIES Carolina Satyr, Little/Viola's Wood-Satyr, Georgia Satyr.

IDENTIFICATION	On the HW below, "gemmed" with a **silver-gray HW patch** containing marginal eye-spots.
HABITAT	Moist grassy areas within woodlands and at the edges of swamps.
RANGE	Also, north to Virginia, west to Kansas, and south into northeastern Mexico.
ABUNDANCE	3 or more broods. **W**: LU, late March–early Nov., especially Aug.–Oct. **N**: LU, late March–early Nov., most common Aug.–Oct. **C**: R, late Feb.–early Nov. **S**: X. **K**: X.
LOCALITIES	Torreya SP, Liberty County; DeLeon Springs, SP, Volusia Co.; Crystal Springs, Pasco Co.
MAJOR FOODPLANT	Spikegrass (*Chasmanthium*) and probably other grasses.
COMMENTS	Can often be separated from the much more common Carolina Satyr in flight by its slightly larger size and paler appearance, but you'll need to wait for it to land to confirm its identity.

Carolina Satyr *Hermeuptychia sosybius* **Plate 24**

SIZE	11/16 inch.
SIMILAR SPECIES	Gemmed Satyr, Georgia Satyr, Little/Viola's Wood-Satyr.
IDENTIFICATION	A small satyr, common throughout Florida's woodlands. Much more at home **within** woodlands than is Little Wood-Satyr. Below, very similar to Little/Viola's Wood-Satyr but note the HW cell-end bar. FW lacks the lower large eye-spot of Little/Viola's Wood-Satyr. Above, uniform dark brown, lacking the eye-spots of Little/Viola's Wood-Satyr.
HABITAT	A wide variety of woodland situations, especially moist forests.
RANGE	Also, north to Virginia, west to Oklahoma, and south into Mexico.
ABUNDANCE	3 or more broods. **W**: A, late Feb.–late Nov., most common Feb.–April, Sept.–Nov. **N**: A, late Feb.–late Nov., most common Feb.–April, Sept.–Nov. **C**: A, early Feb.–Dec., especially Feb.–April, Sept.–Nov. **S**: A, all year, especially March–May, Sept.–Oct., Dec. **K**: RS, Nov.
MAJOR FOODPLANT	St. Augustine grass (*Stenotaphrum secundatum*) and other grasses.
COMMENTS	One of the most frequently seen butterflies along woodland trails.

Georgia Satyr *Neonympha areolata* **Plate 24**

SIZE	> Carolina Satyr.
IDENTIFICATION	On the HW below, note the orange-brown ring surrounding the elliptical, postmedian eye-spots.

HABITAT   Moist grassy clearings in flatwoods, wet prairies, and sometimes sandhills (in northern Florida).

RANGE   Also, north to southeastern Virginia (isolated population in New Jersey) and west to east Texas.

ABUNDANCE   2 or 3 broods. **W**: LR–U, mid April–Sept. **N**: LU, April–Oct., most common Aug.–Sept. **C**: LU–C, late March–early Nov. **S**: LU–C, all year, especially Jan.–March, May–July, Sept.–Oct. **K**: RS, Oct.

LOCALITIES   Blackwater River SF, Santa Rosa Co.; Apalachicola NF; Ralph E. Simmons SF, Nassau Co.; Tiger Bay SF, Volusia Co.; Myakka River SP, Manatee and Sarasota Cos.

MAJOR FOODPLANT   Probably sedges although grasses have also been reported.

COMMENTS   Although its flight is slow, this constantly bobbing satyr can be frustratingly difficult to see clearly.

Little Wood-Satyr *Megisto cymela* and Viola's Wood-Satyr *Megisto viola* **Plate 24**

SIZE   > Carolina Satyr.

SIMILAR SPECIES   Carolina Satyr.

IDENTIFICATION   Medium-brown butterflies that "bounce" along the tops of the grasses, shrubs, and just inside the canopy of small trees. Their characteristic flight, color, and size make them immediately recognizable on the wing. This is good because they rarely rest. When they do, note the two large eye-spots on each wing both above and below. The eye-spots tend to be larger southward. Carolina Satyrs lack eye-spots above and have a HW cell-end bar below that Little/Viola's wood-satyrs lack.

HABITAT   Woodlands including hammocks, edges of swamps, and densely shaded flatwoods.

RANGE   Also, north to southern Canada and west to the Dakotas and east Texas.

ABUNDANCE   1 Brood. **W**: C, late Feb.–mid June, especially late April. **N**: C, late Feb.–early May, most common in April. **C**: U, L, Feb.–April, especially late March–early April. **S**: X. **K**: X.

MAJOR FOODPLANT   Grasses.

COMMENTS   There is very little evidence supporting the idea that Viola's and Little Wood-Satyrs are separate species and good reason to believe that they are not. We list them separately to be consistent with the NABA checklist. In the Florida Panhandle one can find individual wood-satyrs that appear more like typical Little Wood-Satyrs than do some individuals farther south. Farther south, Viola's Wood-Satyr averages slightly larger and brighter than Little Wood-Satyr, with more prominent silver iridescence. Eye-rings tend to be a richer golden color than on Little Wood-Satyrs. The FW postmedian line is usually slightly more curved inwardly than on Little Wood-Satyr, but some Little Wood-Satyrs also have this trait.

Common Wood-Nymph *Cercyonis pegala* Plate 24

SIZE = Cloudless Sulphur.

IDENTIFICATION A large, very dark satyr of open brushy fields with distinctive yellow-orange postmedian FW patches.

HABITAT Brushy fields, prairies, woodland edges, etc.

RANGE Also, north to Nova Scotia and west to California.

ABUNDANCE 1 brood. **W**: LU–LC, late June–early Oct., especially Aug.–early Oct. **N**: LU–LC, late June–early Oct., most common July–Sept. **C**: LU, mid June–mid Oct., especially July–Sept. **S**: X. **K**: X.

LOCALITIES Blackwater River SF, Santa Rosa Co.; Caravelle WMA, Putnam Co.; Ralph E. Simmons SF, Nassau Co.; University of North Florida nature trails, Duval Co.

MAJOR FOODPLANT Grasses.

COMMENTS Females emerge slightly later than males and are longer lived, flying into autumn. Adults land on tree trunks or near the bases of shrubs. When disturbed, they fly into palmettos or shrubs to hide.

Monarchs or Milkweed Butterflies (subfamily Danainae)

Milkweed butterflies are found throughout the tropical world. Many species are distasteful to predators because of the accumulation of toxic chemicals derived from the caterpillar foodplants. They signal this distastefulness to potential predators by sporting bold coloration. For a thorough treatment of this group, see Ackery and Vane-Wright (1984).

Monarch *Danaus plexippus* Plate 25

SIZE 2 inches.

SIMILAR SPECIES Viceroy, Queen.

IDENTIFICATION Probably the best known butterfly of North America. A large orange butterfly with a powerful flight. Often sails with its wings held in a "V." The male has a black scent patch on a HW vein above. Viceroy is smaller and has a weaker flight on shallower wingbeats, often gliding on flat wings. Viceroys have a black postmedian line on the HW. See Queen.

HABITAT Open fields, roadsides, suburban areas. While migrating it can be anywhere.

RANGE Also, all of North America, south to South America. Now established on New Zealand, Australia, Canary Islands, India, etc.

ABUNDANCE 3 or more broods. **W**: C–A, all year, especially, April, July–Dec. **N**: C–A, all year, most common Jan., April, July–Dec. with the peak in Sept. **C**: U–C, all year, especially March, May–June, Oct.–Dec. **S**: U–C, all year, most common in March, May–June, Oct.–Dec. **K**: S, Jan., March, May, Sept.–Dec., especially Oct.–Dec.

MAJOR FOODPLANT Milkweeds (*Asclepias*) and strangler vine (*Morrena odorata*).

GARDEN FOODPLANT Orange [butterfly] milkweed (*Asclepias tuberosa*), tropical milkweed (*Asclepias curassavica*).

COMMENTS Huge numbers of Monarchs move south throughout the East in September-October. Millions of Monarchs from North America eventually overwinter in spectacular communal sites high in the fir-clad Mexican mountains. These enormous roosts are rapidly becoming a major tourist attraction, but face pressures from logging and other development activities that are jeopardizing this vast migratory phenomenon. In very early spring, the overwintering adults mate and begin to move north and lay eggs. Their offspring then continue moving north to repopulate eastern North America. Many of the Monarchs moving down the Atlantic Coast in the fall migrate through parts of Florida. Dense clusters of roosting Monarchs are sometimes seen in October along the Lower St. Johns River and especially at St. Marks NWR in the Panhandle. Many stay all winter along the barrier islands and coastal areas of north-central Florida and the Panhandle. Nonmigratory resident populations reproduce all year in central and southern Florida on tropical milkweed in pastures and gardens. Although it is clear from tagging data that the Monarchs from the center of the continent migrate to the central Mexican mountains, the final destination of most of the Atlantic Coast Monarchs is less certain. To date, very few Monarchs tagged in the northeastern United States have been recovered from the Mexican mountain sites, while two have been recovered in the Bahamas. It is possible that some percentage of the Atlantic Coast Monarchs overwinter either in the West Indies, or fly across the Gulf of Mexico and overwinter somewhere on the

Queen *Danaus gilippus* **Plate 25**

SIZE ≤ Monarch.

SIMILAR SPECIES Monarch, Viceroy.

IDENTIFICATION Queens are a **rich mahogany brown**, darker than Monarchs. This closely related species lacks the Monarch's black subapical band and has **white spots in the FW postmedian area** that are visible either from above or below. Viceroys are smaller, lack the white spots, and have a black HW postmedian line.

HABITAT General in open areas, brushy fields, roadsides, etc.

RANGE Also, north (along the coast) to North Carolina, west to southern California and south throughout tropical Americas.

ABUNDANCE 3 or more broods. **W:** LU, early April–early Nov., most common Sept.–Oct. **N:** LU, early March–early Nov., most common Sept.–Oct. **C:** U–C, Feb.–early Dec., especially Sept.–mid Nov. **S:** C, all year, especially March, Oct.–Dec. **K:** U–C, all year, most common March–May, Sept.–Dec.

MAJOR FOODPLANT Milkweed (*Asclepias*) and milkweed family vines (*Sarcostemma* and *Morrenia*).

GARDEN TIPS Tropical milkweed (*Asclepias curassavica*), white milkweed (*Asclepias tomentosa*), whitevine (*Sarcostemma clausum*).

COMMENTS Like other milkweed butterflies, male Queens possess "hair pencils."

Soldier *Danaus eresimus* **Plate 25**

SIZE ≤ Monarch.

SIMILAR SPECIES Queen, Monarch.

IDENTIFICATION Soldiers are mahogany brown, like Queens (but are brighter, on average), but **lack the white spots in the FW postmedian area**. Instead they either have two faint pale (usually yellowish) spots or no spots at all. Note the **blackened FW veins** (especially near the FW apex). Queens' veins are not blackened. Below, the HW postmedian area is paler, with the appearance of a watermark.

HABITAT Open areas and woodland edges. In central Florida, mostly in the vicinity of orange groves infested with strangler vine (*Morrenia*) where Queens are common.

RANGE Also, south Texas and south through tropical Americas.

ABUNDANCE 3 or more broods. **W:** X. **N:** X. **C:** LR, March–Dec., especially Aug.–Dec. **S:** LU–LC, all year, most common Jan.–Feb., April, June–Aug., Oct.–Nov. **K:** S, May, June, Nov.

LOCALITIES Fern Forest, Broward Co.; Fakahatchee Strand State Preserve, Collier Co.; Chekika unit of Everglades NP, Miami-Dade Co.

MAJOR FOODPLANT Milkweeds (*Asclepias*) and milkweed family vines (*Sarcostemma* and *Morrenia*).

GARDEN TIPS Whitevine (*Sarcostemma clausum*), tropical milkweed (*Asclepias curassavica*), and white milkweed (*Asclepias tomentosa*).

COMMENTS Apparently only established in south Florida since the 1970s, Soldiers move northward as the season progresses and establish ephemeral populations as far north as Orlando.

The Skippers
(family Hesperiidae)

Skippers, which derive their name from their characteristic rapid darting flight, can be the agony and the ecstasy of butterflying. The agony results from trying to identify individual species in the many difficult (some would say impossible) to identify groups. Ecstasy is the result of success. With roughly 3000 species worldwide, there is ample opportunity for pleasure. Skippers are generally distinguishable from the true butterflies by their relatively large bodies (compared to their wings), their relatively small, very angular wings, and by the presence of a thin extension (the apiculus) of the antennal club. There are three subfamilies of skippers in Florida. The spread-winged skippers are generally large (for skippers). When these skippers alight they generally hold their wings open flat—hence the name spread-winged skippers. Although they sometimes hold their wings closed or partially open, the FWs and the HWs are always moved in unison. In contrast, the grass-skippers either alight with their wings completely closed (often) or with the HWs more or less completely open but with the FWs only partially opened, forming a V or U. Giant-Skippers usually hold their wings closed when at rest, but when they do open them, they do so grass-skipper style.

Spread-winged Skippers
(subfamily Pyrginae)

These large-bodied skippers tend to be larger than grass-skippers and usually land with their wings spread flat.

Mangrove Skipper *Phocides pigmalion* **Plate 26**

SIZE	= Silver-spotted Skipper.
SIMILAR SPECIES	Hammock Skipper.
IDENTIFICATION	Very large and dark. Fresh individuals have an **overall cobalt blue iridescence**. Note the lighter **iridescent turquoise blue stripes on the HW and body**. Hammock Skipper can have much iridescent blue above, but is smaller, has bold white spots on the FW, and lacks the lighter iridescent blue on the HW and body.
HABITAT	Mangrove swamps and nearby areas, including tropical hammocks and flower gardens.
RANGE	Also, south through tropical Americas.
ABUNDANCE	3 or more broods. **W:** X. **N:** S. **C:** LU–LC, all year, most common Aug.–Nov. **S:** LU–LC, all year, most common March–April, Sept.–Dec. **K:** U–C, all year, especially Jan., March–May, Sept.–Dec.
LOCALITIES	Biscayne NP, Miami-Dade Co., "Ding" Darling NWR, Lee Co.; Lignumvitae Key State Botanical Site, Monroe Co.; Matheson Hammock, Miami-Dade Co.; Merritt Island NWR, Brevard and Volusia Cos.; North Key Largo Hammocks State Botanical Site, Monroe Co.; Collier-Seminole SP, Collier Co.; Jonathan Dickinson SP, Martin Co.
MAJOR FOODPLANT	Red mangrove (*Rhizophora mangle*).
COMMENTS	Florida's only representative of a sensational tropical group.

Zestos Skipper *Epargyreus zestos* **Plate 26**

SIZE	≤ Silver-spotted Skipper.
SIMILAR SPECIES	Silver-spotted Skipper.
IDENTIFICATION	Looks like a Silver-spotted Skipper without the silver spot (although there is a broad pale median stripe on the HW below), but Silver-spotted Skippers are not normally found on the Florida Keys (soon, neither will be Zestos Skippers—see Comments). Its flight is surprisingly slow compared to a Silver-spotted Skipper and it often lands upside-down under leaves. Fresh individuals have a violaceous sheen below.
HABITAT	Tropical hammocks and their margins.
RANGE	See comments. Also, the Bahamas and eastern Antilles.
ABUNDANCE	3 or more broods. **W:** X. **N:** X. **C:** X. **S:** H. **K:** R, all year, especially March–May, Sept.–Dec.
LOCALITIES	Stock Island Botanical Garden, Monroe Co.
MAJOR FOODPLANT	Milk-pea (*Galactia striata*).
COMMENTS	This species has greatly declined in recent years. This is not sur-

prising since there are almost no hardwood hammocks left on the keys and the few native areas remaining are usually treated with anti-mosquito sprays that kill butterflies. Formerly found on the mainland in south Florida, recently common on the Upper Keys, this species now barely hangs on on the lower Keys.

Silver-spotted Skipper *Epargyreus clarus* Plate 26

SIZE	1 2/16 inch.
SIMILAR SPECIES	Hoary Edge.
IDENTIFICATION	A large, powerful skipper that flashes its **silvered spot in the middle of the HW below** even as it flies. Above the brown-gold FW spots are in an open configuration. The somewhat smaller Hoary Edge has these spots enclosing some dark brown ground color. The Hoary Edge also has a large white patch below, but it is located on the HW margin.
HABITAT	Residential gardens and the margins of hammocks and swamps.
RANGE	Also, north to southern Canada and west to California.
ABUNDANCE	3 or more broods. **W**: LU–LC, late Feb.–mid Nov., most common March–April, July–Sept. **N**: LU–LC, late Feb.–mid Nov., most common March–April, July–Sept. **C**: LU, Feb.–early Dec. **S**: R, all year, especially March–April, Aug. **K**: X.
MAJOR FOODPLANT	Indigo (*Amorpha*), and many other legumes.
GARDEN TIPS	Butterfly-pea (*Clitoria mariana*) and indigo.
COMMENTS	Its large size and distinctive silver patch make this one of Florida's most distinctive skippers.

Hammock Skipper *Polygonus leo* Plate 26

SIZE	≤ Silver-spotted Skipper.
SIMILAR SPECIES	Mangrove Skipper.
IDENTIFICATION	Above, blackish-brown (with blue iridescent sheen) with 3 large white spots on the FW and 3 small subapical spots. Below, blue-tinged gray-brown with a prominent black spot near the base of the HW. Mangrove Skipper lacks the FW white spots, below it is blacker with iridescent blue streaks.
HABITAT	Tropical hammocks, hammock margins, and residential gardens.
RANGE	Also, south through tropical Americas.
ABUNDANCE	3 or more broods. **W**: X. **N**: X. **C**: X. **S**: R–U, all year, most common March–May, Sept.–Dec. **K**: U–C, all year, especially Sept.–Dec.
LOCALITIES	Biscayne NP, Miami-Dade Co., Matheson Hammock Park, Miami-Dade Co.; North Key Largo Hammocks State Botanical Site, Monroe Co.; Collier-Seminole SP, Collier Co.

MAJOR FOODPLANT	Jamaican dogwood (*Piscidia piscipula*) and pongam *(Pongamia pinnata)*.
GARDEN TIPS	Jamaican dogwood and pongam.
COMMENTS	Often pitches under a leaf and lands upside down with its wings closed.

Long-tailed Skipper *Urbanus proteus* Plate 27

SIZE	> Nórthern Cloudywing.
SIMILAR SPECIES	Dorantes Longtail.
IDENTIFICATION	Note the **long, broad "tails."** Above, note the striking blue-green iridescence. See Dorantes Longtail for discussion of separation below.
HABITAT	Open fields and woodland edges, especially brushy and disturbed situations, but migrating individuals may be found in almost any habitat.
RANGE	Also, north to New Jersey, west to southern Arizona and California, and south through tropical Americas.
ABUNDANCE	3 or more broods. **W:** A, all year, most common mid-Aug.–Nov. **N:** A, all year, most common mid-Aug.–Nov. **C:** A, all year, most common Aug.–Nov. **S:** A, all year, especially Jan.–May, Oct.–Dec. **K:** A, all year, most common March–May, Oct.–Dec.
MAJOR FOODPLANT	Many legume family vines including garden beans (*Phaseolus vulgaris*), butterfly-pea (*Clitoria mariana*), and climbing butterfly-pea (*Centrosema virginianum*).
GARDEN TIPS	Garden beans.
COMMENTS	Often a pest of bean farms, the brilliant adults are worth the inconvenience. Worn individuals that have the tails broken off are frequently confused with other skipper species. During the fall huge numbers of Long-tailed Skippers migrate southward into Florida from the north.

Dorantes Longtail *Urbanus dorantes* Plate 27

SIZE	= Northern Cloudywing.
SIMILAR SPECIES	Long-tailed Skipper.
IDENTIFICATION	Immediately identifiable as a longtail by its long tails (unless, of course, its tails are broken off). Above, brown with yellowish spots and no blue-green color. Long-tailed Skipper has iridescent blue-green above. Below, look at the dark brown FW submarginal band. Note how it is almost completely interrupted by a finger of the paler interior ground color pushing through from the inside. Long-tailed Skipper has this band solid through its entire length.

HABITAT	Woodland edges, brushy fields, and gardens.
RANGE	Also, west to southern California and south through tropical Americas.
ABUNDANCE	3 or more broods. **W**: R, immigrant Sept.–Nov. **N**: U–C, all year (but mainly immigrant), most common Sept.–Nov. **C**: A, all year, especially Oct.–Dec. **S**: A, all year, especially Oct.–Dec. **K**: U–C, all year, especially Feb.–April, Sept.–Nov.
MAJOR FOODPLANT	Beggarweeds (*Desmodium*) and other legumes.
GARDEN TIPS	Climbing butterfly-pea (*Centrosema*) and green beans.
COMMENTS	Unlike Long-tailed Skipper, this species rarely lands with its wings open. Northward movement usually occurs in the fall. Established in Florida only since the 1960s and possibly still spreading northward.

Golden-banded Skipper *Autochton cellus* Plate 27

SIZE	≥ Northern Cloudywing.
SIMILAR SPECIES	Hoary Edge.
IDENTIFICATION	A large, dark skipper with very broad, luminous yellow FW bands. FW band of Hoary Edge is a series of orange-brown spots. Below, the Golden-banded Skipper has no white patch.
HABITAT	Wooded ravines with a stream or other water.
RANGE	Panhandle and Gainesville area. Also, discontinuously north to Ohio, west to southeastern Arizona and south into northern Mexico.
ABUNDANCE	2 broods. **W**:LR, April–May, Aug.–Sept. **N**: LR, April–May, Aug.–Sept. **C**: X. **S**: X. **K**: X.
LOCALITIES	Devil's Millhopper State Geological Site, Alachua Co.; San Felasco Hammock State Preserve, Alachua Co.; Torreya SP, Liberty Co.; Florida Caverns SP, Jackson Co.
MAJOR FOODPLANT	Hog peanut (*Amphicarpa bracteata*).
COMMENTS	Males of this stunning skipper perch and defend territories in sunny clearings and along trails through hardwood forests.

Hoary Edge *Achalarus lyciades* Plate 26

SIZE	< Silver-spotted Skipper.
SIMILAR SPECIES	Silver-spotted Skipper.
IDENTIFICATION	A large dark skipper with a conspicuous white patch on the margin of the HW below. Silver-spotted Skipper has more angled wings and its silvered spot is in the middle of the HW below. Above, note the brown-gold spot-band enclosing dark brown ground color.
HABITAT	Sparse woodlands, sandhills and the margins of hammocks.

RANGE Also, north to Massachusetts and west to Missouri and east Texas.

ABUNDANCE 2 broods. **W**:R, April–late Sept., most common April–June, Aug.–Sept. **N**: R, late March–early Oct., especially April–May, Aug.–Sept. **C**: R, early March–early Oct., especially March–April. **S**: X. **K**: X.

LOCALITIES San Felasco Hammock State Preserve, Alachua Co.; Kanapaha Botanical Garden, Alachua Co.; Suwanee River State Park, Suwanee Co.

MAJOR FOODPLANT Butterfly-pea (*Clitoria mariana*) and beggarweeds (*Desmodium*).

COMMENTS More restricted to wooded habitats than the Silver-spotted Skipper and usually flies closer to the ground.

Southern Cloudywing *Thorybes bathyllus* **Plate 28**

SIZE = Northern Cloudywing.

SIMILAR SPECIES Northern Cloudywing, Confused Cloudywing.

IDENTIFICATION A large brown, spread-wing skipper with prominent white markings above and complex dark markings and frosting below. Often lands with its wings folded over its back. Separable from the duskywings by its uniform ground color above (duskywings are heavily mottled) and the bright white line behind the eye. Southern Cloudywings have more extensive and aligned spots than do Northern Cloudywings. Note especially the second spot from the FW margin. This spot is prominent and hourglassed shaped in Southern Cloudywings but is usually a small dot or absent in Northern Cloudywings. Look at the antennal clubs. Southern Cloudywings have a **white patch just where the antennal clubs bend**, Northern Cloudywings lack this white patch. Some Confused Cloudywings can have as extensive spotting as do Southern Cloudywings, but they also lack the white antennal club patch. Below, note the **white or pale gray "face"** of the Southern. Northern has a dark brown or dark gray "face."

HABITAT Sparse woodlands and adjacent dry fields with low brushy areas (for perching).

RANGE Also, north to Massachusetts and Wisconsin and west to east Texas.

ABUNDANCE Probably 2 broods. **W**: C, early March–mid Oct., most common March, Aug.–Sept. **N**: C, late Feb.–late Oct., especially March–April, late Sept.–mid Oct. **C**: U–C, mid-Feb.–Oct., especially March–April, Sept. **S**: R, Feb.–April, Sept. **K**: X.

MAJOR FOODPLANT Legumes, especially beggarweeds (*Desmodium*).

COMMENTS   Males often behave territorially, returning again and again to the same perch. While nectaring, they usually hold their wings partially open.

Northern Cloudywing *Thorybes pylades* **Plate 28**

SIZE   12/16 inch.

SIMILAR SPECIES   Southern Cloudywing, Confused Cloudywing.

IDENTIFICATION   A large skipper, evenly brown above with restricted white spots. See Southern and Confused Cloudywings for discussion of differences.

HABITAT   Sparse woodlands, including scrubs, sandhills, and flatwoods.

RANGE   Also, north to Canada and west to California.

ABUNDANCE   Probably 2 broods. **W**: LR–LU, March–Sept., especially March–April. **N**: U, mid March–Oct., especially March–April. **C**: LU–LC, March–Sept., especially March–April. **S**: LR, March–Sept. **K**: X.

MAJOR FOODPLANT   Legumes, especially beggarweeds (*Desmodium*).

COMMENTS   Behavior is similar to that of Southern Cloudywing, and all three species of cloudywings can be found together.

Confused Cloudywing *Thorybes confusis* **Plate 28**

SIZE   = Northern Cloudywing.

SIMILAR SPECIES   Northern Cloudywing, Southern Cloudywing.

IDENTIFICATION   Called Confused Cloudywing for good reason, the identification of this butterfly is extremely tricky, and many individuals cannot be identified in the field. Spot pattern above varies from usually very restricted (like Northern Cloudywing) to extensive (like Southern Cloudywing). "Face" (palps) tends to be grayish white, as in Southern. The genitalia are diagnostic but for most people this is difficult (actually impossible) to determine in the field (examination of genitalia, usually with a microscope, for species determinations is standard fare for lepidopterists). Although, as indicated above, **many individuals cannot be identified**, individuals strongly exhibiting the following combination of markings can probably be assigned to this species. (*1*) Above with very reduced white markings. In the grouping of the lower three white spots, the central mark (if present at all) is a very thin, pale white line aligned with the spot adjacent to the leading margin (Southern Cloudywing has this spot much thicker and more prominent). (*2*) Face (palps) white (Northern Cloudywing has dark gray or brown palps). (*3*) Antennal clubs with no white at their bend (Southern Cloudywing has a white patch here). (4) White eye-line, continuous over eye (except for very narrow black interruption; Northern Cloudywing usually has less white, and when present, has very wide interruption between white behind and in front of eye).

HABITAT   Sparse, dry woodland, such as scrubs, sandhills, and flatwoods.

RANGE   Also, north to Virginia, west to Kansas and east Texas.

ABUNDANCE   Probably 2 broods. **W**: LU–LC, late Feb.–Oct., most common March–April. **N**: LU–LC, late Feb.–Oct., most common March–April. **C**: LU–LC, Feb.–Oct., especially March–April. **S**: S, Sept. **K**: X.

MAJOR FOODPLANT   Legumes, especially beggarweeds (*Desmodium*).

COMMENTS   While Southern and/or Northern Cloudywings often occur with Confused Cloudywings, this species seems to be more habitat restricted, favoring even drier situations than those species.

Hayhurst's Scallopwing *Staphylus hayhurstii* Plate 31

SIZE   = Tropical Checkered-Skipper.

SIMILAR SPECIES   Common Sootywing.

IDENTIFICATION   A small, very dark spread-winged skipper with even **darker bands forming concentric semicircles on the HW above.** Above, **variably strewn with tiny pale silver or gold flecks.** Also, note the **scalloped HW margin.** Common Sootywing lacks the gray or gold flecks and scalloped HW, has bright white spots above and on the head, and is more uniformly black.

HABITAT   Margins of moist hammocks.

RANGE   Also, north to New Jersey, west to Nebraska and east Texas.

ABUNDANCE   2 or 3 broods. **W**: LR, late March–Oct., most common early Sept. **N**: LR–LU, mid March–early Oct., most common late Aug.–Sept. **C**: LR–LU, March–Oct., especially Sept. **S**: LR, all year, especially March–May, July–Sept. **K**: R, perhaps extirpated, May, Aug.–Sept., Nov.–Dec.

MAJOR FOODPLANT   Bloodleaf (*Iresine diffusa*).

COMMENTS   The most northern member of the large and easily recognizable (due to the scalloped HW and metallic flecking) scallopwing genus. It frequents the dappled shade along trails and the edges of hardwood forests and almost always lands with its wings spread flat.

Duskywings
(genera *Ephyriades* and *Erynnis*)

. . . and rising up like a dark cloud—the duskywings spread across the land, sowing confusion and dissension among butterfliers, the instrument of the Erinnyes revenge.
—The Rites of an Ancient Aurelian. Anonymous. Unpublished.

The duskywings constitute one of our most difficult identification problems. Many species are so similar that it is common to find misidentified museum specimens. Thus the astute observer will often say, "That's a duskywing."

Florida Duskywing *Ephyriades brunneus* **Plate 29**

SIZE	= Northern Cloudywing.
SIMILAR SPECIES	Horace's and Zarucco duskywings.
IDENTIFICATION	Males and females look different, but on both above, note the **semicircle of white spots** on the apical portion of the FW. Males are dark brown with a broad paler brown margin on the HW. Females are a paler brown with a violaceous sheen over the FW. Other duskywings lack the semi-circle of white spots.
HABITAT	Pine rockland.
RANGE	Southern Miami-Dade Co. and the Keys. Also the West Indies, including Bahamas and Cuba.
ABUNDANCE	3 or more broods. **W**: X. **N**: X. **C**: X. **S**: R, all year, most common March–May. **K**: U, all year, especially March–May. Formerly abundant on Big Pine Key, now becoming more scarce.
LOCALITIES	National Key Deer Refuge, Big Pine Key, Monroe Co.; Long Pine Key, Everglades NP.
MAJOR FOODPLANT	Locustberry (*Byrsonima lucida*; Malpighiaceae).
COMMENTS	Although this tropical skipper closely resembles and behaves like other duskywing species, the immature stages differ from the temperate duskywings.

Sleepy Duskywing *Erynnis brizo* **Plate 30**

SIZE	< Northern Cloudywing.
IDENTIFICATION	Medium-sized, this is Florida's only duskywing without white spots above. Also note the broad, chain-like postmedian band on the FW above.
HABITAT	Open woodlands. Scrubs, sandhills, and scrubby flatwoods.
RANGE	Also, north to Massachusetts and Minnesota, west to California.
ABUNDANCE	1 brood. **W**: LR–LU, March–late April, most common in

mid–late March. **N**: LU–LC, late Feb.–early April, especially mid–late March **C**: LR–LU, late Jan.–March, most common mid March. **S**: LR, late Jan.–March. **K**: X.

LOCALITIES   Appalchicola NF, Ocala NF, Marion Co.

MAJOR FOODPLANT   Scrub oaks (*Quercus*).

COMMENTS   Sleepy Duskywings got their name not because of their flight characteristics, but because they lack eye-spots, thus their eyes are closed and they are "sleepy." The typical eastern race occurs in the Panhandle eastward to about Tallahassee. Peninsular Florida is inhabited by an endemic, much darker, form.

Juvenal's Duskywing *Erynnis juvenalis* **Plate 29**

SIZE   = Northern Cloudywing.

SIMILAR SPECIES   Horace's Duskywing.

IDENTIFICATION   Larger size and extensive white spots above (especially the one in the FW cell) separate this species from all Florida's other duskywings but the very similar Horace's. Below, Horace's usually lacks the two pale subapical spots on the HW that Juvenal's **almost** always has. Horace's is more sexually dimorphic than is Juvenal's. Horace's males are less mottled, more uniform, dark brown than Juvenal's males (which usually have much gray overscaling that Horace's lacks), while Horace's females are more boldly mottled than Juvenal's females.

HABITAT   Open oak woodlands and adjacent areas.

RANGE   Also, north to southern Canada, west to Manitoba and east Texas (with scattered populations farther west).

ABUNDANCE   1 brood. **W**: LC, late Feb.–mid April, most common in March. **N**: LC, late Feb.–mid April, most common in March. **C**: LC, late Jan.–early April, especially late Feb.–mid March. **S**: LR, Jan.–mid March. **K**: X.

MAJOR FOODPLANT   Oaks (*Quercus*).

COMMENTS   Males are territorial and quite aggressive. They will "police a beat," chasing even large moving objects such as a person, then return to the same perch.

Horace's Duskywing *Erynnis horatius* **Plate 29**

SIZE   = Northern Cloudywing.

SIMILAR SPECIES   Juvenal's Duskywing, Zarucco Duskywing.

IDENTIFICATION   A large, strong-flying duskywing that is very common and widespread. Extensive strong white spots above and size distinguish it from all but Juvenal's and Zarucco duskywings. Very similar to Juvenal's (see it for distinction) and most easily distinguished from that species in the summer when Juvenal's doesn't fly. Male Horace's are easily confused with Zarucco Duskywing—see below.

HABITAT   Oak woodlands.

RANGE   Also, north to Massachusetts, west to Iowa and central Texas; also in Colorado and New Mexico.

ABUNDANCE   3 or more broods. **W**:C–A, Feb.–late Oct., especially March–April, Aug.–Sept. **N**:C–A, late Jan.–early Nov., most common March–April, Aug.–Sept. **C**: C–A, all year, especially Feb.–March, Sept.–Oct. **S**: C–A, all year, especially Feb.–March, Sept.–Oct. **K**: X.

MAJOR FOODPLANT   Oaks (*Quercus*).

COMMENTS   This is one of the most common skippers in Florida. A number of duskywings are named for Roman poets, as is this species.

Mottled Duskywing *Erynnis martialis* **Plate 30**

SIZE   ≤ Northern Cloudywing.

SIMILAR SPECIES   Wild Indigo Duskywing.

IDENTIFICATION   Not normally seen in Florida. A brighter, more mottled skipper than other duskywings, especially on the HW above. Usually has gray-white apical markings on the FW above that Wild Indigo Duskywing lacks. **Note the narrow and relatively sharply delineated HW postmedian dark band**. Also, multiple gray bands, which other duskywings lack, are usually visible on the abdomen. Fresh individuals have a strong purplish sheen.

HABITAT   Sandhills.

RANGE   Also, north to New York, west to Iowa and east Texas; also in central Colorado.

ABUNDANCE   2 broods. **W**: S, very R, or extirpated, probably March–April and July if present. **N**: S or extirpated. **C**: S or extirpated. **S**: X. **K**: X.

MAJOR FOODPLANT   New Jersey tea (*Ceanothus americanus*).

COMMENTS   This species has declined alarmingly throughout much of its range in eastern North America. Very little is known about this species in Florida. During the past 40 years it has been reported from Escambia, Liberty, and Leon counties. There are also very old records from Volusia County that are questionable. Because of confusion with other duskywings, most literature reports cannot be trusted.

Zarucco Duskywing *Erynnis zarucco* **Plate 30**

SIZE   = Northern Cloudywing.

SIMILAR SPECIES   Wild Indigo Duskywing, Horace's Duskywing.

IDENTIFICATION Note the **pale brown patch** at the end of the FW cell and the **absence of gray overscaling** anywhere. Males are dark and are most similar to male Horace's Duskywings. Note the gray neck on Zarucco males and the absence (or small amount) of white behind the eyes. Horace's males have white behind the eyes and lack the uniform gray neck. Above, Zaruccos usually have the **FW cell (almost) evenly black** and a **cell-spot is usually absent or faint.** See Wild Indigo Duskywing for separation from that species.

HABITAT Flatwoods, scrubs, sandhills, powerline cuts, etc.

RANGE Also, north to southeastern Virginia, west to Arkansas and Louisiana; also in Cuba and Hispaniola.

ABUNDANCE 3 or more broods. **W**: C, Feb.–Oct., especially March–April, Aug.–Sept. **N**: C, late Jan.–late Oct., most common March, July–Sept. **C**: C, late Jan.–late Oct., most common March, Aug.–Oct. **S**: U, late Jan.–late Oct., especially Feb.–early April, Aug.–Sept. **K**: R–U, all year, especially Feb.–May, Sept.–Dec.

MAJOR FOODPLANT Various legumes, including bladderpods (*Sesbania*) and milkpeas (*Galactia*).

COMMENTS Spring forms, which are small and dark, are especially likely to be mistaken for the much rarer Wild Indigo Duskywing. The population on the lower Florida Keys has paler, sometimes white, HW fringes and so resembles Funereal Duskywing.

Wild Indigo Duskywing *Erynnis baptisiae* Plate 30

SIZE ≤ Northern Cloudywing.

SIMILAR SPECIES Horace's Duskywing, Zarucco Duskywing, Mottled Duskywing.

IDENTIFICATION This medium-sized, very variable duskywing, usually with three or four small white spots just past the FW "wrist" above, is rarely seen in Florida. The basal one-half of the FWs is usually very dark and appears "oily." Females are more mottled with more contrast than males. Large, well-marked females can be mistaken for Horace's Duskywing females. Note the small pale spots on the HW margin below. Many females very closely resemble some female Zarucco Duskywings and many individuals may not be separable. Above, Wild Indigo females usually have a faint, pale, straight, and thin HW cell-end bar which Zaruccos either lack or have less defined. Below, Zaruccos are more evenly dark than are Wild Indigos. Wild Indigos average slightly smaller than Zaruccos and tend to have less angled wings.

HABITAT Sparse woodlands and open sites.

RANGE	Also, north to Massachusetts, west to Minnesota and east Texas.
ABUNDANCE	2 or 3 broods. **W**: R, probably early March–early Oct. **N**: R, probably early March–early Oct. **C**: X. **S**: X. **K**: X.
MAJOR FOODPLANT	Wild indigo (*Baptisia*).
COMMENTS	Reported from Liberty, Leon, Jefferson, Hamilton, and Duval counties, this species is easily confused with Zarucco Duskywing, especially in the spring when Zarucco Duskywings are smaller and darker than later in the year.

Common Checkered-Skipper *Pyrgus communis*
Plate 31

SIZE	= Tropical Checkered-Skipper.
SIMILAR SPECIES	Tropical Checkered-Skipper.
IDENTIFICATION	Easily recognized as a checkered-skipper by its black and white checks. To distinguish from Tropical Checkered-Skipper above, look at the FW apex. Tropical has the **apical white spot** of the marginal spot-band present; Common almost always lacks this spot. Look at the FW white cell-end bar. Just beyond it, between the cell-end bar and the median spot-band of white spots, Tropical has another prominent white spot. Common has only a very small white spot here, or lacks this spot entirely. Look at the HW marginal row of white spots. In Tropicals, these spots are smaller than the submarginal white spots, but are not minute. In Commons, they are generally minute. Below, Commons are more clear-cut white and brown than Tropicals, which are tanner and more smudged, and Commons lack a **brown spot in the middle of the HW costa** that Tropicals have.
HABITAT	A wide variety of open situations, usually disturbed.
RANGE	Also, north to southern Canada, west to Washington State, and through Mexico to Argentina.
ABUNDANCE	3 or more broods. **W**: LC, March–early Nov., especially April, Sept. **N**: LU–LC, late Feb.–Nov., most common March–April, Aug.–Sept. **C**: LR–LU, Feb.–Nov., especially March–April, Aug.–Sept. **S**: S, April, July. **K**: X.
MAJOR FOODPLANT	Mallow family (*Malvaceae*), especially broomweed (*Sida acuta*), and Indian hemp (*Sida rhombifolia*).
GARDEN TIPS	Hollyhocks and *Sida*.
COMMENTS	Both checkered-skippers are found throughout much of Florida. In west and north Florida this species is more common, but from central Florida south, Tropicals predominate.

Tropical Checkered-Skipper *Pyrgus oileus* Plate 31

SIZE 9/16 inch.

SIMILAR SPECIES Common Checkered-Skipper.

IDENTIFICATION The extensive white spots on the black background coupled with the blue-tinged hair create the effect of a blue-gray blur as this little skipper whirs by you. Their black and white checks make checkered-skippers distinctive. See Common Checkered-Skipper to distinguish from that species.

HABITAT Mainly disturbed, open situations and the edges of hammocks (more closely associated with woodland edges than Common Checkered-Skipper).

RANGE Also, the entire Gulf Coast and south through the West Indies, Mexico, and tropical Americas.

ABUNDANCE 3 or more broods. **W**: LR–LU, Aug.–Oct. **N**: LU, late March–early Dec., most common Aug.–Oct. **C**: C, all year, especially March–July, Oct.–Dec. **S**: C, all year, especially March–July, Oct.–Dec. **K**: C, all year, especially March–June.

MAJOR FOODPLANT Mallow family (*Malvaceae*), especially broomweed (*Sida acuta*) and Indian hemp (*Sida rhombifolia*).

GARDEN TIPS Broomweed and Indian hemp.

COMMENTS As if distinguishing Tropical and Common checkered-skippers was not difficult enough, males patrolling for females make infrequent stops.

Common Sootywing *Pholisora catullus* Plate 31

SIZE = Tropical Checkered-Skipper.

SIMILAR SPECIES Hayhurst's Scallopwing.

IDENTIFICATION A very small, black spread-winged skipper with a variable number (but usually many) of small, bright **white dots on the head** and wings. Other black skippers lack the white dots on the head.

HABITAT Disturbed open areas, including pastures, edges of cultivated fields, and weedy roadsides.

RANGE Also, north to Massachusetts and North Dakota, west to Washington State, and south into Mexico.

ABUNDANCE 3 broods. **W**: LR, March–Sept., especially Aug.–Sept. **N**: LR, probably late Feb.–early Oct., most common Aug.–Sept. **C**: LR, probably late Feb.–early Oct., especially Aug.–Sept. **S**: X. **K**: X.

MAJOR FOODPLANT Pigweeds (*Amaranthus*) and lambsquarters (*Chenopodium album*).

COMMENTS Infrequently reported from Florida.

Grass-Skippers
(subfamily Hesperiinae)

Grass-skippers are generally smaller than the spread-wing skippers and their flight is harder to follow. They usually fly just over the top of low vegetation. In many species the males have specialized scent patches or stigmas on the FWs. With a color spectrum that ranges mainly from brown to pale orange, many of these are the LBJs (little brown jobs) of the butterfly world. Many beginning butterfliers (and even some experienced butterfliers) avoid this group entirely. While we can't fault this strategy in pain and frustration avoidance, careful study of this large and very interesting group is rewarded by some of the greatest pleasures of butterflying. In addition, because they are understudied, this is the area in which the observations of an amateur can most easily be of importance.

Swarthy Skipper *Nastra lherminier* Plate 32

SIZE	8/16 inch.
SIMILAR SPECIES	Tawny-edged Skipper.
IDENTIFICATION	A very small **dark yellowish-brown** skipper with **slightly paler veining below**. Small worn Tawny-edged Skippers can look very dark below but they usually have pale subapical spots on the FW and lack the pale veining. Above, Swarthy Skippers are plain dark brown while Tawny-edged Skippers have extensive markings. In south Florida see Neamathla Skipper.
HABITAT	Sparsely wooded to open areas with low vegetation and bluestem grasses, such as grassy fields, powerline cuts, roadsides, savannas, and sandhills.
RANGE	Also, north to New York and west to Missouri and east Texas.
ABUNDANCE	3 or more broods. **W**: C, March–Oct., most common Aug.–Sept. **N**: C, March–Oct., most common Aug.–Sept. **C**: C, Feb.–Nov., especially March–April, Sept.–Oct. **S**: U, all year, especially March–April, Sept.–Nov. **K**: X.
MAJOR FOODPLANT	Bluestem grasses (*Andropogon*).
COMMENTS	One of Florida's plainest butterflies—enjoy the intricate tracing of the veins in pale yellow on fresh individuals.

Neamathla Skipper *Nastra neamathla* Plate 32

SIZE	= Swarthy Skipper.
SIMILAR SPECIES	Swarthy Skipper, Eufala Skipper.
IDENTIFICATION	Very similar to the more common and widespread Swarthy

Skipper. Below, Neamathla Skippers are a duller brown **without**
the paler yellow veining. Above, this species generally has
two pale spots in the median FW and especially **two subapical**
FW spots that Swarthy Skippers almost always lack.

HABITAT Low, grassy fields, including disturbed areas.

RANGE Also, east Texas.

ABUNDANCE 3 or more broods. **W:** LR, March–Nov. **N:** LU, March–Oct., espe-
cially Aug.–Sept. **C:** U–C, Feb.–Nov., most common Aug.–Sept. **S:**
LU, all year, especially March–April, Sept.–Oct. **K:** L R,
Sept.–Oct.

MAJOR FOODPLANT Bluestem grasses (*Andropogon*).

COMMENTS Like most skippers, most often seen at flowers, such as the ubiquitous Spanish needles, thistles, and blazing-stars.

Three-spotted Skipper *Cymaenes tripunctus* Plate 32

SIZE = Whirlabout.

SIMILAR SPECIES Eufala Skipper, Obscure Skipper.

IDENTIFICATION This species does have three spots near the FW apex, but so do
many others! Note the **long antennas,** about 1/2 the length of
the FW (but because the antennas are held out at an angle, their
length will seem shorter when viewed from the side—and you
thought that 10th grade geometry wouldn't play a big part in
your life!). Above, often with a **bright tawny base of the FW**
costa. Note the **three white subapical spots that are sepa-**
rate and curve outward. Below, yellowish-brown with faint
and variable postmedian pale spot-band that is usually more distinct than on Eufala Skipper. Eufala Skipper is generally grayer
and paler below, without a bright tawny base of the FW costa
above, with FW subapical white spots that are in a straight line
and almost touching, and with shorter antennas (about 1/3 the
length of the FW). Obscure Skipper has yellower spots above,
panaquin body stripe below.

HABITAT Grassy disturbed woodlands and adjacent areas.

RANGE Also, the West Indies.

ABUNDANCE 3 or more broods. **W:** X. **N:** X. **C:** S. **S:** LC, all year, especially
April–July, Oct.–Dec. **K:** LU, all year, most common
Feb.–March, July–Oct.

LOCALITIES Hugh Taylor Birch SP, Broward Co.; Bauer Park, Miami-Dade
Co.; Stock Island Botanic Garden, Monroe Co.

MAJOR FOODPLANT Grasses.

COMMENTS If you are confused by this skipper, you are in good company.
Close to 1/2 of the south Florida specimens of this species and

Eufala Skipper in a major museum were misidentified, mainly with Three-spotted Skippers being labeled as Eufala Skippers. But the box of Three-spotted Skippers also contained Eufala Skippers and a misidentified Obscure Skipper.

Clouded Skipper *Lerema accius* **Plate 37**

SIZE ≥ Sachem.

SIMILAR SPECIES Zabulon Skipper (female), Dusted Skipper, Dun Skipper (above), Twin-spot Skipper (above).

IDENTIFICATION A very dark, fair-sized skipper. When fresh there is much frosting below. The HW frosting (or, when worn, paler areas) at the margin and at the lower middle of the wing, sets off a dark vertical band that extends from the center of the HW trailing margin. Above, both sexes have **three white subapical FW spots that usually curve outwardly.** Females also have a **smaller, ovate cell spot.** Female Zabulon Skipper has a white apex of the HW below and much more extensive spotting above. Dusted Skipper has white "eye-brows." Above, Dun Skippers are similar but don't have three white FW subapical spots or the ovate cell spot. Twin-spot Skippers do have three white FW subapical spots, but they are in a line, and they lack the ovate cell spot.

HABITAT Can be found in almost any open habitat, including open woodland, but prefers moist grassy areas in or near woods.

RANGE Also, north to Maryland, west to southeastern Arizona, and south to northern South America.

ABUNDANCE 3 or more broods. **W**: U–C, Feb.–Nov., most common late Aug.–early Oct. **N**: C, Feb.–Nov., most common late Aug.–early Oct. **C**: C, all year, especially March–May, Aug.–Sept. **S**: C, all year, most common March–April, July–Oct. **K**: U, all year, especially March–April, Aug.–Sept.

MAJOR FOODPLANT Grasses, especially panic grasses (*Panicum*) and sugarcane (*Saccharum officinarum*).

COMMENTS One of the earliest rising skippers, Clouded Skippers will be seen perching and courting early in the morning before their relatives have woken. Crawling deep into morning glory flowers to reach the nectar, they make an amusing sight. Large numbers often appear in late summer and fall in north Florida.

Least Skipper *Ancyloxypha numitor* **Plate 32**

SIZE ≤ Swarthy Skipper.

SIMILAR SPECIES Southern Skipperling.

IDENTIFICATION   A very small, bright orange skipper **weakly weaving through the grass** is sure to be this species. Contrasting black wings above (in almost all populations) can be detected in flight. Below, Least Skippers are bright orange, with **rounded wings**. Southern Skipperlings fly with much more rapid wing-beats, are even smaller, have little black above, have angular wings, and below have a white stripe.

HABITAT   Open, wet areas, including grassy ditches and the margins of ponds and lakes.

RANGE   Also, north to Canada, west to North Dakota and central Texas.

ABUNDANCE   3 or more broods. **W**: LC, March–Oct., most common April, late Aug.–early Oct. **N**: LC, March–Oct., most common April, late Aug.–early Oct. **C**: LC, mid Feb.–Nov., especially March–April, Aug.–Sept. **S**: LC, all year, especially March–April, Sept.–Oct. **K**: X.

MAJOR FOODPLANT   Aquatic grasses such as southern cutgrass (*Leersia hexandra*) and southern wild rice (*Zizaniopsis miliacea*).

COMMENTS   Pickerelweed is a favorite flower.

Southern Skipperling *Copaeodes minimus* Plate 32

SIZE   < Swarthy Skipper.

SIMILAR SPECIES   Least Skipper.

IDENTIFICATION   A tiny, bright orange skipper with very angular wings. Bright orange with a **narrow white ray on the HW below**. Least Skipper is larger, with more rounded wings, much black above, and without the white ray below.

HABITAT   A wide variety of disturbed, open grassy habitats, but usually not in very wet situations.

RANGE   Also, north to North Carolina, west to Texas, and south to Costa Rica.

ABUNDANCE   3 or more broods. **W**: U, Feb.–Nov., most common Aug.–Sept. **N**: U–C, Feb.–Nov., most common Aug.–Sept. **C**: C, March–Dec., especially Aug.–Sept. **S**: C, all year, especially March–April. **K**: LR, May–Nov.

MAJOR FOODPLANT   Bermuda grass (*Cynodon dactylon*) and other weedy grasses.

COMMENTS   Florida's smallest skipper makes up for its lack of size with its snazzy good looks.

Fiery Skipper *Hylephila phyleus* Plate 33

SIZE   ≤ Sachem.

SIMILAR SPECIES   Whirlabout.

IDENTIFICATION   This common species has the "measles"—many small black spots on the HW below—giving it a fever and making it "fiery." Males are bright orange, with spots varying from faint dull brown to sharp black. Whirlabouts have fewer, larger brown to black blotches. Note the **very wavy black borders on the FW and HW above.** Whirlabout has HW border smooth. Female Fiery Skippers are similar to males but the ground color is dull yellow-brown with a greenish tinge. Above, they are brown with yellow spots. Note the **"arrow" on the HW above.**

HABITAT Lawns and other low open grassy areas such as dry fields, roadsides, and sparse woods.

RANGE Also, north to New Jersey, west to California, and south through Mexico and the West Indies to Argentina.

ABUNDANCE 3 or more broods. **W:** A, late Feb.–Nov., most common March–May, July–Oct. **N:** A, late Feb.–Nov., most common March–May, July–Oct. **C:** A, all year, especially March, June, Aug.–Oct. **S:** A, all year, especially March, June, Aug.–Oct. **K:** A, all year, especially March–May, Sept.–Oct.

MAJOR FOODPLANT Bermuda grass (*Cynodon dactylon*).

COMMENTS Along with Whirlabout and Sachem, one of the three "wizards"—active, orange skippers that are widespread and common throughout the South, and often occur together.

Dotted Skipper *Hesperia attalus* **Plate 34**

SIZE ≥ Sachem.

SIMILAR SPECIES Crossline Skipper, female Sachem.

IDENTIFICATION Large. Below, quite variable, from rich yellowish-brown with well-separated **bold white spots forming a postmedian chevron** on the HW to dull pale brownish-yellow with weak pale spots. Boldly marked individuals are unmistakable but individuals with weak spots could be confused with Crossline Skippers. Note the presence of **two subapical FW spots** (characteristic of hesperia skippers) that Crossline Skipper lacks. Female Sachems below have a more pronounced postmedian spot-band with outwardly concave spots.

HABITAT Dry, grassy woodlands including sandhills and scrubby flatwoods.

RANGE Also, discontinuously north to New Jersey, west to Texas.

ABUNDANCE 2 or 3 broods. **W:** LR, March–May, July–Oct., most common early April, Sept.–early Oct. **N:** LU, March–May, July–Nov., most common early April, Sept.–Oct. **C:** LU, early March–May,

July–early Nov., most common mid March–early April, Sept.–Oct. **S**: R, March–April, Sept.–Oct. **K**: X.

LOCALITIES One-quarter mile west of Lake Delancy Campground, Ocala NF; Withlacoochee SF, Citrus Co.; Jonathan Dickinson SP, Martin Co.
MAJOR FOODPLANT Grasses.
COMMENTS Usually quite wary and difficult to approach.

Meske's Skipper *Hesperia meskei* **Plate 36**
SIZE = Whirlabout.
SIMILAR SPECIES Dotted Skipper, Delaware Skipper, Arogos Skipper.
IDENTIFICATION Yellow-orange to rusty-orange below, often with some sooty overscaling. HW usually with a postmedian spot-band, although this varies from quite prominent and distinct spots to a faint indistinct band. Female above has an unbroken postmedian spot-band. Dotted Skippers are larger and much browner. Below, Delaware and Arogos Skippers lack any HW postmedian band or FW spots. They look very different above.
HABITAT Open dry, grassy flatwoods, pine rockland, sandhills, and adjacent areas.
RANGE Also, discontinuously north to North Carolina and west to east Texas.
ABUNDANCE 2 broods (probably 3 in extreme southern Florida). **W**: LR, May, Sept.–Nov., most common early Oct. **N**: LR, May, Sept.–Nov., most common early Oct. **C**: LR, May, late Sept.–early Oct. **S**: LR, mainly May–June, Oct. in Martin Co.; previously LR all year in southern Miami-Dade, now possibly extirpated. **K**: LR, all year, especially March–May, Dec.
LOCALITIES Suwannee River SP, Suwannee Co.; One-quarter mile west of Lake Delancy Campground, Ocala NF, Marion Co.; Withlacoochee SF, Citrus Co.; Jonathan Dickinson SP, Martin Co.
MAJOR FOODPLANT Grasses.
COMMENTS A wary and elusive skipper, sometimes seen on prickly pear blossoms (*Opuntia humifusa*). The Miami-Dade Co. and Big Pine Key's populations are somewhat duskier below than more northern populations and are now extremely scarce.

Baracoa Skipper *Polites baracoa* **Plate 34**
SIZE = Swarthy Skipper.
SIMILAR SPECIES Tawny-edged Skipper.
IDENTIFICATION A small, dark polites skipper. HW below usually with a chunky pale postmedian band. On the male above, note the short, nar-

row stigma and the dark ray that extends inward from the FW margin past the end of the stigma. Tawny-edged Skipper is slightly larger, usually not so dark below, usually lacks spots on the HW below and, in males, the stigma is thicker and longer and the dark FW ray doesn't extend past the end of the stigma.

HABITAT Sparsely wooded and open situations with low grasses, including lawns.

RANGE Also, Cuba and Hispaniola.

ABUNDANCE 3 or more broods. **W**: R, March–Oct. **N**: LU, late Feb.–early Nov., most common March–April, Sept.–Oct. **C**: LU, early Feb.–mid-Nov., most common March, Sept.–Oct. **S**: LU, all year, especially March–May, Aug.–Oct. **K**: S, Sept.

LOCALITIES Gold Head Branch SP, Clay Co.; Withlacoochee SF, Citrus Co.; Jonathan Dickinson SP, Martin Co.; Fairchild Tropical Garden, Bauer Park, Miami-Dade Co.

MAJOR FOODPLANT Low grasses.

COMMENTS Baracoa Skippers have a great mating dance. Male and female face each other with antennas touching, or almost so. The male starts on the female's right, rapidly dances to her left, then back to her right, then back to her left. The female then waggles her body, tilting her wings first to the left then to the right.

Tawny-edged Skipper *Polites themistocles* **Plate 34**

SIZE ≤ Whirlabout.

SIMILAR SPECIES Crossline Skipper.

IDENTIFICATION A small, dull to darkish skipper below. Below, usually unicolorous drab olive except for tawny orange FW margin and three white spots on the FW subapex (sometimes HW has a faint postmedian band). Male above has intense **thick black stigma** bordering bright orange FW margin. Rest of FW and HW dull brown. Below, usually has sharp contrast between HW color and the brighter FW costal margin. See Crossline Skipper.

HABITAT Sparse woods and open grassy areas with nectar sources, including suburban habitats and roadsides.

RANGE Also, north well into Canada, west to British Columbia and south in the mountains to New Mexico and Arizona.

ABUNDANCE 2, and probably 3, broods. **W**: LU–LC, April–Oct., most common Sept.–Oct. **N**: LU, March–Oct., most common Sept.–Oct. **C**: LU, late Feb.–early Nov., most common Sept.–Oct. **S**: LR, late Feb.–early Nov. **K**: X.

MAJOR FOODPLANT Grasses.

COMMENTS Widespread and quite variable.

Crossline Skipper *Polites origenes* **Plate 34**

SIZE	= Whirlabout.
SIMILAR SPECIES	Tawny-edged Skipper, female Sachem, Dotted Skipper.
IDENTIFICATION	A small to medium-sized dull skipper. Below, distinguished from Tawny-edged Skipper by (*1*) larger size (usually), (*2*) lighter ground color, yellowish-brown, often with a "brassy" look (compared to dull olive for Tawny-edged), (*3*) presence (usually) of at least some (often marked) postmedian spot-band (Tawny-edged Skipper usually lacks a HW postmedian spot-band), and (*4*) less contrast between the HW color and the color of the FW costal margin. Above, the male is distinguished from Tawny-edged Skipper by the **less intense stigma that narrows significantly toward the base of the FW** and by the presence of an **additional pale yellow spot distally adjacent to the stigma**. Female above is very similar to Tawny-edged Skipper but on the HW usually has a broad dark border and a hint of orange. Tawny-edged females lack these features.
HABITAT	Moist grassy areas including savannas, seepage slopes and prairies.
RANGE	Also, north to southern Canada and west to Colorado.
ABUNDANCE	2 broods. **W**: LR–LU, May, late Aug.–Oct., most common Sept. **N**: LU, May, late July–Oct., especially Sept. **C**: LR, late April, late Aug.–Oct., most common Sept. **S**: X. **K**: X.
LOCALITIES	Ralph E. Simmons State Forest, Nassau Co.; Jennings SF, Clay Co.; Apalachicola NF; Kanapaha Botanical Garden, Alachua Co.
MAJOR FOODPLANT	Bluestem grasses (*Andropogon*).
COMMENTS	Best bet is to search on blazing-stars (*Liatris*), in areas where pitcher plants are present, in September.

Whirlabout *Polites vibex* **Plate 33**

SIZE	9/16 inch.
SIMILAR SPECIES	Fiery Skipper.
IDENTIFICATION	Male below, orange-yellow with **large smudged brown or black spots**. These spots are larger and not as numerous as in Fiery Skipper, and tend to be placed at roughly the corners of a square. Male above, note smooth black border on the HW (Fiery Skipper has jagged black border). Female below, dull olive-gray with smudged brown spots.
HABITAT	Disturbed grassy fields, roadsides, woodland edges.
RANGE	Also, north to North Carolina, west to Texas, and south through Mexico to Argentina.
ABUNDANCE	3 or more broods. **W**: C–A, Feb.–Nov., especially April–May,

July–Oct. **N**: C–A, Feb.–Nov., especially April–May, July–Oct. **C**: C–A, all year, especially March, July–Oct. **S**: C–A, all year, especially March, July–Oct. **K**: R or S, June.

MAJOR FOODPLANT Weedy grasses.

COMMENTS One of the most common Florida skippers, its flight pattern lives up to its name.

Southern Broken-Dash *Wallengrenia otho* Plate 35

SIZE ≤ Whirlabout.

SIMILAR SPECIES Northern Broken-Dash.

IDENTIFICATION Similar to Northern Broken Dash but **ground color is a rich reddish brown**. Note the **broad gray FW fringe** contrasting with the buffy HW fringe. Above, both males and females have a **rectangular flag-like yellow spot near the FW center**. Northern Broken-Dash has a yellowish-brown ground color below and dark fringes on both wings.

HABITAT Moist woodland edges and trails and adjacent open areas.

RANGE Also, north to Maryland, west to eastern Oklahoma and Texas and south into Mexico.

ABUNDANCE 2–3 broods. **W**: C, early April–Nov., most common May, Sept.–Oct. **N**: C, early April–Nov., most common May, Sept.–Oct. **C**: C, March–Nov., most common March–April, Sept.–Oct. **S**: U–C, all year, most common March–April, Oct.–Nov. **K**: U, all year, especially March, May, Oct., Dec.

MAJOR FOODPLANT Grasses.

COMMENTS Not that long ago this species and the Northern Broken-Dash were considered to be the same species.

Northern Broken-Dash *Wallengrenia egeremet* Plate 35

SIZE = Whirlabout.

SIMILAR SPECIES Southern Broken-Dash, Little Glassywing, Dun Skipper.

IDENTIFICATION Below, ground color yellowish-brown often with a **violaceous sheen**. HW has a fairly wide, but often indistinct, cream-colored spot-band that is usually **vaguely in the shape of a "3."** Male above, usually has tawny FW margin and two-part **black stigma**. Above, both males and females have a **rectangular flag-like yellow spot near the FW center**. Below, Southern Broken-Dash has a reddish brown ground color. Little Glassywing and Dun Skipper have darker brown ground colors and narrower HW postmedian bands with smaller spots.

HABITAT Sunlit forest clearings and the margins of moist hammocks, swamps, and shrubby places.

RANGE Also, north to southern Canada and west to North Dakota and east Texas.

ABUNDANCE 2 broods. **W**: LU, May–June, Sept.–Oct., most common Sept. **N**: LU, May–June, Sept.–Oct., most common Sept. **C**: LR–LU, April–May, Aug.–Oct., most common Sept. **S**: X. **K**: X.

MAJOR FOODPLANT Grasses.

COMMENTS Along with Little Glassywing and Dun Skipper, one of the "three witches."

Little Glassywing *Pompeius verna* **Plate 35**

SIZE = Whirlabout.

SIMILAR SPECIES Dun Skipper, Northern Broken-Dash, Eufala Skipper, Ocola Skipper.

IDENTIFICATION Below, dark brown ground color with postmedian line of discrete pale spots. Above, dark brown with a large square (female) or rectangular (male) pale spot. Female also has a white spot in the cell (but this can be small). Note **white areas just before the antennal clubs**. Other similar skippers lack these white areas. Dun Skipper below has HW spot-band usually less extensive, usually lacks FW subapical white spots along costa (usually prominent in Little Glassywing). Northern Broken-Dash has a somewhat paler yellowish-brown-mauve ground color and wider postmedian band usually forming a "3." Distinguish from Eufala Skipper by the more extensive white spots above, the much darker ground color below, and the wider wings. Ocola Skipper has the distal one-quarter of its wings below sharply darker and has a striped abdomen.

HABITAT Margins of moist hammocks.

RANGE Also, north to New York and west to Minnesota and Louisiana.

ABUNDANCE 2 broods. **W**: LU, May–June, Aug.–Sept., most common late May, early Sept. **N**: LR, May–June, Aug.–Sept., most common late May, early Sept. **C**: LR, May–June, late Aug.–early Oct., most common early May, mid-Sept. **S**: X. **K**: X.

LOCALITIES Florida Caverns SP, Jackson County; Torreya SP, Liberty Co.; Kanapaha Botanical Garden, Alachua Co.; Gulf Hammock, Levy Co.

MAJOR FOODPLANT Grasses.

COMMENTS This northern species is most frequently seen in the Panhandle region.

SKIPPERS

Sachem *Atalopedes campestris* **Plate 33**

SIZE   11/16 inch.

SIMILAR SPECIES   Whirlabout.

IDENTIFICATION   Male below, note the **squarish brown patch at center of HW bottom margin surrounded by yellow.** Could possibly be confused with a Whirlabout with very faded black spots. Male above, the **large, black rectangular stigma** is unmistakable. Female below, very large, pale yellow postmedian chevron on the HW. Female above, note the **two very large, white hyaline spots on the FW** and the **black patch at the center of the FW.**

HABITAT   Open disturbed fields, roadsides, suburban and urban lots, sandhills.

RANGE   Also, north to New Jersey, west to California, and south through Mexico to Brazil.

ABUNDANCE   3 or more broods. **W:** C, March–Oct., most common April–May, Sept.–Oct. **N:** C, late Feb.–Nov., most common March–May, Sept.–Oct. **C:** C, Feb.–Nov., especially March–May, Sept.–Oct. **S:** C, all year, most common March–May, Sept.–Nov. **K:** LU, all year, most common March and Oct.

MAJOR FOODPLANT   Grasses.

COMMENTS   Widespread, and common. Along with Fiery Skipper and Whirlabout, one of the "three wizards.".

Arogos Skipper *Atrytone arogos* **Plate 36**

SIZE   = Whirlabout.

SIMILAR SPECIES   Delaware Skipper, Byssus Skipper.

IDENTIFICATION   Above, note **broad blackish borders.** Male with orange portion of FW above unmarked, female with black streak in center of orange portion. Below, orange yellow, usually with **white HW fringe** and **whitish HW veins.** Delaware Skipper is brighter orange below (but of course faded individuals are common), with orange or tan (not white) HW fringe and without whitish veining. Byssus Skippers below usually have a paler patch in middle of HW and above have more extensive black areas.

HABITAT   Prairies and sandhills.

RANGE   Also, discontinuously north to New Jersey and west to Colorado.

ABUNDANCE   2 (possibly 3) broods. **W:** LR, probably April–Oct. **N:** LR, April–Oct., especially May, Aug.–Sept. **C:** LR, March–Nov., most common April, July, and Sept. **S:** LR, March–Oct., perhaps extirpated. **K:** X.

LOCALITIES	1/4 mile west of Lake Delancy Campground, Ocala NF, Marion Co. (see Comments); Withlacoochee SF, Citrus Co.(a small number of individuals seen, probably a larger colony exists); Starkey Wilderness Park, Pasco Co.; Bull Creek WMA, Osceola Co.; Jonathan Dickinson SP, Martin Co.
MAJOR FOODPLANT	Lopsided Indian grass (*Sorghastrum secundum*).
COMMENTS	One of the rarest resident skippers of Florida. Unfortunately, the management practices employed within Ocala National Forest site (burned by the U.S. Forest Service) seemed to have caused the species to become even rarer. Once frequent at this site, no adults have been found recently. Hopefully, the population will recover. Recent surveys have found populations at only a few sites in a very restricted number of counties. We don't show it as extirpated in south Florida because it is still possible that there are remnants of the population that inhabited Jonathon Dickinson State Park in Martin Co.

Delaware Skipper *Anatrytone logan* **Plate 36**

SIZE	= Whirlabout, but very variable.
SIMILAR SPECIES	Byssus Skipper.
IDENTIFICATION	An active skipper, **clear bright unmarked yellow-orange below**. Above, orange with black borders and **black FW cell-end bar** and at least some **black veining**. Fringes orange to tan. See Byssus Skipper.
HABITAT	Moist grassy areas, including pond and lake margins and sedge and coastal marshes.
RANGE	Also, north to Massachusetts and Manitoba and west to Montana and New Mexico.
ABUNDANCE	2 (possibly 3) broods. **W**: U–C, April–Oct., especially June–Sept. **N**: U–C, April–Oct., most common June–Sept. **C**: U–C, March–Nov., especially July–early Oct. **S**: U–C, March–Nov., most common July–Oct. **K**: X.
MAJOR FOODPLANT	Wetland grasses such as maidencane (*Panicum hemitomon*) and redtop panicum (*Panicum rigidulum*).
COMMENTS	One of the most common golden skippers in wetland habitats.

Byssus Skipper *Problema byssus* **Plate 36**

SIZE	≥ Sachem.
SIMILAR SPECIES	Delaware Skipper.
IDENTIFICATION	Below bright orange to ochre, usually with a **pale area in middle of HW**. Fringes white to tan. Above, almost always with a **continuous band on FW**. Very rarely, lack of two sub-

apical spots interrupts the band. Below, most individuals show dark shading in the FW margin.

HABITAT A butterfly of the edges of wooded wetlands, savannas, and marshes.

RANGE Also, discontinuously northwest to Iowa.

ABUNDANCE 2 broods. **W**: LR–LU, May and July–Sept., most common Sept. **N**: LU–LC, May–June and July–early Oct., especially Sept. **C**: LU–LC, late April–May, Aug.–Oct., most common Sept. **S**: LU, March–April and Sept.–Oct., especially Sept. **K**: X.

MAJOR FOODPLANT Plumegrasses (*Erianthus*) and eastern gama-grass (*Tripsacum dactyloides*).

COMMENTS Males are territorial early in the morning and again late in the afternoon.

Zabulon Skipper *Poanes zabulon* Plate 37

SIZE = Sachem.

SIMILAR SPECIES Clouded Skipper.

IDENTIFICATION Male below, mainly yellow with HW post-basal **brown patch enclosing yellow at wing base**. Female below, dark rusty brown with vague darker blotches. Note **silvery white HW apex**. Clouded Skippers lack this mark.

HABITAT Margins of moist hammocks, including hammock trails.

RANGE Also, north to Connecticut, west to Kansas and east Texas and south into southern Mexico.

ABUNDANCE Probably 2 broods (possibly 3). **W**: LU, late March–Oct., most common April, Sept. **N**: LR, late March–Oct., especially April, Sept. **C**: LR, late Feb.–Oct., especially March, Sept. **S**: X. **K**: X.

LOCALITIES Florida Caverns SP, Jackson Co.; Torreya SP, Liberty Co.; Suwannee River SP, Suwannee Co.; Kanapaha Botanical Garden, Alachua Co.; Crystal Springs, Pasco Co.

MAJOR FOODPLANT Grasses.

COMMENTS Unlike most grass-skippers, which fly close to the ground, Zabulon Skippers often fly about three or four feet high. The males sally forth from perches on leaves overhanging woodland trails and edges.

Aaron's Skipper *Poanes aaroni* Plate 38

SIZE = Sachem.

SIMILAR SPECIES Broad-winged Skipper, Dion Skipper.

IDENTIFICATION A large dingy orange-brown skipper of marshes and adjacent areas. Below, note the **pale HW ray that goes the width of**

the wing, often flanked by two pale dots. Broad-winged Skipper is similar but has one or two, well-defined white spots on the FW below and is larger. Dion Skipper is usually brighter red-orange and its paler HW ray rarely goes the entire width of the wing.

HABITAT Salt, brackish, and freshwater marshes, pond and lake margins.

RANGE Also, discontinuously north along the coast to New Jersey, and west along the coast to east Texas.

ABUNDANCE 2 broods. **W**: X. (not yet recorded, but probably present). **N**: LU, late March–May and Aug.–Oct., especially Sept. **C**: LU, late Feb.–April and Aug.–Oct., most common Sept. **S**: LU, March–April and Aug.–Oct., especially Sept. **K**: X.

LOCALITIES Osceola NF, Baker Co.; Yankeetown, Levy Co.; Ocala NF; St. Johns Marsh, Brevard Co.; Blue Cypress Conservation Area, Indian River Co.

MAJOR FOODPLANT Maidencane (*Panicum hemitomon*) and probably other grasses.

COMMENTS There are two ecotypes of Aaron's Skipper in Florida, a small dark type associated with salt marshes, and a larger, brighter form found inland in freshwater marshes. It can sometimes be common in its localized colonies.

Yehl Skipper *Poanes yehl* **Plate 38**

SIZE = Sachem.

SIMILAR SPECIES Broad-winged Skipper.

IDENTIFICATION Below, HW bright rusty-orange (male) or orange-brown (female) with **three or four pale postmedian spots** bisected by a faint pale ray. Female above is very similar to Broad-winged Skipper but lacks the narrow yellow ray that species has at the HW outer angle. Male above looks similar to *Euphyes* but, unlike them, black border along leading edge of the HW greatly narrows near the apex.

HABITAT Moist hammocks, canebrakes, and adjacent open areas.

RANGE Also, north to Virginia and west to Arkansas and east Texas.

ABUNDANCE 2 broods. **W**: LR, May and Sept.–Oct., especially Sept. **N**: LR, May and Sept.–Oct., especially Sept. **C**: X. **S**: X. **K**: X.

LOCALITIES University of North Florida nature trails, Duval Co.

MAJOR FOODPLANT Probably switch cane (*Arundinaria gigantea*).

COMMENTS The pale HW spots below seem to become larger with wear, as do those of Broad-winged Skippers. Fresh male Yehls are rather stunning, with their bright rusty-orange color, but older individuals wear a dull yellow-orange garb.

Broad-winged Skipper *Poanes viator* **Plate 38**

SIZE	Very variable, usually > Sachem.
SIMILAR SPECIES	Aaron's Skipper.
IDENTIFICATION	A large, dull-colored, weak-flying marsh skipper. Below, dull orangish-brown with a somewhat pale ray. Usually with two pale spots below the ray and one above it. Usually **lands with its head up** and its body oriented perpendicularly to the ground. Aaron's Skipper is generally smaller and lacks the well-defined FW subapical spot(s) below that this species has.
HABITAT	Margins of swamps, streams, rivers, and lakes.
RANGE	Also, north to Massachusetts, the Great Lakes region, and west to east Texas.
ABUNDANCE	2 broods. **W**: LR, April–May and Sept.–Oct., especially Sept. **N**: LR, late March–May and mid Aug.–Oct., most common Sept. **C**: X. **S**: X. **K**: X.
LOCALITIES	Three Rivers State Recreation Area, Jackson Co.; Torreya SP, Liberty Co.; Lake Alice Wildlife Preserve, University of Florida, Alachua Co.
MAJOR FOODPLANT	Wild rice (*Zizania*).
COMMENTS	Broad-winged Skippers flutter slowly through stands of their foodplants—large grasses whose leaf-edges are armed with small teeth that cut clothing and skin like razors.

Palmetto Skipper *Euphyes arpa* **Plate 39**

SIZE	>> Sachem.
SIMILAR SPECIES	Byssus Skipper.
IDENTIFICATION	A large skipper, orange below with a **golden head** and mantle. Male above with a very long, narrow black stigma.
HABITAT	Sandhills, flatwoods, and prairies.
ABUNDANCE	2 or 3 broods. **W**: LR, April–May, Sept.–Oct. **N**: LR–LU, April–May and Sept.–Oct. **C**: LU, late March–May, Aug.–Oct., most common in Sept. **S**: LU, early March–May, July–Oct. **K**: Probably extirpated, formerly seen in Jan., March–May, Oct., Dec.
LOCALITIES	Apalachicola NF, Liberty Co.; Ocala NF;.Archbold Biological Station, Highlands Co.; Audubon Kissimmee Prairie Sanctuary, Okeechobee Co.; Jonathan Dickinson SP, Martin Co.; Fakahatchee Strand State Preserve, Collier Co.
MAJOR FOODPLANT	Saw palmetto (*Serenoa repens*).
COMMENTS	Obviously, foodplant availability is not the factor limiting populations of this species since saw palmettos are abundant and widespread while Palmetto Skippers are quite scarce. They are

also quite wary. Although common on Big Pine Key during the 1970s, the Palmetto Skipper has not been seen in the lower Keys since the early 1980s.

Palatka Skipper *Euphyes pilatka* Plate 38

SIZE >> Sachem.

SIMILAR SPECIES Broad-winged Skipper.

IDENTIFICATION A **very large** grass-skipper. **Below, rusty-brown,** fairly unicolorous but sometimes with a faint pale postmedian patch. Broad-winged Skipper is not so rusty-colored, has a FW subapical spot that Palatka Skipper lacks, and usually has a pale ray with flanking spots on the HW below.

HABITAT Marshes, flatwoods and pine rockland.

RANGE Also, north along the coast to southeastern Virginia and west along the coast to Mississippi.

ABUNDANCE 2 or 3 broods. **W**: LU, May, Aug.–Oct., most common Sept. **N**: LU, May, Aug.–Oct., especially Sept. **C**: LU, March–Oct., most common March and Sept. **S**: LU–LC, Feb.–early Dec., most common March and Oct. **K**: LU, Jan.–June, Sept.–Oct., Dec., especially March and Oct.

MAJOR FOODPLANT Sawgrass (*Cladium jamaicense*).

COMMENTS Males will behave territorially, perching on sawgrass, but are most frequently seen nectaring at flowers, especially at thistles, usually in a vertical position with their heads up.

Dion Skipper *Euphyes dion* Plate 39

SIZE ≥ Sachem.

SIMILAR SPECIES Delaware Skipper, Broad-winged Skipper, Aaron's Skipper.

IDENTIFICATION A large wetland skipper. Bright orange to duller reddish-orange below with **one or two pale rays on the HW,** the top ray usually not extending the entire width of the wing. Delaware Skipper lacks pale rays and is smaller. Aaron's Skipper is duller with a ray that usually extends the entire width of the wing and is flanked by pale spots. Broad-winged Skipper has a pale HW ray but is duller, its wings are more rounded, and the pale ray is flanked by pale spots.

HABITAT Edges of wetlands.

RANGE Also, north to southern Canada and west to Minnesota and east Texas.

ABUNDANCE 2 broods. **W**: LR, May, Aug.–Oct., most common Sept. **N**: LR–LU, April–May, late July–Oct., especially Sept. **C**: X. **F**: X. **K**: X.

LOCALITIES Apalachicola NF; University of North Florida nature trails, Duval Co.; Kanapaha Botanical Gardens, Alachua Co.

MAJOR FOODPLANT Sedges (*Carex*).

COMMENTS Dion Skippers are closely associated with patches of sedges growing in sunny, open areas, although they may be found nectaring in adjacent upland habitats.

Dukes' Skipper *Euphyes dukesi* Plate 39

SIZE ≥ Sachem.

SIMILAR SPECIES Dion Skipper, Dun Skipper (female above).

IDENTIFICATION Below, a rich orange-brown to sooty-brown with **one or two HW yellow rays** and a **black FW disc**. Above, both sexes are **quite black**, males usually with some tawny-orange along the FW costa and on the HW; females all dark. Dion Skipper is not as dark below, lacks the black FW disc, and above has white spots and is not so blackish. Female Dun Skipper have two small white spots on the FW that female Florida Dukes' Skippers normally lack (other populations of Dukes' Skippers also have these spots).

HABITAT Shady, hardwood swamps.

RANGE Also, the Atlantic coast north to southeastern Virginia, the Mississippi River Valley, and the Great Lakes.

ABUNDANCE 2 broods. **W**: X. **N**: LR, May–early June, Aug.–Oct., especially Sept. **C**: LR, May–early June, Aug.–Oct., most common Sept. **S**: X. **K**: X.

LOCALITIES Caravelle WMA, Putnam Co.; Green Swamp WMA, Sumter Co.

MAJOR FOODPLANT Sedges (*Carex* and *Rhynchospora*).

COMMENTS Unlike most skippers, Duke's Skippers prefer the dappled shade of swamps where they fly slowly through the leaves of grasses and sedges. Males perch in sunlit clearings and patrol just above the tops of sedges. Florida populations are larger and darker than others, and are an endemic subspecies (*E. dukesi calhouni*).

Berry's Skipper *Euphyes berryi* Plate 39

SIZE ≥ Sachem.

SIMILAR SPECIES Byssus Skipper, Palmetto Skipper.

IDENTIFICATION Below, dull brownish-orange with **whitened HW veins**. Male above with much orange, thin FW stigma and a black ray coming in about 1/3 the FW length from the distal border. Females are darker with a FW cell spot and some tawny on the HW. Palmetto Skippers are brighter yellow-orange below, without such pronounced white veins (in some light, Palmetto Skipper HW veins do appear paler), and have golden-yellow heads that

Berry's Skippers lack. Byssus Skipper below can have pronounced whitening of the HW veins but usually has a pale HW postmedian patch that Berry's Skipper lack. Female Palmetto Skippers above lack the FW cell-spot and the tawny HW.

HABITAT   Marshes, savannas, and swamp edges.

RANGE   Also, north to the Carolinas and west to Alabama.

ABUNDANCE   2 broods. **W**: LR, April–May and Aug.–Oct., most common Sept. **N**: LR, April–May, Aug.–Oct., especially Sept. **C**: LR, April–May and Aug.–Oct., most common Sept. **S**: LR, March–April and July–Oct., especially March and Sept. **K**: X.

LOCALITIES   Apalachicola NF, Liberty Co.; Tiger Bay SF, Volusia Co.; Fakahatchee Strand State Botanical Site, Collier Co; Big Cypress National Preserve, Collier Co.

MAJOR FOODPLANT   Sedges (*Carex*).

COMMENTS   A rarely encountered, very poorly known skipper. Although quite local in distribution, one may encounter a number of individuals where it does occur.

Dun Skipper *Euphyes vestris* **Plate 35**

SIZE   ≤ Whirlabout.

SIMILAR SPECIES   Little Glassywing, Northern Broken-Dash, Clouded Skipper (above).

IDENTIFICATION   Dark brown all over. Above, male is **all dark brown** with black stigma. **Head is often bright golden-orange.** Female is all dark brown above with **two small pale spots**. Little Glassywing has a better defined HW spot-band, white at base of antennal clubs, and is very different above. Northern Broken-Dash has paler yellow-brown ground color and HW postmedian band in the shape of a "3." Northern Broken-Dash female above has distinctive elongated pale spot past the FW cell. On the FW above, Dun Skippers lack the three white, outwardly curving, subapical spots that Clouded Skippers have (female Duns often have two white FW subapical spots that do not curve outward).

HABITAT   Moist open situations near hammocks.

RANGE   Also, north to Canada and west to California.

ABUNDANCE   2 broods. **W**: U–C, April–May, Aug.–Oct., especially April and Sept. **N**: U–C, April–May, Aug.–Oct., especially April and Sept. **C**: U–C, March–April, July–Oct., most common Sept. **S**: LR, March–Sept. **K**: X.

MAJOR FOODPLANT   Sedges (*Carex*), especially *Carex lupulina*.

COMMENTS   In Florida, this is the most frequently encountered of the three "witches."

Monk Skipper *Asbolis capucinus* **Plate 42**

SIZE ≤ Silver-spotted Skipper.

SIMILAR SPECIES Palatka Skipper.

IDENTIFICATION A very, very large grass-skipper. Monk Skippers are appropriately garbed in somber attire. Their tawny dark reddish-brown below and rich chestnut above, makes one think of a giant *Euphyes*. Note the white fringe on the HW, especially near the outer angle. Palatka Skipper lacks this, is smaller, and has more contrast between the FW and HW.

HABITAT Gardens and woodland edges near palms.

RANGE Also, Cuba.

ABUNDANCE 3 or more broods. **W**: X. **N**: R immigrant, Aug.–Oct. **C**: LU, April–Nov., especially Sept.–Oct. **S**: U–C, all year, most common March–May, July, Sept.–Oct. **K**: U–C, all year, especially Jan., March–May, July–Oct., and Dec.

LOCALITIES Highlands Hammock State Park, Highlands Co.; Myakka River State Park, Sarasota Co.; Jonanthan Dickinson SP, Martin Co.; Matheson Hammock Park, Miami-Dade Co.

MAJOR FOODPLANT Palms (Arecaceae).

GARDEN TIPS Coconut palm and Christmas palm.

COMMENTS A Cuban species that probably became established in the Florida in the 1940s. The widespread use of palms for urban and suburban landscaping in southern Florida has helped this species spread.

Dusted Skipper *Atrytonopsis hianna* **Plate 37**

SIZE ≥ Sachem.

SIMILAR SPECIES Twin-spot Skipper.

IDENTIFICATION Below, a large dark grass-skipper with much frosting of the marginal wing areas and with a variety of **white postmedian and basal spots on the HW**. Its **"masked" appearance**, due to its dark eye being bordered by the white palps below and a white eye stripe above, separates this species from Florida's other dark skippers with frosting. Northward, individuals lack most of the HW white spots and individuals similar to these may occur in the Florida Panhandle.

HABITAT Flatwoods and prairies.

RANGE Also, north to Vermont, west to Manitoba and New Mexico.

ABUNDANCE 2 broods. **W**: LR, March–May, Aug.–Oct., most common April, Sept. **N**: LR, March–May, Aug.–Oct., especially April, Sept. **C**: LR, March–April, July–Oct., most common April, Sept. **S**: LR, Feb.–April, Aug.–Oct., most common March, Sept. **K**: X.

LOCALITIES   Jay B. Starkey Wilderness Park, Pasco Co.; Jonathan Dickinson SP, Martin Co.

MAJOR FOODPLANT   Bluestem grasses (*Andropogon*).

COMMENTS   Florida populations seem to be declining, which is especially troubling because they (*Atrytonopsis hianna loammi*) are quite distinctive.

Pepper and Salt Skipper *Amblyscirtes hegon* Plate 40

SIZE   ≤ Swarthy Skipper.

IDENTIFICATION   Below, olive-tinged gray-brown ground with prominent cream-colored HW postmedian band. Above, with more extensive white spotting than Common Roadside-Skipper.

HABITAT   Margins of moist hammocks.

RANGE   Also, north to southern Quebec and west to Manitoba and east Texas.

ABUNDANCE   1 brood (partial second brood, July–Aug.). W: LR, May. N: LR, April. C: X. S: X. K: X.

LOCALITIES   Florida Caverns SP, Jackson Co.; Torreya SP, Liberty Co.; Suwannee River SP, Suwannee Co.

MAJOR FOODPLANT   Grasses.

COMMENTS   Little is known about this species in Florida and it has been reported only from Jackson, Liberty, and Suwannee counties.

Lace-winged Roadside-Skipper *Amblyscirtes aesculapius* Plate 40

SIZE   ≤ Whirlabout.

IDENTIFICATION   An arresting underside pattern of **cobwebby white veins and median and postmedian lines** makes this roadside-skipper an easy call.

HABITAT   Moist hammocks, flatwoods, and seepage slopes with canebrakes.

RANGE   Also, north to southeastern Virginia and west to eastern Texas.

ABUNDANCE   2 or 3 broods. W: LR–LU, April–May, Aug.–Oct. N: LR–LU, April–May, July–Oct., especially April, Sept. C: LR, late March–May, July–Oct., especially April, Sept. S: X. K: X.

LOCALITIES   Torreya SP, Liberty Co.; Ralph E. Simmons SF, Nassau Co.; Jennings SF, Clay Co.; Kanapaha Botanical Garden, Alachua Co.; Gulf Hammock, Levy Co.; Alexander Springs, Ocala NF; Kelly Park, Orange Co.

MAJOR FOODPLANT   Cane (*Arundinaria*).

COMMENTS   Look for this beauty in sunny openings in canebrakes or along their edges.

Common Roadside-Skipper *Amblyscirtes vialis*
Plate 40

SIZE	= Swarthy Skipper.
SIMILAR SPECIES	Female Zabulon Skipper, Dusky Roadside-Skipper.
IDENTIFICATION	A **very small black** skipper. Below, frosted on the outer portions of the wings. FW subapical spots are usually wider at costal margin, tending to form a white wedge. Note **strongly checkered fringes**. Zabulon Skippers are much larger and lack checkered fringes. Dusky Roadside-Skipper has bluish scaling on the HW, much weaker FW subapical white spots, and blunt antennal clubs.
HABITAT	Hammock margins.
RANGE	Also, north to Canada and west to California.
ABUNDANCE	2 broods. **W**: LR, April–May, Aug.–Sept., most common April. **N**: X. **C**: X. **S**: X. **K**: X.
LOCALITIES	Torreya SP, Liberty Co.
MAJOR FOODPLANT	Grasses.
COMMENTS	Although locally common in other parts of North America, Common Roadside-Skippers are rarely seen in Florida and are known only from Franklin and Liberty counties.

Dusky Roadside-Skipper *Amblyscirtes alternata*
Plate 40

SIZE	≤ Swarthy Skipper.
SIMILAR SPECIES	Common Roadside-Skipper.
IDENTIFICATION	Small and blackish with very few markings. Below, **bottom 2/3 of HW frosted with bluish scales**. Above, brown with a purplish sheen and with the only pale spots being a few faint FW subapical spots. **Note the blunt antennal clubs, without a tapered extension (apiculus)**. Similar roadside-skippers have antennal clubs that taper at their ends.
HABITAT	Sandhills, flatwoods, and prairies.
RANGE	Also, north to southeastern Virginia and west to east Texas.
ABUNDANCE	2 broods. **W**: LR, late March–April, Aug.–Oct. **N**: LR, March–May, Aug.–Oct. **C**: LR, March, Aug.–Oct. **S**: LR, March, July–Oct. **K**: X.
LOCALITIES	Riverside Island, Ocala NF, Marion Co.; Withlacoochee SF; Jonathan Dickinson SP, Martin Co.
MAJOR FOODPLANT	Grasses.
COMMENTS	A rarely seen species whose life history is very poorly known.

Eufala Skipper *Lerodea eufala* **Plate 32**

SIZE ≤ Whirlabout.

SIMILAR SPECIES Three-spotted Skipper, Swarthy Skipper, Tawny-edged Skipper.

IDENTIFICATION A small, grayish-brown nondescript skipper with a **pale body.** Can often be identified at a distance because it frequently gives two quick "wing-claps" after landing. Below, often with **faint traces of a pale HW postmedian band vaguely shaped like a "3."** There are a series of three white spots on the FW subapex (visible from above and below) that Swarthy Skipper lacks. Above, FW cell often with one or two small pale spots. Swarthy Skipper is darker with pale veining. Three-spotted Skipper is browner, usually with a more developed HW postmedian spot-band below, with longer antennas, and usually with brighter orange-tawny on the costal margin of the FW above.

HABITAT A wide variety of open situations.

RANGE Also, north to southeastern Virginia, west to California, Cuba, Jamaica, and south through Mexico to Argentina.

ABUNDANCE 3 or more broods. **W:** U, March– early Nov., most common Aug.–Oct. **N:** U–C, March–early Nov., most common Aug.–Oct. **C:** : U–C, late Feb.–early Dec., most common Aug.–Oct. **S:** U–C, all year, especially March, Sept.–Oct. **K:** U, all year, especially Sept.–Nov.

MAJOR FOODPLANT Grasses.

COMMENTS You know you've made progress when you get to the point of being confidant about Eufala Skipper identifications!

Twin-spot Skipper *Oligoria maculata* **Plate 37**

SIZE = Sachem.

SIMILAR SPECIES Brazilian Skipper, Clouded Skipper (above), Dun Skipper (above).

IDENTIFICATION Note the **three bold white spots on the rich-brown HW below, two together (the twins), one apart.** Brazilian Skipper is much larger and has bold white or translucent HW spots that angle outward. Above, Dun and Clouded Skippers are similar, see them for discussion.

HABITAT Flatwoods, fields, and the edges of moist hammocks and marshes.

RANGE Also, north along the coast to North Carolina and west along the coast to east Texas.

ABUNDANCE 2 to 3 broods. **W:** U, March–April, Aug.–Oct., most common April and Sept. **N:** U, March–Oct., most common April–May and

SKIPPERS

Sept. **C**: U–C, all year, most common March, Sept. **S**: C, all year, most common March, Sept. **K**: U in lower Keys, all year, especially Jan., March–April, Sept.–Oct.

MAJOR FOODPLANT Bluestem grasses (*Andropogon*).

COMMENTS Thistles are a favorite nectar source.

Brazilian Skipper *Calpodes ethlius* **Plate 42**

SIZE >> Sachem.

SIMILAR SPECIES Twin-spot Skipper.

IDENTIFICATION This very large grass-skipper is a rich reddish-tinged brown below with **three or four large white or translucent spots in an angled line on the HW below.**

HABITAT Wetlands and suburban and urban gardens with cannas.

RANGE Also, north to Virginia, west to southern California, the West Indies and southern Texas, and south to Argentina.

ABUNDANCE 3 or more broods. **W**: R immigrant, Aug.–Oct. **N**: U immigrant, July–Dec., most common Sept.–Oct. **C**: U, all year, especially Aug.–Nov. **S**: U, all year, most common Aug.–Nov. **K**: U, Jan., Sept.–Dec., especially Oct.

MAJOR FOODPLANT Cannas (*Canna*) and alligator flag (*Thalia geniculata*).

GARDEN TIPS Golden canna (*Canna flaccida*), ornamental cannas, and alligator flag. Because of their long tongues, Brazilian Skippers often prefer different nectar plants from other skippers. Orchid trees seem to be a favorite.

COMMENTS Brazilian Skippers are one of Florida's few crepuscular butterflies, although they certainly also can be seen in the middle of the day. These powerful flyers, whose wings make a distinctive raspy noise, are difficult to follow as they buzz in and out of canna stands. It is often easier to locate the caterpillars, rolled up in a canna leaf. In the late 1800s and early 1900s, cannas became a rage in the eastern United States. Consequently, Brazilian Skipper populations exploded, and there are many records from that time period from far north of their current range. But, gardeners soon tired of cannas because something was eating them and making them look very ragged! After the canna fad collapsed, Brazilian Skippers fell back to their more historical range. Today, cannas are becoming more popular again, and Brazilian Skippers are on the move. Become a butterfly gardener and encourage this trend.

Panoquins
(genus *Panoquina*)

The roughly 20 species of panoquins (mainly tropical) can usually be identified as panoquins in the field by a combination of their elongated wings and the presence of a dark line running along the side of the abdomen. We have three species.

Salt Marsh Skipper *Panoquina panoquin* Plate 41

SIZE	= Sachem.
IDENTIFICATION	A very long-winged, yellow-brown skipper with **paler yellow veining** and **a cream-colored streak distal to the HW cell below**.
HABITAT	Salt marshes and adjacent fields.
RANGE	Also, north along the coast to Connecticut and west along the coast to east Texas.
ABUNDANCE	3 or more broods. **WF:** LU, April–Nov., most common Aug.–Oct. **N:** LU, April–Dec., especially Aug.–Oct. **C:** LC, Feb.–Dec., most common March, Sept.–Oct. **S:** LU–LC, all year, most common March, Sept.–Oct. **K:** LR–LU in the lower Keys, probably all year, especially Nov.–Dec.
LOCALITIES	Stokes Landing Conservation Area, S. Johns Co.; Yankeetown, Levy Co.; Merritt Island NWR, Brevard and Volusia Cos.; Canaveral National Seashore, Brevard Co.; J.N. "Ding" Darling NWR, Lee Co.; Collier-Seminole SP, Collier Co.; Flamingo, Everglades NP.
MAJOR FOODPLANT	Saltgrass (*Distichlis spicata*) and saltmarsh cordgrass (*Spartina alterniflora*).
COMMENTS	Although colonies are local, individuals can be abundant. Occasional individuals stray far inland.

Obscure Skipper *Panoquina panoquinoides* Plate 41

SIZE	≤ Whirlabout.
SIMILAR SPECIES	Twin-spot Skipper, Salt Marsh Skipper, Three-spotted Skipper.
IDENTIFICATION	This tiny inhabitant of salt marshes is smaller than Salt Marsh Skipper and duller brown. On the HW below there are usually **two small white spots** in the lower postmedian area. The intensity of these spots varies from bold, to obvious (as in the individual on plate 41), to faint, to absent. Unlike Salt Marsh

Skipper, there is no cream-colored streak on the HW below. Twin-spot Skipper is larger, has a richer, reddish-brown ground color, lacks paler veining, and has three FW subapical white spots (Obscure Skipper has two). Three-spotted Skipper has longer antennas, usually has more white spots in the postmedian band and has three FW subapical spots.

HABITAT Salt marshes and adjacent areas.

RANGE Also, south through the West Indies and south Texas to South America.

ABUNDANCE 3 or more broods. **W**: LR, April–Oct., especially April, Sept. **N**: LR, April–Oct., especially April, Sept. **C**: LU, March–Dec., especially March, Sept.–Oct. **S**: All year, LU, especially Feb.–March, Sept.–Oct. **K**: LU, all year, most common Jan., Sept.–Oct., Dec.

LOCALITIES Yankeetown, Levy Co.; Collier-Seminole SP, Collier Co.; North Key Largo Hammocks State Botanical Site, Monroe Co.; Cactus Hammock, Big Pine Key, Monroe Co.

MAJOR FOODPLANT Seashore dropseed (*Sporobolus virginicus*) and other salt marsh grasses.

COMMENTS Skipping obscure nonharlequin-garbed butterflies will deprive one of a panoramic view of the lepidopteran landscape.

Ocola Skipper *Panoquina ocola* Plate 41

SIZE ≥ Sachem.

IDENTIFICATION Note the long and narrow wings. Plain, dull yellowish-brown below with **distal one-quarter of wings darker brown**. Sometimes with purple sheen when fresh. Note the **striped abdomen**. Above, the white or yellowish median pale spot is bullet-shaped.

HABITAT Almost any open moist areas, including salt marsh, flatwoods, and gardens.

RANGE Also, north to Maryland, west to Texas, and south through the West Indies and Mexico to South America.

ABUNDANCE 3 or more broods. **W**: A, Feb.–Dec., most common Aug.–Oct. **N**: A, Feb.–Dec., most common Aug.–Oct. **C**: A, all year, especially Aug.–Oct. **S**: A, all year, especially March, July–Dec. **K**: R, June, Sept.–Oct., Dec.

MAJOR FOODPLANT Aquatic and semiaquatic grasses, such as torpedo-grass (*Panicum repens*).

COMMENTS In the late summer and fall, Ocola Skipper becomes one of the most common butterflies in Florida, with many individuals moving in a southerly direction during this time.

Giant-Skippers
(subfamily Megathyminae)

The aptly named giant-skippers are big, fat, and powerful. If you are so lucky as to have one whirr by you, you will hear the quite audible sound made by their wingbeats. There are many species in the Southwestern United States and northern Mexico, but only two species in Florida.

Yucca Giant-Skipper *Megathymus yuccae* Plate 42

SIZE	≥ Silver-spotted Skipper.
IDENTIFICATION	A huge, big-bodied skipper. Very dark brown-black below with some marginal frosting, a white spot near the leading edge of the HW, and tan-yellow HW fringe.
HABITAT	Open situations with yuccas, especially scrubby flatwoods, sandhills, dry hammocks, and coastal dunes.
RANGE	Also, north to Virginia and west to southern California and northern Mexico.
ABUNDANCE	1 brood. W: LU, Feb.–April. N: LU, Feb.–April. C: LR–LU, Feb.–May. S: LR, Feb.–May. K: X.
LOCALITIES	Apalachicola NF; Torreya SP, Liberty Co.; Gold Head Branch SP, Clay Co.; Riverside Island, Ocala NF, Marion Co.; Jonathan Dickinson SP, Martin Co.
MAJOR FOODPLANT	Yucca.
GARDEN TIPS	Spanish bayonet (*Yucca aloifolia*).
COMMENTS	Many active butterfliers have never seen a wild adult. Look for males on the trunks of pines, on low vegetation, or even on the ground. It is usually much easier to find caterpillars by looking for the young caterpillars' silk nests among the yucca leaf tips or the older caterpillars' silk-covered tubes attached to the yucca roots.

Cofaqui Giant-Skipper *Megathymus cofaqui* Plate 42

SIZE	= Silver-spotted Skipper.
SIMILAR SPECIES	Yucca Giant-Skipper.
IDENTIFICATION	Similar to Yucca Giant-Skipper but HW below is paler gray, white spot near the leading margin is much less prominent, and there are a variable number of other small white spots in the postmedian area.
HABITAT	Open situations with yuccas, especially sandhills and dry hammocks.

RANGE	Also, north to the Carolinas.
ABUNDANCE	2 broods. **W**: LR, March–April, Aug.–Oct. **N**: LU, March–April, Aug.–Oct. **C**: LU, Feb.–March, Aug.–Oct. **S**: LR, March–Oct. **K**: X.
LOCALITIES	Torreya SP, Liberty Co.; Ralph E. Simmons SF, Nassau Co.; Welaka SF, Putnam Co.; Riverside Island, Ocala NF, Marion Co.; Withlacoochee SF.
MAJOR FOODPLANT	Yucca.
GARDEN TIPS	Yucca (*Yucca filamentosa*) and Spanish bayonet (*Yucca aloifolia*).
COMMENTS	Even less known than Yucca Giant-Skipper, Cofaqui Giant-Skippers are rarely seen, in part because of their crepuscular nature. Adults perch on tree trunks and other vegetation during the day and become active in late afternoon, flying into dusk. If the proper habitat is nearby, they can sometimes be found resting near building lights.

SPECIES OCCURRING IN FLORIDA ONLY AS STRAYS

Cuban Kite-Swallowtail *Eurytides celadon*
Not Illustrated.

SIZE < Pipevine Swallowtail.

SIMILAR SPECIES Zebra Swallowtail.

IDENTIFICATION Above, basal area of FW has more extensive white than does Zebra Swallowtail. Note the **uneven FW marginal band**. In Zebra Swallowtail this band is smooth. **Lacks red HW median stripe** below that Zebra Swallowtail has.

RANGE Cuba.

ABUNDANCE Several reports, none certain. If it occurs in Florida at all, it is as an extremely rare stray to the Keys. Most likely in May, during its major flight in Cuba.

Androgeus Swallowtail *Papilio androgeus*
Not Illustrated.

SIZE ≥ Eastern Tiger Swallowtail.

SIMILAR SPECIES Giant Swallowtail (male), Pipevine Swallowtail (female).

IDENTIFICATION Males: note the extremely wide yellow bands on the FW above and especially on the HW above covering the entire base of the HW. Below, FW lacks cream-colored marginal spots that Giant Swallowtail has. Female is dark with iridescent blue area on HW above and **five short pointed tails**.

HABITAT Overgrown citrus plantations.

RANGE West Indies, including Cuba, and Mexico south through tropical Americas. Formerly found in Broward and Miami-Dade Counties, Florida.

ABUNDANCE There is no current population in Florida. Formerly April–Oct.

MAJOR FOODPLANT Citrus.

COMMENTS A colony of this tropical species became established in southern Florida in 1976 and then disappeared by 1983. May occur as a stray or again become established.

Clouded Sulphur *Colias philodice* Not Illustrated, see *Butterflies through Binoculars: The East.*

SIZE	= Checkered White.
SIMILAR SPECIES	Orange Sulphur.
IDENTIFICATION	A strong-flying medium-sized sulphur of open fields. Since sulphurs almost always land with their wings closed, it is difficult to get a good view of their upper wing surfaces. Above, which can be seen in flight, is clear lemon-yellow with **no orange patches**. Both sexes have black FW borders above but females have yellow spots within the border. Orange Sulphur has at least some orange above. Some female Clouded and Orange Sulphurs lack the yellow and/or orange pigments and are off-white with the usual black pattern. They can be distinguished from Cabbage Whites by their less swerving flight patterns, their off-white appearance, and their black markings. Although Clouded Sulphur females generally have a narrower black FW border than Orange Sulphur females, distinguishing the white females in the field may not be possible.
HABITAT	Open fields, roadsides, suburban areas, etc.
RANGE	Most of North America.
ABUNDANCE	A few old records from north Florida.
MAJOR FOODPLANT	White clover (*Trifolium repens*).
COMMENTS	Most reports of this species from Florida are really of Orange Sulphurs with very little orange.

Yellow Angled-Sulphur *Anteos maerula* **Plate 9**

SIZE	≥ Cloudless Sulphur.
SIMILAR SPECIES	Cloudless Sulphur.
IDENTIFICATION	Seen well, the reticulated greenish-white underside with prominent veining, and curved wing shape, distinguish angled-sulphurs from Giant-Sulphurs (*Phoebis*). Above bright (male) or dull (female) yellow.
HABITAT	Generally distributed in open tropical areas, as a stray it could occur anywhere.
RANGE	West Indies, including Cuba, and Mexico south to Peru.
ABUNDANCE	Rare stray to the Florida Keys and south Florida. Most likely in Sept.
MAJOR FOODPLANT	Cassias.
COMMENTS	A very large yellow sulphur with a very powerful flight. Very rarely immigrates into the Keys (presumably from Cuba) in numbers (as in 1973).

Orbed Sulphur *Phoebis orbis* Not Illustrated.

SIZE ≤ Cloudless Sulphur.

SIMILAR SPECIES Cloudless Sulphur, Statira Sulphur, White Angled-Sulphur.

IDENTIFICATION Usually smaller than other giant-sulphurs. Above, male is pale yellowish-white with a bright orange patch at the FW base. Female deep orange above. Below, pale orange, with strong markings and with a strong and well-defined red-brown border on the FW outer margin. Below, both sexes have the FW apical line broken, as in Cloudless Sulphur, not straight, as in Large Orange Sulphur.

RANGE Cuba and Hispaniola.

ABUNDANCE 1 record (Cuban subspecies), April 25, 1973, Big Pine Key, Florida.

MAJOR FOODPLANT Not known to breed in Florida, but uses dwarf poinciana (*Poinciana pulcherrima*) in Cuba. This plant is cultivated in Florida as an ornamental.

Boisduval's Yellow *Eurema boisduvaliana* Plate 9

SIZE ≤ Checkered White.

SIMILAR SPECIES Sleepy Orange, Little Yellow, Mexican Yellow.

IDENTIFICATION Note "tails," bright orange-yellow above, yellow below. Sleepy Orange is deep orange above and lacks "tails." Little Yellow is smaller and below lacks tails and HW diagonal line. Mexican Yellow (not recorded from Florida, but an immigrant to eastern U.S. from the Southwest) is pale yellow to white above, has a more angular "face" on the FW above.

HABITAT Tropical forest and scrub.

RANGE West Indies and Mexico south to Costa Rica.

ABUNDANCE Several old records and, more recently. 1 record from Sept. 20, 1973, Stock Island, Florida.

MAJOR FOODPLANT Probably sennas.

COMMENTS May be increasing its range in the West Indies; if so, more strays to south Florida are possible.

Shy Yellow *Eurema messalina* Plate 6

SIZE ≤ Little Yellow.

SIMILAR SPECIES Little Yellow, Mimosa Yellow.

IDENTIFICATION White above with a narrow FW black border (visible through wing). Below there is a **black subapical spot on the FW** and the FW disc is white. Some Little Yellows are white above, but they lack the strong black subapical FW spot below and their FW discs are not cleanly white.

HABITAT Edges of tropical hammocks and thickets.

RANGE West Indies, including Cuba and the Bahamas.

ABUNDANCE 1 record from Sanford, Seminole Co. in October 1887. Perhaps that individual's presence in Florida was assisted by a human, but given the proximity of the Bahamas, where it is common, who knows?

MAJOR FOODPLANT *Cassia.*

COMMENTS Even more than Mimosa Yellow, the aptly named Shy Yellow remains inaccessible, weaving deftly through the brushy edges of woodlands on indefatigable wing muscles.

Disguised Scrub-Hairstreak *Strymon limenia*
Plate 15

SIZE < Gray Hairstreak.

SIMILAR SPECIES Mallow Scrub-Hairstreak.

IDENTIFICATION This stray is very similar to the common Mallow Scrub-Hairstreak but is more brown than gray (but worn Mallow Scrub-Hairstreaks can appear brownish). Note the characteristic HW cell-end bar that looks like a pale continuation of the postmedian band, being much thinner and fainter than the distal two spots and, especially, the **extra black spot along the HW trailing margin**. In addition, note the HW black cell-spot, as black and prominent as the two black spots on the HW leading margin. Mallow Scrub-Hairstreak usually has this spot somewhat paler, less prominent, and with some reddish scales. Also, look at the two black spots on the HW leading margin. Disguised Scrub-Hairstreak has the more distal spot larger while Mallow Scrub-Hairstreak has the two spots about the same size. If you are exceptionally lucky and the butterfly opens its wings, note the diagnostic **red outer angle lobes above**.

HABITAT Disturbed, weedy fields and roadsides.

RANGE Cuba, Hispaniola, Puerto Rico, Jamaica, and St. Thomas.

ABUNDANCE Rare stray and temporary colonist (in the early 1970s) in the Florida Keys. Reported March, April, May, December. We know of no records since 1976.

MAJOR FOODPLANT Unknown.

Caribbean (or Cuban) Peacock *Anartia chrysopelea*
Not Illustrated.

SIZE ≤ Common Buckeye.

SIMILAR SPECIES Male Mimic.

IDENTIFICATION A small, black-brown nymphalid with a median white stripe on the FW, a central white blotch on the HW, and a small tail. Above, note the orange-red submarginal dashes. Male Mimics are larger and have subapical white spots and no tail.

RANGE Cuba.

ABUNDANCE A few records from 1972–1973 from Key West and Big Pine Key.

MAJOR FOODPLANT Fogfruit (*Lippia*).

Mimic *Hypolimnas misippus* **Plate 43**

SIZE Between Common Buckeye and Red-spotted Purple.

SIMILAR SPECIES Male, Caribbean Peacock; Female, Monarch, plain tiger.

IDENTIFICATION Males and females look very different. Males above are black with a few bold white spots and are distinctive. Below, males have approximately the same white spots on a brown background. Caribbean Peacocks lack Mimic's white apical spot and are brown, not black. Mimic females are orange with a black FW apex and a subapical white stripe. Monarchs lack the bold white stripes. Females very closely mimic the widespread Old World species, the plain tiger (*Danaus chysippus*). Although plain tigers do not naturally occur in Florida, they are exhibited by butterfly zoos and may occasionally escape. Look closely at the HW black border. On female Mimics this border is quite even, while on plain tigers it becomes irregularly wider at the HW apex.

HABITAT Open tropical areas.

RANGE West Indies, Venezuela and the Guianas, Africa, and Asia.

ABUNDANCE Very rare stray to south Florida.

MAJOR FOODPLANT Morning glory (*Ipomea*), purslanes (Portulacaceae) and mallows (Malvaceae). There is a report from the 1880s of this species using purslane as a caterpillar foodplant in Florida.

COMMENTS Apparently an immigrant to the New World in historic times, either unaided or assisted by boats over trade routes. Generally considered to be rare throughout the West Indies. Almost all Florida records are old, but one was seen and photographed at Royal Palm Hammock, Everglades NP, in November 1986 (see photo on plate 43).

Pale Cracker *Hamadryas amphichloe* **Plate 43**

SIZE ≤ Red-spotted Purple.

IDENTIFICATION Above, mottled bluish-gray with much white mottling on the apical half of the FW. Below, similar, but ground color is gray-white. Usually lands on tree-trunks with wings spread and head down.

HABITAT   Edges of tropical woodlands.

RANGE   West Indies, including Cuba, and Mexico south to Peru.

ABUNDANCE   Rare stray to extreme southern Florida.

MAJOR FOODPLANT   Unknown, but possibly *Dalechampia*.

COMMENTS   The misnamed Pale Cracker (it's not paler than many crackers) is a great find in Florida. The most recent sightings have been from Broward Co. (1984), northern Key Largo (1988) and Palm Beach Co. (1990).

Orion *Historis odius* Plate 43

SIZE   = Eastern Tiger Swallowtail.

IDENTIFICATION   Very large. Mottled chestnut below, brown-orange above with broad black borders.

RANGE   West Indies, including Cuba, and Mexico south to South America.

ABUNDANCE   There are a few old and questionable reports and possible recent sightings from Broward County and the Keys.

MAJOR FOODPLANT   Cecropia (*Cecropia*).

Many-banded Daggerwing *Marpesia chiron* Plate 23

SIZE   ≥ Common Buckeye.

IDENTIFICATION   Banded dark-brown on light-brown, with characteristic dagger-wing tails.

RANGE   West Indies, including Cuba, and southern Texas south through the American tropics.

ABUNDANCE   There are old reports of this butterfly from Miami and one more recent record, Nov. 7, 1985, from Big Pine Key.

MAJOR FOODPLANT   Figs (*Ficus*) and other Moraceae.

Antillean Daggerwing *Marpesia eleuchea* Plate 23

SIZE   > Common Buckeye.

SIMILAR SPECIES   Ruddy Daggerwing.

IDENTIFICATION   Looks like a small Ruddy Daggerwing. Above, very similar but the **FW median line is angled** at the bottom of the cell. Ruddy Daggerwing has this line straight across the wing. Below, note the white spot where the HW postmedian line reaches the trailing margin and the **lack of white on the underside of the body.** Ruddy Daggerwing lacks the white spot and has a bright white body, contrasting strongly with the wings.

HABITAT   Native habitat is woodland edges and clearings.

RANGE   Bahamas, Cuba, Hispaniola, and Jamaica.

ABUNDANCE   There are a number of old reports—probably the result of confusion with Ruddy Daggerwings—and one more recent record from Sugarloaf Key, Oct. 14, 1973.

MAJOR FOODPLANT   Figs (*Ficus*).

Tiger Mimic-Queen *Lycorea cleobaea* Not Illustrated.

SIZE   = Monarch.

IDENTIFICATION   Large with horizontal stripes of black and orange.

HABITAT   Tropical woodlands.

RANGE   West Indies, including Cuba, and Mexico south through tropical Americas.

ABUNDANCE   Very rare stray from Cuba to southern Florida.

MAJOR FOODPLANT   Milkweeds (*Asclepias*), papaya (*Carica papaya*) and other tropical plants.

COMMENTS   May have reproduced in Florida at least once. Formerly common and widespread in Cuba, now much rarer.

Mercurial Skipper *Proteides mercurius* Plate 43

SIZE   ≥ Silver-spotted Skipper.

IDENTIFICATION   A very large skipper with **golden head and thorax**. HW below and abdomen with much pale mottling.

HABITAT   Tropical and subtropical woodlands and gardens near watercourses.

RANGE   West Indies, including Cuba, and Mexico south through tropical Americas.

ABUNDANCE   There have been a few reports of this species from Florida.

MAJOR FOODPLANT   Various tree and shrub legumes.

Funereal Duskywing *Erynnis funeralis* Plate 43

SIZE   = Northern Cloudywing.

SIMILAR SPECIES   Zarucco Duskywing.

IDENTIFICATION   Extremely similar to Zarucco Duskywing, but **HW fringe is boldly white** (but note that Zaruccos on the lower Keys often have whitish fringes).

HABITAT   A wide variety of open situations, from woodland edges, to brushy fields, to thorn scrub.

RANGE   Southwestern Louisiana west to southern California and south to southern South America.

ABUNDANCE   Rare stray to the Panhandle.

COMMENTS   Reports from the Florida Keys probably are referable to Zarucco Duskywing.

Reversed Roadside-Skipper *Amblyscirtes reversa*
Not Illustrated, see *Butterflies through Binoculars: The East.*

SIZE   ≥ Swarthy Skipper.

IDENTIFICATION   Below, **chestnut with yellow veins** and other pale markings. Often has a wavy yellow ray splitting the pale spots.

HABITAT   Moist woodlands with cane.

RANGE   Northeastern Georgia to southeastern Virginia.

ABUNDANCE   There is a single recent specimen labeled Gulf Hammock, Levy County. Although this region has been intensively searched before and since, no additional individuals have been reported. This species has been reported from a number of areas very far removed from the major range in the Carolinas and northern Georgia (e.g., Illinois and southern Alabama) and the foodplant is abundant in the Gulf Hammock area.

MAJOR FOODPLANT   Cane (*Arundinaria*).

Violet-banded Skipper *Nyctelius nyctelius* **Plate 43**

SIZE   = Whirlabout.

IDENTIFICATION   Below, the HW has alternating pale and dark bands, the pale bands with a violaceous sheen when fresh. A black spot is near the middle of the HW leading margin. Abdomen with black and white rings. Above, FW with a double cell-spot.

HABITAT   Disturbed grassy areas.

RANGE   West Indies, including Cuba, and southern Texas south through tropical Americas.

ABUNDANCE   1 record from Key Largo, May 10, 1974.

MAJOR FOODPLANT   Coarse grasses.

DUBIOUSLY OCCURRING SPECIES

The following species have been recorded from Florida but are likely to have been mislabeled, misidentified, to have been transported to Florida by human agency, or need further verification for other reasons.

Apricot Sulphur *Phoebis argante* Not Illustrated.

COMMENTS There are a few specimens of this species in the American Museum of Natural History (New York, NY) labeled as having been collected in the Sarasota, Florida area. There is reason to believe that these are incorrectly labeled. Apricot Sulphurs do occur in Cuba, but are rare there.

Ruddy Hairstreak *Electrostrymon sangala* Not Illustrated.

COMMENTS There is one record, from the vicinity of Grassy Key, in February 1982. Since it is not found in the West Indies, it is unlikely that this delicate tropical butterfly arrived in Florida under its own volition. Perhaps it was transported on a produce ship from South America. The specimen upon which this record was based was originally misidentified as the closely related Latin American *Electrostrymon endymion* and is illustrated as such in Minno and Emmel (1993).

Banded Orange Heliconian *Dryadula phaetusa* Not Illustrated.

COMMENTS A number of these tropical butterflies were supposedly captured in 1932 in the vicinity of Miami and on Key Largo. However, the validity of these unusual records is questionable and there have been no recent sightings. This species does not occur in the West Indies. Since Banded Orange Heliconians are commonly exhibited at butterfly zoos, someone may eventually see an escaped individual.

Great Spangled Fritillary *Speyeria cybele* Not Illustrated, see *Butterflies through Binoculars: The East.*

COMMENTS There are several older reports of this large butterfly from the vicinity of Gainesville, Florida.

Cramer's Eighty-eight *Diaethria clymena* Not Illustrated.

COMMENTS There are several old, and untrustworthy, reports of this striking South American butterfly in Florida, but at least one record is convincing—a single worn adult found visiting damp soil at Royal Palm Hammock in Everglades NP in 1944. This species does not occur in the West Indies, and so it is likely that this individual was transported to Florida by human agency.

Manuel's Skipper *Polygonus manueli* Not Illustrated.

COMMENTS Most Florida records of this tropical skipper have confused the very similar Hammock Skipper with this species. However, there are at least two old specimens of this species that are labeled as having been collected in Florida—they may be mislabeled. Since this species is not found in Cuba or the Bahamas, individuals reaching Florida are probably transported by human agency, although it is possible that tropical storm assisted strays occasionally reached Florida from the Lesser Antilles or Central America.

Tanna Longtail *Urbanus tanna* Not Illustrated.

COMMENTS A Tanna Longtail recorded from Lake Wales, Polk Co. in 1993 is probably mislabeled. Even if it actually was found there, it seems very unlikely that it flew from Mexico or Venezuela under its own power.

Variegated Skipper *Gorgythion begga* Not Illustrated.

COMMENTS Twice reported from Key Largo, this tropical species does not occur in the West Indies.

Dreamy Duskywing *Erynnis icelus* Not Illustrated, see *Butterflies through Binoculars: The East.*

COMMENTS Several old specimens are labeled from the Panhandle. There are no recent sightings.

Hobomok Skipper *Poanes hobomok* Not Illustrated, see *Butterflies through Binoculars: The East.*

COMMENTS There are a few old specimens, captured during the late nineteenth century and labeled as from the Panhandle. There have been no other reports or recent sightings.

Bell's Roadside-Skipper *Amblyscirtes belli* Not Illustrated, see *Butterflies through Binoculars: The East.*

COMMENTS A recent report, from Suwanee River State Park, needs substantiation.

Descriptions and Checklists
for Selected Butterflying Localities

THE FOLLOWING LOCALITIES HAVE BEEN CHOSEN for the diversity and for the abundance of their butterfly fauna. In addition, they are easily accessible to a large percentage of the people of Florida. They can serve as excellent starting points for your butterflying experiences. Most of the species recorded from Florida have been seen in at least one of these localities. In almost all cases they are protected by law.

PANHANDLE REGION
APALACHICOLA NATIONAL FOREST
FRANKLIN, LEON, LIBERTY, AND WAKULLA COUNTIES
At nearly 570,000 acres, Apalachicola NF is one of the largest natural areas in Florida. Habitats include sandhills, pine flatwoods, hammocks, pitcher plant savannas, canebrakes, hardwood, cypress, and white cedar swamps, bayheads, and ravines. The butterflies of this region are equally diverse and interesting.

Silver Lake Camp located eight miles southwest of Tallahassee is the most developed site with electricity, flush toilets, and hot showers. A fee is charged at this area. Take State Road (S.R.) 20 west, go south on S.R.-260. More primitive camp sites are located along the Ochlockonee River, including Porter Lake, Whitehead Lake, Mack Landing, Hitchcock Lake, and Wood Lake. Other primitive camps in the western part of the forest include Camel Lake (F.S. 105), White Oak Landing (F.S. 115), Cotton Landing (F.S. 123), Wright Lake (flush toilet and cold showers), and Hickory Lake (both off F.S. 101). Trails in the forest including the Vinzant Horse Trail (29 miles), Munson Hills Mountain Bicycling Trail (10 miles), and the Florida National Scenic Trail (60 miles). Numerous canoeing opportunities are available on the Apalachicola and Ochlockonee rivers and their tributary streams. The pitcher plant savannas just north of Sumatra are also good places to view butterflies, especially during the fall. There are hundreds of miles of unpaved forest service roads to explore. Often white cedars can be found where the roads cross over blackwater streams such as F.S. 114 east of Sumatra. Apalachicola NF is so large and diverse that nearly all of the panhandle butterflies are likely to be found here. Among the rarer species, the Falcate Orangetip has been found a few times around the edges of bottomland forests along the Ochlockonee River. Henry's Elfin also can be found in the same habitat and season. Hessel's Hairstreak is a butterfly that makes an ephemeral appearance and that may occasionally be seen flitting among the tops of white cedars that frequently grow along the banks of blackwater streams and rivers. Berry's Skipper is locally abundant in some of the savanna areas north of Sumatra.

Other interesting species to watch for at Apalachicola NF are Coral Hairstreak, Banded Hairstreak, King's Hairstreak, Striped Hairstreak, Southern Hairstreak, 'Olive' Juniper Hairstreak, Eastern Pine Elfin, Eastern Tailed-Blue, Summer Azure, 'Edwards' Spring Azure, Texan Crescent, Silvery Checkerspot, Eastern Comma, Mourning Cloak, Goatweed Leafwing, Appalachian Brown, Gemmed Satyr, Georgia Satyr, Little Wood-Satyr, Common Wood-Nymph, Golden-banded Skipper, Hoary Edge, Dotted Skipper, Meske's Skipper, Crossline Skipper, Little Glassywing, Zabulon Skipper, Yehl Skipper, Broad-winged Skipper, Palmetto Skipper, Dion Skipper, Dusted Skipper, Pepper and Salt Skipper, Common Roadside-Skipper, Yucca Giant-Skipper, and Cofaqui Giant-Skipper.

Precautions: Some roads may be impassable during the rainy season. Take care during the fall and spring game hunting seasons.

DIRECTIONS Apalachicola NF extends from 10 to 60 miles southwest of Tallahassee. Access to the forest may be made from S.R. 20 (runs eastwest along the northern part of the forest), S.R. 65 (north-south road through the western part of the forest), and U.S. 319 (north-south road along eastern edge of forest). For more information call 850-942-9300 or write to Apalachicola National Forest, USDA Forest Service, 227 N. Bronough Street, Tallahassee, FL 32301. Field headquarters are located in Bristol (West District) and Crawfordville (East District).

BLACKWATER RIVER STATE FOREST

OKALOOSA AND SANTA ROSA COUNTIES

The Blackwater River SF consists of nearly 190,000 acres, and is the largest state forest in Florida. Together with the nearby Conecuh NF in Alabama, Blackwater River SF contains the world's largest contiguous area of longleaf pine/wiregrass vegetation. This ecosystem once covered 60 million acres across the southeastern U.S. Less than 3 million remain. Habitats present at Blackwater River SF include sandhills, pine flatwoods, pitcher plant seeps, canebrakes, hardwoods, cypress, and white cedar swamps, hammocks, and ravines. The butterflies of the western panhandle are poorly known. Some species present in Alabama may eventually be found in Blackwater River SF.

Blackwater River SP lies adjacent to the state forest, about 15 miles northeast of Milton. The park has a developed campground with electricity, flush toilets, and hot showers. The Blackwater River SP charges entrance and camping fees. Take U.S. 90 to Harold, turn north on County Road (C.R.) 23. Park is located on the east side of C.R. 23 about 3.5 miles north of U.S. 90. Primitive camps in Blackwater River SF include Bear Lake off S.R. 4 east of Munson, Bryant Bridge C.R. 21 at the Blackwater River, Camp Lowry off C.R. 28 northwest of Munson, Camp Paquette off C.R. 25 north of Munson, Hurricane Lake off C.R. 18 northeast of Munson, Juniper Bridge S.R. 191 at Juniper Creek south of Munson, Karick Lake off C.R. 38 northeast of Munson, Kennedy Bridge off C.R. 24 at Blackwater River, and Red Rock C.R. 21 at Juniper Creek. The forest has hundreds of miles of dirt roads and trails, including a segment of the Florida National Scenic Trail, to explore. Some of the best canoeing in Florida may be enjoyed on Coldwater Creek, Sweetwater/Juniper Creek, and especially the Blackwater River.

The expansive Blackwater River SF probably contains most of the butterflies found in the panhandle region. The Eastern Tailed-Blue is a rare Florida butterfly that is found in the sandhills of the forest. During late summer and fall Common Wood-Nymphs are abundant in the same habitat. Other unusual butterflies to watch for are the Harvester, Banded Hairstreak, King's Hairstreak, Striped Hairstreak, Southern Hairstreak, 'Olive' Juniper Hairstreak, Hessel's Hairstreak, Henry's Elfin, Eastern Pine Elfin, Summer Azure, 'Edwards' Spring Azure, Texan Crescent, Eastern Comma, Mourning Cloak, Goatweed Leafwing, Southern Pearly-eye, Appalachian Brown, Gemmed Satyr, Georgia Satyr, Little Wood-Satyr, Golden-banded Skipper, Hoary Edge, Dotted Skipper, Meske's Skipper, Crossline Skipper, Northern Broken-Dash, Little Glassywing, Zabulon Skipper, Yehl Skipper, Dukes' Skipper, Dusted Skipper, Pepper and Salt Skipper, Common Roadside-Skipper, Yucca Giant-Skipper, and Cofaqui Giant-Skipper.

Precautions: Take care during the fall and spring game hunting seasons.

DIRECTIONS Blackwater River SF lies about 30 miles northeast of Pensacola. The forest is a maze of small paved and dirt roads. Access to the forest is from U.S. 90 via S.R. 4, S.R. 189, C.R. 21, and S.R. 191. The forest headquarters are located in Munson near the junction of S.R. 4 and S.R. 191. For more information call 850-957-4201 or write to Blackwater River State Forest, Route 1 Box 77, Milton, FL 32570.

FLORIDA CAVERNS STATE PARK

JACKSON COUNTY

The Chipola River basin is a special biogeographic zone in Florida where plants and butterflies of northern affinity are found in disjunct populations. Florida Caverns SP has 1300 acres of diverse magnolia/beech forest and bottomland swamps. Below the forests and hills the caverns in the park are magnificent and extensive. Even the Chipola River disappears underground for a few hundred yards. The park has a developed campground with electricity, flush toilets, and hot showers. Entrance and camping fees are charged. The nature trail is 1.5 miles. A canoe trail on the Chipola River runs for 52 miles.

The Silvery Checkerspot and the Golden-banded Skipper are two rare butterflies that may be seen in the park. Other rarities to watch for are the Falcate Orangetip, Harvester, Coral Hairstreak, Banded Hairstreak, King's Hairstreak, Striped Hairstreak, Southern Hairstreak, Henry's Elfin, Eastern Pine Elfin, Summer Azure, 'Edwards' Azure, Texan Crescent, Eastern Comma, Mourning Cloak, Appalachian Brown, Gemmed Satyr, Common Wood-Nymph, Hoary Edge, Northern Broken-Dash, Little Glassywing, Zabulon Skipper, Yehl Skipper, Dukes' Skipper, Pepper and Salt Skipper, Common Roadside-Skipper, Yucca Giant-Skipper.

DIRECTIONS The park is located about 65 miles northwest of Tallahassee. From I-10 take Exit 20 or 21 to Marianna. The park is located 3 miles north of Marianna off S.R. 167. For more information call 850-482-1228 or write to Florida Caverns State Park, Marianna, FL 32446.

MACLAY STATE GARDENS

LEON COUNTY

During the summer, the gardens attract large numbers of butterflies from the surrounding hardwood forests. The gardens are laid out around Lake Hall, providing a range of habitats to explore. An entrance fee is charged from Jan. 1–April 30. Several trails wind through the gardens and hammocks. The nearby Lake Overstreet Addition (880 acres) property offers an additional 5 miles of trails.

Many common lawn and garden butterflies may be seen in the formal gardens. Among the rarer butterflies that may be present are the Harvester, Banded Hairstreak, Striped Hairstreak, 'Olive' Juniper Hairstreak, Eastern Tailed-Blue, Summer Azure, Eastern Comma, Gemmed Satyr, Hoary Edge, Little Glassywing, Zabulon Skipper, and Yehl Skipper. **DIRECTIONS** Located in Tallahassee, a few miles north of I-10 (Exit 30) on the west side of Thomasville Road (U.S. 319). For more information call 850-487-4556 or write to Maclay State Gardens, 3540 Thomasville Road, Tallahassee, FL 32308

PINE LOG STATE FOREST

BAY AND WASHINGTON COUNTIES

This forest consists of about 6910 acres of slash pine plantations, sandhills, bayheads, and swamps. Adjacent to the forest on the east is Moore's Pasture Unit (42,675 acres) of Point Washington Wildlife Mangement Area. Moore's Pasture is an extensive tract of wet flatwoods and swamps.

There is a developed campground with electricity, flush toilets, and hot showers located in the northwest corner of the forest, about 1/2 mile south of Ebro on the west side of S.R. 79. A camping fee is charged. Both Pine Log and Moore's Pasture Unit are traversed by miles of unpaved roads. At Pine Log, a nature trail loops south from the campground. A section of trail along Pine Log Ceek is beautiful and excellent for butterflies.

The Cofaqui Giant-Skipper is an uncommon butterfly found at Pine Log SF. Other choice species to look for are similar to those found at Maclay State Gardens (above).

Precautions: Some roads may be impassable during the rainy season. Game hunting is permitted in Moore's Pasture Unit during fall and spring.

DIRECTIONS The forest is located about 30 miles northwest of Panama City. Access is from S.R. 79. For more information call 850-747-5639 or write to District Forester, Pine Log State Forest, 715 West 15th Street, Panama City, FL 32401.

POINT WASHINGTON STATE FOREST

BAY, WALTON, AND WASHINGTON COUNTIES

This large natural area consists of about 98,530 acres of scrub, sandhills, flatwoods, hammocks, swamps, bayheads, marshes, wet prairies, and estuarine habitats. Several separate parcels are included in the forest. No camping is permitted at Point Washington SF, but the many miles of unpaved roads provide access to remote sites.

This forest has a nice selection of flatwoods and swamp butterflies. **Precautions:** Take care during the fall and spring game hunting seasons.

DIRECTIONS The main portions of Point Washington WMA are located about 30 miles or less west of Panama City. Access is off U.S. 98 and S.R. 331, S.R. 283, S.R. 395, and S.R. 79. For more information call 850-747-5639.

ROCKY BAYOU STATE RECREATION AREA
(also known as FRED GANNON STATE RECREATION AREA)

OKALOOSA COUNTY

This is a small park (360 acres) located on the northern edge of Choctawatchee Bay. The main habitats are sand pine scrub and hammocks.

The park has a developed campground with electricity, flush toilets, and hot showers. Entrance and camping fees are charged. Red Cedar Trail, Rocky Bayou Trail, and Sand Pine Trail along Puddin Head Lake are located in the park. The lake was created when beavers impounded a small stream that runs through a ravine.

Look for hairstreaks on the scrub oaks during early summer at Rocky Bayou. Other choice species may include Summer Azure, Little Glassywing, and Yucca Giant-Skipper.

DIRECTIONS The park is located about 15 miles northeast of Fort Walton Beach. Access is off S.R. 20, about 3 miles east of Niceville on the north side of the road. For more information call 850-833-9144 or write to Fred Gannon Rocky Bayou State Recreation Area, P.O. Box 597, Niceville, FL 32578.

ST. GEORGE ISLAND STATE PARK

FRANKLIN COUNTY

This is one of the most scenic parks in Florida. St. George Island SP preserves nearly 2000 acres of beaches, dunes, flatwoods, hammocks, and freshwater and salt marshes. One can walk or bike the entire eastern end of St. George Island within the park.

The park has a developed campground with electricity, flush toilets, and hot showers. Entrance and camping fees are charged. A nature trail (2.5 miles) loops east from the campground through a nice pineland. There are also many miles of park roads and the beach to explore.

During late summer and fall, the park is alive with Gulf Fritillaries, Cloudless Sulphurs, Monarchs, and Long-tailed Skippers. Potential uncommon species include 'Olive' Juniper Hairstreak, Summer Azure, Georgia Satyr, Little Wood-Satyr, and Yucca Giant-Skipper. The park is located on the eastern end of St. George Island about 70 miles southwest of Tallahassee. Take U.S. 98 to East Point. Turn south on S.R. 300, cross the long toll-free bridge over Apalachicola Bay to St. George Island, then head east at the stop sign. S.R. 300 ends at the park. For more information call 850-927-2111 or write to Dr. Julian G. Bruce, St. George Island State Park, P. O. Box 62, East Point, FL 32328.

ST. MARKS NATIONAL WILDLIFE REFUGE

JEFFERSON, TAYLOR, AND WAKULLA COUNTIES

This large natural area consists of 66,540 acres of pine flatwoods, hammocks, bayheads, canebrakes, swamps, and freshwater and salt marshes. St. Marks is a gathering point for countless monarchs during the fall. A butterfly festival celebrating the monarch migration is held every year in October. The refuge is divided into three management units: St. Marks (eastern end), Wakulla (central), and Panacea (western end). The visitor center, an interesting lighthouse, and the main butterfly viewing areas are located in the St. Marks Unit. Six butterfly trails have been designated in the St. Marks Unit, especially around impoundments created for ducks and other water fowl. Butterfly trails include Double Dikes (less than 1 mile), Stoney Bayou Pool #1 (about 3 miles), Mounds Pool #2 (under 2 miles), Mounds Trail (about 1 mile), Picnic Pond (less than 2 miles), and the Lighthouse Area (less than 3/4 mile). A 41-mile segment of the Florida National Scenic Trail also passes through the eastern end of St. Marks. Many other trails are found in the Wakulla and Panacea units. The refuge does not have camping facilities. Mosquitoes and other biting flies are often very abundant.

Monarchs, Cloudless Sulphurs, and Gulf Fritillaries are often incredibly abundant at St. Marks during the fall. A good selection of wetland species is also present.

Precautions: Some areas of the refuge are open to game hunting during the fall and spring.

DIRECTIONS Located about 20 miles south of Tallahassee. From Newport on U.S. 98, turn south on C.R. 59 on the east of the St. Marks River. The road ends at the St. Marks Unit. Access to the Wakulla Unit is about 10 miles west of Newport. Turn south on C.R. 365, which ends at the refuge. The Panacea Unit is located around the town of Panacea, about 23 miles west of Newport. S.R. 372A heading west out of Pancea leads to trails around Otter Lake. For more information call 850-925-6121 or write to St. Marks National Wildlife Refuge, P.O. Box 68, St. Marks, FL 32355.

TOP SAIL HILL STATE PRESERVE

WALTON COUNTY

Top Sail Hill is a spectacular, but little-known park consisting of 1470 acres of beaches, dunes, sand pine scrub, pine flatwoods, swamps, and salt marsh.

No camping is permitted in the park. There are many miles of beaches, dirt roads, and trails to explore.

Some of the more unusual butterflies to watch for at Top Sail Hill are the 'Olive' Juniper Hairstreak, Summer Azure, Georgia Satyr, Little Wood-Satyr, Common Wood-Nymph, Golden-banded Skipper, Hoary Edge, and Palmetto Skipper.

DIRECTIONS Top Sail Hill is located about 12 miles east of Destin on the south side of U.S. 98. For more information call 850-233-5110.

TORREYA STATE PARK

LIBERTY COUNTY

DESCRIPTION This interesting park preserves 2540 acres of sandhills, hammocks, swamps, ravines, and canebrakes. The landscape is of rolling hills and ravines richly covered by a diverse forest of hardwoods including beech and magnolia. The Torreya tree is a rare plant found only in a few places in the Panhandle. Many of the trees have recently died from an undetermined disease.

Camping and Butterfly Sites: The park has a developed campground with electricity, flush toilets, and hot showers. Entrance and camping fees are charged. Over 15 miles of trails are designated in the park. The short Weeping Ridge Trail loops off from the campground. The Stone Bridge Trail makes a broad circle through the park, crossing Rock Creek, and the Confederate Gun Pits, and skirts the Apalachicola River in a few spots.

BUTTERFLIES Rare butterflies that have been seen at Torreya include Eastern Tailed-Blue, Spring Azure, Coral Hairstreak, Pepper and Salt Skipper, Common Roadside-Skipper, Wild Indigo Duskywing, and Golden-banded Skipper. In the sandhill at the park entrance you may find Pipevine Swallowtail, Zebra Swallowtail, Southern Dogface,

Coral Hairstreak, Eastern Tailed-Blue, Variegated Fritillary, Hoary Edge, Southern Cloudywing, Northern Cloudywing, Confused Cloudywing, Juvenal's Duskywing, Horace's Duskywing, Zarucco Duskywing, Yucca Giant-Skipper, and Cofaqui Giant-Skipper. The rare roadside-skippers have been seen in grassy areas around the gun pits and along the ridge trail. Summer Azures, Question Marks, Eastern Commas, and Zabulon Skippers may be seen around the campground trails.

SPECIES LIST Pipevine Swallowtail C, Zebra Swallowtail C, Black Swallowtail U, Giant Swallowtail U, Eastern Tiger Swallowtail C, Spicebush Swallowtail C, Palamedes Swallowtail C, Cabbage White R, Southern Dogface U, Cloudless Sulphur A during late summer and fall, Barred Yellow U–C, Little Yellow C, Sleepy Orange U–C, Great Purple Hairstreak U, Coral Hairstreak R, Banded Hairstreak U, King's Hairstreak U, Striped Hairstreak U, Southern Hairstreak U, Henry's Elfin U, Eastern Pine Elfin R, White M Hairstreak U, Red-banded Hairstreak C, Gray Hairstreak C, Ceraunus Blue C, Eastern Tailed-Blue U, "Edwards" Spring Azure R, Summer Azure C, American Snout U, Gulf Fritillary A during late summer and fall, Variegated Fritillary C, Texan Crescent U, Phaon Crescent C, Pearl Crescent C, Question Mark U–C, Eastern Comma U–C, Mourning Cloak R, Red Admiral U–C, American Lady U–C, Common Buckeye C, Red-spotted Purple C, Viceroy C, Hackberry Emperor A, Tawny Emperor A, Southern Pearly-eye U, Gemmed Satyr U, Carolina Satyr C–A, Little Wood-Satyr C–A, Monarch C, Silver-spotted Skipper C, Long-tailed Skipper A during late summer and fall, Golden-banded Skipper U, Hoary Edge U, Southern Cloudywing C, Northern Cloudywing C, Confused Cloudywing C, Juvenal's Duskywing C, Horace's Duskywing C, Zarucco Duskywing C, Wild Indigo Duskywing R, Swarthy Skipper C, Clouded Skipper C, Fiery Skipper C, Tawny-edged Skipper C, Whirlabout C, Southern Broken-Dash C, Little Glassywing U, Sachem U, Delaware Skipper C, Byssus Skipper C, Zabulon Skipper U, Broad-winged Skipper R, Pepper and Salt Skipper R, Lace-winged Roadside-Skipper U, Common Roadside-Skipper R, Yucca Giant-Skipper U, Cofaqui Giant-Skipper R.

Precautions: Ticks are often abundant along the trails.

DIRECTIONS The park is located about 40 miles west of Tallahassee. From S.R. 20 take S.R. 12 north from Bristol. In about 6 miles turn north on C.R. 271 then west on C.R. 1641 to the park. From I-10 take Exit 24 north about 2 miles to C.R. 269. Turn south, then west on C.R. 1641. For more information call 850-643-2674 or write to Torreya State Park, Route 2, Box 70, Bristol, FL 32321.

WAKULLA SPRINGS STATE PARK

WAKULLA COUNTY

Wakulla Springs containes one of the world's largest and deepest springs. The park preserves 2900 acres of flatwoods, hammocks, bayheads, swamps. An entrance fee is charged at the gate.

No camping is permitted in the park, but the park does offer a magnificent lodge with dining facilities that was built in 1937. Several trails loop around the central park for a total of about 5 miles.

The butterflies present at the park are mostly forest species. All of the swallowtails are common. Carolina Satyrs, Question Marks, and American Ladies can also be found along the trails. Choice species to watch for include Harvester, 'Olive' Juniper Hairstreak, Summer Azure, Texan Crescent, Eastern Comma, Appalachian Brown, Gemmed Satyr, Goldenbanded Skipper, Hoary Edge, Crossline Skipper, Little Glassywing, Zabulon Skipper, Yehl Skipper, and Dukes' Skipper.

DIRECTIONS Wakulla Springs is located about 14 miles south of Tallahassee. The park is situated on the south side of S.R. 267 about 5 miles west of Wakulla. From Tallahassee take U.S. 319 south, turn south on S.R. 61, then east on S.R. 267. Or use S.R. 363 to Wakulla and turn west on S.R. 267 to the park. For more information call 850-922-3632 or write to Edward Ball Wakulla Springs State Park, 1 Spring Drive, Wakulla Springs, FL 32305.

NORTH PENINSULA

ANASTASIA ISLAND STATE RECREATION AREA

ST. JOHNS COUNTY

Anastasia Island State Recreation Area is one of the most popular parks in Florida. The preserve features 1500 acres of broad sandy beaches, sea oats covered dunes, sand pine scrub, coastal hammocks, and salt marshes. The park provides habitat for the endangered Anastasia beach mouse as well as interesting butterflies. Many of the trees near the beach have been pruned and dwarfed by the strong winds and salt-laden air into natural bonsai. This is a must-see park if you're visiting the St. Augustine area.

Anastasia Island SRA has a developed campground with electricity, flush toilets, and showers. Entrance and camping fees are charged. The 1-mile long nature trail loops through a coastal hammock. There are also plenty of butterfly viewing opportunities along the 8 miles of service roads through the park

The beaches and dunes are a harsh environment and have a reduced butterfly fauna. During the fall, migrating butterflies such as Great Southern Whites, Cloudless Sulphurs, Common Buckeyes, and Long-tailed Skippers are commonly seen on blanket flower and Spanish needles. Monarchs are especially fond of seaside goldenrod flowers. Look for Southern Hairstreaks on the dwarf oaks and 'Sweadner's' Juniper Hairstreaks on red cedars near the parking lot in April. You also may see Mangrove Buckeyes, Salt Marsh Skippers, and Obscure Skippers near the dunes and salt marsh in the park.

Precautions: Mosquitoes and sandflies may be abundant during the summer wet season.

DIRECTIONS The park is located a few miles southeast of St. Augustine on S.R. A1A. For more information call 904-461-2000 or write to Anastasia State Recreation Area, 13406 A1A South, St. Augustine, FL 32084

AMELIA ISLAND STATE RECREATION AREA

NASSAU COUNTY

This small park provides easy viewing of coastal habitats and butterflies. There are 230 acres of beaches, dunes, coastal hammocks, and salt marshes to explore on the southern end of Amelia Island. The park is only for daytime use.

In weedy areas near the parking lots and along the roads look for Checkered Whites, Cloudless Sulphurs, Barred Yellows, Sleepy Oranges, Gray Hairstreaks, Ceraunus Blues, Gulf Fritillaries, Phaon Crescents, American Ladies, Painted Ladies, Common Buckeyes, White Peacocks, Long-tailed Skippers, Dorantes Longtails, Tropical Checkered-Skippers, Fiery Skippers, Whirlabouts, Eufala Skippers, and Ocola Skippers. Swallowtails such as the Pipevine, Zebra, Giant, Spicebush, and Palamedes can be enjoyed around the coastal hammock. Also around the hammock watch for Southern Hairstreaks, White M Hairstreaks, Red-banded Hairstreaks, Red Admirals, Hackberry Emperors, Tawny Emperors, Silver-spotted Skippers, and Northern Cloudywings. Near the salt marshes or beach, Great Southern Whites, Eastern Pygmy-Blues, and Salt Marsh Skippers should be found.

Precautions: Mosquitoes and sandflies may be abundant during the summer wet season.

DIRECTIONS The park is located about 20 miles northeast of Jacksonville. From I-95 take Exit 129 (A1A) east to Fernandina Beach, then south about 9 miles to just before the bridge across the Nassau River. For more information call 904-251-2320 or write to Amelia Island State Recreation Area, c/o Little Talbot Island State Park, 12157 Heckscher Drive, Jacksonville, FL 32226.

CARY STATE FOREST

DUVAL AND NASSAU COUNTIES

Cary SF has 3400 acres of flatwoods dotted with small isolated swamps. Other interesting habitats include hammocks, pitcher plant seeps, canebrakes, bayheads, and wet prairies.

Generally the forest is open to daytime use only. The two nature trails near the environmental center total 1.2 miles. The north trail goes through pine flatwoods and over a boadwalk through a cypress swamp to Moccasin Slough Road. The south trail cuts across more flatwoods and a swamp to Fox Squirrel Road. Cary SF has at least 18 miles of forest roads for hiking. Especially interesting are Chicken Farm Road, Red Root Road, and No Catch Road. Check out the pitcher plant seeps along the powerline for skippers.

The flatwood habitats at Cary SF harbor a good assortment of local butterflies. More wooded seeps with canebrakes will have Southern Pearly-eyes and Lace-winged Roadside-Skippers.

Precautions: Mosquitoes may be abundant during the summer wet season. Take care during the spring and fall hunting seasons. All of the roads are unpaved and may not be passable to regular vehicles, especially during the summer rainy season.

DIRECTIONS The forest is located 6 miles north of Baldwin on U.S. 301 near Bryceville. For more information call 904-266-9349 or write to Cary State Forest, 8719 West Beaver Street, Jacksonville, FL 32220.

CEDAR KEY SCRUB STATE RESERVE

LEVY COUNTY

As you travel S.R. 24 from Gainesville to Cedar Key notice the tremendous changes in habitat that unfold in a relatively short span. From the sandhills of the northern Brooksville Ridge the road crosses wet flatwoods then passes through an ancient dune ridge on the Cedar Key Scrub S.R. before reaching the salt marshes along the coast. The reserve contains 4880 acres of sand pine scrub, flatwoods, hammocks, bayheads, and swamps. The Cedar Keys National Wildlife Refuge protects several small islands off Cedar Key. These delicate islands are off limits to pedestrians and are only accessible by boat. The Cedar Keys State Museum (1710

Museum Drive) in Cedar Key gives a great introduction to the rich history of this part of Florida.
The reserve is for daytime use only. There are several parking areas and trailheads that are easily accessible off S.R. 24.
The scrub butterflies to watch for in the reserve include Zebra Swallowtails and Yucca Giant-Skippers. Also look for Yucca Giant Skippers on the island of Cedar Key around stands of Spanish bayonet. Wetter sites such as swamps and wet hammocks are the homes of Henry's Elfins, Southern Pearly-Eyes, Appalachian Browns, and some wetland skippers.

Precautions: Biting insects may be abundant during the summer wet season.

DIRECTIONS The preserve is located on S.R. 24 about 55 miles southwest of Gainesville. Look for signs a short way west of Rosewood. For more information call 352-543-5567 or write to Cedar Key Scrub State Reserve, P.O. Box 187, Cedar Key, FL 32625.

DEVIL'S MILLHOPPER STATE GEOLOGICAL SITE

ALACHUA COUNTY

A short walk through a shady hammock brings you to the edge of a huge sinkhole 120 feet deep. As the trail descends to the bottom of the sinkhole the air cools and ferns blanket the ground. Another loop traverses rich forest and pine flatwoods around the rim of the sink. The park is for daytime use only. No fees are charged for enjoying this 60 acre wonder of nature.

Along the 1/2-mile long trail you're likely to encounter a good selection of swallowtails. Rare species to watch for include Harvester, Goatweed Leafwing, Golden-banded Skipper, Hoary Edge, and Little Glassywing.

DIRECTIONS The park is located in northwestern Gainesville. From I-75 take Exit 77 (S.R. 222 or NW 39th Avenue) east to NW 43rd Street. Go north 1 3/4 miles to NW 53rd Avenue. Turn west and look for the entrance on the north side of the road after 1/4 mile. For more information call 352-955-2008 or write to Devil's Millhopper State Geological Site, 4732 Millhopper Road, Gainesville, FL 32606

FAVER DYKES STATE PARK

ST. JOHNS COUNTY

This mostly wooded park is nestled along Pellicer Creek. Faver Dykes SP contains 1450 acres of hammocks, pine flatwoods, bayheads, swamps, and salt marshes. The landscape is low and wet. Bald Eagles frequently soar above the marshes along the creek.

The park has a developed campground with electricity, flush toilets, and showers. Camping fees are charged. The 2.5-mile long hiking trail as well as the park roads provide some of the best butterfly viewing opportunities.

Along with the usual swallowtails and sulphurs, you may glimpse Henry's Elfins visiting willow flowers or perching on dahoon hollies in the swamps. Salt Marsh Skippers and Great Southern Whites mix with the Delaware Skippers on Spanish needles and other flowers. The woods are often alive with Carolina Satyrs and Little Wood-Satyrs in the spring.

DIRECTIONS The park is located about 15 miles south of St. Augustine. From I-95 take Exit 92 (U.S. 1) south to S.R. 204. Head east on S.R. 204 to the entrance. For more information call 904-794-0997 or write to Faver-Dykes State Park, 1000 Faver-Dykes Road, St. Augustine, FL 32086.

FORT CLINCH STATE PARK

NASSAU COUNTY

Fort Clinch SP lies at the northern tip of Amelia Island, Florida's northernmost Atlantic barrier island. This fort guarded the entrance to the St. Marys River and was occupied by the Union Army during the Civil War. Fort Clinch has 1380 acres of beaches, dunes, salt marshes, and coastal hammocks. The beaches are particularly beautiful and fine for swimming.

The park has two camping areas with electricity, flush toilets, and showers. Entrance and camping fees are charged. The Willow Pond Nature Trail runs 1.5 miles through a coastal hammock. In addition there are 6 miles of park roads suitable for hiking and butterflying.

Among the more interesting butterflies to look for at Fort Clinch are 'Sweadner's' Juniper Hairstreaks, Salt Marsh Skippers, and Yucca Giant-Skippers. Falcate Orangetips are found on similar islands farther north, but have not yet been found in this part of Florida.

DIRECTIONS The park is located about 30 miles northeast of Jacksonville. From I-95 take Exit 129 (A1A) east to Fernandina Beach. Follow A1A north in Fernandina Beach to the junction of S.R. A1A and Atlantic Avenue. For more information call 904-277-7274 or write to Fort Clinch State Park, 2601 Atlantic Avenue, Fernandina Beach, FL 32034.

ST. JOHNS COUNTY

French colonists founded Fort Caroline near Jacksonville in 1564. Most were Huguenots seeking religious freedom in the New World. But Florida was to be Spanish territory. After skirmishes with Spanish soldiers based in St. Augustine, the French counterattacked with overwhelming numbers, only to have their ships wrecked by a severe storm. Many of the survivors surrendered, but were executed at the site now known as matanzas or slaughters. The Castillo de San Marcos in St. Augustine became a major base of operations for the Spanish. A fortified outpost was erected with slave labor on Rattlesnake Island along the Matanzas River south of St. Augustine to protect the city from attack by the English and French. This interesting park contains 230 acres of beaches, dunes, coastal hammocks, and salt marshes.

The park is for daytime use only. One can stroll along the beach on the ocean side of the park, view the coastal hammock on a winding nature trail, or ride a ferry to the restored outpost across the river on Rattlesnake Island. There is no charge for entering the park or for the boat ride.

This is an easy park in which to view coastal butterflies such as the Great Southern White, Eastern Pygmy-Blue, Salt Marsh Skipper, and Yucca Giant-Skipper. Occasionally you may see Cassius Blues or Monk Skippers around the coastal hammock. Look on the red cedar trees around the parking lot for 'Sweadner's' Juniper Hairstreaks.

DIRECTIONS The park is located 14 miles south of St. Augustine off S.R. A1A just north of the bridge across the Matanzas Inlet. For more information call 904-471-0116 or write to Fort Matanzas National Monument, 8635 A1A South, St. Augustine, FL 32086.

GOETHE STATE FOREST

ALACHUA AND LEVY COUNTIES

Goethe SF contains some magnificent tracts of old growth longleaf pine. The 49,230 acres of flat or gently rolling land are crisscrossed by unpaved roads. Habitats present include sandhills, pine flatwoods, canebrakes, bayheads, wet prairies, and swamps. An interesting diversity of wild flowers, birds, and butterflies occurs in the forest.

The forest is for daytime use only. The best butterfly viewing opportunities are along the unpaved roads such as Black Prong Road, Cow Creek Road, or Gas Line Road. The Tidewater hiking trail is 5.5 miles long.

In the flatwoods look for stands of flowering redroot during the summer. You're likely to find a large assortment of butterfly species visiting this wetland plant. Around swamps or wet hammocks with cane brakes look for Great Purple Hairstreaks and Henry's Elfins.

Precautions: Take care during the spring and fall hunting seasons. You may need a 4-wheel drive vehicle to drive the during the summer rainy season.

DIRECTIONS The forest is located about 30 miles southwest of Gainesville. Take S.R. 121 southwest to just north of Lebanon Station. Access can also be made on Black Prong Road from C.R. 343 and C.R. 326, Gas Line Road off C.R. 336, or several roads off C.R. 337. For more information call 352-447-2202 or write to Goethe State Forest, 8250 SE County Road 336, Dunnellon, FL 34431.

GOLD HEAD BRANCH STATE PARK

CLAY COUNTY

This 2120 acre park is officially known as Mike Roess Gold Head Branch State Park. Gold Head Branch SP lies on a sandy ridge known as the Trail Ridge. Some of the highest elevations in Florida are found in the vicinity of the park. The main habitat is longleaf pine/turkey oak sandhills with small patches of sand pine scrub. This high dry sandy land is pockmarked with sinkholes that have filled with water to become lakes. Marshes and wet prairies occur around the edges of the lakes. There is also a deep ravine with a nature trail in the park. A diverse hammock of woody trees and shrubs covers the ravine.

The park has a developed campground with electricity, flush toilets, and showers. Entrance and camping fees are charged. Nature trails are 2 miles, 3 miles, and 13.5 miles. A 29-mile segment of the Florida Trail passes through the park, but only 3 miles are open to non-Florida Trail Association members.

In the sandhills near the park entrance look for Dotted Skippers, Meske's Skippers, and giant-skippers, in addition to a good assortment of more common species. Wandering the shady path down into and along the ravine keep an eye out for Gemmed Satyrs flying among the much more numerous Carolina Satyrs. At the bottom of the ravine trail you may glimpse a Zabulon Skipper.

DIRECTIONS Gold Head Branch State Park lies about 35 miles northeast of Gainesville or 40 miles southwest of Jacksonville. Take S.R. 21 six miles north of Keystone Heights. The park is on the east side of the road. For more information call 352-473-4701 or write to Gold Head Branch State Park, 6239 State Road 21, Keystone Heights, FL 32656.

LEVY COUNTY

This 25,000 acre unit lies just southwest of the Goethe State Forest near the town of Lebanon Station. Sandhills, pine flatwoods, canebrakes, bayheads, wet prairies, and swamps are the major habitats represented. There is a primitive camp area in the southeastern section of the forest. Butterflying is especially good along the power line. Many miles of unpaved roads make for easy hiking and butterfly watching.

Gulf Hammock WMA is one of the southernmost localities for Little Glassywings. It's also a great place to see swallowtails, satyrs, and other common butterflies. Try looking at patches of flowers along Butler Road, especially where streams cross. During the fall, the sandhills often have lots of wildflowers that are attractive to many butterflies.

Precautions: Take care during the spring and fall hunting seasons. All of the roads are unpaved and may not be passable to regular vehicles, especially during the summer rainy season.

DIRECTIONS The forest is located about 30 miles southwest of Gainesville. Take S.R. 121 southwest to U.S. 19 at Lebanon Station. Access roads such as Butler Road and King Road run west off U.S. 19, a few miles south of Lebanon Station. For more information call 352-447-2202 or write to Goethe State Forest, 8250 SE County Road 336, Dunnellon, FL 34431.

JENNINGS STATE FOREST

CLAY COUNTY

Jennings SF covers 20,570 acres of the Trail Ridge, a relatively high sandy topographic feature of northeastern Florida. The North Fork of Black Creek and its tributaries, home of the endemic Black Creek crayfish, have carved ravines and small valleys in the ridge. The area is characterized by sandhills, sand pine scrub, hammocks, pine flatwoods, seeps, canebrakes, bayheads, wet prairies, and swamps. Along with interesting butterflies, you may see Red-Headed Woodpeckers, Sherman's fox squirrels, or the rare St. John's Susan sunflower.

Jennings has quite a number of rare butterflies. When sundial lupines are in bloom during March in the sandhills, look for Frosted Elfins perching on the flowers. Very rare Eastern Tailed-Blues occur in the sandhills at Jennings along with Dotted Skippers and Meske's Skippers. Around patches of yucca, there may be Cofaqui or Yucca giant-skippers. Look for very rare Arogos Skippers and Dusted Skippers in grassy areas in the sandhills and flatwoods of the forest. Where seeps form on the sides of the sandhills there are often open areas with carnivorous plants, club mosses, and a variety of terrestrial orchids. This is prime habitat for Georgia Satyrs and Crossline Skippers. In shaded canebrakes you're likely to see Southern Pearly-eyes and Lace-winged Roadside-Skippers. **Precautions:** Take care during the spring and fall hunting seasons. All of the roads are unpaved and may not be passable to regular vehicles, especially during the summer rainy season.

DIRECTIONS The forest is located near Middleburg, about 20 miles SW of Jacksonville. From Jacksonville, take I-295 to S.R. 21 (Blanding Boulevard) south. There are three access points to the forest. To get to the main parking area, from Middleburg turn west on S.R. 220 A (Old Jennings Road) then north on Live Oak Lane according to the signs. Access to the southern part of the forest is from C.R. 218 west of Middleburg. Turn north on Nolan Road and follow the signs to the parking area. To get to the northern part of the forest, turn north on C.R. 217 from C.R. 218, then east on Long Branch Road. For more information call 904-529-2359 or write to Jennings State Forest, 8719 West Beaver Street, Jacksonville, FL 32220.

MORNINGSIDE NATURE CENTER

ALACHUA COUNTY

Morningside Nature Center has about 280 acres of pine flatwoods, sandhills, hammocks, and swamps. Prescribed burning is used to manage the upland habitats. The sandhills are especially brilliant with wildflowers and butterflies during the fall following a spring burn.

No camping is permitted, but the park has a nature center with butterfly attracting plantings, a pioneer homestead/farm, and nature trails looping through sandhills, flatwoods, and swamps. The park is free. This is one of the best butterflying sites in Gainesville.

A good assortment of local species can be found, including Little Metalmark, and Neamathla Skipper.

DIRECTIONS The park is located in eastern Gainesville off S.R. 26 (University Avenue). For more information call 352-334-2170 or write to Morningside Nature Center, 3540 East University Avenue, Gainesville, FL 32601.

OSCEOLA NATIONAL FOREST

BAKER AND COLUMBIA COUNTIES

Osceola NF lies along the southern fringe of the Okeefenokee Swamp. Of the three national forests in Florida, this is probably the least visited and least known. With names like Big Gum Swamp, Buckhead Swamp, Impassable Bay, and Pinhook Swamp you get the idea that much of this area is wet and difficult terrain. Most of the 193,100 acres are covered by swamps and wet flatwoods. However, you will also find some sandhill habitat near Ocean Pond and canebrakes, pitcher plant seeps, bayheads, and wet prairies scattered throughout the forest.

The park has a developed campground with electricity, flush toilets, and showers on the northern shore of Ocean Pond off F.S. Road 268. Camping fees are charged. Showers and water are also available at Olustee Beach picnic and swimming area on the southern shore of Ocean Pond. Twenty-two miles of the Florida National Scenic Trail passes through the forest. For a shorter hike, trailheads are located off U.S. 90 at the Olustee Battlefield State Historic Site and on the road to Ocean Pond Campground making a nice 6-mile segment. Big Gum Swamp Wilderness has 13,000 acres of wet flatwoods and swamps. Access is mostly from the old tram roads used to haul cypress and other valuable timber to the mills.

Precautions: Take care during the spring and fall hunting seasons. All of the roads are unpaved and may not be passable to regular vehicles, especially during the summer rainy season.

Swallowtails and other forest butterflies such as Question Marks, Red Admirals, and Red-spotted Purples, are abundant at Osceola NF. This is a good locality to observe Southern Pearly-Eyes, Appalachian Browns, Gemmed Satyrs, Georgia Satyrs, Common Wood-Nymphs, Aaron's Skippers, Yehl Skippers, Broad-winged Skippers, and Lace-winged Roadside-Skippers.

DIRECTIONS The forest is located about 40 miles west of Jacksonville. From I-75 take Exit 82 (U.S. 90) east about 12 miles to Olustee. From I-295 take I-10 west to Exit 45 (U.S. 90), then head west to Olustee. Turn north on C.R. 250A, the main forest road. For more information call 904-752-2577 or write to Osceola National Forest, P.O. Box 70, Olustee, FL 32072.

PAYNES PRAIRIE STATE PRESERVE

ALACHUA COUNTY

Paynes Prairie is a round basin formed from collapsed caverns that has at various times been a lake or a marsh/wet prairie system. In 1774, William Bartram visited the Paynes Prairie area and wrote about the plants and animals as well as a large Indian village that stood near the current town of Micanopy. In 1871, an underground drain known as Alachua Sink became plugged and the prairie became a lake. Steam boats ferried passengers and supplies between Gainesville and Micanopy. Twenty years later the sink opened again and the steamers were left stranded overnight. This beautiful park has 21,050 acres of pine flatwoods, hammocks, old fields, canebrakes, swamps, and freshwater marsh. Small herds of grazing bison and "Cracker" horses can often be seen from the prairie observation tower at the southern visitor center.

The park has a developed campground with electricity, flush toilets, and showers at the southern or Lake Wauberg entrance. Entry and camping fees are charged at the Lake Wauberg unit. The 3.5-mile long nature trail passes through a diverse hardwood hammock and other habitats. At the northern entrance, part of the Gainesville-Hawthorne Rail Trail runs along the rim of Paynes Prairie. This 17-mile trail is often alive with butterflies visiting Spanish Needles and other flowers. A shorter trail takes visitors to Alachua Sink where Sweetwater Branch disappears below ground. During the dry season, the sink is often filled with hundreds of alligators of various sizes.

Butterflies that have been seen at Paynes Prairie include Pipevine Swallowtail, Zebra Swallowtail, Black Swallowtail, Giant Swallowtail, Eastern Tiger Swallowtail, Spicebush Swallowtail, Palamedes Swallowtail, Checkered White, Cloudless Sulphur, Barred Yellow, Little Yellow, Sleepy Orange, Great Purple Hairstreak, Southern Hairstreak, White M Hairstreak, Red-banded Hairstreak, Gray Hairstreak, Ceraunus Blue, Summer Azure, Little Metalmark, American Snout, Gulf Fritillary, Zebra (Heliconian), Phaon Crescent, Pearl Crescent, Question Mark, Red Admiral, American Lady, Painted Lady, Common Buckeye, Red-spotted Purple, Viceroy, Goatweed Leafwing, Hackberry Emperor, Tawny Emperor, Southern Pearly-Eye, Gemmed Satyr, Carolina Satyr, Little Wood-Satyr, Monarch, Queen, Silver-spotted Skipper, Long-tailed Skipper, Dorantes Longtail, Southern Cloudywing, Northern Cloudywing, Confused Cloudywing, Hayhurst's Scallopwing, Juvenal's Duskywing, Horace's Duskywing, Zarucco Duskywing, Common Checkered-Skipper, Tropical Checkered-Skipper, Swarthy Skipper, Neamathla Skipper, Clouded Skipper, Least Skipper, Southern Skipperling, Fiery Skipper, Tawny-edged Skipper, Whirlabout, Southern Broken-Dash, Northern Broken-Dash, Little Glassywing, Sachem, Delaware Skipper, Byssus Skipper, Aaron's Skipper, Yehl Skipper, Dun Skipper, Lace-winged Roadside-Skipper, Eufala Skipper, Twin-spot Skipper, Brazilian Skipper, Ocola Skipper, and Yucca Giant-Skipper.

DIRECTIONS There are two separate entrances to the park. The southern entrance at Lake Wauberg is off U.S. 441, 10 miles south of Gainesville. To get to the north entrance and the Gainesville-

Hawthorn Trail take S.R. 26 (University Avenue) east in Gainesville.
Turn south on S.E. 15th Street (Kincaid Road) and watch for signs to
the park at the 90° turn to the east. For more information call 352-
466-3397 or write to Paynes Prairie State Preserve, Route 2, Box 41,
Micanopy, FL 32667.

SAN FELASCO HAMMOCK STATE PRESERVE

ALACHUA COUNTY

Rolling hills and rich woodlands best describe the San Felasco Hammock State Preserve. There are 6900 acres of sandhills, hammocks,
canebrakes, sinkholes, and swamps on the preserve. From the southern
trailhead, the path starts in the sandhill and descends into a beautiful
hammock with canebrakes in the wetter areas. The northern trailhead
passes through a nice sandhill then loops around diverse hammocks
and a large swamp.

This is one of the best places in northern Florida to see uncommon butterflies such as the Harvester, Golden-banded Skipper, Hoary Edge, Hayhurst's Scallopwing, Lace-winged Roadside-Skipper, and Yucca Giant-
Skipper.

DIRECTIONS The park is located just northwest of Gainesville. The
entrance is off NW 63rd Boulevard (Millhopper Road) about 3 3/4 miles
west of Devils Millhopper State Geological Site. For more information call
352-462-7905 or write to San Felasco Hammock State Preserve, c/o
Devil's Millhopper State Geological Site, 4732 Millhopper Road,
Gainesville, FL 32601.

RALPH E. SIMMONS STATE FOREST
(formerly ST. MARYS RIVER STATE FOREST)

NASSAU COUNTY

DESCRIPTION The Simmons SF is located on the bluffs overlooking the
St. Marys River. This blackwater river begins in the Okeefenokee
Swamp in Georgia and flows east, forming Florida's northern boundary.
There are 3640 acres of sandhills, pine flatwoods, hammocks, canebrakes, bayheads, pitcher plant seeps, and swamps. The forest is crisscrossed by miles of unpaved roads, most of which are closed to vehicles,
except during hunting events. To see this wonderful natural area, you
need to hike, bike, or horseback ride a long distance to get to the back
country. The St. Marys River Canoe Trail starts from S.R. 121 five miles
north of Macclenny and extends 51 miles to Hilliard.

About 7 miles of this looping, winding, river pass through the northern edge of the Simmons SF. The forest is primarily for daytime use only, but there are primitive camps along the river for canoers.

BUTTERFLIES Look for Frosted Elfins on stands of sundial lupine in March. Also Goatweed Leafwings are sometimes common here. The adults perch on the ground and occasionally visit mud puddle areas. The powerline and recently burned sandhills often have an abundance of flowers that attract numbers of butterflies.

SPECIES LIST Pipevine Swallowtail C, Zebra Swallowtail C, Black Swallowtail U–C, Giant Swallowtail R, Eastern Tiger Swallowtail C, Spicebush Swallowtail C, Palamedes Swallowtail C, Orange Sulphur R, Southern Dogface R, Cloudless Sulphur C–A, Barred Yellow C–A, Little Yellow C, Sleepy Orange U–C, Great Purple Hairstreak U, Frosted Elfin U, White M Hairstreak U, Red-banded Hairstreak U, Gray Hairstreak C, Ceraunus Blue C, Summer Azure U, 'Edwards' Spring Azure R, Little Metalmark U, Gulf Fritillary C–A, Zebra (Heliconian) U, Variegated Fritillary U, Phaon Crescent U, Pearl Crescent C, Question Mark U, Red Admiral U, American Lady U, Common Buckeye C, Red-spotted Purple U, Viceroy C, Goatweed Leafwing U–C, Southern Pearly-eye U, Appalachian Brown U, Gemmed Satyr U, Carolina Satyr C, Georgia Satyr U, Little Wood-Satyr C, Common Wood-Nymph C, Monarch C, Queen U, Silver-spotted Skipper U, Long-tailed Skipper C, Dorantes Longtail U, Southern Cloudywing C, Northern Cloudywing C, Confused Cloudywing U, Sleepy Duskywing U, Juvenal's Duskywing C, Horace's Duskywing C, Zarucco Duskywing C, Common Checkered-Skipper U, Tropical Checkered-Skipper U, Swarthy Skipper C, Clouded Skipper C, Least Skipper U, Southern Skipperling U, Fiery Skipper C, Tawny-edged Skipper C, Crossline Skipper U, Whirlabout U, Southern Broken-Dash C, Sachem U, Delaware Skipper U, Byssus Skipper U, Yehl Skipper R, Palatka Skipper R, Dion Skipper R, Dun Skipper U, Lace-winged Roadside-Skipper U, Eufala Skipper U, Twin-spot Skipper U, Brazilian Skipper U, Ocola Skipper C–A, Cofaqui Giant-Skipper R.

Precautions: Take care during the spring and fall hunting seasons. Ticks are often abundant, especially in the hammocks.

DIRECTIONS The forest is located about 30 miles northwest of Jacksonville off U.S. 301. Just before the bridge across the St. Marys River/Georgia State Line in Boulogne take Lake Hampton Road east 1 3/4 mile to the powerline crossing entrance. Proceed another mile east on Lake Hampton Road, then turn north on Penny Haddock Road to the main entrance. For more information call 904-845-3597 or write to Ralph E. Simmons State Forest, 8719 West Beaver Street, Jacksonville, FL 32210.

SUWANNEE RIVER STATE PARK

HAMILTON, MADISON, AND SUWANNEE COUNTIES

This beautiful park is located at the confluence of the Withlacoochee and Suwannee rivers. There are 2010 acres of sandhills, pine flatwoods, hammocks, canebrakes, wet prairies, and swamps to explore. During the winter dry season when the river is low, the eroded limestone along the banks is especially interesting.

The park has a developed campground with electricity, flush toilets, and showers. Entrance and camping fees are charged. The Florida National Scenic Trail and Big Oak Trail pass through the park. There are also nature trails along the river.

Along the roadsides and firelanes at the park entrance you're likely to find the Pipevine Swallowtail, Zebra Swallowtail, Spicebush Swallowtail, Palamedes Swallowtail, Gray Hairstreak, Hoary Edge, Southern Cloudywing, Northern Cloudywing, Confused Cloudywing, Sleepy Duskywing, Juvenal's Duskywing, Horace's Duskywing, Zarucco Duskywing, Swarthy Skipper, Yucca Giant-Skipper, and Cofaqui Giant-Skipper. In hammocks on the bluffs above the river look for the Harvester, Great Purple Hairstreak, Banded Hairstreak, Striped Hairstreak, Southern Hairstreak, White M Hairstreak, Red-banded Hairstreak, Summer Azure, American Snout, Question Mark, Red Admiral, Red-spotted Purple, Hackberry Emperor, Tawny Emperor, Carolina Satyr, and Little Wood-Satyr. Bell's Roadside-Skipper has been reported from the park, but needs substantiation. The Southern Pearly-Eye, Gemmed Satyr, and Lace-winged Roadside-Skipper are likely to be in the vicinity of switch cane as well.

DIRECTIONS   The park is located about 65 miles east of Tallahassee or 15 miles west of Live Oak. From I-10 take Exit 38 (C.R. 255) north to U.S. 90, then east about 6 miles. The park is located along the Suwannee River on the north side of the road. Or take U.S. 90 west from Exit 39. For more information call 850-362-2746 or write to Suwannee River State Park, 29185 County Road 132, Live Oak, FL 32060.

CENTRAL FLORIDA

BLUE SPRING STATE PARK, VOLUSIA COUNTY

VOLUSIA COUNTY

DESCRIPTION   This park is named for the large and beautiful spring that issues from the base of high sandy hills and flows into the St. Johns River. Every winter dozens of manatees congregate in the relatively warm spring water. Blue Spring SP encompasses 2485 acres of sand pine scrub, hammocks, swamps, and weedy lawns that was at one time an orange grove in front of the ancient Thursby house. This is one of the most popular parks in Florida for camping, swimming, and wildlife viewing.

Camping and Butterfly Sites: The park has a developed campground with electricity, flush toilets, and hot showers. A primitive camp is located in a magnificent live oak hammock along the St. Johns River. There is a nature trail along the spring run that extends from the river to the pool where the sparkling water emerges from the ground. Another trail begins at the main parking lot and heads south through an oak hammock and skirts the bottomland swamps along the river. The park charges entrance and camping fees. Canoeing is available on the St. Johns River.

BUTTERFLIES   For the best assortment, check the scrubby areas of the park, such as around the entrance and campground, wetter areas around the hammocks, and the grassy area in front of the Thursby House, and along the park roads.

SPECIES LIST   Pipevine Swallowtail U, Zebra Swallowtail C, Black Swallowtail U, Giant Swallowtail C, Eastern Tiger Swallowtail C, Spicebush Swallowtail C, Palamedes Swallowtail C, Great Southern White U, Southern Dogface U, Cloudless Sulphur A, Barred Yellow A, Little Yellow C, Sleepy Orange C, Southern Hairstreak C, White M Hairstreak C, Red-Banded Hairstreak C, Gray Hairstreak C, Ceraunus Blue C, Gulf Fritillary A, Zebra (Heliconian) C, Phaon Crescent A, Pearl Crescent C, Red Admiral U, American Lady U, Common Buckeye U–A, White Peacock U, Red-spotted Purple U, Viceroy U, Hackberry Emperor C, Carolina Satyr A, Viola's Wood-Satyr C, Monarch C, Queen U, Silver-spotted Skipper U, Long-tailed Skipper A, Dorantes Longtail A, Southern Cloudywing U, Northern Cloudywing U, Sleepy Duskywing U, Juvenal's Duskywing U, Horace's Duskywing C, Zarucco Duskywing U, Tropical Checkered-Skipper U, Neamathla Skipper U, Clouded Skipper C, Southern Skipperling U–C, Fiery Skipper C, Whirlabout C, Southern Broken-Dash C, Sachem U, Monk Skipper U, Eufala Skipper U, Brazilian Skipper U, Ocola Skipper A.

Precautions: Mosquitoes may be abundant during the summer wet season.

DIRECTIONS   The park is located about 30 miles north of Orlando. Take I-4 north to the U.S. 92/17 Exit just before Lake Monroe. Proceed north on U.S. 92/17 about 8 1/4 miles to Orange City. Turn west on French Avenue. The park entrance is 2 1/2 miles farther on the south side of the road. For more information call 904-775-3663 or write to Blue Spring State Park, 2100 West French Avenue, Orange City, FL 32763.

BROOKER CREEK PRESERVE

PINELLAS COUNTY

DESCRIPTION This 8500 acre park lies adjacent to the Hillsborough County Line in northeastern Pinellas County. Scrubby flatwoods, hammocks, and swamps are the main habitats represented. Guided butterfly walks are offered on weekends and NABA members conduct 'an annual 4th of July butterfly count at Brooker Creek.

SPECIES LIST Pipevine Swallowtail U, Zebra Swallowtail C, Black Swallowtail U, Giant Swallowtail C, Eastern Tiger Swallowtail C, Spicebush Swallowtail C, Palamedes Swallowtail C, Checkered White U, Great Southern White U, Cloudless Sulphur A, Barred Yellow A, Little Yellow C, Sleepy Orange U–C, Dainty Sulphur C, Banded Hairstreak U, Red-banded Hairstreak C, Southern Hairstreak U, White M Hairstreak U, Gray Hairstreak C, Ceraunus Blue C, Gulf Fritillary A, Variegated Fritillary U, Zebra (Heliconian), C, Phaon Crescent A, Pearl Crescent C, Question Mark U, American Lady U, Red Admiral U, Common Buckeye C, White Peacock A, Red-spotted purple U, Viceroy C, Carolina Satyr A, Georgia Satyr U, Monarch C, Queen C, Silver-spotted Skipper C, Longtailed Skipper A, Southern Cloudywing U, Tropical Checkered-Skipper C, Common Checkered-Skipper U, Sleepy Duskywing U, Juvenal's Duskywing U, Horace's Duskywing C, Zarucco Duskywing C, Swarthy Skipper U, Neamathla Skipper U, Clouded Skipper C, Least Skipper C, Southern Skipperling U/C, Fiery Skipper C, Baracoa Skipper U, Tawnyedged Skipper U, Whirlabout C, Southern Broken-Dash C, Sachem U–C, Delaware Skipper U, Palmetto Skipper U, Eufala Skipper U–C; Twinspot Skipper U–C, Brazilian Skipper U, Ocola Skipper A, and Yucca Giant-Skipper U.

DIRECTIONS The park is located about 20 miles northeast of Tampa. For more information call 813-943-4000 or write to Brooker Creek Preserve, 1001 Lora Lane, Tarpon Springs, Florida 34689.

BULL CREEK WILDLIFE MANAGEMENT AREA

OSCEOLA COUNTY

The landscape throughout much of Osceola County is low, wet, and flat. The vegetation is mostly pine flatwoods intermingled with isolated cypress swamps and bottomland hardwoods along the creeks and rivers. Bull Creek WMA has large tracts of flatwoods with widely spaced longleaf pine and a patchwork understory of grassy prairie, saw palmetto, and gallberry. Crabgrass Creek runs along the northern part of the property and Bull Creek and associated streams drain the south. Near Billy Lake there is dry sandy ridge with sand pine scrubs, xeric hammocks, and scrubby flatwoods. Over 17 miles of the Florida National Scenic Trail run through this 23,500 preserve. There's also an 8.6-mile interpretive drive on Loop Road.

Primitive camping is allowed in designated areas near the game check station, along Crabgrass Creek, and at the southern end of the property near Billy Lake.

There are some beautiful habitats to explore for butterflies at Bull Creek. Look for Arogos Skippers, Georgia Satyrs, and Little Metalmarks in the grassy prairies near the game check station and along Loop Road. Also small depressional wetlands with an abundance of flowering redroot are likely to be hopping with diverse butterflies such as swallowtails, sulphurs, hairstreaks, and skippers. Delaware Skippers, Palmetto Skippers, Berry's Skippers, and many others are quite fond of redroot.

Precautions: Take care during the spring and fall hunting seasons. All of the roads are unpaved and may not be passable to regular vehicles, especially during the summer rainy season.

DIRECTIONS The park is located about 30 miles west of Melbourne. From I-95 take U.S. 192 west. About 7 miles west of C.R. 419, turn south on Crabgrass Road and follow this turning dirt trail to the entrance. For more information call 352-732-1225 or write to Bull Creek WMA, c/o Florida Game and Fresh Water Fish Commission, 1239 SW 10th Street; Ocala, FL 34474.

BULOW PLANTATION RUINS STATE HISTORIC SITE

FLAGLER COUNTIES

During the early 1800s sugar cane, cotton, rice, and indigo were grown on plantations along the Atlantic coast of Florida. John James Audubon and other naturalists visited the Bulow Plantation, which was at that time a lonely outpost on the frontier. The plantation was destroyed in 1836 during the Second Seminole Indian War. Today parts of the coquina rock foundations of the buildings and remains of the sugar mill can still be seen. The park vegetation varies from hardwood hammocks with live oaks hundreds of years old to pine flatwoods and marshes along Bulow Creek. There are two nature trails of 1/2 and 3 1/2 miles in length in this 3340 acre park. A short canoe ride south on Bulow Creeks takes one out into the extensive saltmarshes of the Halifax Creek portion of the Intracoastal Waterway.

Swallowtails and satyrs frequent the hammock trails and edges of the plantation grounds. Along Bulow Creek it's possible to find both fresh-

water and salt marsh species of skippers. Look for Henry's Elfin on blooming willows and around dahoon holly trees in the swamps. **DIRECTIONS** The park is located about 16 miles north of Daytona Beach. From I-95 take S.R. 100 east 1/4 to S.R. 5A (Old Kings Road). Turn south onto Old Kings Road. The park entrance is on the east side of the road, about 3 1/2 miles south of S.R. 100.
For more information call 904-517-2084 or write to Bulow Plantation Ruins State Historic Site, P.O. Box 655, Bunnell, FL 32010.

HIGHLANDS HAMMOCK STATE PARK

HARDEE AND HIGHLANDS COUNTIES

Highlands Hammock SP lies on the Lake Wales Ridge, an ancient topographic feature of central Florida. The ridge has some of the highest elevations and most desert-like scrubs in peninsular Florida. Unfortunately, this land was well-suited for orange groves, and more recently, housing tracts. Many rare and endangered species of plants and animals occur in the small parcels of sand pine scrub habitats that were left undeveloped on the ridge. The U.S. Fish and Wildlife Service is buying up many of these natural areas to create a National Scrub Preserve at the southern end of the ridge. Highlands Hammock SP is a mosaic of sand pine scrub, flatwoods, hammocks, and swamps. The park encompasses 5540 acres.

Highlands Hammock SP has a developed campground with electricity, flush toilets, and hot showers. Eight short nature trails and boardwalks wind through parts of the lush hammocks and swamps. The Cypress Swamp Trail begins off the main road. This approximately 2000 foot long boardwalk meanders through a magnificent cypress swamp. The Fern Garden Trail passes through a hydric hammock with an abundance of ferns. More than 30 species of ferns occur in the park. Some of the live oaks at Highlands Hammock are estimated to be 1000 years old. There are also paved and unpaved roads as well as an 11-mile equestrian trail to explore. We recommend that you make reservations at least six months in advance if you're planning to camp at this popular park, especially during the winter and spring. Entrance and camping fees are charged.

Tiger, Spicebush, and Palamedes swallowtails may be incredibly abundant around the hammocks and swamps at Highlands Hammock, and often puddle in groups on the dirt roads. The park is the southernmost known locality for Henry's Elfins. Look for these small brown butterflies visiting willow blossoms in the spring. The road to the group camping site cuts through flatwoods and scrub. Patches of redroot in wet areas of the flatwoods attract masses of butterflies, including the Pipevine Swallowtail, Zebra Swallowtail, Black Swallowtail, Gray Hairstreak, Gulf Fritillary, Silver-spotted Skipper, cloudywings, Horace's Duskywing, Zarucco Duskywing, Tropical Checkered-Skipper, Neamathla Skipper, Clouded Skipper, Fiery Skipper, Tawny-edged Skipper, Whirlabout, Southern Broken-Dash, Sachem, Delaware Skipper, Palmetto Skipper, Monk Skipper, Eufala Skipper, Twin-spot Skipper, and Ocola Skipper. You may also see Little Metalmarks, Common Buckeyes, and Georgia Satys in open areas through the flatwoods. The scrubby area around the group camping site is home to Southern Dogfaces, Little Yellows, Banded Hairstreaks, Southern Hairstreaks, Ceraunus Blues, Sleepy Duskywings, Juvenal's Duskywings, and Yucca Giant-Skippers.

DIRECTIONS The park is located at the northern end of Sebring. From U.S. 27 turn west on C.R. 634. The park entrance is about 4 miles from U.S. 27. For more information call 941-386-6094 or write to Highlands Hammock State Park, 5931 Hammock Road, Sebring, FL 33872.

JAY B. STARKEY WILDERNESS PARK

PASCO COUNTY

The Starkey Wilderness Park is an oasis of natural habitats in a rapidly urbanizing landscape. This 8620-acre park serves as a wellfield and provides outdoor recreation opportunites. The park has outstanding examples of pine flatwoods, sandhills, hammocks, sand pine scrub, small cypress ponds, wet prairies, and bottomland swamp habitats.

The Starkey Wilderness Park has a developed campground with electricity, flush toilets, and hot showers. Cabins are also available but must be reserved well in advance of your trip. Camping fees are charged. A 1.3-mile nature trail loops to the east of the campground and has a short branch to the Pithlachoascotee River. A 3-mile paved bikeway traverses the center of the property. There is also an 8-mile long equestrian trail that starts near the campground.

Patches of weedy plants along the bikeway such as fogfruit and Spanish needles attract large numbers of butterflies. Palamedes Swallowtails, Dainty Sulphurs, Common Buckeyes, White Peacocks, Horace's Duskywings, Fiery Skippers, and Whirlabouts are often abundant along the bikeway. Baracoa Skippers may be seen visiting flowers near the beginning of the bikeway. To find the rarer butterflies, make short trips off the bikeway into the different plant communities. In the palmetto and wiregrass prairies look for Arogos Skippers, Palmetto Skippers, Twin-spot Skippers, and Dusted Skippers. You may find Sleepy Duskywings, Juvenal's Duskywings, Dotted Skippers, Meske's Skippers, and giant skippers in the scrub and sandhill areas of the park. Hairstreaks, such as Southern Hairstreak, White M Hairstreak, Red-banded Hairstreak, and Gray Hairstreak, often visit the blooming palmettos in early summer.

Precautions: Mosquitoes may be abundant during the summer wet season.

DIRECTIONS The park is located about 15 miles northwest of Tampa. From U.S. 19 at New Port Richie take S.R. 54 east to Elfers, then C.R. 587 north and follow the signs to the park. For more information call 813-834-3247 or write to Jay B. Starkey W.P., 7750 North Congress Street, New Port Richey, FL 34653.

LAKE KISSIMMEE STATE PARK

POLK COUNTY

Lake Kissimmee forms the headwaters of the Everglades system. Water flows southward through the Kissimmee River into Lake Okeechobee and then into the Everglades proper. The park has 5860 acres of pine flatwoods, scrubby flatwoods, scrub, hammocks, prairies, and freshwater marshes. There are 13 miles of the Florida National Scenic Trail in two loops to explore. Entrance and camping fees are charged.

The park has a developed campground with electricity, flush toilets, and hot showers set in a wonderful live oak hammock near Lake Kissimmee.

In the scrubbby flatwoods around the park entrance you may encounter the threatened Florida Scrub Jay as well as a good assortment of butterflies, possibly including Little Metalmarks, Palmetto Skippers, and Yucca Giant-Skippers. On the nature trail through the wetter flatwoods there are prairies with a diversity of wildflowers. Here you may find Georgia Satyrs, Arogos Skippers, Palmetto Skippers, Monk Skippers, and Twin-spot Skipper. In the hammocks around the campground and picnic area look for swallowtails, Great Purple Hairstreaks, Southern Hairstreaks, White M Hairstreaks, and Monk Skippers. Marshy areas around the lake are frequented by Black Swallowtails, White Peacocks, Queens, Soldiers, Viceroys, Least Skippers, Delaware Skippers, Byssus Skippers, Brazilian Skippers, and Ocola Skippers. These butterflies are fond of pickerelweed and buttonbush flowers.

DIRECTIONS The park is located about 65 miles south of Orlando. From U.S. 27 in Lake Wales take S.R. 60 east about 8 miles. Turn north on Boy Scout Road then east on Camp Mack Road and follow the signs to the park. For more information call 941-696-1112 or write to Lake Kissimmee State Park, 14248 Camp Mack Road, Lake Wales, FL 33853.

MERRITT ISLAND NATIONAL WILDLIFE REFUGE

BREVARD AND VOLUSIA COUNTIES

Merritt Island has a regular pattern of low sandy ridges that support scrub vegetation interspersed with wet swales. The edges along the Indian River Lagoon and Banana River are mostly mangroves and salt marshes. The refuge flanks the western and northern sides of the Kennedy Space Center, most of which is off limits to the general public. Merritt Island NWR forms a buffer zone between the Space Center and population centers to the west. In addition, the Canaveral National Seashore lies just north of the refuge. Within this area is a blending of tropical and temperate species as well as salt-tolerant and freshwater plant communities. The refuge preserves 139,155 acres of beaches, dunes, scrub, hammock, flatwoods, salt marshes, and mangroves. No camping is provided at the refuge, but there are three nature trails through hammocks and salt marshes. Black Point Wildlife Drive just northwest of the Visitor Center takes you on a scenic tour of flatwoods and saltmarshes. Hiking trails include the Oak Hammock Trail (1/2 mile) and Palm Hammock Trails (2 miles) located about a mile east of the visitor center.

Around the coastal hammocks look for the Giant Swallowtail, Red-banded Hairstreak, Red Admiral, Carolina Satyr, Clouded Skipper, and Southern Broken-Dash. The Little Yellow, Southern Hairstreak, Olive Hairstreak, Gray Hairstreak, Gulf Fritillary, Common Buckeye, Northern Cloudywing, Sleepy Duskywing, and Yucca Giant-Skipper are likely to be seen around the scrubs, dunes, and coastal oak forests. At the edges of mangroves and salt marshes the Great Southern White, Eastern Pygmy-Blue, Mangrove Buckeye, and Salt Marsh Skipper are often abundant.

Precautions: Mosquitoes and sand flies may be abundant during the summer wet season.

DIRECTIONS Merritt Island is located about 40 miles east of Orlando. From I-95 take Exit 80 (S.R. 406) east into Titusville. This road becomes S.R. 402. Continue across the bridge to Merritt Island. The Visitor Center is located about 4 miles east of Titusville on the south side of the road. For more information call 407-861-0667 or write to Merritt Island NWR, P.O. Box 6504, Titusville, FL 32782-6504

MYAKKA RIVER STATE PARK

MANATEE AND SARASOTA COUNTIES

Myakka River SP is a very popular birding as well as a butterfly-viewing site. The marshes along the Myakka River attract a diversity of wading birds. The park has 37,125 acres of pine flatwoods, hammocks, swamps, marshes, and large tracts of prairie, one of Florida's most endangered habitats. Twelve miles of the Myakka River pass through the park. Myakka River has a developed campground with electricity, flush toilets, and hot showers. It's easy to walk along the park roads and watch for butterflies on flowers along the verge. A dirt path at the powerline crossing runs east to the magnificent prairies. Entrance and camping fees are charged. Canoes and canoe rentals are available. A general assortment of butterflies can be seen that possibly include Arogos, Palmetto, and Dusted skippers.

Precautions: Mosquitoes may be abundant during the summer wet season. Bring plenty of water for the prairie walk especially during the summer.

DIRECTIONS The park is located about 15 miles southeast of Sarasota. From I-75 take Exit 37 (S.R. 70 east). The park entrance is on the north side of the road, just east of the Myakka River. For more information call 941-365-0100 or write to Myakka River State Park, 13207 State Road 72, Sarasota, FL 34241-9542.

OCALA NATIONAL FOREST

LAKE, MARION, AND PUTNAM COUNTIES

DESCRIPTION Ocala NF is a huge natural area (383,225 acres) that lies at the northern end of the Lake Wales Ridge. The forest has the largest intact tracts of sand pine scrubs in the world. This community typically has a dense canopy of sand pine and a thick understory of scrub oaks and other shrubs. Many endangered plants occur in scrub. Equally important is the beautiful stand of a longleaf pine sandhill known as Riverside Island located in the northern part of the forest. Unlike the scrub, the sandhill community is open and park-like with an abundance of wiregrass and a great diversity of wildflowers covering the ground. Although scrub and sandhill communities both occur on excessively drained sandy ridges, the plant species and to some extent the butterflies found in each are mostly different. The landscape in this part of Florida is rolling hills interspersed with sinkholes. Also found in abundance at Ocala NF are pine flatwoods, hammocks, prairies, swamps, and marshes. The western and northern boundaries of the forest are formed by the scenic Oklawaha River, while the St. Johns River and Lake George make up the eastern boundary. There are more than 600 ponds and lakes in the forest. Alexander, Juniper, Salt, and Silver Glen springs are among the largest and most beautiful in the state. Ocala NF is divided and managed by two different ranger districts with headquarters in Silver Springs and Eustis.

Camping and Butterfly Sites: The forest has developed campgrounds with electricity, flush toilets, and showers at Dorr Lake, Juniper Springs, and Salt Springs. Primitive camping is also available at Lake Delancy, Grassy Pond, River Forest, Clearwater Lake, Island Ponds, Big Bass Lake, Lake Catherine, Halfmoon Lake, Mill Dam, Lake Eaton, Fore Lake, and Johnson Field. sixty-seven miles of the Florida National Scenic Trail pass through Ocala NF. Some of the best canoeing in Florida is possible on the numerous lakes, springs, and rivers in the forest. There are also one 20-mile and two 40-mile equestrian trails.

Ocala NF has four wilderness areas for the serious explorer. Little Lake George Wilderness at the northern end of the forest is low and wet. This area contains an exceptional tract of pond pine flatwoods that can be viewed from F.S. Road 77 East. Juniper Prairie Wilderness is best viewed by canoe starting at Juniper Springs and ending at S.R. 19. A nice stand of Atlantic white cedar, the food plant of Hessel's Hairstreak, occurs just east of the canoe takeout. Although the cedar occurs naturally at Ocala NF, we're still trying to find the butterfly at this southern location. The nearest known populations of plants and butterflies are in the Panhandle. Billies Bay Wilderness and Alexander Springs Wilderness are in the southeastern part of the forest. Much of these areas are inaccessible wet flatwoods and swamps. Check with personnel at the Lake George or Seminole Ranger Districts about restrictions before going off road into the wilderness.

Alexander Springs is a popular swimming area during the torrid summer months. The nature trail at Alexander Springs passes through hammocks with canebrakes. Look for Southern Pearly-eyes, Gemmed Satyrs, and Lace-winged Roadside-Skippers around the canebrakes. Other butterflies that are likely to be encountered visiting lyre-leaved sage and other flowers are swallowtails, Great Purple Hairstreaks, Banded Hairstreaks, Southern Hairstreaks, White M Hairstreaks, Red-banded Hairstreaks, Question Marks, Red Admirals, Red-spotted Purples, Carolina Satyrs, Viola's Wood-Satyrs, Silver-spotted Skippers, Long-tailed Skippers, Horace's Duskywings, Southern Broken-Dashes, and Northern Broken-Dashes.

The vegetation at Big Scrub camp is mostly sand pine scrub. This area would be a desert if rain was a little less plentiful. Zebra Swallowtails, Banded Hairstreaks, Striped Hairstreaks, Southern Hairstreaks, and Eastern Pine Elfins occur in this habitat at Ocala NF.

Hopkins Prairie is a wonderful marsh/wet prairie system that blazes yellow and pink in the summer from the abundant wildflowers. Butterflies to watch for at this site are Black Swallowtail, Red Admiral, White

Peacock, Viceroy, Queen, Least Skipper, Delaware Skipper, Byssus Skipper, Aaron's Skipper, Palatka Skipper, and Ocola Skipper.

Juniper Springs has a number of springs with sand boils billowing in the bottom of aqua-colored pools. There are several nice trails at Juniper Springs. The Florida Trail passes through mature sand pine scrub at this site and goes on for miles. Look for hairstreaks on blooming palmettos in early summer. Later in the fall, the pink-flowered shrub, garberia, attracts Great Purple Hairstreaks, Cloudless Sulphurs, Southern Dogfaces, and many other butterflies. There is another short trail that loops through a hydric hammock and around the springs. Watch for Appalachian Browns and Gemmed Satyrs in this habitat. These butterflies and others can also be viewed from a canoe down the beautiful Juniper Run. Numerous swallowtails and other butterflies frequent the stands of lyre-leaved sage around the parking lot in the spring.

In the longleaf pine sandhill just west of the Lake Delancy campground look for Pipevine Swallowtail, Zebra Swallowtail, Southern Dogface, Cloudless Sulphur, Barred Yellow, Little Yellow, Gray Hairstreak, Ceraunus Blue, Gulf Fritillary, Phaon Crescent, Pearl Crescent, Common Buckeye, Goatweed Leafwing, Monarch, Queen, Long-tailed Skipper, Southern Cloudywing, Northern Cloudywing, Confused Cloudywing, Sleepy Duskywing, Juvenal's Duskywing, Horace's Duskywing, Zarucco Duskywing, Swarthy Skipper, Fiery Skipper, Dotted Skipper, Meske's Skipper, Whirlabout, Dusted Skipper, Dusky Roadside-Skipper, Eufala Skipper, and Cofaqui Giant-Skipper. This area supported a strong colony of the Arogos Skipper in the mid 1990s, but large-scale prescribed burning in recent times may have negatively affected the population. The elusive Eastern Pine Elfin is sometimes abundant on blooming wild cherries or at mud puddles in the extensive sand pine scrub a few miles east of Lake Delancy.

The area around Lake Dorr in the southern part of the forest is mostly hammock and swamp. The lake also has a marshy fringe. Look for Red Admirals, Viceroys, Little Wood-Satyrs, Least Skippers, Delaware Skippers, Aaron's Skippers, Brazilian Skippers, and Ocola Skippers on blooming pickerelweed, buttonbush, or Spanish needles around the edges of Lake Dorr. Henry's Elfins and other hairstreaks are highly attracted to willow blossoms in the spring.

Sand pine scrub, hammocks, and swamps occur at Salt Spring. These habitats support an abundance of swallowtails, sulphurs, and skippers. Among the more interesting butterflies at Salt Spring is the Juniper Hairstreak. Adults of this small green hairstreak perch near the tops of the red cedars near the spring and occasionally visit flowers like Spanish needles.

Precautions: Mosquitoes, deer flies, and sand flies may be abundant during the spring and summer. Take precautions during the fall and spring game hunting seasons.

SPECIES LIST   Pipevine Swallowtail C, Zebra Swallowtail C, Black Swallowtail U, Giant Swallowtail U, Eastern Tiger Swallowtail C, Spicebush Swallowtail C, Palamedes Swallowtail C, Checkered White C, Cabbage White U, Orange Sulphur U, Southern Dogface C, Cloudless Sulphur A, Barred Yellow A, Little Yellow C, Sleepy Orange U, Dainty Sulphur U, Great Purple Hairstreak U, Banded Hairstreak U, Striped Hairstreak U, Southern Hairstreak U–C, Juniper Hairstreak U, Henry's Elfin U, Eastern Pine Elfin U, White M Hairstreak U–C, Red-banded Hairstreak C, Gray Hairstreak C, Ceraunus Blue C, Little Metalmark C, American Snout U, Gulf Fritillary A, Zebra (Heliconian) C, Variegated Fritillary U, Phaon Crescent C, Pearl Crescent C, Question Mark U–C, Red Admiral U–C, American Lady U–C, Painted Lady U, Common Buckeye C, White Peacock U–C, Red-spotted Purple U, Viceroy C, Goatweed Leafwing R, Hackberry Emperor U, Tawny Emperor U, Southern Pearly-eye U, Appalachian Brown U, Gemmed Satyr U, Carolina Satyr A, Georgia Satyr U, Little Wood-Satyr C, Common Wood-Nymph U, Monarch U–C, Queen U–C, Silver-spotted Skipper U, Long-tailed Skipper A, Dorantes Longtail U–C, Southern Cloudywing C, Northern Cloudywing U–C, Confused Cloudywing U–C, Hayhurst's Scallopwing U, Sleepy Duskywing C–A, Juvenal's Duskywing C, Horace's Duskywing C, Zarucco Duskywing C, Common Checkered-Skipper U, Tropical Checkered-Skipper U, Swarthy Skipper U, Neamathla Skipper U–C, Clouded Skipper C, Least Skipper C, Southern Skipperling U–C, Fiery Skipper C, Dotted Skipper U, Meske's Skipper R, Baracoa Skipper U, Tawny-edged Skipper U, Whirlabout C, Southern Broken-Dash C, Northern Broken-Dash U, Sachem U–C, Arogos Skipper R, Delaware Skipper U, Byssus Skipper U, Aaron's Skipper U, Yehl Skipper R, Palmetto Skipper U, Palatka Skipper U, Dukes' Skipper R, Dun Skipper U, Dusted Skipper U, Lace-winged Roadside-Skipper R, Dusky Roadside-Skipper R, Eufala Skipper U–C, Twin-spot Skipper U–C, Brazilian Skipper U, Ocola Skipper A, Yucca Giant-Skipper U, Cofaqui Giant-Skipper R.

DIRECTIONS   The forest is located about 50 miles northeast of Orlando and is accessible from both I-75 and I-95 by S.R. 40. From I-75 at Ocala, take S.R. 40 (Exit 69) east. From I-95 take S.R. 40 (Exit 88) west toward Astor. S.R. 19 runs north/south through Ocala NF between Umatilla and Palatka. For more information contact the Forest Supervisor at the Lake George District Ranger, Route 2, Box 701, Silver Springs,

SAVANNAS STATE PRESERVE

MARTIN AND ST. LUCIE COUNTIES

This park extends for 13 miles on the west bank of the Indian River and covers about 5120 acres. There is a narrow strip of sand pine scrub and scrubby flatwoods. Much of the preserve is pine flatwoods, small hammocks, and the largest fresh water marsh system of coastal southeastern Florida.

The park has a developed campground with electricity, flush toilets, and hot showers. Entrance and camping fees are charged. Butterflies such as White Peacocks can be abundant around the campground and picnic area. There is a 3/4-mile long nature trail looping from the campground. Another 2 1/2-mile long trail on the west side of the park will accommodate butterflying as well as hiking, biking, or horseback riding.

BUTTERFLIES In weedy areas around the campground and scrubby areas in the park, look for a general assortment of widespread butterflies. The marshes of the preserve are beautiful, but are best seen by canoe or small boat. Great Southern Whites, Viceroys, Least Skippers, Delaware Skippers, Salt Marsh Skippers, and Ocola Skippers are often abundant around wetland areas of Savannas.

Precautions: Mosquitoes and sandflies may be abundant during the summer wet season.

DIRECTIONS The park is located about 6 miles south of Fort Pierce. From U.S. 1 turn east on S.R. 712 (Midway Road) 1.3 miles. For more information call 561-468-3985 or write to Savannas State Preserve, c/o Ft. Pierce Inlet State Recreation Area, 905 Shorewinds Drive, Fort Pierce, FL 34949.

TOMOKA STATE PARK

VOLUSIA COUNTY

This lovely park is situated on a peninsula formed by the Tomoka and Halifax rivers. There are about 1540 acres of live oak hammocks, swamps, and marshes. The ancient Timucuan Indian village of Nocoroco was located here. Indigo and sugar cane plantations prevailed during American Revolutionary War times.

The park has a developed campground with electricity, flush toilets, and hot showers. Camping and entrance fees are charged. The nature trails are 1/2 mile, 6 miles, and 3 miles long. There is also a 3.3-mile canoe trail in the park. Tomoka is a meeting place for fresh water and salt marsh butterflies. You may see dozens of Hackberry Emperors and Tawny Emperors perching around hackberry trees. Look for Great Southern Whites, Baracoa Skippers, Delaware Skippers, Palatka Skippers, Salt Marsh Skippers, and Ocola Skippers on pickerelweed, fogfruit, or Spanish needle flowers.

Precautions: Mosquitoes and sandflies may be abundant during the summer wet season.

DIRECTIONS The park is located about 10 miles north of Daytona Beach. From Ormond Beach, take S.R. 5A (North Beach Street) about 3 miles. For more information call 904-676-4050 or write to Tomoka State Park, 2099 North Beach Street, Ormond Beach, Fl 32174.

WITHLACOOCHEE STATE FOREST

CITRUS, HERNANDO, PASCO, AND SUMTER COUNTIES

Withlacoochee SF is made up of several separate tracts totaling about 147,900 acres. The forest is located partly on the Brooksville Ridge, a major physiographic feature of west-central Florida. The habitat in the forest varies from dry sandhills, to moist pine flatwoods, bayheads, hammocks, canebrakes, and swamps. Limestone is close to the surface in this part of Florida, enriching the soils. Many of the hammocks have a high diversity of trees and shrubs. The Brooksville ridge also has rich phosphate deposits and extensive surface mining occurs in this region.

The forest has developed campgrounds with electricity, flush toilets, and hot showers at Tillis Hill Recreation Area, Holder Mine Recreation Area, Silver Lake Recreation Area, River Junction Recreation Area, Hog Island Recreation Area, and Croom Motocycle Recreation Area. Fees are charged at the more developed campgrounds.

The Citrus Unit of Withlacoochee SF is most easily accessible off C.R. 480, about 10 miles east of U.S. 98. Forest Road T.R. 13 is the main north-south road. The entire tract is gridded by unpaved roads, some of which may not be passable without a 4-wheel drive vehicle. These roads are easy for hiking, however. In addition, the Citrus Hiking Trail loops for 46 miles through the property. This area has nice sandhills, hammocks, and some sand pine scrub. Southern Dogfaces are often abundant here, but also keep an eye out for rare Arogos Skippers and Dusky Roadside-Skippers. The Holder Mine Recreation Area, Mutual Mine Recreation Area, and Tillis Hill Recreation Area are located in the Citrus Unit. The Tillis site is popular for horseback riding and dog field-trials.

The Croom Tract is accessible via several roads off S.R. 50 to the south or roads off S.R. 476 to the north. This site has the Hog Island, Iron Bridge

Areas. There are over 30 miles of trails looping through the Croom tract. The Croom Unit has ravines, prairies, sandhills, and bluffs along the Withlacoochee River. The Withlacoochee State Trail was an old railroad line. Through the state rails-to-trails program, a 41-mile stretch of railroad tracks has been converted into a trail for hiking, biking, and horseback riding. The trail begins off Croom Rital Road and runs parallel to the Withlacoochee River. The section that crosses S.R. 476 just east of the Withlacoochee River near Istachatta is a famous area to view hairstreaks. In a single trip it's possible to see the Great Purple Hairstreak, Banded Hairstreak, Striped Hairstreak, Southern Hairstreak, Juniper Hairstreak, White M Hairstreak, Red-banded Hairstreak, and Gray Hairstreak. Sweet clover growing along the former railroad is especially attractive to these butterflies.

The Jumper Creek Unit has about 10,000 acres of hardwood hammocks, flatwoods, marshes, and swamps. Access is off C.R. 470 on the west side of Lake Panasoffkee. Butterflies can easily be viewed visiting wildflowers along Kettle Island Road and Rear Island Road.

MeKethan Lake has a diverse hardwood forest surrounding a small lake. This popular picnic site is located on U.S. 41, just north of S.R. 476. Butterflies can be observed along the paved road or the 2-mile long nature trail at this site. This is one of the best places in Florida to find Banded Hairstreaks, Striped Hairstreaks, and Southern Hairstreaks, as well as Cofaqui Giant-Skippers. Just a few miles south of MeKethan Lake on U.S 41, the Colonel Robbins Recreation Area has a 2.5-mile long nature trail.

The Richloam Unit consists of nearly 50,000 acres of relatively flat, but fertile soil. Much of the area is used for forestry and timber production. There are 14 miles of hiking trails through flatwoods, hammocks, and swamps. Of special interest are herds of "Cracker" ponies and cattle that are descended from stock brought to Florida hundreds of years ago by the Spanish. Richloam can be accessed via S.R. 50.

Chinsegut Nature Center Wildlife and Environmental Area is not part of the Withlacoochee SF, but is located nearby. From U.S. 41, take Lake Lindsey Road west a few miles and watch for signs to the park. This site has a butterfly garden around the nature center as well as nature trails through hammocks, sandhills, May's Prairie, and a cypress swamp.

Precautions: Take precautions during the fall and spring game hunting seasons.

DIRECTIONS   The forest is located about 45 miles northeast of Tampa. For more information call 352-754-6777 or write to Withlacoochee State Forest, 15019 Broad Street, Brooksville, FL 34601.

SOUTH FLORIDA

BIG CYPRESS NATIONAL PRESERVE

COLLIER COUNTY

This little-explored area has a nice selection of wetland species. This is also an excellent area to see Palatka Skippers, Berry's Skippers, and Twin-spot Skippers as they nectar at roadside thistles in March–April. Try the roadsides along Burns Road (about 8 miles east of Monroe Station). The preserve is located north and south of route 41 about 50 miles west of Miami.

BLOWING ROCKS PRESERVE

MARTIN COUNTY

This Nature Conservancy Preserve encompasses 75 acres containing beaches, dunes, tropical hammocks, and mangroves. A highly eroded shelf of limestone flanks the beach. During high tides, the incoming waves force sea water through tubular solution holes. The jets of water blown skyward make a spectacular display. In addition to the interesting butterflies, three species of sea turtles nest here, and manatees are often seen on the bayside of the preserve during winter. The preserve is for daytime use only. A nice butterfly garden of native flowers planted around the visitor center attracts numerous delightful butterflies. Tropical species such as the Florida White, Statira Sulphur, Mangrove Buckeye, Ruddy Daggerwing, Mangrove Skipper, and Hammock Skipper may be seen at the preserve. Look for the Giant Swallowtail, Great Southern White, Dainty Sulphur, Fulvous Hairstreak, Julia (Heliconain), Zebra (Heliconian), White Peacock, Monk Skipper, and Brazilian Skipper feeding at flowers in the garden or flying along the trails.

DIRECTIONS The park is located about 15 miles north of Palm Beach, just north of the Palm Beach County line. Take I-95 (Exit 59; S.R. 706 or Indiantown Road) east to U.S. 1. Turn north on U.S. 1 then east on C.R. 707. The preserve is about 2 miles from U.S. 1. For more information call 561-744-6668 or write to Blowing Rocks Preserve, 574 South Beach Road, Hobe Sound, FL 33455.

CAMP OWAISSA BAUER

MIAMI-DADE COUNTY
by Roger L. Hammer
Camp Owaissa Bauer is a 110-acre Miami-Dade County park with tropical hardwood hammock and pine rockland habitats accessible by trails.

The park is noted by butterfly enthusiasts for its populations of Dina Yellows and Mimosa Yellows, both of which can be observed along trails that bisect pine rockland and along the margins of hardwood hammock habitat.

DIRECTIONS The park is located at 17001 Southwest 264th Street, in Homestead. The main entrance is on the north side of Bauer Avenue just east of Krome Boulevard. The park is available by group reservation but is open to public visitation when not closed due to reservation. To inquire, phone the park office at 305-247-6016.

CASTELLOW HAMMOCK NATURE CENTER

MIAMI-DADE COUNTY
by Roger L. Hammer

DESCRIPTION Castellow Hammock is a 60-acre preserve owned and operated by Miami-Dade Park & Recreation Department. Habitats include tropical hardwood hammock, pine-hammock transition zone, overgrown pine rockland, and an extensive planting of native landscape plants around the nature center building. The perimeter of the hammock harbors weedy plant species that typify disturbed sites. A nature trail offers visitors access to the interior of the hammock.

BUTTERFLIES Park naturalists and visiting butterfly enthusiasts identified 67 species within Castellow Hammock prior to Hurricane Andrew in 1992. There have been no comprehensive surveys of butterflies at the park since the hurricane. The shady interior of the hammock is not prime butterfly habitat, except for occasional satyrs, but the hammock trail, open canopy gaps, and hammock margins are prime locations for a variety of species. In these open areas, visitors will likely encounter Zebra (Heliconians), Julia (Heliconians), Gulf Fritillaries, Giant Swallowtails, Cloudless Sulphurs, Orange-barred Sulphurs, Large Orange Sulphurs, Cassius Blues, Long-tailed Skippers, Dorantes Longtails, Three-spotted Skippers, and other species. The park is noted for harboring small populations of Dina Yellows and Dingy Purplewings, and these can occasionally be observed along the hammock margin nectaring on lantana and other flowers. Dina Yellows are most commonly found on the eastern side of the park along S.W. 157 Avenue in the vicinity of the caterpillar foodplant Mexican alvaradoa (*Alvaradoa amorphoides*). During the summer, Malachites have been seen nectaring on Mexican clover (*Richardia grandiflora*) flowers growing in the park lawn, and these small pink flowers are also attractive to White Peacocks, Checkered Whites, Barred Yellows, Baracoa Skippers, and a host of other species. Ruddy Daggerwings can be seen nectaring on wild coffee (*Psychotria nervosa*) blossoms or around their caterpillar foodplants, strangler fig (*Ficus aurea*) and shortleaf fig (*Ficus citrifolia*).

SPECIES LIST Polydamas Swallowtail U, Zebra Swallowtail R, Black Swallowtail U, Giant Swallowtail C, Palamedes Swallowtail R, Florida White C, Checkered White U–C, Great Southern White C, Cloudless Sulphur C, Orange-barred Sulphur C, Large Orange Sulphur C, Statira Sulphur R, Barred Yellow C, Little Yellow U, Mimosa Yellow R, Dina Yellow U–C, Sleepy Orange U, Dainty Sulphur C, Atala R, White M Hairstreak U, Gray Hairstreak C, Martial Scrub-Hairstreak R, Fulvous Hairstreak U–C, Red-banded Hairstreak C, Gray Ministreak R, Cassius Blue C, Ceraunus Blue C, Gulf Fritillary C, Zebra (Heliconian) C–A, Julia (Heliconian) C, Variegated Fritillary R, Phaon Crescent C, Pearl Crescent U, Red Admiral R, Common Buckeye C, Mangrove Buckeye R, White Peacock C, Malachite R, Viceroy R, Dingy Purplewing U, Florida Purplewing R, Ruddy Daggerwing C, Florida Leafwing R, Carolina Satyr U, Georgia Satyr R, Monarch C, Queen C, Silver-spotted Skipper R, Hammock Skipper C, Long-tailed Skipper C, Dorantes Longtail C, Florida Duskywing U, Horace's Duskywing U, Tropical Checkered-Skipper C, Three-spotted Skipper C, Clouded Skipper C, Southern Skipperling C, Fiery Skipper C, Baracoa Skipper C, Whirlabout U, Southern Broken-Dash C, Sachem U, Palmetto Skipper R, Twin-spot Skipper R, Brazilian Skipper U, Eufala Skipper U, Ocola Skipper R.

DIRECTIONS Take U.S. 1 south to Hainlin Mill Drive (S.W. 216 Street). Turn right (west) and drive 5 miles to Farm Life Road (S.W. 162 Avenue). Turn left and drive 1/2 mile to park entrance on left. From Florida's Turnpike (Homestead Extension) take the "Cutler Ridge Blvd.—S.W. 216 Street" Exit. Turn right at the second traffic light off the exit (S.W. 216 Street), proceed to U.S. 1 and continue west as above. For more information call 305-247-6007 or write to Castellow Hammock Preserve, 22301 SW 162 Avenue, Miami, FL 33170-3905.

COLLIER-SEMINOLE STATE PARK

COLLIER COUNTY

Collier-Seminole SP is a meeting place for saltwater and freshwater plants and animals as well as tropical and temperate species. The park contains 6440 acres of salt marsh, mangroves, cypress swamps, hammocks, and flatwoods.

The park has a developed campground with electricity, flush toilets, and hot showers. The 6 1/2-mile long nature trail begins near the boat launch. Look for Cuban Crescents and Salt Marsh Skippers in the salt marsh at the trail head. The trail then enters a hammock with tropical

trees such as strangler fig, the host plant of the Ruddy Daggerwing, and
transverses a nice cypress and hardwood swamp.

Collier-Seminole SP is one of the southernmost localities for Tiger and Spicebush swallowtails. Tiger Swallowtails from the northern U.S. look downright puny by comparison with these southern populations. Spicebush Swallowtails in the park are also quite different even from those in northern Florida, in having very large pale spots bordering the upper wings. These swallowtails mixed with tropical butterflies make this a must-see park to explore.

Precautions: This is one of the buggiest parks in Florida. If camping, make sure your tent has netting fine enough to keep out the sand flies or no-see-ums. Mosquitoes, sand flies, deerflies, and horseflies may be incredibly abundant during the summer wet season.

DIRECTIONS The park is located about 17 miles south of Naples on U.S. 41 (Tamiami Trail). The well-marked entrance is on the west side of the road. For more information call 941-394-3397 or write to Collier-Seminole State Park, 20200 East Tamiami Trail, Naples, FL 34114.

CORKSCREW SWAMP SANCTUARY

COLLIER COUNTY
by Roberta Wooster

DESCRIPTION Corkscrew Swamp Sanctuary is an 11,000-acre wildlife oasis amidst the urban sprawl and agricultural fields of southwest Florida. The Sanctuary contains the largest stand of virgin bald cypress forest in North America. Other habitats included by the 2-mile boardwalk are pine flatwoods, wet prairies, and sawgrass marshes. The butterfly population is assisted by the lack of mosquito spraying in this part of the county. In addition, the sanctuary has an aggressive program of exotic plant control and prescribed burning. Sanctuary personnel have made strong efforts around the visitor center area to use native vegetation both for nectar and for caterpillar foodplant resources. Over 60 species of butterflies have been recorded at Corkscrew Swamp Sanctuary. Numbers are dependent upon the wet season and dry season changes in vegetation.

SPECIES LIST Zebra Swallowtail U, Black Swallowtail C, Giant Swallowtail, U, Eastern Tiger Swallowtail C, Florida White R, Great Southern White, A, Orange Sulphur C, Cloudless Sulphur C, Orange-barred Sulphur C, Barred Yellow C, Little Yellow U, Dainty Sulphur C, Gray Hairstreak U, Mallow Scrub-Hairstreak R, Red-banded Hairstreak C, Cassius Blue, U, Ceraunus Blue U, Little Metalmark, C, Gulf Fritillary A, Julia (Heliconian) C, Zebra (Heliconian) A, Variegated Fritillary U, Cuban Crescent R, Phaon Crescent A, Pearl Crescent A, Question Mark R, Red

Admiral C, Common Buckeye C, White Peacock A, Viceroy A, Ruddy Daggerwing C, Tawny Emperor U, Carolina Satyr C, Georgia Satyr C, Little Wood-Satyr R, Common Wood-Nymph R, Monarch U, Queen A, Soldier C, Silver-spotted Skipper C, Long-tailed Skipper C, Dorantes Longtail C, Hayhurst's Scallopwing U, Zarucco Duskywing U, Tropical Checkered-Skipper C, Clouded Skipper U, Least Skipper C, Southern Skipperling C, Fiery Skipper C, Whirlabout C, Sachem C, Delaware Skipper U, Zabulon Skipper U, Aaron's Skipper U, Palmetto Skipper U, Twinspot Skipper C, Brazilian Skipper A, Salt Marsh Skipper C.

DIRECTIONS The preserve is located about midway between Fort Myers and Naples. From I-75 take C.R. C-846 (Exit 17 or Immokalee Road) east about 15 miles, turn north (left) onto Sanctuary Road and watch for signs. The entrance is on the west side of the road. For more information call 941-657-3771 or write to Corkscrew Swamp Sanctuary, 375 Sanctuary Road, Naples, FL 34120.

DEERING ESTATE AT CUTLER

MIAMI-DADE COUNTY

This newly opened county park has the potential to be one of the top butterflying localities in south Florida. Its 420 acres include 150 acres of tropical hardwood hammocks, the largest extant hardwood hammock on the mainland, 150 acres of pine rocklands, and 120 acres of mangrove swamps. Recent attempts to reestablish Schaus' Swallowtail on mainland south Florida have centered on this park, and, at least as of this writing, it is possible to see this federally endangered species on naturalist led tours. Other tropical hardwood hammock specialists, including purplewings, are also possibilities.

DIRECTIONS To reach the park, take Old Cutler Road to SW 168th Street. Turn east to the park entrance. For more information call 305-235-1668 or write to Deering Estate at Cutler, 16701 SW 72nd Avenue, Miami, FL 33157.

J.N. "DING" DARLING NATIONAL WILDLIFE REFUGE

LEE COUNTY

Ding Darling NWR is a famous viewing area for shore and wading birds located on Sanibel Island. The refuge contains 6310 acres including coastal hammocks, salt marshes, and mangrove habitats. Ding Darling was a political cartoonist who also had a passion for conservation. He was awarded Pulitzer prizes in 1923 and 1942. In 1934, he was appointed

Wildlife Service. In this capacity he was responsible for securing millions of dollars for wildlife habitat, and established the Migratory Bird Conservation Commission and the Federal Duck Stamp Program. For many years Darling had a winter home on Captiva Island. The refuge on Sanibel Island was dedicated to Ding Darling in 1978. The preserve has a visitor center, hiking and canoe trails, and a 5-mile wildlife drive.

The refuge is for daytime use only. A nice selection of butterflies can often be seen in the butterfly garden at the visitor center. The 5-mile wildlife viewing drive loops through the central part of the preserve. Frequent stops can be made to explore for butterflies. Weedy roadsides with patches of flowers are some of the best places to see butterflies along the wildlife drive. As you explore the mangrove and salt marsh areas of the refuge, watch for Eastern Pygmy-Blues, Cuban Crescents, Mangrove Buckeyes, Mangrove Skippers, Salt Marsh Skippers, and Obscure Skippers.

Precautions: Mosquitoes and other biting insects are often abundant during the torrid summer months.

DIRECTIONS The refuge is located west of Fort Myers on Sanibel Island. Take S.R. 867 (McGregor Boulevard) west from Fort Myers, over the toll bridge and on to the island. Turn west onto Periwinkle Way, north on Tarpon Road, then west on Sanibel-Captiva Road. For more information call 941-472-1100 or write to J. N. "Ding" Darling N.W.R, 1 Wildlife Drive, Sanibel, FL 33957.

EVERGLADES NATIONAL PARK

COLLIER, MIAMI-DADE, AND MONROE COUNTIES

DESCRIPTION Everglades National Park covers a whopping 1,507,850 acres of the southern tip of the Florida Peninsula. Although most of the area is wetland habitats such as freshwater and salt marshes, swamps, and mangroves, there are also tiny tree islands, prairies, tropical hammocks, and pine rocklands. Along with the exquisite butterflies are colorful tree snails, crocodiles, and some of the most unique birding opportunities in the U.S.

Camping and Butterfly Sites: The park has a developed campground and a small hotel at Flamingo. Camping is also available at Long Pine Key (no showers) and at Chekika (no electricity). Entrance and camping fees are charged at the main entrance. Camping is restricted to the least buggy winter months at Flamingo. Some of the more interesting butterfly viewing sites are as follows:

Gulf Coast Visitor Center

The highlight of this area is the mature mangrove forest. Butterflies may abound in weedy areas with Spanish needles and along roadsides. This is a good place to see Mangrove Buckeyes, Mangrove Skippers, Salt Marsh Skippers, and other tropical butterflies.

Shark Valley

This area features Everglades marshes and the Shark River Slough, a shallow slow moving river 50 miles wide. For a small fee, a park tram takes visitors to an observation deck overlooking the marshes and slough. Among the butterflies to be seen in this part of the park are Black Swallowtails, White Peacocks, Viceroys, Monarchs, Queens, Soldiers, Least Skippers, Delaware Skippers, Byssus Skippers, Aaron's Skippers, Palatka Skippers, Twin-spot Skippers, Brazilian Skippers, and Ocola Skippers.

Chekika

Chekika has a diversity of habitats including Everglades marshes, tree islands, and a tropical hammock. Marsh butterflies such as White Peacocks, Least Skippers, Delaware Skippers, Aaron's Skippers, Palatka Skippers, and hammock species, such as Tawny Emperors and Soldiers, may be seen along the short trails through the park.

Royal Palm Hammock

This is one of the most popular wildlife viewing areas in the United States. There are two trails leading from the mahogany lined parking lot. Anhinga Trail skirts Taylor Slough. The boardwalk takes you over ponds and marshes with an abundance of alligators and water birds. Look for butterflies visiting the blossoms of pickerelweed and buttonbush. The Gumbo Limbo Trail loops through the beautiful hardwood hammock. Purplewings were once abundant in this forest, but have disappeared in recent times.

Long Pine Key

Long Pine Key is an island of rocky pine flatwoods habitat surrounded by Everglades marshes and prairies. The grasses and shrubs in the understory of the pine forest burn easily and are subjected to frequent lightening-induced as well as prescribed fires. Watch for Bartram's Scrub-Hairstreaks, Little Metalmarks, Florida Leafwings, Georgia Satyrs, Florida Duskywings, and Palmetto Skippers along roadsides and trails in this area.

This 1/2-mile long trail winds through pine rockland habitat and crosses the edge of a tropical hammock. Butterflies of special interest are similar to those of Long Pine Key.

Pa-hay-okee Overlook

A short boardwalk passes through sawgrass marsh dotted with dwarf cypress trees and leads to an observation tower at Pa-hay-okee, the Seminole word for the Everglades. Watch for Black Swallowtails, White Peacocks, Viceroys, Georgia Satyrs, Monarchs, Queens, Soldiers, Least Skippers, Delaware Skippers, Byssus Skippers, Aaron's Skippers, Palatka Skippers, Brazilian Skippers, and Ocola Skippers in this area.

Mahogany Hammock Trail

At this viewing site, a 1/2-mile long boardwalk passes through a nice tropical hammock containing many mahogany trees. Look for Florida Whites and Hammock Skippers along the trail and edges of the hammock.

West Lake Trail

The weedy lawn around West Lake is home to Great Southern Whites, Barred Yellows, Little Yellows, Dainty Sulphurs and other widespread species.

Snake Bight Trail

Few brave the hordes of mosquitoes along this 2-mile trail that leads to a salt marsh and an observation deck overlooking Florida Bay, but the butterflies, occasional crocodile, and scenery are well worthwhile. Butterflies that may be seen in this area include Great Southern Whites, Martial Scrub-Hairstreaks, Mallow Scrub-Hairstreaks, Eastern Pygmy-Blues, Cuban Crescents, Mangrove Buckeyes, Queens, Soldiers, Mangrove Skippers, Three-spotted Skippers, Salt Marsh Skippers, and Obscure Skippers.

Mrazek Pond

This terrific birding area has mangroves and weedy vegetation near a brackish pond. Look for Great Southern Whites, Barred Yellows, Mallow Scrub-Hairstreaks, Cassius Blues, and others on Spanish needles.

Flamingo Recreation Area

From the campground/hotel complex are some relatively easy trails to Bear Lake, Christian Point, Rowdy Bend, Eco Pond, and a coastal prairie.

204 At times Great Southern Whites are so abundant around Flamingo it would appear the area was in the midst of a snow storm. Other butterflies that may be seen are Mallow Scrub-Hairstreaks, Eastern Pygmy-Blues, Cuban Crescents, Mangrove Buckeyes, Queens, Mangrove Skippers, Salt Marsh Skippers, and Obscure Skippers.

Wilderness Waterway

This nearly 100-mile long trail is not for the inexperienced canoeist. Permits must be obtained from the park staff before attempting the trail. Here lies a tropical adventure through the mangroves of the Ten Thousand Islands from the Gulf Coast Visitor Center southeast to Flamingo. Large Orange Sulphurs, Mangrove Skippers, and other tropical butterflies may be seen along the trail.

Precautions: Mosquitoes and sand flies may be incredibly abundant during the summer wet season in Everglades National Park.

SPECIES LIST Polydamas Swallowtail R, Zebra Swallowtail R, Black Swallowtail U, Giant Swallowtail U, Eastern Tiger Swallowtail R, Spicebush Swallowtail R, Palamedes Swallowtail C, Florida White R–U, Checkered White R, Cabbage White R, Great Southern White A, Southern Dogface R, Cloudless Sulphur A, Orange-barred Sulphur U, Large Orange Sulphur C, Barred Yellow C, Little Yellow C, Mimosa Yellow R, Sleepy Orange, Dainty Sulphur C, Atala R, Southern Hairstreak R, White M Hairstreak U, Red-banded Hairstreak C, Gray Hairstreak C, Martial Scrub-Hairstreak R, Bartram's Scrub-Hairstreak R, Mallow Scrub-Hairstreak U, Eastern Pygmy-Blue U, Cassius Blue C, Miami Blue R or H, Ceraunus Blue C, Little Metalmark C, Gulf Fritillary C, Julia (Heliconian) C, Zebra (Heliconian) C, Variegated Fritillary R–U, Cuban Crescent R, Phaon Crescent C–A, Pearl Crescent C, Red Admiral U–C, American Lady U, Painted Lady R, Common Buckeye C, Mangrove Buckeye U, White Peacock A, Malachite R, Viceroy C, Dingy Purplewing R, Florida Purplewing R, Ruddy Daggerwing U, Florida Leafwing R, Hackberry Emperor R, Tawny Emperor R, Carolina Satyr C, Georgia Satyr U, Monarch C, Queen C, Soldier U–C, Mangrove Skipper U–C, Zestos Skipper H, Silver-spotted Skipper R, Hammock Skipper U, Long-tailed Skipper A, Dorantes Longtail C–A, Hayhurst's Scallopwing R–U, Florida Duskywing U, Juvenal's Duskywing R, Horace's Duskywing U, Tropical Checkered-Skipper U–C, Swarthy Skipper U, Neamathla Skipper U, Three-spotted Skipper U–C, Clouded Skipper C, Least Skipper C, Southern Skipperling U, Fiery Skipper C, Baracoa Skipper U, Whirlabout C, Southern Broken-Dash U, Sachem U, Delaware Skipper U, Byssus Skipper R, Aaron's Skipper R, Palmetto Skipper R, Palatka

Skipper U, Berry's Skipper R, Monk Skipper U–C, Dusted Skipper R, Dusky Roadside-Skipper R, Eufala Skipper U, Twin-spot Skipper C, Brazilian Skipper U–C, Salt Marsh Skipper U, Obscure Skipper U, Ocola Skipper A.

DIRECTIONS There are four access points to the park. Along Tamiami Trail (U.S. 41) there are two entrances; the Gulf Coast Visitor Center near Everglades City/Chokoloskee, and Shark Valley located about 20 miles west of Miami. The Chekika entrance is on the west side of S.R. 997 about 8 miles north of Homestead. The main park entrance is west of Florida City. Follow the Turnpike to Florida City. Turn west on Palm Drive (S.R. 9336). At "Robert Is Here" fruit stand turn south and then west to the park according to the signs. For more information call 305-242-7700 or write to Everglades National Park, 40001 State Road 9336, Homestead, FL 33034-6733.

FAIRCHILD TROPICAL GARDENS

MIAMI-DADE COUNTY

This spectacular garden specializes in palms, cycads, and other tropical plants. There are 70 acres with winding paths to explore. As wild parrots screech from the fruiting tropical trees you may see beautiful Atala butterflies flitting about. Look on coontie and other cycads to see the brilliant red and yellow caterpillars. Other tropical butterflies that have been found on the grounds are Polydamas Swallowtails, Florida Whites, Statira Sulphurs, Fulvous Hairstreaks, Malachites, Dingy Purplewings, Mangrove Skippers, Hammock Skippers, Baracoa Skippers (often common), and Monk Skippers. An entrance fee is charged.

DIRECTIONS The garden is located adjacent to Matheson Hammock off Old Cutler Road in Coral Gables. For more information call 305-667-1651 or write to Fairchild Tropical Gardens, 10901 Old Cutler Road, Coral Gables, FL 33156.

FAKAHATCHEE STRAND STATE PRESERVE

COLLIER COUNTY

The Fakahatchee Strand is one of the wildest places in Florida. There are 69,090 acres of tropical hammocks, pine flatwoods, swamps, and marshes to explore. This is an easy place in which to get lost, so bring a knowledgeable guide or two compasses. Many rare orchids, bromeliads, royal palms, and other plants are found in Fakahatchee Strand. The strand is mostly a swamp about 20 miles long and 3–5 miles wide that drains the Big Cypress Swamp. Butterfly viewing is best done along

W. J. Janes Memorial Scenic Drive, which winds for 11 miles through the preserve. Around the hammocks and swamps look for Florida Whites, Ruddy Daggerwings, White Peacocks, Zebras (Heliconian) and Queens. In the marshes and pineland around the park entrance you may find Aaron's Skippers, Palmetto Skippers, Palatka Skippers, and Berry's Skippers visiting flowers such as pickerelweed.

Precautions: Mosquitoes and other biting insects are often abundant during the wet season. Keep a watchful eye for the abundant water moccasins and rattlesnakes that may lay along roadsides and trails.

DIRECTIONS The preserve is located about 35 miles southeast of Naples. Take I-75 heading east of Naples to Exit 14A (S.R. 29). Go south about 14 miles to the hamlet of Copeland and follow W. J. Janes Memorial Scenic Drive west to the preserve. An alternate route is U.S. 41 (Tamiami Trail) heading south from Naples, then turn north on S.R. 29 to Copeland. For more information call 941-695-4593 or write to Fakahatchee Strand State Preserve, P.O. Box 548, Copeland, FL 34137.

FERN FOREST REGIONAL PARK

BROWARD COUNTY

DESCRIPTION This 245-acre park is a small remnant of the forests that once covered southeastern Florida. The habitats represented include hammock, swamp, and old field. The grounds around the visitor center have been planted with flowers attractive to butterflies.

BUTTERFLIES The park has a mixture of tropical and temperate butterflies. At least 47 species have been recorded from this site so far. Fern Forest is an especially good place to see Malachites and Ruddy Daggerwings. The Cypress Creek Trail is a 1/2-mile boardwalk through a hammock and swamp. The Prairie Overlook Trail loops through more hammocks and an old field. A 20-foot observation platform overlooks the field. Fern Forest is open for daytime use only.

SPECIES LIST Zebra Swallowtail U, Giant Swallowtail U–C, Palamedes Swallowtail U–C, Checkered White U, Great Southern White U–C, Cloudless Sulphur A, Orange-barred Sulphur U, Barred Yellow C, Little Yellow U, Sleepy Orange U, Dainty Sulphur C, Red-banded Hairstreak C, Fulvous Hairstreak U, Gray Hairstreak C, Mallow Scrub-Hairstreak U, Cassius Blue C, American Snout R, Gulf Fritillary A, Julia (Heliconian) A, Zebra (Heliconian) A, Phaon Crescent C, Pearl Crescent C, Red Admiral C, Common Buckeye C, White Peacock A, Malachite U, Viceroy U, Ruddy Daggerwing A, Carolina Satyr A, Monarch C, Queen U, Soldier A, Silver-spotted Skipper R, Long-tailed Skipper A, Dorantes Longtail A, Horace's Duskywing C, Tropical

Checkered-Skipper C, Three-spotted Skipper C, Clouded Skipper C, Southern Skipperling C, Fiery Skipper C, Whirlabout C, Sachem C, Monk Skipper C, Eufala Skipper U, Brazilian Skipper U, and Ocola Skipper A.

DIRECTIONS The park is located just north of Fort Lauderdale. From I-95 take Exit 34 west about 2 miles to Lyons Road. Turn south on Lyons Road and watch for the park entrance on the west side of the road. For more information call 954-970-0150 or write to Fern Forest Nature Center, 201 Lyons Road South, Coconut Creek, FL 33063.

HUGH TAYLOR BIRCH STATE RECREATION AREA

BROWARD COUNTY

DESCRIPTION Hugh Taylor Birch has one of the few tropical hammocks left in Broward County. The park contains 180 acres of beach, tropical hammock, and mangrove habitats. This is one of the better spots to find Statira Sulphurs. Other unusual tropical butterflies that have been found in the park are Florida Whites, Lyside Sulphurs, Atalas, Miami Blues, and Malachites. Viewing is best from along the paved road that loops through the park or from the path of the defunct tram. An entrance fee is charged. Only group camping is provided by the park.

SPECIES LIST Zebra Swallowtail R, Giant Swallowtail U, Florida White U–C, Great Southern White C–A, Cloudless Sulphur C, Orange-barred Sulphur C, Large Orange Sulphur C, Statira Sulphur U–C, Lyside Sulphur S, Barred Yellow U–C, Dainty Sulphur C, Atala U–C, White M Hairstreak U, Red-banded Hairstreak C, Fulvous Hairstreak U, Gray Hairstreak U, Cassius Blue C, Miami Blue H, Ceraunus Blue U, Gulf Fritillary C–A, Julia (Heliconian) C–A, Zebra (Heliconian) C, Phaon Crescent C, Common Buckeye U, Mangrove Buckeye U, White Peacock C–A, Malachite U, Ruddy Daggerwing U, Monarch U, Queen U, Soldier U, Mangrove Skipper U, Hammock Skipper U, Long-tailed Skipper C–A, Dorantes Longtail C–A, Horace's Duskywing C, Tropical Checkered-Skipper C, Three-spotted Skipper C, Clouded Skipper U, Southern Skipperling U, Fiery Skipper C, Whirlabout C, Sachem U, Monk Skipper C, Brazilian Skipper U, Ocola Skipper C–A.

DIRECTIONS The park is located in downtown Fort Lauderdale at the corner of East Sunrise Boulevard (S.R. 838) and Atlantic Boulevard (S.R. A1A). The entrance is on Sunrise Boulevard just east of the Intracoastal Waterway. For more information call 954-564-4521 or write to Hugh Taylor Birch State Recreation Area, 3109 East Sunrise Boulevard, Fort Lauderdale, FL 33304.

JONATHAN DICKINSON STATE PARK

MARTIN COUNTY

DESCRIPTION   Jonathan Dickinson State Park was named for a shipwrecked Quaker who wrote an account of the ordeal. The park contains 11,575 acres of scrub, flatwoods, hammocks, prairies, swamps, and mangroves. The eastern side includes part of the Atlantic Coastal Ridge and is covered by sand pine scrub. The endangered four-petaled pawpaw, a host plant of the Zebra Swallowtail, grows on the ridge. A terrific view can be had from the 25 foot tall observation tower located on Hobe Mountain at the top of the ridge. Yucca Giant-Skippers as well as rare red widow spiders may be seen along the path leading to the tower. Beautiful tracts of flatwoods stretch westward to the lower, estuarine part of the Loxahatchee River. Mangroves form a dense shrubbery along the banks of the river.

Camping and Butterfly Sites: The park has a developed campground with electricity, flush toilets, and hot showers. In addition to the Hobe Mountain Trail, there are two nature trails to explore. The Kiching Creek Trail loops west of the picnic area through a south Florida flatwoods. The trail cuts across a mosaic of grassy prairies dotted with orchids, shallow ponds, and patches of saw palmetto. Look for Arogos Skippers, Dotted Skippers, Meske's Skippers, and Dusted Skippers visiting patches of flowers. The River Trail winds along the Loxahatchee River through flatwoods, mangroves, and freshwater swamps. The park charges entrance and camping fees. Canoeing on the river and canoe rentals are available.

Precautions: Mosquitoes may be abundant during the summer wet season.

SPECIES LIST   Zebra Swallowtail C, Black Swallowtail U, Giant Swallowtail U, Eastern Tiger Swallowtail U, Palamedes Swallowtail C, Great Southern White U–A, Southern Dogface U, Cloudless Sulphur A, Barred Yellow U–C, Little Yellow C, Sleepy Orange U, Dainty Sulphur U–C, Southern Hairstreak U, White M Hairstreak U, Red-banded Hairstreak C, Gray Hairstreak C, Ceraunus Blue U, Little Metalmark U, Gulf Fritillary C–A, Julia (Heliconian) U, Zebra (Heliconian) C, Phaon Crescent U, Pearl Crescent U, Red Admiral U, American Lady U, Common Buckeye C, White Peacock C, Viceroy C, Carolina Satyr C, Monarch U–C, Queen U, Soldier U, Long-tailed Skipper A, Dorantes Longtail A, Sleepy Duskywing U, Juvenal's Duskywing U, Horace's Duskywing C, Zarucco Duskywing C, Tropical Checkered-Skipper U, Neamathla Skipper U, Clouded Skipper C, Least Skipper C, Fiery Skipper C, Meske's Skipper U, Tawny-edged Skipper U, Whirlabout C, Southern Broken-Dash C, Sachem U,

Arogos Skipper R, Delaware Skipper U, Palmetto Skipper U, Palatka Skipper U, Monk Skipper U, Dusted Skipper U–C, Eufala Skipper U, Twin-spot Skipper U, Brazilian Skipper U, Ocola Skipper C–A, Yucca Giant-Skipper R. **DIRECTIONS** The park is located about 20 miles north of West Palm Beach. From I-95 take Exit 60 (C.R. 708) east toward Hobe Sound. Turn south on U.S. 1. The park entrance is located about 3 miles south on the west side of the road. For more information call 561-546-2771 or write to Jonathan Dickinson State Park, 16450 SE Federal Highway, Hobe Sound, FL 33455.

LOXAHATCHEE NATIONAL WILDLIFE REFUGE

PALM BEACH COUNTY

This 221-square-mile refuge represents the northernmost section of the Everglades. Most of 145,750 acres are freshwater marshes dotted with tree islands, but there are also numerous water lily sloughs, wet prairies, and some hammocks and cypress swamps. Large numbers of ducks and other water birds use the refuge. Given that most of the refuge is everglades, wetland butterflies dominant the fauna.

The refuge is open for daytime use only. The Cypress Swamp Boardwalk winds for nearly 1/2 mile through a nice swamp. Look for butterflies visiting flowers such as Spanish Needles along the Marsh Trail that circles about 1 mile on levees surrounding an impoundment. The canoe trail makes a 5.5-mile loop through the refuge. Butterflies that you're most likely to see at Loxahatchee NWR include Black Swallowtails, Palamedes Swallowtails, Great Southern Whites, Cloudless Sulphurs, Barred Yellows, Little Yellows, Sleepy Oranges, Dainty Sulphurs, White M Hairstreaks, Red-banded Hairstreaks, Fulvous Hairstreaks, Gray Hairstreaks, Cassius Blues, Ceraunus Blues, Little Metalmarks, Gulf Fritillaries, Julias (Heliconian), Zebras (Heliconian), Phaon Crescents, Pearl Crescents, Red Admirals, American Ladies, Common Buckeyes, White Peacocks, Viceroys, Ruddy Daggerwings, Carolina Satyrs, Georgia Satyrs, Monarchs, Queens, Soldiers, Long-tailed Skippers, Dorantes Longtails, Horace's Duskywings, Zarucco Duskywings, Tropical Checkered-Skippers, Neamathla Skippers, Clouded Skippers, Least Skippers, Southern Skipperlings, Fiery Skippers, Whirlabouts, Southern Broken-Dashes, Sachems, Delaware Skippers, Aaron's Skippers, Palatka Skippers, Monk Skippers, Eufala Skippers, Twin-spot Skippers, Brazilian Skippers, and Ocola Skippers.

Precautions: Mosquitoes and other biting insects are often abundant.

DIRECTIONS The refuge is located west of Boynton Beach. From I-95 take Exit 44 (S.R. 804) west to U.S. 441. Turn south on U.S. 441 for about

2 miles, then turn west onto Lee Road. For more information call 407-734-8303 or write to Loxahatchee National Wildlife Refuge, 10216 Lee Road, Boynton Beach, FL 33437.

MATHESON HAMMOCK PARK

MIAMI-DADE COUNTY

Matheson Hammock is a small slice of tropical paradise located within 8 miles of the heart of Miami. The park has 630 acres of tropical trees and shrubs that harbor one of the best populations of Florida Whites. The nature trail, on the west side of Old Cutler Road, winds through a nice hardwood hammock, home to tropical butterflies such as the Large Orange Sulphur, Florida White, Malachite, Ruddy Daggerwing (usually common), and Hammock Skipper. Look along the hammock edges for hairstreaks and blues. The coastal part of Matheson Hammock has a mature mangrove swamp where the Mangrove Skipper is often abundant.

DIRECTIONS   The park is located adjacent to Fairchild Tropical Gardens in Coral Gables off Old Cutler Road. For more information call 305-666-6979 or write to Matheson Hammock Park, 9610 Old Cutler Road, Coral Gables, FL 33156.

NAVY WELLS PINELAND PRESERVE

MIAMI-DADE COUNTY
   by Roger L. Hammer

This 400-acre pine rockland habitat is the site of the Florida Keys Aqueduct Authority (FKAA) well-field so that a portion of the property is not open to the public. A network of trails offers easy access into the preserve from the FKAA parking lot. The preserve is known to harbor small populations of Florida Leafwings and Bartram's Scrub-Hairstreaks as well as other more common species that typify pine rockland habitat.

DIRECTIONS   The preserve is located on Southwest 192nd Avenue and Southwest 354th Street in Homestead.

SECRET WOODS REGIONAL PARK

BROWARD COUNTY

Secret Woods Nature Center is located along the New River in a very urban part of Florida. There are 55 acres of hammocks, hardwood swamps, and mangroves in the park. The visitor center has wildlife plantings with native plants attractive to butterflies. Two short trails

(Laurel Oak Trail and New River Trail) loop through the hammock and over the mangrove swamp via a boardwalk. The park is open for daytime use only.

Secret Woods has an abundance of common south Florida butterflies. Among the more interesting butterflies are Statira Sulphurs, which may be seen on the New River Trail, Ruddy Daggerwings, Soldiers, and Fulvous Hairstreaks.

DIRECTIONS The park is located in Fort Lauderdale. From I-95 take Exit 27 (S.R. 84) west about a mile. The park is located on the north side of the road on the east side of the New River. For more information call 954-791-1030 or write to Secret Woods Nature Center, 2701 West State Road 84, Dania, FL 33312.

TREETOPS REGIONAL PARK

BROWARD COUNTY

DESCRIPTION Located on the southern end of Pine Island Ridge, Treetops Park contains 358 acres of hammock and freshwater marsh. The upland habitat is a mixture of huge live oaks, cabbage palm, and South Florida slash pine. The hammocks contain both tropical trees and shrubs such as mastic and wild coffee as well as temperate plants. There are four nature trails including a 1000 foot boardwalk over a freshwater marsh. The trail behind the Nature Center goes to the Pine Ridge area and is a good choice for seeing Malachites.

BUTTERFLIES The park is a good place to see tropical butterflies such as the Julia (Heliconian), Zebra (Heliconian), White Peacock, Malachite, Ruddy Daggerwing, and Monk Skipper, as well as temperate species like the Tawny Emperor and Red Admiral.

SPECIES LIST Polydamas Swallowtail R, Black Swallowtail U, Giant Swallowtail U–C, Palamedes Swallowtail C, Checkered White U, Great Southern White U, Cloudless Sulphur C–A, Orange-barred Sulphur U, Barred Yellow U, Sleepy Orange U, Dainty Sulphur C, Southern Hairstreak U, White M Hairstreak U, Gray Ministreak R, Fulvous Hairstreak U, Gray Hairstreak C, Mallow Scrub-Hairstreak U, Cassius Blue C, Little Metalmark U, Gulf Fritillary A, Julia (Heliconian) A, Zebra (Heliconian) A, Phaon Crescent A, Pearl Crescent C, Red Admiral U–C, American Lady U, Common Buckeye U–C, White Peacock C–A, Malachite U–C, Viceroy C, Ruddy Daggerwing U–C, Tawny Emperor U, Carolina Satyr C, Monarch U–C, Queen U–C, Soldier U–C, Long-tailed Skipper C–A, Dorantes Longtail C–A, Horace's Duskywing C, Tropical Checkered-Skipper C, Swarthy Skipper U, Neamathla Skipper U, Three-spotted Skipper C, Clouded Skipper C, Least Skipper C, Southern Skipperling C,

Fiery Skipper C, Whirlabout C, Southern Broken-Dash C, Sachem U, Delaware Skipper U, Monk Skipper U, Eufala Skipper U, Twin-spot Skipper U, Brazilian Skipper U, Ocola Skipper C–A.

DIRECTIONS The park is located just west of Fort Lauderdale. From I-75 take Griffin Road (Exit 7) east about 4 miles. Or, take I-95 to Griffen Road. Go west about 7 miles. Take a right onto SW 100th Avenue, go about 1/2 mile. Tree Tops is on the right. Go to the end of the road to the Nature Center and Administration building. For more information call 954-370-3750 or write to Treetops Regional Park, 3900 SW 100th Avenue, Davie, FL 33328.

KEYS

Unfortunately, habitat loss and mosquito control spraying has caused very serious declines in butterfly populations on the Florida Keys. Some of the rarest butterflies in the U.S. can still be found on the remaining fragments of habitats that still exist in protected parkland. But for how long? Butterflies may also be found in weedy disturbed areas, along bikeways, roadsides, or utility lines, and around remnants of hammocks and other natural areas. Butterflies recorded from the main islands are listed below.

BISCAYNE NATIONAL PARK

MIAMI-DADE COUNTY

DESCRIPTION Biscayne NP encompasses a narrow band of mangroves on the mainland, Biscayne Bay, and the northernmost Florida Keys. The park headquarters is located on the mainland, about 9 miles east of Florida City. Visitor centers are also located on Elliott Key and on Adams Key. The park offers scuba and snorkeling tours, but you will need to bring or rent a boat to get onto the islands. The keys in Biscayne NP are vegetated with tropical hammocks, mangrove swamps, and salt marshes. The largest island is Elliott Key. On the 7-mile trip across Biscayne Bay from the park headquarters you may see porpoises, sponge fishermen, or manta rays. Camping is permitted on the grounds around the Elliott Key visitor center and bathrooms with showers are provided. The nature trail makes a rectangular circuit east to the ocean side of the island and back. Another trail, Spite Highway, runs north-south down the middle of the island.

SPECIES LIST FOR ELLIOTT KEY Polydamas Swallowtail U, Giant Swallowtail U, Schaus' Swallowtail U–C, Bahamian Swallowtail R, Florida White U, Checkered White R, Great Southern White A, Cloudless Sulphur C, Orange-barred Sulphur R, Large Orange Sulphur A, Statira Sulphur R, Lyside Sulphur R or S, Barred Yellow U, Little Yellow U,

Mimosa Yellow R, Sleepy Orange R, Dainty Sulphur U, Silver-banded Hairstreak R, Red-banded Hairstreak R, Gray Hairstreak U, Martial Scrub-Hairstreak U, Mallow Scrub-Hairstreak U, Eastern Pygmy-Blue U, Cassius Blue C, Miami Blue R or H, Ceraunus Blue U, American Snout R, Gulf Fritillary C, Julia (Heliconian) C, Zebra (Heliconian) C, Cuban Crescent U, Phaon Crescent C, Pearl Crescent U, Red Admiral U, American Lady U, Common Buckeye U, Mangrove Buckeye U, White Peacock U, Malachite R, Viceroy R, Florida Purplewing U, Ruddy Daggerwing U, Monarch U–C, Queen U–C, Soldier R, Mangrove Skipper U, Zestos Skipper R or H, Hammock Skipper U, Long-tailed Skipper U–C, Dorantes Longtail U–C, Tropical Checkered-Skipper U, Neamathla Skipper R, Three-spotted Skipper U, Clouded Skipper U, Southern Skipperling R, Fiery Skipper U–C, Southern Broken-Dash U, Sachem U, Monk Skipper U, Brazilian Skipper U, Obscure Skipper U, and Ocola Skipper R.

Precautions: Bring plenty of water and insect repellant. Biting insects are often excedingly abundant on the islands from May through December. Also, watch for diamondback rattlesnakes on the rocky trails.

DIRECTIONS The park is located in Biscayne Bay, just south of Miami. From the Florida Turnpike, take Exit 2 (Campbell Drive) east. Turn south on Tallahassee Road, then east on Lucy Street to the park. For more information call 305-230-7275 or write to Biscayne National Park, 9700 SW 328th Street, Homestead, FL 33030.

KEY LARGO HAMMOCKS STATE BOTANICAL SITE

MONROE COUNTY - KEY LARGO

There are two roads leading out of Florida City on the mainland onto Key Largo. The main road is U.S. 1 or the Overseas Highway. After the 1935 hurricane wiped out Henry Flagler's railroad to Key West, the line was converted into the Overseas Highway. A second road, County Road 905-A has a toll bridge over Card Sound leading to some magnificent butterflying areas on northern Key Largo. The Ocean Reef Club, an upscale development, occupies the northern-most tip of Key Largo. Most of the land between the Ocean Reef Club and the entry point of U.S. 1 onto Key Largo is state or federally owned. After passing over the Card Sound bridge, C.R. 905-A crosses mangroves and the Crocodile Lake area. If you are lucky, you may see one of the endangered crocodiles. At the stop sign you must turn right (south) to get to Key West. Key Largo Hammocks State Botanical Site contains 2340 acres of tropical hammocks, mangroves, and salt marshes. This preserve lies on the ocean side of C.R. 905-A from the Ocean Reef Club, south past the old radar base. In order to hike on the property, one must first check in with the ranger at John Pennekamp State Park, about 15 miles south of Key Largo Hammocks at mile marker 102.5.

BUTTERFLIES Along the roadsides or on the trails through the hammocks you may see a Schaus' Swallowtail, Bahamian Swallowtail, Lyside Sulphur, Mimosa Yellow, Amethyst Hairstreak, Silver-banded Hairstreak, Gray Ministreak, Miami Blue, or Florida Purplewing. But, realistically, you almost certainly won't. Around the salt marshes and mangroves look for Great Southern Whites, Eastern Pygmy-Blues, Cuban Crescents, Mangrove Buckeyes, Queens, Soldiers, Mangrove Skippers, Salt Marsh Skippers, and Obscure Skippers.

SPECIES LIST FOR KEY LARGO Polydamas Swallowtail R, Giant Swallowtail U, Schaus' Swallowtail R, Bahamian Swallowtail R, Florida White U, Checkered White R, Great Southern White U–A, Orange Sulphur R, Cloudless Sulphur C, Orange-barred Sulphur R, Large Orange Sulphur C, Statira Sulphur R, Lyside Sulphur R or S, Barred Yellow U–A, Little Yellow U, Mimosa Yellow R, Dina Yellow R, Sleepy Orange R, Dainty Sulphur U–C, Amethyst Hairstreak R or H, Silver-banded Hairstreak R, Red-banded Hairstreak R, Gray Hairstreak U, Martial Scrub-Hairstreak R, Mallow Scrub-Hairstreak U, Eastern Pygmy-Blue U, Cassius Blue U–A, Miami Blue R or H, Ceraunus Blue U, American Snout R, Gulf Fritillary C, Julia (Heliconian) C, Zebra (Heliconian) C, Cuban Crescent R, Phaon Crescent C, Pearl Crescent U, Red Admiral U, American Lady U, Common Buckeye U, Mangrove Buckeye U, Tropical Buckeye R, White Peacock U, Malachite R, Viceroy R, Dingy Purplewing R, Florida Purplewing R, Ruddy Daggerwing U, Monarch U–C, Queen U–C, Soldier R, Mangrove Skipper U, Zestos Skipper R or H, Hammock Skipper U, Long-tailed Skipper U–C, Dorantes Longtail U–C, Florida Duskywing R, Tropical Checkered-Skipper U–C, Neamathla Skipper R, Three-spotted Skipper U, Clouded Skipper U, Southern Skipperling R, Fiery Skipper U–C, Southern Broken-Dash U, Sachem U, Monk Skipper U, Brazilian Skipper U, Obscure Skipper U, and Ocola Skipper R.

Precautions: Mosquitoes and sand flies are often exceedingly abundant in the hammocks and mangroves.

DIRECTIONS From U.S. 1 in Florida City take Card Sound Road (C.R. 905-A) over the toll bridge to the stop sign. Entry points are located across the road from the stop sign, immediately south of the Ocean Reef Club, and at the old radar installation a few miles to the south. Check first with the rangers at John Pennekamp State Park before going on the property. For more information about the preserve call 305-451-1202 or write to Key Largo Hammocks State Botanical Site, State Road 905, Key Largo, FL 33037.

MONROE COUNTY - KEY LARGO

This spectacular underwater park protects 61,530 acres of coral reefs, sea-grass beds, and other fragile marine habitats. The visitor center on Key Largo has a huge coral reef display tank, terrestrial plant and animal exhibits, and educational programs. Excellent examples of tropical hammocks and mangroves are located just a short distance from the visitor center. This is one of the most visited parks in the U.S.

The park has a developed campground with electricity, flush toilets, and hot showers. All of the Florida Keys Parks are extremely popular, especially in winter and spring. We recommend that you make reservations at least six months in advance if you're planning to camp. The nature trail winds through a beautiful tropical hammock. The park charges entrance and camping fees.

Rare tropical butterflies have been seen at John Pennekamp SP such as endangered Schaus' Swallowtails, Florida Whites, and Florida Purplewings. However, these species are not really to be expected. At the edges of the tropical hammock look for the Giant Swallowtail, Large Orange Sulphur, Miami Blue, Cuban Crescent, Ruddy Daggerwing, Hammock Skipper, Southern Broken-Dash, and Monk Skipper. Mangrove Skippers are likely to be seen near the mangrove swamp or perching on shrubs around the tropical hammock. Hairstreaks are often attracted to the flowers of seagrape planted around the parking lot.

Precautions: Mosquitoes and sand flies are often exceedingly abundant.

DIRECTIONS The park is located just north of the City of Key Largo at mile marker 102.5. For more information call 305-451-1202 or write to John Pennekamp Coral Reef State Park, P.O. Box 487, Key Largo, FL 33037.

LIGNUMVITAE KEY STATE BOTANICAL SITE

MONROE COUNTY - LIGNUMVITAE KEY

DESCRIPTION This 280-acre island has relics of Calusa Indian, Spanish, and plantation cultures and today has exemplary tropical hammocks, mangroves, and salt marshes. The island's name is derived from the magnificent *Lignum vitae,* or tree-of-life, a host plant of the rare Lyside Sulphur. Lignumvitae Key lies 1 mile north of the main Keys chain in Florida Bay. Guided tours of the Historic Matheson House Museum and the surrounding tropical hammocks are offered by Florida Park Service rangers.

BUTTERFLIES The island offers some of Florida's rarest butterflies.

Keep watch for Schaus' Swallowtails, Florida Whites, Martial Scrub-Hairstreaks, Miami Blues, Florida Purplewings, Ruddy Daggerwings, Mangrove Skippers, and Hammock Skippers along the nature trail or around the perimeter of the Matheson House lawn.

SPECIES LIST Black Swallowtail R, Giant Swallowtail U–C, Schaus' Swallowtail R, Florida White U, Checkered White R, Great Southern White A, Cloudless Sulphur C, Large Orange Sulphur C, Statira Sulphur R, Barred Yellow U–C, Little Yellow U, Dainty Sulphur U–C, Gray Hairstreak U, Martial Scrub-Hairstreak U, Mallow Scrub-Hairstreak U, Eastern Pygmy-Blue U–C, Cassius Blue A, Miami Blue R or H, Ceraunus Blue U, Gulf Fritillary C, Julia (Heliconian) C, Zebra (Heliconian) C, Cuban Crescent U, Phaon Crescent U, Painted Lady R, Mangrove Buckeye U, White Peacock U–C, Malachite R, Florida Purplewing U, Ruddy Daggerwing U, Georgia Satyr R, Monarch U, Queen U, Mangrove Skipper U, Zestos Skipper R, Hammock Skipper U, Long-tailed Skipper C, Dorantes Skipper C, Zarucco Duskywing R, Tropical Checkered-Skipper U, Monk Skipper C, and Obscure Skipper U.

Precautions: Mosquitoes and other biting insects may be incredibly abundant on Lignumvitae Key. Long sleeve shirts, long pants, and plenty of insect repellent are highly recommended.

DIRECTIONS A tour boat operated by the Florida Park Service ferries visitors between U.S. 1 on the north or bay side of Indian Key Fill (Mile Marker 78.5) and Lignumvitae Key. Tour reservations can be made by calling 305-664-9814. For more information call 305-664-4815 or write to Lignumvitae Key State Botanical Site, P.O. Box 1052, Islamorada, FL 33036.

NATIONAL KEY DEER REFUGE, BIG PINE KEY

MONROE COUNTY
by Mark Salvato

DESCRIPTION Established in 1957, National Key Deer Refuge was the result of conservation efforts designed to protect the remaining herd of fewer than 50 key deer. In response, the population of this endangered animal has since risen to approximately 300 individuals. Big Pine Key is the largest member in the chain of keys that make up the refuge. This key's variety of ecosystems includes dense mangrove, pine rockland, hardwood hammocks and fresh water wetlands. Thus, allowing Big Pine Key to qualify as a butterfly enthusiasts paradise. However, due to decades of fire suppression and urban development, much of the habitat within and adjacent to the refuge has been drastically altered. Furthermore, Watson's Hammock and parts of Cactus Hammock on Big Pine along with No Name Key are the only populated areas within the Lower Keys not targeted by year-round mosquito control chemical applications.

BUTTERFLIES As is the case throughout the Florida Keys, loss of habitat has jeopardized many of the butterflies in Key Deer. Any detailed observations made in the Lower Keys offer the amateur a chance to make important contributions to what is known about the natural histories of the areas' butterflies. This makes visiting Key Deer Refuge very exciting. Over 70 species have been reported from within the refuge, the majority of these can be seen on Big Pine. The rainy season runs from May to October, and, in general, this is also the period of greatest butterfly abundance, but there are exceptions. Research the species of interest to you before you make this trip.

Watson's Hammock (located on northwestern Big Pine) is the most undisturbed area within the key. This part of the refuge gives one an opportunity to explore all of the major habitats, with transition zones between tropical pineland, hardwood hammock, and mangrove communities. Watson's best access point is the trail/fire break that begins at the west end of Higgs Road (west off of Key Deer Boulevard). Here a typical over-story of southern Florida slash pine is maintained, interrupted by grass savanna and a patchy under-story of tropical and temperate shrubs, such as saw palmetto, coconut, and thatch palms. The exposed porous oolite rock substrate supports a variety of shrubs such as locustberry, host to Florida Duskywings, and sweet acacia. Narrow-leaved croton is abundant here, its year-round blooms provide an important nectar source for a wide array of species, including Bartram's Scrub-Hairstreak, which uses the plant as its sole caterpillar foodplant. Species of *Cassia* prosper at the pineland edges, serving as hosts for assorted sulphurs. Large Orange Sulphurs and Florida Leafwings can be seen in the distance, scaling the canopy top in search of mates. Balloon-vine, caterpillar foodplant for Miami Blues, is common here within Watson's pineland and in disturbed areas across Big Pine. Wild limes and torchwood become increasingly more common in the ecotones between pineland and the denser hardwood hammock, these serve as hosts for Giant Swallowtails, the Lower Keys' lone extant swallowtail species. Zebra (Heliconians) and Gulf Fritillaries frequent the hardwood hammock and can be viewed visiting passion-vines. A variety of tropical species, such as Dingy and Florida purplewings, and Many-banded Daggerwings, have been found here, albeit rarely.

Cactus Hammock located immediately upon entry to Big Pine Key (across from the fishing lodge) offers easier access to a variety of butter-flies. Great Southern Whites cover the mangroves here, especially in their years of cyclic eruption. The abundance of pepper-grass, Spanish needles, mallows, and milk-pea provides nectar to a wide array of species. Bay cedars, located along the coastlines, support the largest population of Martial Scrub-Hairstreaks in the U.S. Saltwort and glasswort are abundant in the salt marsh areas, and here you can find Eastern Pygmy-Blues sporadically using them.

At Blue Hole (located on north Key Deer Boulevard) numerous flow-ering shrubs such as lantana and rattlebox teem with assorted skippers and blues. The invasive Brazilian pepper is common on Big Pine and will likely have Fulvous Hairstreaks nearby.

SPECIES LIST   Giant Swallowtail C, Florida White C, Great Southern White A, Yellow Angled-Sulphur S, Cloudless Sulphur A, Orange-Barred Sulphur C, Large Orange Sulphur C, Orbed Sulphur S, Barred Yellow A, Little Yellow A, Sleepy Orange C, Dainty Sulphur C, Gray Hairstreak U, Martial Hairstreak C, Bartram's Scrub-Hairstreak C, Mallow Scrub-Hairstreak C, Disguised Scrub-Hairstreak S, Fulvous Hairstreak C, Red-banded Hairstreak U, Eastern Pygmy-Blue C, Cassius Blue C, Nickerbean Blue C, Miami Blue R or H, Ceraunus Blue A, Little Metalmark U, Gulf Fritillary A, Julia (Heliconian), U, Zebra (Heliconian) C, Variegated Fritillary U, Phaon Crescent U, Pearl Crescent A, Painted Lady U, Red Admiral U, Common Buckeye A, Mangrove Buckeye C, Tropical Buckeye R, White Peacock A, Caribbean Peacock S, Malachite U, Dingy Purplewing R, Florida Purplewing R, Many-banded Daggerwing S, Florida Leafwing C, Georgia Satyr U, Monarch C, Queen C, Mangrove Skipper A, Zestos Skipper R, Hammock Skipper C, Long-tailed Skipper C, Dorantes Longtail C, Florida Duskywing A, Zarucco Duskywing U, Tropical Checkered-Skipper A, Three-spotted Skipper C, Clouded Skipper U, Fiery Skipper A, Meske's Skipper R, Southern Broken-Dash C, Sachem C, Palmetto Skipper U, Palatka Skipper U, Monk Skipper C, Eufala Skipper U, Twin-spot Skipper C, Brazilian Skipper U, Salt Marsh Skipper U, Obscure Skipper C, and Ocola Skipper U.

DIRECTIONS   Follow U.S. 1 south through the Keys. National Key Deer starts at mile marker 32 on Big Pine Key. Cactus Hammock is located at mile marker 32, the area lies on the south side of U.S. 1 and follows the coastline north for about 1 mile. Key Deer Boulevard intersects U.S. 1 after mile marker 31 and runs north. Higgs Road and Blue Hole are both about 2 miles north on Key Deer Boulevard. Follow Key Deer Boulevard past Blue Hole for less than 2 a mile to reach a self-guided nature trail. Turn left off Key Deer Boulevard onto Higgs Road and follow it to its end to enter the unmarked Watson's Hammock. For more information call 305-872-2239 or write to National Key Deer Wildlife Refuge, P.O. Box 430510, Big Pine Key, FL 33043-0510.

Other Portions of the Refuge

NO NAME KEY, MONROE COUNTY Contains only relict pineland, fire suppression has given rise to hardwood hammock. This is the best location in the lower Keys to observe Mangrove Buckeyes. It also maintains a large year-round density of pierid species, especially Great Southern Whites.

SUGARLOAF KEY, MONROE COUNTY As in the salt marshes of Cactus Hammock, glassworts and saltworts are used by Eastern Pygmy-Blues. American Lady, and Ruddy and Antillean daggerwings have been reported only from this part of National Key Deer Refuge.

LONG KEY STATE RECREATION AREA

MONROE COUNTY - LONG KEY

Located in the middle keys, this 1085-acre park has interesting tropical hammocks, mangroves, and salt marshes.

The park has a developed campground with electricity, flush toilets, and hot showers located on the beach. We recommend that you make reservations at least six months in advance if you're planning to camp. The park has a nature trail through a lush tropical hammock and a board walk over a mangrove bordered lagoon. A canoe trail winds through some of the mangrove lagoons. Canoe rentals are available. The park charges entrance and camping fees.

In the tropical hammocks of Long Key you may glimpse the Giant Swallowtail, Florida White, Large Orange Sulphur, Zebra (Heliconian), Ruddy Daggerwing, Zestos Skipper, or Hammock Skipper. Around the salt marshes look for the Great Southern White, Eastern Pygmy-Blue, Cuban Crescent, Mangrove Buckeye, Queen, Mangrove Skipper, Salt Marsh Skipper, and Obscure Skipper. Weedy areas along the roads often have an abundance of flowers attractive to many butterflies. Look for the Amethyst Hairstreak, Silver-banded Hairstreak, Martial Scrub-Hairstreak, Mallow Scrub-Hairstreak, Miami Blue, and Three-spotted Skipper on Spanish Needles and other weedy plants.

Precautions: Mosquitoes and sand flies are often exceedingly abundant in the hammocks and mangroves.

DIRECTIONS The park is located on Long Key at mile marker 67.5. For more information call 305-664-4815 or write to Long Key State Recreation Area, P.O. Box 776, Long Key, FL 33001.

STOCK ISLAND BOTANICAL GARDEN

MONROE COUNTY

This small tropical garden and hammock supports many uncommon butterflies. Take a leisurely stroll along the short winding paths. Look to the treetops for blues and hairstreaks. Closer to the ground, you may find large skippers perching on the undersides of leaves of shrubs. Patches of Spanish needles around the parking lot often attract many butterflies as well.

You may find rare or interesting tropical butterflies such as the Orange-barred Sulphur, Amethyst Hairstreak, Fulvous Hairstreak, Mallow Scrub-Hairstreak, Miami Blue, Malachite, Ruddy Daggerwing, Mangrove Skipper, Zestos Skipper, Hammock Skipper, Three-spotted Skipper, or Monk Skipper in this 5-acre garden.

DIRECTIONS The garden is located on Stock Island. Turn north off the Overseas Highway just before the bridge to Key West. The parking lot is a short distance beyond the county buildings.

Checklist of Florida Butterflies

Swallowtail, Pipevine
  Polydamas
  Zebra
  Cuban
  Black
  Giant
  Schaus'
  Bahamian
  Androgeus
  Eastern Tiger
  Spicebush
  Palamedes
White, Florida
  Checkered
  Cabbage
  Great Southern
Orangetip, Falcate
Sulphur, Orange
Dogface, Southern
Sulphur, Cloudless
  Orange-barred
  Large Orange
  Statira
  Lyside
Angled-Sulphur, Yellow
Yellow, Barred
  Boisduval's
  Little
  Mimosa
  Shy
  Dina
Orange, Sleepy
Sulphur, Dainty
Harvester

Atala
Hairstreak, Great Purple
  Amethyst
  Silver-banded
  Coral
  Banded
  King's
  Striped
  Southern
Elfin, Frosted
  Henry's
  Eastern Pine
Hairstreak, Juniper
  Hessel's
  White M
Scrub-Hairstreak, Gray
  Martial
  Bartram's
  Mallow
  Disguised
Hairstreak, Fulvous
  Red-banded
Ministreak, Gray
Pygmy-Blue, Eastern
Blue, Cassius
  Miami
  Nickerbean
  Ceraunus
Tailed-Blue, Eastern
Azure, Spring
  Summer
Metalmark, Little
Snout, American
Fritillary, Gulf

(Heliconian), Julia
  Zebra
Fritillary, Variegated
Checkerspot, Silvery
Crescent, Texan
  Cuban
  Phaon
  Pearl
Question Mark
Comma, Eastern
Mourning Cloak
Lady, American
  Painted
Red Admiral
Mimic
Buckeye, Common
  Mangrove
  Tropical
Peacock, White
  Caribbean
Malachite
Red-Spotted Purple
Viceroy
Purplewing, Dingy
  Florida
Cracker, Pale
Daggerwing, Many-
  banded
  Ruddy
  Antillean
Leafwing, Florida
  Goatweed
Emperor, Hackberry
  Tawny

Pearly-eye, Southern
Brown, Appalachian
Satyr, Gemmed
  Carolina
  Georgia
Wood-Satyr, Little
  Viola's
Wood-Nymph, Common
Monarch
Queen
Soldier
Skipper, Mangrove
  Mercurial
  Zestos
  Silver-spotted
  Hammock
  Long-tailed
Longtail, Dorantes
Skipper, Golden-banded
  Hoary Edge
Cloudywing, Southern
  Northern
  Confused
Scallopwing, Hayhurst's
Duskywing, Florida
  Sleepy
  Juvenal's
  Horace's

  Mottled
  Zarucco
  Funereal
  Wild Indigo
Checkered-Skipper,
  Common
  Tropical
Sootywing, Common
Skipper, Swarthy
  Neamathla
  Three-spotted
  Clouded
  Least
Skipperling, Southern
Skipper, Fiery
  Dotted
  Meske's
  Baracoa
  Tawny-edged
  Crossline
  Whirlabout
Broken-Dash, Southern
  Northern
Glassywing, Little
Sachem
Skipper, Arogos
  Delaware
  Byssus

  Zabulon
  Aaron's
  Yehl
  Broad-winged
  Palmetto
  Palatka
  Dion
  Dukes'
Dash, Black
Skipper, Berry's
  Dun
  Monk
  Dusted
Roadside-Skipper,
  Pepper and Salt
  Lace-winged
  Reversed
  Common
  Dusky
Skipper, Eufala
  Twin-spot
  Brazilian
  Salt Marsh
  Obscure
  Ocola
  Violet-banded
Giant-Skipper, Yucca
  Cofaqui

Organizations Concerned with Butterflies

The North American Butterfly Association (NABA) promotes public enjoyment, awareness, and conservation of butterflies and all aspects of recreational, nonconsumptive butterflying, including field identification, butterfly gardening, and photography. North American Butterfly Association publishes a full-color magazine, *American Butterflies*; a newsletter *Butterfly Gardening News*; has chapters throughout North America (there are currently 5 chapters in Florida) and runs the annual NABA 4th of July Butterfly Counts. These one-day counts, held mainly in June–July (centered on the 4th of July period) are growing rapidly. Currently about 350 counts are conducted each year, at sites across North America. They are a fun filled way to help monitor butterfly populations, to learn about butterfly identification, and to meet other butterfliers.

There are currently five NABA chapters in Florida. Information about NABA and its Florida chapters can be found at:

NABA
4 Delaware Road
Morristown, NJ 07960
Web site: *http://www.naba.org*

The Lepidopterists' Society is an international organization devoted to the scientific study of all lepidoptera. The Society publishes the *Journal of the Lepidopterists' Society* as well as the *News of the Lepidopterists' Society*.

Lepidopterists' Society
1608 Presidio Way
Roseville, CA 95661
Web site: *http://www.furman.edu*

Southern Lepidopterists Society promotes the scientific study of all lepidoptera. The Society publishes the *Southern Lepidopterists' News*.

Southern Lepidopterists' Society
c/o Jeffrey R. Slotten
5421 NW 69th Lane
Gainesville, FL 32653

The Xerces Society is an international organization dedicated to the global protection of habitats for all invertebrates, including butterflies. The Society publishes *Wings*.

Xerces Society
4828 Southeast Hawthorne Boulevard
Portland, OR 97215

The Nature Conservancy buys land to preserve natural diversity and owns more than 1300 preserves—the largest private system of nature sanctuaries in the world.

The Nature Conservancy
1815 Lynn Street
Arlington, VA 22209
Web site: *http://www.tnc.org*

NABA 4th of July Butterfly Counts in Florida

EACH YEAR, THE NORTH AMERICAN BUTTERFLY ASSOCIATION (NABA) sponsors the 4th of July Butterfly Counts. The time in the field and the social occasion can be lots of fun, plus the data generated may prove useful in tracking the fate of many of our butterfly species. Included here are all the counts held in Florida in 1998. Because the count compilers tend to be fairly stable, I have also included their names and addresses. Contact a compiler if you are interested in joining future counts; most compilers will welcome your participation regardless of your level of butterflying ability. For the most current information on NABA 4th of July Counts, visit the NABA web site at *www.naba.org*.

Alva (Lee Co.)
Mark Salvato, 1109 NW 41st Ave. #5, Gainesville, FL 32609

Archer
Mark Salvato, 1109 NW 41st Ave. #5, Gainesville, FL 32609

Big Pine Key, Monroe Co.
Mark Salvato, 1109 NW 41st Ave. #5, Gainesville, FL 32609

Christmas
Randy Snyder, 1584 Outlook St., Orlando, FL 32806

Coral Gables
Robert Kelley, Box 249085, Math & Computer Sciences, University of Miami, Coral Gables, FL 33124

Corkscrew Swamp Sanctuary
Robbie Wooster, 7380 Rookery Ln., Naples, FL 34120

Disney Wilderness Preserve
Byrum Cooper, 115 Lameraux Rd., Winter Haven, FL 33884

Highlands Hammock
Alana Edwards, 3206 Palm Dr., Delray Beach, FL 33483

Homestead
Michael Hennessey, 5800 Merton Ct., Apt. 280, Alexandria, VA
22311

Kissimmee Prairie Sanctuary
Byrum Cooper, 115 Lameraux Rd., Winter Haven, FL 33884

Manatee County East
J.Y. Miller, 3621 Bay Shore Rd., Sarasota, FL 34234

Manatee County West
J.Y. Miller, 3621 Bay Shore Rd., Sarasota, FL 34234

Palm Beach County Central
Alana Edwards, 3206 Palm Dr., Delray Beach, FL 33483

Palm Beach County North
Alana Edwards, 3206 Palm Dr., Delray Beach, FL 33483

Palm Beach County South
Alana Edwards, 3206 Palm Dr., Delray Beach, FL 33483

Palm Harbor
Lois Weber, 4243 Lake Ave., Palm Harbor, FL 34684

Pasco County
Sandra Deese, 8009 Laurel Vista Loop, Port Richey, FL 34668

St. Petersburg
Tim Adams, 1291 Amber Lea Dr. E., Dunedin, FL 34698

Sanibel
Dee Serage, Sanibel-Captiva Cons. Fdn., PO Box 839, Sanibel, FL
33957

Sarasota County East
Paul Nenninger, 4928 San Jose Dr., Sarasota, FL 34235

Sarasota County West
J.Y. Miller, 3621 Bay Shore Rd., Sarasota, FL 34234

Tarpon Springs West
Lois Weber, 4243 Lake Ave., Palm Harbor, FL 34684

Wekiva River
Randy Snyder, 1584 Outlook St., Orlando, FL 32806

Glossary

ANTENNAL CLUB The thickened end of the antenna. Great Southern Whites, Plate 4, photo 3, have turquoise antennal clubs.

APEX The tip of the wing. Male Mimics, Plate 43, photo 2, have a small white spot at the FW apex. Female Zabulon Skippers, Plate 37, photo 7, have a white HW apex.

APICAL Referring to the area at the tip of the wing.

BASAL Referring to the area near the base of the wing, adjacent to the body. Great Purple Hairstreaks, Plate 11, photo 2, have red basal spots.

CELL The central area of the wing, bounded on all sides by veins. Common Buckeyes, Plate 21, photo 2, have two orange bars in each FW cell.

CELL-END BAR A thin bar of color along the vein bounding the outer edge of the cell, contrasting with the ground color of the wing. Goatweed Leafwings, Plate 23, photo 2, have a dark FW cell-end bar.

COSTAL MARGIN (COSTA) The leading edge of the FW.

DISC The central area of the wing including, but larger than, the cell.

DISTAL Away from the body.

DORSAL Toward the back. The dorsal wing surface is the upper surface.

FOREWINGS (FWs) The leading pair of wings.

FRINGES Scales that stick out from the edges of the wing membranes. Funereal Duskywing, Plate 43, photo 5, has a white HW fringe.

FRONS The area in the front of the head between the eyes.

GROUND COLOR The basic or background color of the wing.

HINDWINGS (HWs) The rear pair of wings.

HYALINE Translucent.

LEADING MARGIN The margin of the HW that is on top as the butterfly sits upright.

MARGIN Any of the wing edges, but usually referring to the outer margin.

MARGINAL LINES, BANDS or SPOTS A series of lines or spots along the outer margin. Coral Hairstreak, Plate 13, photo 1, has red HW marginal spots.

MEDIAN About one-half of the way out the wing, passing the distal end of the cell.

OUTER MARGIN The wing edge farthest from the body, it is more or less perpendicular to the ground as the butterfly sits upright.

POSTMEDIAN The wing regions farther from the body than (distal to) the median region. Silver-banded Hairstreak, Plate 12, photo 3, has a white postmedian line on its HW.

POSTMEDIAN BAND A series of spots or lines in the postmedian region of the wing, either darker or paler than the ground color. Red-banded Hairstreak, Plate 14, photo 5, has a postmedian band that is partially red.

STIGMA A structure, usually black and visible, on the FWs of most grass-skippers, formed by specialized scales. Male Sachems, Plate 33, photo 9, have a prominent black stigma in the center of the FW.

SUBAPICAL Referring to the region just before the tip of the wing.

SUBMARGINAL Referring to the region just before the area at the outside edge of the wing.

VENTRAL Toward the belly. The ventral wing surface is the lower wing surface.

VEINS A series of visibly raised structural elements on the wings that serve as wing struts. The branching pattern of the veins is important in lepidopteran systematics. Monarchs, Plate 25, photo 1, have the veins covered with black scales.

Bibliography

Ackery, P.R. and Vane-Wright, R.I. 1984. *Milkweed Butterflies*. London: British Museum.

Ajilvsgi, G. 1990. *Butterfly Gardening for the South*. Dallas: Taylor Publishing Co.

Bagget, H.D. 1982. Lepidoptera. In *Rare and Endangered Biota of Florida* Vol 6, Invertebrates. R. Franz (ed), 75–77. Gainesville: University of Florida Press.

Bell, C.R. and Taylor, B.J. 1982. *Florida Wild Flowers and Roadside Plants*. Chapel Hill: Laurel Hill Press.

Burns, J.M. 1964. *Evolution in Skipper Butterflies of the Genus* Erynnis. Berkeley: University of California Press.

Calhoun, J.V. 1995. "The biogeography and ecology of *Euphyes dukesi* in Florida." *J. Lep. Soc.* 49:6–23 .

Calhoun, J.V. 1996a. "Conquering soldiers: The successful invasion of Florida by *Danaus eresimus*." *Holarctic Lep*. 3:7–18.

Calhoun, J.V. 1996b. "Possible relict populations of *Chlosyne nycteis* in the Florida panhandle." *Holarctic Lep*. 3:69–71.

Calhoun, J.V. and Slotten, J. 1997. "Notes on the occurrence of *Satyrium titus* in northern Florida." *Holarctic Lep*. 4:51–54.

Catling, P.M. and Calhoun, J.V. 1997. "Genus *Megisto* in Florida and the taxonomic status of *Megisto viola*." *Holarctic Lep*. 4:27–33.

Clench, H.K. 1976. "*Nathalis iole* in the southeastern United States and the Bahamas." *J. Lep. Soc.* 30:121–126.

Dickson, J.D. III, Woodbury, R.O., and Alexander, T.R.. 1953. "Checklist of the flora of Big Pine Key, Florida and surrounding keys." *Quarterly J. Florida Academy of Sciences* 16:181–197.

Emmel, T.C. 1994. "Schaus' Swallowtail: A Beleaguered Aristocrat Teeters on the Edge of Extinction in the Florida Keys." *American Butterflies* February:18–22.

Gerberg, E.J. and Arnett, Jr., R.H. 1989. *Florida Butterflies*. Baltimore: Natural Science Publications.

Glassberg, J. 1998. "Go get set on your marks: Black-eyed Blues." *American Butterflies* Summer: 34–36.

230 Glassberg, J. 1999. *Butterflies through Binoculars: The East*. New York: Oxford University Press.

Griffiths, Chris. 1994. "A passion for *Passiflora*." *American Butterflies* November:12–19.

Howe, W.H. 1975. *The Butterflies of North America*. New York: Doubleday.

Kimball, C.P. 1965. *The Lepidoptera of Florida*. Gainesville: Florida Department of Agriculture.

Klots, A.B. 1951. *A Field Guide to the Butterflies of North America East of the Great Plains*. Boston: Houghton Mifflin.

Lenczewski, B. 1980. *Butterflies of Everglades National Park*. National Park Service, Homestead, Florida. Report T-588.

Lenczewski, B., Smith, D.S., and Leston, D. 1980. *Butterflies of Everglades National Park*. (a checklist) Florida National Parks and Monuments Assn., Homestead, FL.

Leston, D., Smith, D.S., and Lenczewski, B. 1982. "Habitat, diversity, and immigration in a tropical island fauna: the butterflies of Lignumvitae Key, Florida." *J. Lep. Soc.* 36:241–255.

Minno M.C. 1992. "Butterflies of the Archibold Biological Station, Highlands County, Florida." *J. Lep. Soc.* 46:138–158.

Minno, M.C. 1995. "Definitive destination: Ocala National Forest, Florida." *American Butterflies* Winter:4–11.

Minno, M.C. and Emmel, T.C. 1993. *Butterflies of the Florida Keys*. Gainesville: Scientific Publishers.

Minno, M.C., Emmel, T.C., and Calhoun, J.V. 1994. "Lepidoptera." In *Rare and Endangered Biota of Florida*, Vol. IV, Invertebrates. Deyrup, M. and Franz, R. (eds.), 574–623. Gainesville: University Press of Florida.

Minno, M.C. and Minno, M. 1999. *Florida Butterfly Gardening*. Gainesville: University Press of Florida.

NABA. 1995. *Checklist and English Names for North American Butterflies*. Morristown, NJ: North American Butterfly Assn.

New, T.R. 1991. *Butterfly Conservation*. New York: Oxford University Press.

Nijhout, H.F. 1991. *The Development and Evolution of Butterfly Wing Patterns*. Smithsonian Institution Press.

Norton, B.G. 1987. *Why Preserve Natural Variety?* Princeton University Press.

Opler, P.A. 1992. *A Field Guide to Eastern Butterflies*. Boston: Houghton-Mifflin.

Opler, P.A. and Krizek, G.O. 1984. *Butterflies East of the Great Plains*. Baltimore: Johns Hopkins University Press.

Pyle, R.M. 1981. *The Audubon Society Field Guide to North American Butterflies.* New York: Knopf.

Pyle, R.M. 1992. *Handbook for Butterfly Watchers.* Boston: Houghton-Mifflin.

Riley, N.D. 1975. *A Field Guide to the Butterflies of the West Indies.* London: Collins.

Salvato, M. 1998. "The Florida Keys: A paradise endangered." *American Butterflies* Winter:26–35.

Schwartz, A. 1989. The butterflies of the Lower Florida Keys. *Milwaukee Public Museum Contribution in Biology and Geology,* No. 73.

Smith, D.S., Miller, L.D., and Miller, J.Y. 1994. *The Butterflies of the West Indies and South Florida.* London: Oxford University Press.

Stamp, N.E. and Casey, T.M., eds. 1993. *Caterpillars: Ecological and Evolutionary Constraints on Foraging.* New York: Chapman and Hall.

Tekulsky. M. 1985. *The Butterfly Garden.* The Harvard Common Press.

Walker, T.J. 1978. "Migration and re-migration of butterflies through north peninsula Florida: quantification with malaise traps." *J. Lep. Soc.* 32:178–190.

Williams, C.B. 1930. *The Migration of Butterflies.* Oliver and Boyd.

Williams, C.B. 1958. *Insect Migration.* London: Collins.

Worth, R. A. et.al. 1996. "Notes on the biology of *Strymon acis bartrami* and *Anaea troglodyta floridalis* in south Florida." *Holarctic Lep.* 3:62–65.

Xerces Society/Smithsonian Institution. 1990. *Butterfly Gardening.* San Francisco: Sierra Club Books.

Photographic Credits

EXCEPT FOR THE 29 PHOTOGRAPHS noted below, all photographs were taken by Jeffrey Glassberg. J.G. used a Minolta 7000i automatic-focusing camera equipped with a 100 mm macro lens and a 1200AF ring flash. Film was Kodachrome ASA 64. Other photo credits are the following.

Plate 1 Pipevine Swallowtail, above, Jaret Daniels
Polydamas Swallowtail, above, Ron Boender

Plate 3 Bahamian Swallowtail, below, James L. Nation, Jr.
Bahamian Swallowtail, above, Thomas C. Emmel

Plate 15 Disguised Scrub-Hairstreak, Joe Spano

Plate 16 Miami Blue, below and ♂ above, Harry N. Darrow
Nickerbean Blue, ♀ above, Jane Ruffin

Plate 17 Variegated Fritillary, above, Jaret Daniels

Plate 20 Tawny Emperor, below, Jane Ruffin

Plate 22 Red-spotted Purple, above, Jaret Daniels
Dingy Purplewing, Peter W. Post

Plate 23 Goatweed Leafwing, below and above, Jaret Daniels

Plate 36 Meske's Skipper, ♂ above, Derb Carter

Plate 37 'Florida' Dusted Skipper, below, Marc C. Minno

Plate 43 Mimic, ♂ below, Charlie Rose
Mimic, ♀ above, Philip Nordin
Mercurial Skipper, Valerie Giles
Orion, Valerie Giles
Pale Cracker, Linas Kudzma

Plate 44 All photos this plate by Marc and Maria Minno except fogfruit and narrow-leaved croton by Jeffrey Glassberg

Index

Page numbers in **boldface** refer to color plates.

Field Notes

Field Notes

Field Notes